Fodor's

WITHDRAWN

BAHAMAS

WELCOME TO THE BAHAMAS

Made up of 700 islands—some busy and bustling, some isolated and inhabited by no one but hermit crabs and seagulls—the Bahamas offers an alluring mix of land and sea activities. From Nassau to Eleuthera, you can play golf on a seaside fairway, dive dramatic wrecks and reefs, and sail in crystal clear water. Accommodations run the gamut from simple inns to sophisticated retreats, from practical fishing lodges to romantic honeymoon hideaways. And for those who look a little closer, there's a fascinating and diverse culture to be explored.

TOP REASONS TO GO

★ **Beaches.** The powdery, soft sand creates some of the world's best strands.

★ **Boating.** Ideal conditions draw small dinghies, serious sailboats, and luxury yachts.

★ **Family Fun.** From sprawling water parks to horseback rides along the beach.

★ **Out Islands.** Quiet and uncrowded, these islands are hard to reach but worth the trip.

★ **Fishing.** From fly-casting for tarpon and bonefish to fighting with a giant marlin.

Fodor's BAHAMAS

Publisher: Amanda D'Acierno, *Senior Vice President*

Editorial: Arabella Bowen, *Editor in Chief*; Linda Cabasin, *Editorial Director*

Design: Tina Malaney, *Associate Art Director*; Chie Ushio, *Senior Designer*

Photography: Jennifer Arnow, *Senior Photo Editor*; Mary Robnett, *Photo Researcher*

Production: Linda Schmidt, *Managing Editor*; Evangelos Vasilakis, *Associate Managing Editor*; Angela L. McLean, *Senior Production Manager*

Maps: Rebecca Baer, *Senior Map Editor*; Mark Stroud and Henry Colomb (Moon Street Cartography), David Lindroth, *Cartographers*

Sales: Jacqueline Lebow, *Sales Director*

Marketing & Publicity: Heather Dalton, *Marketing Director*; Katherine Punia, *Publicity Director*

Business & Operations: Susan Livingston, *Vice President, Strategic Business Planning*; Sue Daulton, *Vice President, Operations*

Fodors.com: Megan Bell, *Executive Director, Revenue & Business Development*; Yasmin Marinaro, *Senior Director, Marketing & Partnerships*

Copyright © 2016 by Fodor's Travel, a division of Penguin Random House LLC

Writers: Bob Bower, Julianne Hoell, Jessica Robertson, Jamie Werner

Editors: Douglas Stallings (Lead Editor), Bethany Cassin Beckerlegge

Production Editor: Evangelos Vasilakis

30th Edition

ISBN 978-1-101-87854-5

ISSN 1524–7945

All details in this book are based on information supplied to us at press time. Always confirm information when it matters, especially if you're making a detour to visit a specific place. Fodor's expressly disclaims any liability, loss, or risk, personal or otherwise, that is incurred as a consequence of the use of any of the contents of this book.

SPECIAL SALES

This book is available at special discounts for bulk purchases for sales promotions or premiums. For more information, e-mail specialmarkets@penguinrandomhouse.com.

PRINTED IN THE UNITED STATES OF AMERICA

10 9 8 7 6 5 4 3 2 1

CONTENTS

CONTENTS

MAPS

ABOUT THIS GUIDE

Fodor's Recommendations

Everything in this guide is worth doing—we don't cover what isn't—but exceptional sights, hotels, and restaurants are recognized with additional accolades. **Fodor's Choice★** indicates our top recommendations, and **Best Bets** call attention to notable hotels and restaurants in various categories. Care to nominate a new place? Visit Fodors.com/contact-us.

Trip Costs

We list prices wherever possible to help you budget well. Hotel and restaurant price categories from **$** to **$$$$** are noted alongside each recommendation. For hotels, we include the lowest cost of a standard double room in high season. For restaurants, we cite the average price of a main course at dinner or, if dinner isn't served, at lunch. For attractions, we always list adult admission fees; discounts are usually available for children, students, and senior citizens.

Hotels

Our local writers vet every hotel to recommend the best overnights in each price category, from budget to expensive. Unless otherwise specified, you can expect private bath, phone, and TV in your room. *For expanded hotel reviews, facilities, and deals, visit Fodors.com.*

Top Picks	Hotels &
★ **Fodor's**Choice	**Restaurants**
	⊡ Hotel
Listings	⇗ Number of
✉ Address	rooms
✉ Branch address	⏍Ⓞ⏌ Meal plans
☎ Telephone	✕ Restaurant
🖷 Fax	⪪ Reservations
⊕ Website	⌂ Dress code
✐ E-mail	▭ No credit cards
▨ Admission fee	Ⓢ Price
⊘ Open/closed	
times	**Other**
Ⓜ Subway	⇨ See also
⊹ Directions or	☞ Take note
Map coordinates	🏌 Golf facilities

Restaurants

Unless we state otherwise, restaurants are open for lunch and dinner daily. We mention dress code only when there's a specific requirement and reservations only when they're essential or not accepted. *To make restaurant reservations, visit Fodors.com.*

Credit Cards

The hotels and restaurants in this guide typically accept credit cards. If not, we'll say so.

EUGENE FODOR

Hungarian-born Eugene Fodor (1905–91) began his travel career as an interpreter on a French cruise ship. The experience inspired him to write *On the Continent* (1936), the first guidebook to receive annual updates and discuss a country's way of life as well as its sights. Fodor later joined the U.S. Army and worked for the OSS in World War II. After the war, he kept up his intelligence work while expanding his guidebook series. During the Cold War, many guides were written by fellow agents who understood the value of insider information. Today's guides continue Fodor's legacy by providing travelers with timely coverage, insider tips, and cultural context.

EXPERIENCE THE BAHAMAS

1

WHAT'S WHERE

1 New Providence and Paradise Islands. Nassau and nearby Paradise Island are the most action-packed places in the Bahamas. From flashy megaresorts Atlantis and Baha Mar to fine dining and high-end shopping, development here is unrivaled on any of the other islands.

2 Grand Bahama Island. Urban and deserted vibes mix to create a quieter alternative to fast-paced Nassau. Lucaya has shopping, gambling, golfing, and beach parties, but old-island fishing settlements and vast expanses of untouched nature appeal to adventurous travelers.

3 The Abacos. Shallow, translucent waters, top-notch marinas, and idyllic, historic settlements spread over 120 miles of cays (some uninhabited) give the Abacos the apt title of "Sailing Capital of the Bahamas."

4 Andros, Bimini, and the Berry Islands. In the northwest corner of the Bahamas, these islands share many characteristics, most notably their reputation for excellent fishing and diving. Each exudes a casual, old-island atmosphere and abundant natural beauty.

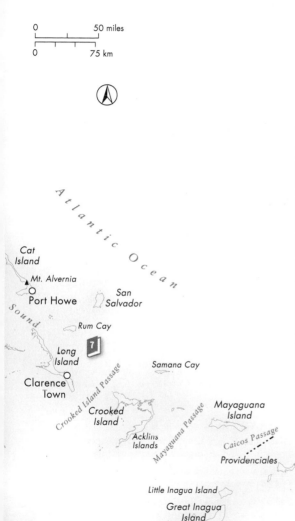

0 |———|———| 50 miles

0 |———|———| 75 km

Atlantic Ocean

Cat
Island

▲ Mt. Alvernia
○
Port Howe   San
                     Salvador
Sound

    Rum Cay

Long
Island   **7**
○   Samana Cay
Clarence
Town   *Crooked Island Passage*
        Crooked
        Island   Mayaguana
                            Island
            Acklins
            Islands   *Mayaguana Passage*
                    Caicos Passage
                        Providenciales

Little Inagua Island

Great Inagua
Island
        Lake
        Rose

5 **Eleuthera and Harbour Island.** The Nantucket of the Bahamas, Harbour Island—rimmed by its legendary pink-sand beach—is the chicest Out Island. Eleuthera is the opposite, with historic churches and pretty fishing villages, unpretentious inns, and a few upscale, intimate beach resorts.

6 **The Exumas.** Hundreds of islands skip like stones across the Tropic of Cancer, all with gorgeous white beaches and the most beautiful water in the Bahamas. Mainland Great Exuma has friendly locals and great beach parties.

7 **The Southern Out Islands.** The Bahamas' southernmost islands have so few visitors and so many natural wonders. Cat Island boasts the highest natural point in the country, San Salvador marks Christopher Columbus's discovery of the Western world, and Inagua is home to one of the largest flamingo colonies in the world.

NEED TO KNOW

BAHAMAS

★ Nassau

Atlantic Ocean

Caribbean Sea

AT A GLANCE

Capital: Nassau

Population: 383,600

Currency: Bahamian dollar; pegged to the U.S. dollar

Money: ATMs common on main islands, nonexistent on others. U.S. dollar widely accepted. Bring cash to small islands.

Language: English

Country Code: 1 242

Emergencies: 919

Driving: On the left

Electricity: 120v/60 cycles; plugs are U.S. standard two- and three-prong

Time: Same as New York

Documents: Up to 90 days with valid passport; immigration preclearance returning to U.S.

Mobile Phones: GSM (1900 bands)

Major Mobile Companies: BTC

WEBSITES

Bahamas Ministry of Tourism: ⊕ www.bahamas. com

Bahamas Out Islands Promotion Board: ⊕ www. myoutislands.com

Bahamas Visitors Guide: ⊕ www.bahamas visitorsguide.com

GETTING AROUND

✈ **Air Travel:** Nassau's Lynden Pindling International Airport and Freeport's Grand Bahama International Airport are principal gateways.

🚌 **Bus Travel:** Some larger islands have public buses, locally called "jitneys," to get around the island. Other islands, like Exuma, do not have public buses.

🚗 **Car Travel:** Rental cars are a fun way to explore the islands, though some have few roads. Be warned: you might have to settle for a rusty heap that doesn't have working seat belts and you'll hit a lot of potholes.

PLAN YOUR BUDGET

	HOTEL ROOM	MEAL	ATTRACTIONS
Low Budget	$225	$15	The Pompey Museum of Slavery and Emancipation, $5
Mid Budget	$350	$25	Half-day snorkel cruise, $60
High Budget	$475	$45	Atlantis Aquaventure Pass (cruise passengers only), $150

WAYS TO SAVE

Conch it up. This pricey delicacy is an inexpensive staple in the Bahamas, available everywhere.

Fly free with hotel booking. The Bahamas Ministry of Tourism often sponsors promotions.

Sail away . . . slowly. The Bahamas' old-fashioned mail boats are an interesting and inexpensive way to get to the Out Islands.

Kid freebies. On its website, the Bahamas Ministry of Tourism often runs promotions offering freebies for tots and tykes.

PLAN YOUR TIME

Hassle Factor	Medium. The majority of the Bahamas' smaller islands require a puddle-jumper from Nassau or Freeport, and visits here must certainly be preplanned.
3 days	Relax poolside or beachside at your Bahamas resort. Take a day to explore the island and do some sightseeing.
1 week	Enjoy and explore one of the Bahamas' principal islands: Grand Bahama Island or New Providence Island (Nassau). Take a small plane to one of the Out Islands to experience the real Bahamas.
2 weeks	Choose Nassau as your base and island hop through the Bahamas. First visit Andros (by plane or ferry); then fly to The Abacos, Eleuthera, The Exumas, and more.

WHEN TO GO

High Season: Mid-December through mid-April is the most fashionable and most expensive time to visit, when the weather is typically sunny and warm. Good hotels are often booked far in advance, and everything is open—and busy. On more touristy islands, spring breakers are most numerous in February and March.

Low Season: From July to late October, temperatures can grow oppressively hot and the weather muggy, with high risk of tropical storms. However, diving and fishing conditions are at their best. Most resorts remain open, offering deep discounts.

Value Season: From late April to June and again November to mid-December, hotel prices drop 20% to 50% from high-season prices. There are chances of scattered showers, but expect sun-kissed days and comfortable nighttime temperatures with fewer crowds.

BIG EVENTS

December–January: Junkanoo celebrations take place on Boxing Day and New Year's Day with festivities that include parades, music, dancing, and food.

February–October: Wooden sloop regattas complete with big parties on land take place—on a different island each month.

June–August: The annual Junkanoo Summer festival is held on Saturdays throughout July in Nassau.

December: The Bahamas International Film Festival in Nassau. ⊕ www.bintlfilmfest.com

READ THIS

■ *Islands in the Stream,* Ernest Hemingway. Parts take place in Bimini.

■ *Thunderball: James Bond Series,* Ian Fleming. Bond's 9th outing.

■ *The Noble Pirates,* Rima Jean. A fictional historical romance.

WATCH THIS

■ *Casino Royale.* The 21st James Bond film.

■ *Splash.* Tom Hanks encounters a nude Daryl Hannah.

■ *Cocoon.* Alien encounter filmed in Bahamas.

EAT THIS

■ *Cracked conch*: pounded, battered, and then fried.

■ *Conch salad*: diced with chopped onion, bell pepper, lime, sour orange, and local peppers.

■ *Guava duff*: compote in sweet dough, with a sweet rum or brandy sauce.

■ *Johnnycake*: thick, slightly sweet cornmeal flatbread.

■ *Peas 'n' rice*: white rice with salt pork, thyme, tomato paste, and pigeon peas.

■ *Bahamian mac 'n' cheese*: baked with cream, Daisy cheese, and butter.

BAHAMAS TODAY

Development is no longer on the back burner in the Bahamas. The largest project, the Baha Mar overhaul of the Cable Beach strip on New Providence, is years behind schedule but will finally open in 2015, and it's bound to have a huge impact on tourism to the country. Many other new projects are under way across the islands, and Bahamians have used this slow period as an opportunity to spruce up existing properties and improve an infrastructure that was starting to show signs of age and neglect.

The British Feel Remains

From driving on the left side of the road (albeit mostly in left-hand drive cars) to tea parties to wig-wearing lawyers strolling into court, the Bahamas still has a decidedly British air about it. The country gained independence from England in 1973, but old colonial habits die hard. Bahamians learn British spelling in school, and the country still uses the Westminster style of government. That said, a constant diet of American media has had an impact on the country. Bahamians measure temperature in Fahrenheit instead of Celsius, and although the English gentleman's cricket is the national sport, you'll be hard-pressed to find a local who understands the game, much less plays it.

A Playground for the Rich and Famous

With its near-perfect year-round weather, modern infrastructure and amenities, and proximity to the United States, it's no wonder that the Bahamas is a home away from Hollywood for many celebrities. Sean Connery lives behind the gates of the exclusive Lyford Cay community on New Providence Island. Johnny Depp owns his own private island in the Exumas, as do Tim McGraw and Faith Hill, David Copperfield, and Nicolas Cage, who also owns a home on Paradise Island. Mariah Carey owns a private Eleuthera estate; the island is also home to Lenny Kravitz, whose mother, actress Roxie Roker, grew up there.

Many Different Destinations

The majority of the 6 million tourists who visit the Bahamas each year experience only Nassau, Paradise Island, or perhaps Grand Bahama. But with more than 700 islands, there's so much more to see and do. Each island offers a different flavor and none of them have the hustle and bustle of big-city life experienced in the capital. The farther south you venture, the slower

WHAT WE'RE TALKING ABOUT

Bahamians are passionate about their politics. Despite elections only every five years, everyone is continually vocal about which party will win and which scandals will and will not sway voters.

The Bahamas has a parliamentary system, much like England's. As elsewhere in the British Commonwealth, there is a governor general who serves as the Queen's representative. A prime minister leads the government and bicameral legislature. The upper chamber is called the Senate, whose members are appointed by the prime minister in consultation with the opposition. Members of the lower chamber, the House of Assembly, are elected directly. Perry Christie and the Progressive Liberal Party unseated Hubert Ingraham and the Free National Movement Party for a second time in the pace. Locals have distinct looks, dialects, and surnames on each island. White Americans and British settled in the Abacos and north Eleuthera, and their strong accents—putting an *h* where there isn't one and omitting one where there should be—help tell them apart from expats. Long Island is home to a large "conchy joe" population, white Bahamians who might have had a black great grandpa. Tell someone you're a Knowles and they'll want to know if you're a Long Island Knowles or an Eleuthera Knowles.

Still Developing

Bay Street, once Nassau's Madison Avenue, is on the road to recovery after years of neglect. The esplanade just west of downtown is undergoing a major transformation with new and renovated hotels, and western New Providence continues to be developed. The Lynden Pindling International Airport is now a modern gateway that truly welcomes visitors. And following a number of false starts, the multibillion-dollar Baha Mar transformation of the Cable Beach strip is now a reality. As Nassau continues to develop, the Out Islands remain untouched, preserving the quaint nature that attracts adventure travelers each year.

Not the Caribbean

Even though the country gets lumped in with the Caribbean in glossy travel brochures and on cruise itineraries, it is not geographically a part of it. Rather than being situated in the Caribbean Sea, the islands of the Bahamas are in the Atlantic Ocean. In fact, more Bahamians have traveled to nearby South Florida than to the Caribbean. But from a cultural and political point of view, the Bahamas is aligned with the neighboring islands. The country is a full member of the Caribbean Community (CARICOM) and Bahamians will cheer on their Caribbean brothers and sisters in any sporting match.

Sustainable Development

The government works closely with the Bahamas National Trust to identify and develop protected green spaces, adding more and more land each year to the National Park System, and any developer interested in putting up a sizable or potentially environmentally sensitive project anywhere in the country is required to pay for and submit an Environmental Impact Assessment before consideration is granted.

2012. The Democratic National Alliance, led by a former FNM cabinet minister, was the first fringe party to run a full slate of candidates in 2012, and all three parties are likely to be the forerunners in 2017.

Even the most patriotic Bahamian will admit that the country's jewel—downtown Nassau—had lost its luster. As the economy slumped, particularly east of East Street, once-spectacular stores had given way to tacky T-shirt shops or have been left vacant, and sidewalks and building facades had suffered. A resurgence is now under way. New restaurants and bars have been popping up, live music and handmade crafts are available at Pompey Square, and extensive renovations and new construction are creating a complete resurgence west of the British Colonial Hilton.

BAHAMAS TOP ATTRACTIONS

Junkanoo

(A) The Bahamas' answer to Rio de Janeiro's Carnaval and New Orleans' Mardi Gras, Junkanoo is a festival of parades and parties held in Nassau on Boxing Day (the day after Christmas) and New Year's Day. Groups compete with elaborate, colorful costumes and choreographed routines to distinctly Bahamian music created by goatskin drums, clanging cowbells, shrieking whistles, and brass bands.

Pink Sand

(B) Head to Eleuthera, Harbour Island, or Cat Island to experience pink-sand beaches. The pink hue comes from the shell of a microscopic sea creature living on the coral reefs offshore. Waves crush the pink and red shells and wash them onto the beach. The most famous pink beach is on the northern side of Harbour Island.

Coral Reefs

(C) The Bahamas is home to the world's third-largest barrier reef. If diving along the Andros Barrier Reef is too advanced for you, no worries: there are many opportunities right offshore to explore the magnificent undersea world surrounding the Bahamas. Colorful coral, sea fans, and marine creatures abound; take an underwater camera, since the only things you're allowed to bring back to the surface are photographs and memories.

Fish Fry

No matter which island you're visiting, there's bound to be a fish fry in full swing at least one night of the week. Clusters of wooden shacks and stalls fry up snapper, goggle eye, or jack fish, served with fries or a thick chunk of sweet island bread. Each stall plays its own music, creating a cacophony of sound; groups gather around wooden tables to play dominoes or to catch up on the local sip-sip (gossip).

The fish fry at Arawak Cay in Nassau is open daily, but on the other islands they can be a once-a-week occurrence.

Conch

(D) Conch, pronounced "konk," is popular for more than just its distinctive, spiral-shape shells; this sea creature, essentially a giant snail, is one of the mainstays of Bahamian cuisine. Firm white conch meat is tenderized, then turned into a variety of dishes. There's cracked conch, conch salad, conch chowder, and the popular appetizer, conch fritters. Islanders often claim that conch has two other magical powers—as a hangover cure (when eaten straight from the shell with hot peppers, salt, and lime) and as an especially tasty aphrodisiac.

Rake 'n' Scrape

(E) Generations ago, many Bahamians didn't have the money to buy instruments, so they made music using whatever was at hand. Someone played a saw, someone else made a bass out of string and a tin tub, and another musician kept the beat by shaking a plastic jug filled with rocks or dried beans, or beating a goat-skin drum. Today the best place to hear authentic Rake 'n' Scrape is on Cat Island, where the style is said to have been born.

Rum Drinks

(F) The Bahamas has a long history with rum, dating back to the days of bootlegging during the United States Prohibition. Rum consumption is perfectly legal nowadays, and Bahamian bartenders have mixed up some rum-infused concoctions that have become synonymous with tropical vacations: Bahama Mama, Yellow Bird, and the Hurricane. If you're in Green Turtle Cay in Abaco, pop into Miss Emily's Blue Bee Bar, where the Goombay Smash was born.

ISLAND FINDER

	NEW PROVIDENCE AND PARADISE ISLANDS	GRAND BAHAMA ISLAND	THE ABACOS	ELEUTHERA	HARBOUR ISLAND	THE EXUMAS	THE OTHER OUT ISLANDS
BEACHES							
Activities and Sports	●	●	●	◖	◖	◖	◖
Deserted	○	◖	◖	●	○	◖	●
Party Scene	●	◖	◖	○	●	◖	○
Pink Sand	○	○	○	●	●	○	◖
CITY LIFE							
Crowds	●	◖	○	○	◖	○	○
Urban Development	●	◖	◖	○	○	○	○
ENTERTAINMENT							
Bahamian Cultural Events and Sights	●	◖	◖	○	◖	○	◖
Hot Restaurant Scene	●	◖	○	○	●	○	○
Nightlife	●	◖	○	○	◖	○	○
Shopping	●	●	◖	○	◖	◖	○
Spas	●	◖	○	○	○	◖	○
Casinos	●	◖	○	○	○	○	○
LODGING							
Luxury Hotels and Resorts	●	●	◖	◖	●	◖	◖
Condos	●	◖	◖	◖	◖	◖	◖
NATURE							
Wildlife	◖	●	●	◖	○	●	●
Ecotourism	◖	●	●	◖	○	●	●
SPORTS							
Golf	●	●	◖	○	○	●	○
Scuba and Snorkeling	●	●	●	●	●	●	●
Fishing	●	●	●	●	●	●	●

●: noteworthy; ◖ some; ○: little or none

THE BAHAMAS' BEST BEACHES

by Jessica Robertson

There's no feeling as invigorating as putting the first footprints on a powdery sand beach. With 800 miles of beachfront across the Bahamas, you could be the first to leave your mark even if you head out at sunset. But if your idea of a perfect beach day includes tropical drinks, water sports, and pulsating music, most islands have those, too.

pictured: Gold Rock Beach, Grand Bahama

BEACH PLANNING

With so many spectacular stretches of sand in the Bahamas, how do you increase your odds of stumbling upon the best ones?

Decide whether you want a deserted island experience or a beach with lots of amenities. For beaches with bathrooms, water sport activities, and pick-up volleyball games, you'll find the most options on New Providence, Paradise Island, and Grand Bahama. The Exumas, Harbour Island, Bimini, and the Abacos have a good mix of secluded sand and beach parties. The farther south you travel, the more deserted the beaches become. You might have the sand entirely to yourself on Eleuthera or any of the southern Out Islands.

Waters in the Bahamas are calm, for the most part. But when weather picks up, so do the waves. That said, most of the Atlantic-side beaches are protected by coral reefs offshore, so waves are broken up before they reach you. More good news: these natural barriers break up shells, creating powder-fine white—and in some cases pink—sand. Most of the noteworthy beaches that don't face the Atlantic are in bays and coves where you'll rarely find a ripple in the water. These are the beaches to visit with small children and if you're a serious shell seeker.

If you're traveling with children, shade is a must. When you venture away from the hotel, head for a beach lined with tall casuarinas trees. Although considered invasive nuisances by locals because the carpet of needles they shed prevent any other native foliage to grow, they do provide the best shade from the relentless Bahamian sunshine.

Pink Sands Beach, Harbour Island

PINK SAND

❶ **Club Med Beach, Eleuthera.** The island's less famous (and less crowded) pink sand beach got its name from the European resort that once overlooked it. The Atlantic-side beach has baby's-bottom-soft pink sand and lots of shady casuarinas pines.

❷ **Fine Beach, Cat Island.** Twelve miles of fine, powdery pink sand lie just north of Greenwood Beach. Despite the pristine beauty of this Atlantic-side beach, you'll likely be the only one here on any given day.

❸ **Greenwood Beach, Cat Island.** Eight miles of pink sand stretch along the Atlantic Ocean at the southeast tip of Cat Island. This remote beach is never crowded, so even on a busy beach day you'll find your own spot for swimming, strolling, or sunbathing.

❹ **Lighthouse Beach, Eleuthera.** Ask any Eleutheran to point you to his or her favorite beach, and you'll probably end up on a long drive south to Bannerman Town on roads with more potholes than asphalt. But when you get to Lighthouse Beach, you'll know you weren't led astray. Caves, cliffs, and a long-abandoned, centuries-old lighthouse make for fun exploring on the 3 mi of pink sand that curve around the island's southern point.

❺ **Pink Sands Beach, Harbour Island.** Finely crushed shells give this 3-mi stretch of sand its spectacular hue, and the wide, flat topography is ideal for sunbathing or galloping along on horseback.

Chat 'N' Chill, Stocking Island, the Exumas

Great Exuma

BEACH PARTIES

❶ **Cabbage Beach, Paradise Island.** The fun and activities from the Bahamas' largest resort, Atlantis, spill over onto 3-mi Cabbage Beach. This is the best spot on Paradise Island for Jet Skis, banana boats, or parasailing. Dreadlocked men carrying cardboard boxes of fresh coconuts will crack one open and create your very own intoxicating concoction. If you're not staying at one of the resorts lining the beach, you can access it just east of the Riu Palace.

❷ **Guana Cay Beach, the Abacos.** On Sunday afternoon, head to Nippers, on the north side of the beach, and wonder at all the people. Locals and tourists alike come out for the legendary all-day pig roast. Grab a drink and find a perch at the bar, beach, or bi-level pool.

❸ **Lucaya Beach, Grand Bahama.** If you're looking for water sports, tropical music, and drinks served beachside, this 7.5-mi stretch of white sand is a good place to lay your towel. The most action is right in front of the Our Lucaya resort, but if you head west, you can barhop at the hotels, restaurants, and beach bars lining the strip.

❹ **Stocking Island, the Exumas.** On Sunday, everyone heads to Stocking Island for the pig roast at Chat 'N' Chill. The music is good, the food is spectacular, and the drinks flow. Play volleyball, go snorkeling just offshore, or sit under a tree with a fresh bowl of conch salad and an infamous Goombay Smash.

WORTH THE TREK

❶ **Gold Rock Beach, Grand Bahama.** This seemingly endless stretch of sand near the Lucayan National Park is extraordinarily peaceful. As the tide goes out, wide, rippled sand banks pop out of the water, giving the illusion that you could walk out to the horizon. To access the beach, leave your car at the park and walk about a half hour over a low bridge crossing the mangrove swamps. Note, however, that there are planks missing in some parts of the bridge.

❷ **Sandy Cay, the Exumas.** The southernmost Exuma cay only gets more spectacular as the tide goes out. The main beach is exquisite, but it's the sand bar that emerges at low tide that makes this location well worth the short boat ride from William's Town, the southernmost settlement on Little Exuma. Starfish, sand dollars, and shells usually dot the tidal beach, and the kaleidoscopic crystal-clear water surrounding it is breathtaking. It's no wonder scenes from *Pirates of the Caribbean* were filmed here.

❸ **Surfer's Beach, Eleuthera.** The Bahamas aren't known as a surfer's paradise, but Surfer's Beach near Gregory Town, Eleuthera, is one of the sport's best-kept secrets. Even if you don't hang ten, this beautiful beach makes the treacherous journey worthwhile. Unless you're in an off-road vehicle, you'll probably have to abandon your car halfway down rough-and-bumpy Ocean Boulevard and walk nearly a mile up and over cliffs to the beach.

FODOR'S CHOICE BEST BEACHES

❶ Fernandez Bay Beach, Cat Island

Why: The odds of being the only one on this sparsely populated island's most amazing beach are definitely stacked in your favor, even though it's home to a small resort. White sand lines the crescent-shaped cove from end to end.

Claim to fame: Nothing yet. It's just waiting for you to come and discover beach perfection.

Don't miss: The beach faces west, so sundown here is spectacular.

❷ Cape Santa Maria Beach, Long Island

Why: The sand on Cape Santa Maria Beach is shimmering white and powder fine, and goes on for more than 4 mi. Lined with swaying palms, this flat beach on the northwest coast of Long Island is postcard-perfect.

Claim to fame: Christopher Columbus named this cape after one of three ships he used to sail from Spain.

Don't miss: The chance to catch dinner when the tidal flats rise out of the turquoise water at low tide.

❸ Pink Sands Beach, Harbour Island

Why: The vibrant 3-mi pink sand beach and extraordinary palette of blues and aquamarines in the ocean make a stunning backdrop for a sunrise or sunset stroll.

Claim to fame: Martha Stewart, Nicole Kidman, and Brooke Shields have stayed at the beach's posh Pink Sands resort.

Don't miss: A chance for a seaside canter. Just look for the dreadlocked man with the horses, and pick your mount.

❹ Treasure Cay Beach, the Abacos

Why: One of the widest stretches of powdery white sand in the Bahamas, the beach at Treasure Cay is 3½ mi long and borders a shallow aquamarine bay that's perfect for swimming. Activities and a restaurant are on one end, and a deserted oasis on the other.

Claim to fame: Voted the Best Beach in the Caribbean in 2004 by readers of *Caribbean Travel and Life* magazine.

Don't miss: The sand dollars that line the sand as the tide gently rolls out.

KIDS AND FAMILIES

It might not be an exaggeration to say that the Bahamas is a playground for children—or anyone else who likes building castles in the sand, searching for the perfect seashell, and playing tag with ocean waves.

While water-related activities are the most obvious enticements, these relaxed and friendly islands also offer a variety of land-based options, particularly in Nassau and on adjacent Paradise Island. For tales of the high seas, **Pirates of Nassau** has artifacts and interactive exhibits of the original pirates of the Caribbean.

The **Ardastra Gardens, Zoo and Conservation Center** is home to a variety of animals. Some you'd expect to find in the Bahamas—like the world-famous marching flamingos; others—like the pair of jaguars and Madagascar lemurs—are endangered creatures from faraway places.

Let the kids pick out their favorite straw-hat-wearing pony at the **Surrey Horse Pavilion** on Prince George Wharf and take a leisurely clip-clopping ride through the old city of Nassau. For a few extra dollars, most guides will extend your tour beyond the typical route to include other sites. Keep your guidebook handy to verify facts; guides are trained but often add their own twist on history, which can be entertaining to say the least.

Of course, megaresort **Atlantis** is always a crowd pleaser, with everything from pottery painting to remote-control-car making and racing, to an 8,000-square-foot, state-of-the-art kids camp and the Bahamas' and Caribbean's largest casino and water park.

Both Nassau and Freeport, on Grand Bahama Island, offer the chance to have close encounters of the dolphin kind. **Blue Lagoon Island Dolphin Encounter,** off Paradise Island, lets you stand waist deep in a protected pool of water and interact with trained dolphins, or put on snorkeling gear and swim with them. In Freeport, **UNEXSO** (one of whose founders was Jacques Cousteau) has a similar program at Sanctuary Bay, a refuge for dolphins. After a performance of backflips and other tricks, these intelligent creatures literally snuggle up to be petted. Older children and adults also can spend a day learning how these remarkable creatures are trained.

For water-sports enthusiasts, snorkeling, parasailing, and boating opportunities abound. In the Exumas, rent a powerboat and take the kids to Big Major's Cay to see the famous **swimming pigs.** Don't forget some scraps! Kids will also get a kick out of the hundreds of **iguanas** on nearby Allan's Cay and the **giant starfish** near mainland Great Exuma.

Much of the Bahamas' most incredible scenery is underwater, but kids of all ages can enjoy the scenes beneath the sea without even getting wet. At **Stuart Cove's Dive Bahamas** in Nassau, kids 12 and up can go 15 feet under with a SUB (Scenic Underwater Bubble) and zoom around the reefs. **Seaworld Tours'** semisubmarine explores Nassau Harbour and Paradise Island for an hour and a half with sightseeing above and below water.

FLAVORS OF BAHAMAS

You'll find food from all over the world in Nassau and Freeport restaurants, but you'll be missing out if you don't try the local cuisine. There's nothing fancy about Bahamian food, just fresh ingredients and peppery spices you'll remember long after your trip is over.

Breakfasts include standard American fare like hearty eggs, bacon, and pancakes, or Bahamian favorites such as chicken souse, boil' fish, or stew' fish, served with grits and johnnycake. At lunch you'll likely find variations on a few standards: fresh fish, conch, or chicken sandwiches, or hamburgers sided with french fries, coleslaw, or local favorites like peas 'n' rice or baked macaroni and cheese with locally grown goat or bird peppers. At dinner you'll find fish, fried chicken, and pasta.

"Steamed" fish means cooked with tomatoes, peppers, and onions. Order any fish "Bahamian style" and it will be baked and smothered in tomatoes and spices.

Conch

(A) You'll find conch, the unofficial dish of the Bahamas, prepared in a variety of ways, on nearly every menu. The sea snail has a mild flavor and taste and texture similar to calamari. The safest way to ease into conch is conch fritters, tasty fried dough balls packed with chunks of conch. Conch chowder is traditionally tomato based; cracked conch is battered and fried; grilled conch is wrapped in a foil packet with lime juice, pepper, onion, tomato, and a bit of butter and cooked on top of the barbecue; and, perhaps the most popular entrée, conch salad is akin to ceviche. Fresh-caught conch is diced and mixed with chopped onions and red or green bell peppers. The mix is drizzled with fresh lime and sour orange juice, and spiced with finely minced local hot peppers.

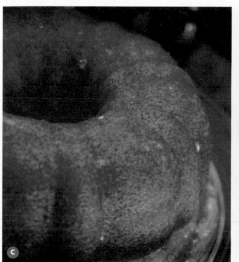

Guava Duff

This local favorite is similar to English pudding. A guava fruit compote is folded into a sweet dough and wrapped up in aluminum foil, and then steamed or boiled for as long as three hours. It's topped with a sweet rum or brandy sauce.

Johnnycake

(B) Despite its name, johnnycake is not actually a dessert but a thick, heavy, slightly sweet bread that's typically served alongside souses, soups, and stews.

Mac 'n' Cheese

If you order a side of macaroni, don't expect anything resembling Kraft mac and cheese. Bahamians bake their macaroni noodles in a mixture of cream, Daisy cheese, and butter.

Peas 'n' Rice

This popular side dish is made of white rice cooked with salt pork, thyme, a dab of tomato paste, and fresh or canned pigeon peas.

Rum Cake

(C) Given Bahamians' long-standing love affair with rum, it's no surprise that rum cake is an all-time favorite in the islands. Rum is mixed into the batter and then poured in a syrupy glaze over the fresh-out-of-the-oven cake. Don't worry about getting drunk; the alcohol cooks off when it bakes.

Souse, Boil', or Stew'

(D) A peppery bowl of chicken souse or boil' fish—the clear broth has a lime-and-goat-pepper base with pieces of chicken or meaty fish, onions, and potatoes—is an authentic breakfast dish. Variations include pig-feet and sheep-tongue souse, which are more of an acquired taste. You'll also find stew' fish or conch on most menus. The soup in bowls of stew is a Bahamian variation on the traditional French roux made with flour, water, and browning sauce, and seasoned with pepper and fresh thyme.

IT'S 5 O'CLOCK SOMEWHERE

Rum has played a particularly interesting role in Bahamian history since the days of the U.S. Prohibition, when entrepreneurial Bahamians got rich smuggling liquor across the Atlantic from Britain; a ready supply less than 50 miles away made the island nation a key trans-shipment point for contraband.

The Bahamas still has two breweries, and two rum distilleries. **Kalik**, brewed on the southwestern end of New Providence at Commonwealth Brewery, is a nice, light ale and comes in regular, Kalik Lite, Kalik Radler (including a nonalcoholic version), and, for the serious drinker, the stronger Kalik Gold. The beer was awarded four Monde Selection Gold Medals. Commonwealth also has a distillery, turning out **Ole Nassau** and **Ron Ricardo** rums. Brewery and distillery tours are not available there, but you're encouraged to tour the artisanal John Watling's Distillery located on the site of the former Buena Vista

hotel in Nassau. After your tour, take a seat, enjoy the breeze off the harbor, and enjoy their signature Rum Dum cocktail. The newer **Sands Beer**, brewed on Grand Bahama, comes in regular and light. The line recently expanded to include stouts and lagers. Tours are available at this 20-acre brewery (*242/352–4070*).

Bahamian Cocktails

Bahama Mama. Light rum, coconut rum, vanilla-infused rum, orange and pineapple juices.

(A) Goombay Smash. Light rum, coconut rum, pineapple juice, a dash of Galliano, grenadine. Created at Miss Emily's Blue Bee Bar on Green Turtle Cay, where her daughter and granddaughter still serve them daily.

Rum Punch. Campari, light rum, coconut rum, orange and pineapple juices.

Sky Juice. Gin, fresh coconut water, condensed milk, a sprinkle of nutmeg. Served

over crushed ice. In Grand Bahama, this concoction is called Gully Wash.

Best Beach Bars

(B) Chat 'N' Chill, the Exumas. The restaurant and 9-acre playground—an amazing white-sand beach is the Exumas' party central, particularly for the famous all-day Sunday pig roasts and the Friday-night bonfire beach bash. Play volleyball in the powdery sand, slam the notorious Goombay Smash, order what's cooking on the outdoor grill—fresh fish, ribs—or chat and chill.

Mackey's Sand Bar and Tiki Bar, South Bimini. Boat in or take the shuttle from Bimini Sands Resort to this party place where you can get sand between your toes just as easily inside—where sand carpets the floor—as well as outside. Play a little volleyball, take a dip in the pool, or snorkel right off the beach between cold Kaliks.

(C) Nippers, the Abacos. Guana Cay's infamous party spot is a lively bar with spectacular views of the Abaco Great Barrier Reef. The Frozen Nipper—a slushy rum-and-fruit-juice beverage—goes down well on a hot day. Don't miss the Sunday pig roasts, which draw everyone on the island.

Pete's Pub, Abaco. This beachside tiki hut in Little Harbour is jumping from 11 am to sunset. Take a dip in the shallow harbor or luxuriate on the beach with a cup of their special rum punch—the Blaster.

Tony Macaroni's, Grand Bahama. Follow up Tony's famous roasted conch with a Gully Wash (fresh coconut water, condensed milk, gin, a sprinkle of nutmeg) on Taino Beach, arguably the island's most spectacular. There's usually great live music at this thatch-roof shack.

GREAT ITINERARIES

ISLAND-HOPPING FOR 1 WEEK

The Bahamas is comprised of more than 700 islands, yet many visitors experience just one in a single visit. With limited scheduled transportation between the islands, it's difficult to island-hop without going back to Nassau for each leg, but this itinerary shows how you can use mail boats, speed boats, and scheduled flights to experience Nassau, Paradise Island, Rose Island, Sandals Island, mainland Exuma, and a handful of the Exuma cays and do it all in just a week, provided you arrive in Nassau on a Monday since the mail boat to George Town leaves on Tuesday.

1 Day: Nassau

Explore the sprawling marine habitat, face your fears on the exhilarating waterslides (including a clear acrylic slide that plunges through a shark tank), and get up close with sea lions and dolphins at the iconic Atlantis Resort. A new policy limits Aquaventure access to resort guests or cruise-ship passengers (with a day pass) so you'll need to plan on at least one night in the sprawling resort or at Comfort Suites next door. Dine at one of the 21 restaurants on-property, and then dance the night away at Aura nightclub.

1 Day: Mail Boat Passage

On Day 2, head downtown and take in the history, architecture, culture, and (most important of all) the food of historic Nassau on the Bites of Nassau Food Tour. With your belly full, head to the eastern side of Potter's Cay Dock to the *Grand Master* mail boat ☎ *(242/393–1041)*. Once you get your tickets (no need to book in advance), head over to the colorful stalls to enjoy a game of dominoes

and an ice cold Sands or Kalik beer. The mail boat, which leaves port between 4 and 5:30 every Tuesday afternoon, will be your transportation, overnight accommodations, and dinner restaurant on your way to George Town, Exuma, all for less than $60 per person one-way. Don't expect anything fancy; you'll get only a basic bunk in one of two small and stark—but air-conditioned—cabins. For dinner it's a plate full of the same hearty meal enjoyed by the crew.

1 Day: George Town, Exuma

Following your 14-hour overnight passage—complete with unbelievable sunsets, a strong possibility of dolphin spotting, and space shared with everything from cars to mail to sheep and goats—you'll arrive in George Town bright and early. Make Club Peace and Plenty your first stop for a Bahamian breakfast staple: boiled fish and johnny cake. Drop your bags at your prebooked accommodations, and take the water taxi from the Government Dock for a day of sun and fun at Chat 'N' Chill on Stocking Island, just a mile offshore. Swim with some wild stingrays that pop in daily for lunch, and treat yourself to tropical libations and conch salad prepared right before your eyes. When you're done chatting and chilling, head back over to the mainland for a restful night, as there's not likely to be much going on outside of Fish Fry Friday or the annual Regatta.

1 Day: Exuma Cays

The next day, island-hop the stunning Exuma Cays on a half-day excursion with Four C's Adventures (*see Sports and the Outdoors in Exuma Cays*). Skim through the azure, crystal clear waters from island to island, feeding iguanas on Allan's Cay, petting the swimming pigs on Big Major

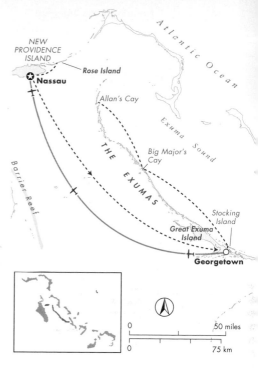

Cay, taking the perfect selfie at one of the beautiful beaches, and snorkeling in ocean blue holes. Catch the last scheduled flight back to Nassau, where you'll spend another night.

1 Day: Rose Island

Just 8 miles off the eastern coast of New Providence lies Rose Island. A popular weekend boating drop for locals, the long island is uninhabited. Book a night at the new Sandy Toes Retreat (☎ 363–8637 ⊕ *www.sandytoesroseisland.com*; starting at $795 a night), a beautifully appointed two-bedroom cottage with unbelievable ocean views. Your boat transportation is included, and once the excursion day-trippers leave at 3:45, you'll have the island to yourself.

1 Day: Nassau

Catch the 20-minute boat ride back to Nassau, and head west to wrap up your island-hopping week with a luxurious massage on the Sandals resort private island. A day pass gives you access to an array of restaurants, unlimited beverages, and all the amenities, including a private offshore island where you can be pampered in a tiki hut as the waves break on the northern shore, explore the three beaches, or lounge in the pool, and either head home late in the afternoon or early evening or spend one final night on New Providence.

TIPS

Because of the mail boat schedule, this itinerary should begin on a Monday.

The *Grand Master* departs Tuesday between 4 and 5:30. Just show up a few hours early to buy your passenger ticket.

Mail boat has two rooms with six bunks each and no shower facilities onboard.

Arrange provisioning for your meals on Rose Island, or stop at a food store in Nassau and stock up.

GREAT ITINERARIES

ISLAND-HOPPING FOR TWO WEEKS

While you could easily spend two weeks soaking up the sun, snorkeling, scuba diving, beach combing, and enjoying local cuisine on any single island, this itinerary let's you see more of the Bahamas, taking you to Nassau, the Exuma Cays, Grand Bahama, and the Abacos over two weeks.

1 Day: Nassau

Plan on arriving early and dropping your bags at your hotel. Explore downtown Nassau this morning by foot, stopping in at the National Art Gallery, the Straw Market, and the Graycliff Cigar Factory, then rent a scooter and head west. Baha Mar is a good spot to take a break and grab a drink, then continue west. Have lunch at Dino's Gourmet Conch Salad stand and carry on to Clifton Heritage National Park, where you can immerse yourself in the slave and plantation history and snorkel out to the Atlas underwater statue just offshore.

2 Days: Ship Channel Cay, Exuma

Powerboat Adventures offers an exciting day trip to a private island called Ship Channel Cay, near the top of the Exuma Cays. Enjoy a day feeding iguanas and stingrays, watching the shark feeding, and snorkeling in the beautiful waters. When the day-trippers head back to Nassau, wave good-bye from the dock and retreat to your private cottage for a night on a deserted island. After breakfast, head to the side of the island few day-trippers even know exists for a day of complete sunbathing privacy. Lunch and an open bar are provided, and you'll head back to Nassau in the afternoon with the day-trippers. Try your luck tonight in one of the world-class casinos at Atlantis or Baha Mar and spend one more night in Nassau.

2 Days: Grand Bahama

Fly to Grand Bahama, where you'll spend two nights, and head to UNEXSO to swim with dolphins in their natural open-ocean habitat. Once back on land, head next door to Port Lucaya Marketplace for some shopping, drinks, live music, and dinner in Count Basie Square. The next morning, rent a car and venture east to the Lucayan National Park, timing your visit for low tide. After exploring the fascinating caves, walk across the street along the boardwalk over the mangroves to Gold Rock Beach. You can walk for miles along the rippled sand and lounge in the tide pools.

1 Day: Treasure Cay, Abaco

Catch the 8:30 am Pinder's Ferry from McClean's Town, Grand Bahama, to Crown Haven at the northern tip of Abaco. The Great Abaco Express charter bus will take you the 45-minute drive into Treasure Cay, where you'll spend the night. Grab a towel and relax on the world-famous pink-sand beach.

2 Days: Green Turtle Cay, Abaco

Indulge in one of the delicious cinnamon buns from Café La Florence near the marina before you catch the ferry to nearby Green Turtle Cay, where you'll spend the night. Head out for a memorable scuba or snorkel day trip with Brendals; you'll likely experience another wild-dolphin encounter. The next morning, brush up on Bahamian history as you wander around New Plymouth by golf cart. Be sure to stop in at Miss Emily's Blue Bee Bar for an authentic Goombay Smash. Get the last ferry (4:30 pm) back to Treasure Cay and take a taxi south to Marsh Harbour for the night.

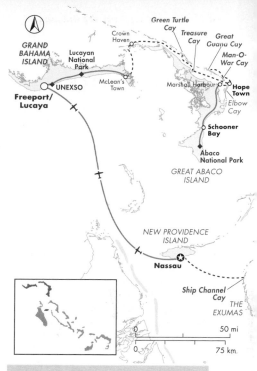

2 Days: Hope Town

Rent a small speedboat and head over to Elbow Cay, making the lighthouse your first stop. The views from the top are breathtaking. Cruise on over to Hope Town to explore the quaint town by foot. Enjoy a spectacular sunset and incredible dinner at FireFly. The next morning head back out in your boat to Tahiti Beach, and then have lunch over at Lubber's Landing on Lubber's Quarters, where you'll hang out on the beach or bar, enjoy an evening bonfire, and spend the night in one of the very private cottages.

1 Day: Man O' War and Guana Cays

At your leisure, head out to Man O' War Cay to watch the men build traditional wooden boats. Lunch is at Nippers on nearby Great Guana Cay. Expect huge crowds if you happen to catch it on a Sunday, but otherwise you'll likely have the sprawling bar, pool, and beach to yourself. Before sundown, head back to Marsh Harbour to check into a hotel.

1 Day: Schooner Bay

Rent a car and drive south to Schooner Bay. Book a room and dinner well in advance at one of the upscale bonefishing lodges in the area so you can try your hand at bonefishing on the world-famous marls. After dinner walk out to the observation deck for a night of stargazing.

1 Day: Southern Abaco

Early the next morning, head deep into the Abaco National Park at the southernmost tip of the island with DSB excursions, where you'll explore caves and abandoned plantation buildings, climb to the top of the lighthouse, and picnic on a beach that probably hasn't been seen by anyone else in a very long time. Drive back to Marsh Harbour and fly home direct or via Nassau.

TIPS

If you're not comfortable handling a speedboat, you can do this island-hopping itinerary using Albury's Ferry service, but you will have to go back and forth to Marsh Harbour to make connections.

Prebook your Great Abaco Express charter ($10 per person) to Treasure Cay (☎ 242/646-7072) or risk being stuck in Crown Haven.

WHEN TO GO

The Bahamas enjoys sunny days, refreshing breezes, and moderate-to-warm temperatures with little change from season to season. That said, the most pleasant time to visit is from December through May, when temperatures average 70°F–75°F. It stands to reason that hotel prices during this period are at their highest—around 30% higher than during the less popular times. The rest of the year is hot and humid and prone to tropical storms; temperatures hover around 80°F–85°F. Temperatures in Freeport, Bimini, and the Abacos are nearly the same: a degree or two cooler in spring and fall, and a degree or two warmer in summer. As you head down to the more southern islands, expect temperatures to be about a degree or two warmer than the capital year-round.

Whether you want to join it or avoid it, be advised that spring break takes place primarily from the end of February to late March (and sometimes up to mid-April). This means a lot of vacationing college students, beach parties, sports events, and entertainment, mainly in New Providence, Grand Bahama, and Hope Town, Abaco.

Hurricane Season

Hurricane season is from June 1 through November 30, with greatest risk of a storm from August through October. Meteorology being what it is, you generally know days in advance if the area you're traveling to will be affected. Check with your hotel if a storm is on the horizon—the islands are so spread out that, just as most of the United States was unaffected when Katrina hit New Orleans, one island could be experiencing hurricane-force winds while it's nice and sunny in another.

The Bahamas has been relatively lucky when it comes to hurricanes. Nassau, the capital and central hub of the country, has not had a direct devastating hit in many decades. A glancing blow from a storm can result in some downed trees and power lines as well as localized flooding, but Bahamians have learned how to prepare for these situations and within days manage to get things pretty much back to normal. The country enforces strict building codes to guard against major structural damage from the 100-mile-an-hour winds a hurricane can bring with it. Even in the Out Islands, where more storms have come aground, the worst damage is caused by tidal flooding, which washes away quickly.

Most hotels have meticulously detailed hurricane plans that are put into action once a major storm is headed toward the country. If the storm is a major category system, extra flights are lined up to help evacuate tourists, and some hotels have hurricane policies that offer guests free stays at a later date if their vacation is interrupted by Mother Nature.

GREAT WATER ADVENTURES

In an archipelago nation named for shallow seas that amaze even astronauts in space, don't miss having a close marine encounter. Water adventures range from a splash at the beach to shark diving. Or stay between the extremes with fishing and snorkeling.

by Justin Higgs

WHERE TO DIVE AND SNORKEL IN THE BAHAMAS

Although most water in the Bahamas is clear enough to see to the bottom from your boat, snorkeling or diving gets you that much closer to the country's true natives. Coral reefs, blue holes, drop-offs, and sea gardens abound.

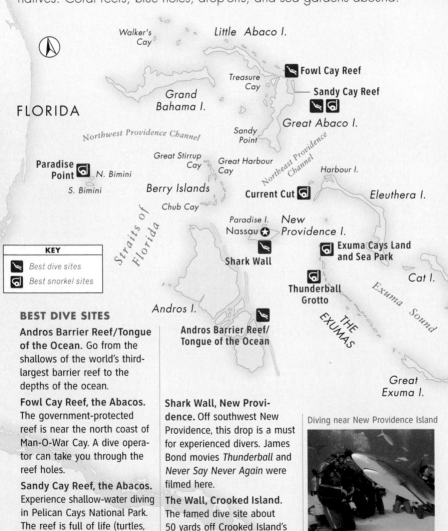

BEST DIVE SITES

Andros Barrier Reef/Tongue of the Ocean. Go from the shallows of the world's third-largest barrier reef to the depths of the ocean.

Fowl Cay Reef, the Abacos. The government-protected reef is near the north coast of Man-O-War Cay. A dive operator can take you through the reef holes.

Sandy Cay Reef, the Abacos. Experience shallow-water diving in Pelican Cays National Park. The reef is full of life (turtles, spotted eagle rays, tarpon), thanks to its protected status.

Shark Wall, New Providence. Off southwest New Providence, this drop is a must for experienced divers. James Bond movies *Thunderball* and *Never Say Never Again* were filmed here.

The Wall, Crooked Island. The famed dive site about 50 yards off Crooked Island's coast drops from 45 feet to thousands.

Diving near New Providence Island

BEST SNORKEL SITES

Current Cut, Eleuthera.
Near the Current settlement in North Eleuthera there is great drift snorkel with the right tide.

Exuma Cays Land and Sea Park. This 176-sq-mi park was the first of its kind. Since the park is protected and its waters have essentially never been fished, you can see what the ocean looked like before humanity.

Paradise Point, Bimini. Off northern Bimini, this area is rich in sea life and is famous for the underwater stone path some believe marks the road to the lost city of Atlantis. Dolphins and black coral gardens are just offshore.

Sandy Cay Reef, the Abacos. The water surrounding this reef is just 25-feet deep, making it great for snorkeling or diving.

Thunderball Grotto, the Exumas. This three-story limestone-ceiling cave at the northern end of the Exumas chain was featured in the James Bond movie of the same name.

Diving near Bimini

EXTREME DIVING ADVENTURES

Various outfitters on Grand Bahama and New Providence offer shark dives. With **Caribbean Divers** (☎ 242/373–9111 ⊕ www.bellchannelinn.com) and **UNEXSO** in Grand Bahama and **Stuart Cove's** in New Providence, you'll watch dive masters feed reef sharks which brush by you—no cage included. Dive masters control the ferocity and location of the frenzy, so the sharks' attention is on the food.

Incredible Adventures (☎ 800/644–7382 ⊕ www.incredible-adventures.com) in Grand Bahama offers cage diving with tiger sharks. You'll sit in the water as giant sharks come breathtakingly close, the only thing between you a few strips of metal.

Feeding sharks when humans are present make these dives controversial, especially when multiple sharks are involved and there's the possibility of a frenzy. Dive operators doing these extreme adventures are experienced and knowledgeable about shark-feeding patterns and signs of aggression, but partake in these dives at your own risk.

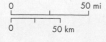

San Salvador

Rum Cay

Long I.

Crooked Island Passage

Samana Cay

The Wall
Crooked I.

Mayaguana Passage

Mayaguana I.

Acklins I.

0   50 mi
0   50 km

Little Inagua I.

Great Inagua I.

French Angelfish	Four-Eyed Butterflyfish	Grunt
Nassau Grouper	Parrotfish	Queen Triggerfish
Sergeant Major	Snapper	Iang
Barracuda*	Lionfish*	Shark*

*dangerous fish

WHAT YOU'LL SEE UNDER THE SEA

Reefs in the Bahamas are alive with colorful life. Vibrant hard corals—such as star, brain, staghorn, and elk—and waving purple sea fans are home to schools of myraid fish, some pictured above. Be on the lookout for lionfish; a prick from the fins of this poisonous fish is painful and could send you to the hospital. The most common sharks in the Bahamas are nurse sharks (typically non-threatening to humans) and Caribbean reef sharks. The deeper you dive, the bigger and more varied shark species get.

Generally, the further the reef is from a developed area the more abundant the marine life, but even sites around developed islands might surprise you.

ISLAND-HOPPING

The Bahamas is a boater's paradise, with shallow protected waters and secluded, safe harbors. In small island groups, travel takes just a few hours, even minutes. The Abacos archipelago and the Exuma Cays are the best and most convenient islands to hop.

THE ABACOS

If you're cruising from Florida, clear customs in West End, Grand Bahama; the Abaco Cays start just north.

Grand Cay, at the northern end of the chain, has a small community of 200 people. Most yachters find the anchorage off the community dock adequate, and the docks at Rosie's Place can take boats up to 80 feet. Double anchors are advised to handle the harbor's tidal current.

Fox Town, on the "mainland" of Little Abaco, is a good fuel stop, the first if you're traveling east from West End. Farther south, stock up on provisions in **Coopers Town,** Little Abaco's largest community. Just northeast is an 80-slip marina at **Spanish Cay.**

Cruising south, **Green Turtle Cay** has excellent yachting facilities. The Green Turtle Club dominates White Sound's northern end, whereas Bluff

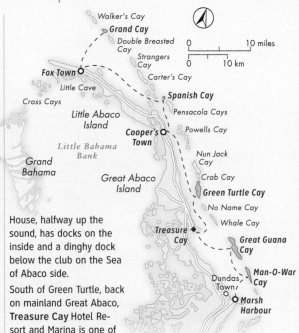

House, halfway up the sound, has docks on the inside and a dinghy dock below the club on the Sea of Abaco side.

South of Green Turtle, back on mainland Great Abaco, **Treasure Cay** Hotel Resort and Marina is one of the largest marinas on the island. Here you can play golf, dine, or relax on a beautiful beach.

Straight back out in the Sea of Abaco is **Great Guana Cay** and its gorgeous 7-mi strip of pristine sand. On Sunday don't miss the famous pig roast at Nippers Bar. Just south is New England–style charmer **Man-O-War Cay,** a boatbuilding settlement with deserted beaches and 28-slip Man-O-War Marina. Fowl Cay

Park offers great snorkeling and diving just to the north.

Back on Great Abaco, **Marsh Harbour** is the capital and most populated settlement in the Abacos. Boaters consider it one of the easiest harbors to enter. It has several full-service marinas, including the 190-slip Boat Harbour Marina and the 80-slip Conch Inn Marina. This is the stop to catch up on banking and business needs. There are great restaurants and shops, too.

Fishing near Green Turtle Cay

Exuma Cays Land and Sea Park

THE EXUMA CAYS

To really get off the beaten path, the Exuma Cays are where it's at. This 120-mi archipelago is made up of small cays, many of which are still uninhabited or privately owned, and interspersed with sand banks and spits. Throughout is excellent diving and snorkeling. Boaters usually stock up and clear customs in Nassau, cross the yellow banks to the north of the chain, and slowly make their way south.

BOAT TOURS

These outfitters will take you on island-hopping adventures.

Captain Plug. ☎ 242/577–0273 ⊕ www.captplug.com. $500 for a full day of island hopping in the Abacos.

Four C's Adventures. ☎ 242/464–1720 ⊕ www.exumawatertours.com. $1400 or $160 per person for a full day excursion to the Exuma Cays from Great Exuma.

Powerboat Adventures. ☎ 242/363–2265 ⊕ www.powerboatadventures.com. $200 per person to the Exuma Cays from Nassau.

Highbourne Cay at the chain's northern end has a marina and food store. You can explore many of the surrounding cays by tender if you prefer to dock here. Nearby, **Allan's Cay** is home to hundreds of iguanas that readily accept food.

Norman's Cay has an airstrip and Norman's Cay Beach Club has a fantastic restaurant and bar. Just south is the 176-sq-mi **Exuma Cays Land and Sea Park.** It has some of the country's best snorkeling and diving. Warderick Wells Cay houses the park headquarters, which has nature trail maps and a gift shop. Just below, **Compass Cay** has a marina known for its friendly nurse sharks and a small convenience store. **Pipe Creek,** which winds between Compass and Staniel Cays, has great shelling, snorkeling, diving, and bonefishing. **Staniel Cay** is the hub of activity in these parts and a favorite destination of yachters. That's thanks to the Staniel Cay Yacht Club, the only full-service marina in the cays. It makes a good base for visiting **Big Major's Cay,** where wild pigs swim out to meet you,

Ship Channel Cay
Allan's Cay
Highbourne Cay
Lang Cay
Norman's Cay
Shroud Cay
Hawksbill Cay
Cistern Cay
Exuma Cays Land and Sea Park
Waderick Wells Cay
Halls Pond Cay
Bolls Cay
O'Brian's Cay
Compass Cay
Pipe Creek
Joe Cay
Thomas Cay
Big Major's Cay
Thunderball Grotto
Staniel Cay

0 ___ 10 miles
0 ___ 10 km

and **Thunderball Grotto,** a beautiful marine cave that snorkelers (at low tide) and experienced scuba divers can explore.

BONEFISHING

WHAT IS BONEFISHING?
Bonefishing is the fly-fishing sport of choice in the Bahamas. The country is full of pristine shallow flats and mangroves where stealthy "gray ghosts"—silvery white, sleek fish—school in large groups. Hooking one is a challenge, as the fish are fast, strong, and perfectly camouflaged to the sand and water.

To catch bonefish you need the right mix of knowledge, instinct, and patience. Guides are the best way to go, as their knowledge of the area and schooling patterns gives them an uncanny ability to find bonefish quickly.

EQUIPMENT
Basics include a fly-fishing rod and reel and the right lure. Experienced anglers, guides, and fishing-supply dealers can help you gear up with the best and latest technology. Bonefishing is catch and release, so always use barbless hooks and work quickly when removing them to avoid stressing the fish. Wear comfortable, light clothing that protects much of your body from the sun, as you'll be out for hours without shade.

In many places you can just walk offshore onto the flats. Some anglers use shallow draft boats with a raised platform in the back, where they pole into extremely shallow areas.

BEST PLACES TO BONEFISH
Bonefish hang out in shallow flats and mangrove areas. Andros, Bimini, and the Exumas have the best bonefishing; Abaco, Eleuthera, and Long Island also provide excellent adventures. If you have the time, visit the southernmost islands, like Crooked, Acklins, or Inagua, where these gray ghosts are "uneducated" to anglers.

WHERE TO STAY

Bonefishing lodges are common in the Bahamas and often include top-notch guides. Accommodations are usually basic. Here are our top bonefishing lodges:

- **Andros Island Bonefishing Club**

- **Bishop's Bonefish Resort, Grand Bahama**

- **Crooked Island Lodge**

- **Peace and Plenty Bonefish Lodge, the Exumas**

- **Rickmon Bonefish Lodge, the Abacos**

- **Small Hope Bay Lodge, Andros**

(left pg) Bonefishing in Andros.
(right) A prize catch.

OTHER TYPES OF FISHING

Make sure you are familiar with fishing regulations before you begin your adventure. Visit ⊕ *www.bahamas-travel.info.*

DEEP-SEA FISHING

Deep water is just a few miles off most islands, where anglers try for large ocean fish—tuna, wahoo, mahi mahi, shark, and marlin. Like bonefishing, the fight is what most anglers are after; however, a day on the ocean can provide a great meal. The Abacos has great deep-sea fishing, and many tournaments are held there each year.

REEF/SHOAL FISHING

Fishing with a rod, or Bahamian "handlining" can be a great family fishing adventure. Anchoring near a shoal or reef, or even trolling with a lure, can be relaxing. The Out Islands are home to shoals, reefs, and wrecks that are less visited by fishing enthusiasts.

SPEARFISHING

Most reefs are okay for free-dive spear fishing, but spear guns (guns that fire spears) are illegal in the Bahamas. Spear is the traditional Bahamian fishing method, so reefs close to more developed islands tend to have fewer fish. The Out Islands still have lesser-known spots good for spearfishing.

SAILING

Sailing is popular in the
Bahamas, and there are many
regattas held here throughout
the year. The Abacos, the sailing capital of the Bahamas,
also host an open regatta,
inviting all classes of boats
and sailors to join in for a
week of island hopping and
racing. Large sailboats are
available for charter in Marsh
Harbour and Hope Town.

NEW PROVIDENCE AND PARADISE ISLANDS

WELCOME TO NEW PROVIDENCE AND PARADISE ISLANDS

TOP REASONS TO GO

★ **Beach-hop:** New Providence beaches, though less secluded than those on the Out Islands, still tempt travelers with their balmy breezes and aquamarine water. Choose between the more remote beaches on the island's western end, action-packed strips on Cable Beach, or public beaches in downtown Nassau.

★ **Dine with the best of 'em:** New Providence is the country's culinary capital. Eat at a grungy local dive for one meal, then feast in a celebrity-chef restaurant for the next.

★ **Experience Atlantis:** Explore the world's largest outdoor aquarium, splash around in the something-for-everyone water park, or dine at one of the 40-plus restaurants, all while never leaving the resort property.

★ **Celebrate Junkanoo:** This uniquely Bahamian carnival takes place the day after Christmas and again on New Year's Day. If you miss it, there are smaller parades in Marina Village on Paradise Island each Wednesday and Saturday at 9:30 pm.

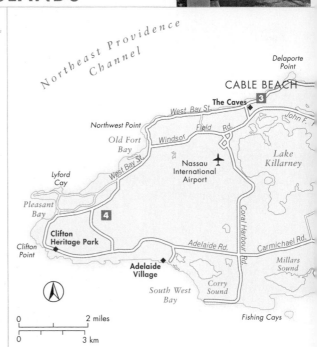

1 Nassau. Pink buildings dating back to the colonial era are interspersed with modern-day office complexes; horses pull their wooden carriages alongside stretch limousines; and tourists browse the local craft-centric straw market or shop for luxurious handbags at Gucci, all in this historic capital city.

2 Paradise Island. P. I. (as locals call the island) is connected to downtown Nassau's east end by a pair of bridges. Atlantis is a beachfront resort complete with a gamut of dining options, a huge casino, and some of the region's fanciest shops. Most memorable, however, are the water-based activities, slides, and aquariums which make it a perfect family destination. Love it or despise it, it's today's face of paradise.

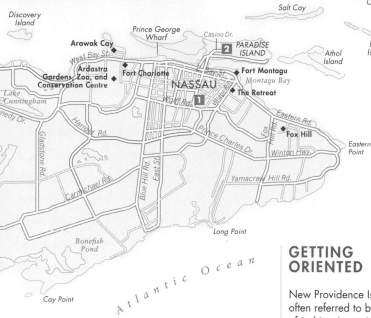

GETTING ORIENTED

New Providence Island is often referred to by the name of its historic capital city, Nassau. More than two-dozen hotels and at least twice as many restaurants lure more than 2 million tourists to the city—and nearby Paradise Island and Cable Beach—annually. The heart of commerce and government and the bulk of the country's 378,000 people are crammed onto the 21-mile-by-7-mile island, less than 200 miles from Miami. Venturing outside the three main tourist areas will give you a better idea of true Bahamian life and a glimpse at some less visited but worth-the-trek attractions.

3 Cable Beach. The crescent-shaped stretch of sand west of Nassau is being transformed into Baha Mar, a 1,000-acre destination to rival Paradise Island. Four brand-new resorts; a top-class golf course; the largest casino in the Caribbean; a sprawling upscale spa; a snorkeling sanctuary; and a vast array of restaurants, bars, and nightlife guarantee there is something to suit everyone. A short walk west of the resort complex are a smattering of restaurants and cafés.

4 Western New Providence. West of Cable Beach's high-rise hotels, New Providence becomes primarily residential, with small restaurants and bars along the way. West Bay Street hugs the coastline, providing spectacular ocean views. This part of the island is the least developed, so it's the perfect spot to find a secluded beach or go bird-watching.

Updated
by Jessica
Robertson

An incongruous mix of glitzy casinos and quiet shady lanes, splashy megaresorts and tiny settlements that recall a distant simpler age, land development unrivaled elsewhere in the Bahamas, and vast stretches of untrammeled territory. This is New Providence Island, a grab-bag destination. The island, home to two-thirds of all Bahamians, provides fast-paced living, nightlife that goes on until dawn, and high-end shopping strips. And when all the hustle and bustle becomes too much, it's easy to find quiet stretches of sandy white beach where the only noise is the waves rolling in.

In the course of its history, the island has weathered the comings and goings of lawless pirates, Spanish invaders, slave-holding British Loyalists who fled the United States after the Revolutionary War, Civil War–era Confederate blockade runners, and Prohibition rum-runners. Nevertheless, New Providence remains most influenced by England, which sent its first royal governor to the island in 1718. Although Bahamians won government control in 1967 and independence six years later, British influence is felt to this day.

Nassau is the nation's capital and transportation hub, as well as its banking and commercial center. The fortuitous combination of tourist-friendly enterprise, tropical weather, and island flavor with a European overlay has not gone unnoticed: each year more than 2.5 million cruise-ship passengers arrive at Nassau's Prince George Wharf.

There's a definite hustle and bustle in this capital city that's not found elsewhere in the country, but that doesn't mean you have to follow suit. From shark diving and snorkeling to bicycle tours, horseback riding, tennis, and golf, active pursuits abound in New Providence. Avid watersports fans will find a range of possibilities, including paddleboarding, sailing, kayaking, and deep-sea fishing. Or simply cruise the clear Bahamian waters for a day trip or an evening ride.

PLANNING

2

WHEN TO GO

With the warm Gulf Stream currents swirling and balmy trade winds blowing, New Providence is an appealing year-round destination. Temperatures usually hover in the 70s and 80s and rarely get above 90°F on a midsummer's day or below 60°F on a winter's night. June to October tend to be the hottest and wettest months, although rain is often limited to periodic afternoon showers.

The best time to visit the island is December to May, especially if you're escaping the cold. Don't mind the locals, who'll likely tell you it's too chilly to hit the beach in winter, but you may want to pack a light sweater if you plan on dining outdoors. Visitors from colder climates may find the humid summer days and nights a bit stifling. Be aware that tropical depressions, tropical storms, and hurricanes are a possibility in New Providence during the Atlantic hurricane season from early June to late November. Expect to pay between 15% and 30% less off-season at most resorts.

TOP FESTIVALS

WINTER **Bahamas International Film Festival.** In early December, the Bahamas International Film Festival in Nassau celebrates cinema in paradise, with screenings, receptions, and movie-industry panels. ⊠ *Nassau* ⊕ *www. bintlfilmfest.com.*

Christmas Jollification. This ongoing arts-and-crafts fair with Bahamian Christmas crafts, food, and music is held at the Retreat in Nassau the third weekend in November. ⊠ *Nassau* ⊕ *www.bnt.bs.*

Junior Junkanoo Parade. The island's schoolchildren compete for bragging rights in the Junior Junkanoo Parade in mid-December. The parade starts at 6 pm and kids in preschool through high school dress up in crepe paper costumes and put on an exciting show.

Junkanoo. Once Christmas dinner is over, the focus shifts to Junkanoo. The first major parade of the season starts just after midnight in downtown Nassau. There's a second parade on New Year's Day. ⊠ *Nassau.*

SPRING **International Dog Show & Obedience Trials.** In Nassau, watch dogs of all classes compete at the International Dog Show & Obedience Trials, held mid-March. Check *www.bahamaskennelclub.org* for location.

SUMMER **Junkanoo Summer Festival.** Bay Street is transformed during the annual Junkanoo Summer festival held every Saturday night 7 pm–midnight during the month of July. Watch some of the island's top Junkanoo groups and sample local foods. ⊠ *Nassau* ⊕ *www.bahamas.com/ summerfestivals.*

Fox Hill Festival. The Nassau Fox Hill Festival in early August pays tribute to Emancipation with church services, Junkanoo parades, music, cookouts, games, and other festivities.

FALL **International Cultural Weekend.** Eat and drink your way around the world at the International Cultural Weekend, hosted at the Botanic Gardens the third weekend of October.

GETTING HERE AND AROUND

AIR TRAVEL

Lynden Pindling International Airport (NAS) is 8 miles west of Nassau. Many major U.S. airlines fly to Nassau from several different gateways; in addition, the nation's flag carrier, Bahamasair, flies to Nassau from four airports in Florida: Fort Lauderdale (FLL), Miami (MIA), Orlando (MCO), and West Palm Beach (PBI). There is no public bus service from the airport to hotels. Many smaller airlines depart from Nassau to the other islands of the Bahamas. Major car-rental companies are represented at the airport. A taxi ride for two people from the airport to downtown Nassau costs $27; to Paradise Island, $42 (this includes the $1 bridge toll); and to Cable Beach, $25. Each additional passenger is $3, and excess baggage costs $2 a bag.

BOAT AND FERRY TRAVEL

Water taxis travel between Prince George Wharf and Paradise Island during daylight hours at half-hour intervals. The one-way cost is $3 per person, and the trip takes 12 minutes. Nassau is also the primary hub for Bahamas mailboats and ferries to the Out Islands.

BUS TRAVEL

The frequent jitneys are the cheapest choice on routes such as Cable Beach to downtown Nassau. Fare is $1.25 each way, and exact change is required. Hail one at a bus stop, hotel, or public beach. In downtown Nassau jitneys wait on Frederick Street and along the eastern end of Bay Street. Bus service runs throughout the day until 7 pm.

CAR TRAVEL

Rent a car if you plan to explore the whole island. Rentals are available at the airport, downtown, on Paradise Island, and at some resorts for $55–$120 per day. Gasoline costs between $5 and $6 a gallon. Remember to drive on the left. Virgo Car Rental, a local company, doesn't have a website or an airport rental desk, but it does offer a courtesy shuttle to its nearby office.

Contacts Avis Rent A Car. ✉ *Lynden Pindling International Airport, Nassau* ☎ *242/377–7121* ⊕ *www.avis.com.* **Budget Rent-A-Car.** ✉ *Lynden Pindling International Airport, Nassau* ☎ *242/377–9000* ⊕ *www.budget.com.* **Dollar/ Thrifty Rent A Car.** ✉ *Lynden Pindling International Airport, Nassau* ☎ *242/377–8300* ⊕ *www.dollar.com.* **Hertz Rent-A-Car.** ✉ *Lynden Pindling International Airport, Nassau* ☎ *242/377–8684* ⊕ *www.hertz.com.* **Virgo Car Rental.** ☎ *242/377–1275.*

SCOOTER TRAVEL

Two people can rent a motor scooter for about $65 for a half day, $85 for a full day.

TAXI TRAVEL

Unless you plan to jump all over the island, taxis are the most convenient way to get around. The fare is $9 plus $1 bridge toll between downtown Nassau and Paradise Island, $20 from Cable Beach to Paradise Island (plus $1 toll), and $18 from Cable Beach to Nassau. Fares are for two passengers; each additional passenger is $3. It's customary to tip taxi drivers 15%.

Contacts **Bahamas Transport.** ⊠ *Nassau* ☏ *242/323–5111.* **Taxi Cab Union.** ⊠ *Nassau* ☏ *242/323–5818.*

HOTELS

If you want to mix with locals and experience a little more of Bahamian culture, choose a hotel in downtown Nassau. Its beaches are not dazzling; if you want to be beachfront on a gorgeous white strand, stay on Cable Beach or Paradise Island's Cabbage Beach. Reasons to stay in Nassau include proximity to shopping and affordability (although the cost of taxis to and from the better beaches can add up).

The plush Cable Beach and Paradise Island resorts are big and beautiful, glittering and splashy, and have the best beaches, but they can be overwhelming. In any case, these big, top-dollar properties generally have more amenities than you could possibly make use of, a selection of dining choices, and a full roster of sports and entertainment options. Stay in Cable Beach if you don't plan to visit Nassau or Paradise Island often; you need to take a cab, and the costs add up.

RESTAURANTS

Foodies will delight in New Providence's restaurant range, from shabby shacks serving up the kind of food you'd find in any Bahamian's kitchen, to elegant eateries where jackets are required and the food rivals that found in any major city. You'll recognize celebrity chef names like Todd English, Jean-Georges Vongerichten, and Nobu Matsuhisa, all of whom have restaurants on Paradise Island.

Eating out can get expensive, particularly in resort restaurants, so a budget-friendly strategy is having brunch at one of the myriad all-you-can-eat buffets at the larger hotels on Paradise Island and Cable Beach, then a light snack to hold you over until dinnertime.

Note: A gratuity (15%) is often added to the bill automatically.

HOTEL AND RESTAURANT PRICES

Restaurant prices are based on the median main course price at dinner, excluding gratuity (typically 15%) and VAT (7/5%), which are automatically added to the bill. Hotel prices are for two people in a standard double room in high season, excluding service and 6%–12% hotel tax plus 7.5% VAT.

WHAT IT COSTS IN DOLLARS			
$	$$	$$$	$$$$
Restaurants	under $20	$20–$30	$31–$40	over $40
Hotels	under $200	$200–$300	$301–$400	over $400

VISITOR INFORMATION

The Ministry of Tourism operates tourist information booths at the airport, open daily from 8:30 am to 11:30 pm, and at Festival Place, which is adjacent to Prince George Wharf and open daily from 9 am to 5 pm. The Ministry of Tourism's People-to-People Program sets you up with a Bahamian family with similar interests to show you local culture firsthand.

Contacts Ministry of Tourism. ☎ 242/302–2000 ⊕ www.bahamas.com. **People-to-People Program.** ☎ 242/324–9772 ⊕ www.bahamas.com/people-to-people.

EXPLORING

NASSAU

Nassau's sheltered harbor bustles with cruise-ship activity, while a block away Bay Street's sidewalks are crowded with shoppers who duck into air-conditioned boutiques and relax on benches in the shade of mahogany and lignum vitae trees. Shops angle for tourist dollars with fine imported goods at duty-free prices, yet you'll find a handful of stores overflowing with authentic Bahamian crafts, food supplies, and other delights.

With a revitalization of downtown ongoing, Nassau is trying to recapture some of its past glamour. Nevertheless, modern influences are completely apparent: fancy restaurants and trendy coffeehouses have popped up everywhere. These changes have come partly in response to the growing number of upper-crust crowds that now supplement the spring breakers and cruise passengers who have traditionally flocked to Nassau. Of course, you can still find a wild club or a rowdy bar, but you can also sip cappuccino while viewing contemporary Bahamian art or dine by candlelight beneath prints of old Nassau, serenaded by soft, island-inspired calypso music.

A trip to Nassau wouldn't be complete without a stop at some of the island's well-preserved historic buildings. The large, pink colonial-style edifices house Parliament and some of the courts, while others, like Fort Charlotte, date back to the days when pirates ruled the town. Take a tour via horse-drawn carriage for the full effect.

TOP ATTRACTIONS

Arawak Cay. Known to Nassau residents as "The Fish Fry," Arawak Cay is one of the best places to knock back a Kalik beer, chat with locals, watch or join in a fast-paced game of dominoes, or sample traditional Bahamian fare. You can get small dishes such as conch fritters or full meals at one of the pastel-color waterside shacks. Order a fried snapper served up with a sweet homemade roll, or fresh conch salad (a spicy mixture of chopped conch—just watching the expert chopping is a show as good as any in town—mixed with diced onions, cucumbers, tomatoes, and hot peppers in a lime marinade). The two-story Twin Brothers and Goldie's Enterprises are two of the most popular places. Try their fried "cracked conch" and Goldie's famous Sky Juice (a sweet but potent gin, coconut-water, and sweet-milk concoction sprinkled with nutmeg). Local fairs and craft shows are often held in the adjacent field. ⊠ W. Bay St. and Chippingham Rd., Nassau.

John Watling's Distillery. The former Buena Vista Estate which featured in the James Bond film *Casino Royale* has been painstakingly transformed and taken back to its glory days, emerging as the new home of

The Royal Bahamas Police Force Band performs in front of Government House.

the John Watling's Distillery. Parts of the home date back to 1789 and the actual production of the line of John Watling's artisanal rums, gins, vodkas, and liquors are handmade, hand bottled, and hand labeled just as they would have been in that era. Take a self-guided tour through the grounds and working estate to learn the fascinating history of the home and then walk out back to watch the rum production line from an overhead mezzanine. Sit in the Red Turtle Tavern with an internationally acclaimed Rum Dum or just a great mojito and pick up a unique Bahamian souvenir in the on-site retail store. ⊠ *17 Delancy St., Nassau* ☎ *242/322–2811* ⊕ *www.johnwatlings.com* ⊠ *Free* ☉ *Sat.–Thurs. 10–6, Fri. 10–9.*

Fodor's Choice **National Art Gallery of the Bahamas.** Opened in 2003, the museum houses
★ the works of esteemed Bahamian artists such as Max Taylor, Amos Ferguson, Brent Malone, John Cox, and Antonius Roberts. The glorious Italianate colonial mansion, built in 1860 and restored in the 1990s, has double-tiered verandas with elegant columns. It was the residence of Sir William Doyle, the first chief justice of the Bahamas. Don't miss the museum's gift shop, where you'll find books about the Bahamas as well as Bahamian quilts, prints, ceramics, jewelry, and crafts. ⊠ *West and W. Hill Sts., across from St. Francis Xavier Cathedral, Nassau* ☎ *242/328–5800* ⊕ *www.nagb.org.bs* ⊠ *$10* ☉ *Tues.–Sat. 10–4, Sun. noon–4.*

FAMILY **Pirates of Nassau.** Take a self-guided journey through Nassau's pirate days in this interactive museum devoted to such notorious members of the city's past as Blackbeard, Mary Read, and Anne Bonney. Board a pirate ship, see dioramas of intrigue on the high seas, hear historical

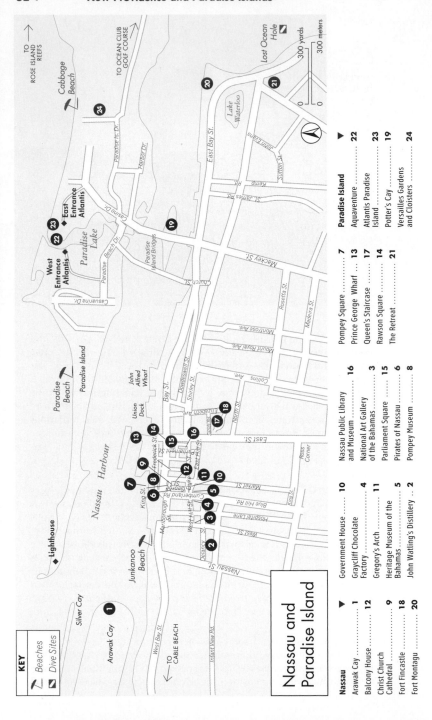

Nassau and Paradise Island

KEY

⌇ Beaches

▨ Dive Sites

Nassau ▶

Arawak Cay **1**
Balcony House **12**
Christ Church Cathedral **9**
Fort Fincastle **18**
Fort Montagu **20**

Government House **10**
Graycliff Chocolate Factory **4**
Gregory's Arch **11**
Heritage Museum of the Bahamas **5**
John Watling's Distillery .. **2**

Nassau Public Library and Museum **16**
National Art Gallery of the Bahamas **3**
Parliament Square **15**
Pirates of Nassau **6**
Pompey Museum **8**

Pompey Square **7**
Prince George Wharf ... **13**
Queen's Staircase **17**
Rawson Square **14**
The Retreat **21**

Paradise Island ▶

Aquaventure **22**
Atlantis Paradise Island **23**
Potter's Cay **19**
Versailles Gardens and Cloisters **24**

narration, and experience sound effects re-creating some of the gruesome highlights. It's a fun and educational (if slightly scary) family outing. Be sure to check out the offbeat souvenirs in the Pirate Shop. ⊠ *George and King Sts., Nassau* ☎ *242/356-3759* ⊕ *www.piratesof-nassau.com* ✉ *$13* ⊙ *Mon.–Sat. 9–6, Sun. 9–12:30.*

The Retreat. Nearly 200 species of exotic palm trees grace the 11 verdant acres appropriately known as The Retreat, which serves as the

PIRATES OF THE BAHAMAS

Pirates roamed the waters of the Bahamas, hiding out in the 700 islands, but they especially liked New Providence Island. Edward Teach, or Blackbeard, even named himself governor of the island. He scared enemy and crew alike by weaving hemp into his hair and beard and setting it on fire.

headquarters of the Bahamas National Trust. Stroll in blessed silence through the lush grounds, and be on the lookout for native birds. It's a perfect break on a steamy Nassau day. The Retreat hosts the Jollification—the unofficial start to the Christmas season—the third weekend in November. Carols, festive food and drinks, a kids' holiday craft center, and local artisans selling native and Christmas crafts make this a must-do event. ⊠ *Village Rd., Paradise Island* ☎ *242/393-1317* ✉ *$2* ⊙ *Weekdays 9–5.*

WORTH NOTING

Balcony House. A delightful 18th-century landmark—a pink two-story house named aptly for its overhanging balcony—this is the oldest wooden residential structure in Nassau and its furnishings and design recapture the elegance of a bygone era. A mahogany staircase, believed to have been salvaged from a ship during the 19th century, is an interior highlight. A guided tour through this fascinating building is an hour well spent. ⊠ *Market St. and Trinity Pl., Nassau* ☎ *242/302-2621* ✉ *Donations accepted* ⊙ *Mon.–Wed. and Fri. 9:30–4:30, Thurs. 9:30–1.*

Christ Church Cathedral. It's worth the short walk off the main thoroughfare to see the stained-glass windows of this cathedral, which was built in 1837, when Nassau officially became a city. The white pillars of the church's spacious, airy interior support ceilings beamed with dark wood handcrafted by ship builders. The Crucifixion depicted in the east window's center panel is flanked by depictions of the Empty Tomb and the Ascension. Be sure to spend a few minutes in the small, flower-filled Garden of Remembrance, where stone plaques adorn the walls. Sunday Mass is held at 7:30, 9, 11:15 am, and 6 pm. Drop by the cathedral Christmas Eve and New Year's Eve to see the glorious church at night, and hear the music and choir. Call ahead to find out the time of the service. ⊠ *George and King Sts., Nassau* ☎ *242/322-4186* ⊕ *www. christchurchcathedralbahamas.com* ⊙ *Daily 8:30–5.*

Fort Fincastle. Shaped like the bow of a ship and perched near the top of the Queen's Staircase, Fort Fincastle—named for Royal Governor Lord Dunmore (Viscount Fincastle)—was completed in 1793 to be a lookout post for marauders trying to sneak into the harbor. It served as a lighthouse in the early 19th century. A 15- to 20-minute tour costs just $1 per person and includes the nearby Queen's Staircase. The fort's 126-foot-tall water tower, which is more than 200 feet above sea level (and the island's highest point), is closed at this writing. ⊠ *Top of Elizabeth Ave. hill, south of Shirley St., Nassau* ☎ *242/356–9085* ◻ *Free* ◔ *Daily 8–4.*

Fort Montagu. The oldest of the island's three forts, Montagu was built of local limestone in 1741 to repel Spanish invaders. The only action it saw was when it was occupied for two weeks by rebel American troops— among them a lieutenant named John Paul Jones—seeking arms and ammunition during the Revolutionary War. The small fortification is quite simple, but displays a lovely elevated view of Nassau Harbour. The second level has a number of weathered cannons. A recently renovated and restored public beach looks out upon Montagu Bay, where many international yacht regattas and Bahamian sloop races are held annually. ⊠ *East of Bay St. on Eastern Rd., Nassau* ◻ *Free.*

Government House. The official residence of the Bahamas governor-general, the personal representative of the Queen since 1801, this imposing pink-and-white building on Duke Street is an excellent example of the mingling of Bahamian-British and American colonial architecture. Its graceful columns and broad circular drive recall the styles of Virginia or the Carolinas. But its pink color, distinctive white quoins (cross-laid cornerstones), and louvered wooden shutters (to keep out the tropical sun) are typically Bahamian. Here you can catch the crisply disciplined but beautifully flamboyant changing of the guard ceremony, which takes place every second Saturday of the month at 11 am. The stars of the pomp and pageantry are members of the Royal Bahamas Police Force Band, who are decked out in white tunics; red-striped black trousers; and spiked, white pith helmets with red bands. The drummers sport leopard skins. There is a tea party open to the public from 3 to 4 pm on the last Friday of the month from January to June as part of the People-to-People program. Dress is casual but elegant—no shorts, jeans, or tennis shoes. Musicians, poets, and storytellers provide entertainment. Be sure to note the larger-than-life statue of Christopher Columbus on the grounds overlooking Nassau. ⊠ *Duke and George Sts., Nassau* ☎ *242/356–5415 ceremony schedule, 242/397–8816 tea party, 242/322–2020 Government House.*

FAMILY   **Graycliff Chocolate Factory.** Go behind the scenes at this boutique chocolate factory, and you can make your own sweet souvenirs. The tour lasts about an hour, and after watching master chocolatiers in action and learning the history of chocolate production around the world, guests enter the chocolate classroom where they get to design their own creations, including a signature Graycliff chocolate bar. There is also a kids' classroom for younger chocolate lovers. ⊠ *Graycliff Hotel, W. Hill St., Nassau* ☎ *242/302–9150* ⊕ *www.graycliff.com* ◻ *$49.95* ◔ *Mon.–Sat. 11:15.*

Gregory's Arch. Named for John Gregory (royal governor 1849–54), this arch, at the intersection of Market and Duke streets, separates downtown from the "over-the-hill" neighborhood of Grant's Town, where much of Nassau's population lives. Grant's Town was laid out in the

1820s by Governor Lewis Grant as a settlement for freed slaves. Visitors once enjoyed late-night mingling with the locals in the small, dimly lighted bars; nowadays you should exhibit the same caution you would if you were visiting the commercial areas of a large city. Nevertheless, it's a vibrant section of town where you can rub shoulders with Bahamians at a funky take-out food stand or down-home restaurant. ⊠ *Nassau.*

FAMILY **Heritage Museum of The Bahamas.** So many artifacts are on display in this small but interesting museum that you can easily spend an hour wandering. Opt for a guided tour, or use the audio tour to take in everything at your own pace. You'll learn about Bahamian history from the days of pirates through the days of slavery to the present. One of the best exhibits is the life-size replica of the old Bay Street General Store. Quite by a series of coincidences, the collection box from the oldest church ended up in this museum—right across the street from the remains of the very same church. ⊠ *8–14 W. Hill St., Nassau* ☎ *242/302–9150* 🖻 *$12.50 self-guided tour, $18.50 guided tour* ⊗ *Mon.–Sat. 9–5.*

Nassau Public Library and Museum. The octagonal building near Parliament Square was the Nassau Gaol (the old British spelling for jail), circa 1797. You're welcome to pop in and browse. The small prison cells are now lined with books. The museum has an interesting collection of historic prints and old colonial documents. Computers with Internet access are available for rent ($1 for 15 minutes, $4 for an hour). ⊠ *Shirley St. between Parliament St. and Bank La., Nassau* ☎ *242/322–4907* ⊕ *www.bahamaslibraries.org* 🖻 *Free* ⊗ *Weekdays 10–5:45, Sat. 10–3:45.*

Parliament Square. Nassau is the seat of the national government. The Bahamian Parliament comprises two houses—a 16-member Senate (Upper House) and a 38-member House of Assembly (Lower House)—and a ministerial cabinet headed by a prime minister. If the House is in session, sit in to watch lawmakers debate. Parliament Square's pink, colonnaded government buildings were constructed in the late 1700s and early 1800s by Loyalists who came to the Bahamas from North Carolina. The square is dominated by a statue of a slim young Queen Victoria that was erected on her birthday, May 24, in 1905. In the immediate area are a handful of magistrates' courts. Behind the House of Assembly is the Supreme Court. Its four-times-a-year opening ceremonies (held the first weeks of January, April, July, and October) recall the wigs and mace-bearing pageantry of the Houses of Parliament in London. The Royal Bahamas Police Force Band is usually on hand for the event. ⊠ *Bay St., Nassau* ☎ *242/322–2041* 🖻 *Free* ⊗ *Weekdays 10–4.*

Pompey Museum. The building, where slave auctions were held in the 1700s, is named for a rebel slave who lived on the Out Island of Exuma in 1830. The structure and historic artifacts inside were destroyed by fire in December 2011, but have been painstakingly re-created and new exhibits have been acquired and produced. Exhibits focus on the issues of slavery and emancipation and highlight the works of local artists. A knowledgeable, enthusiastic young staff is on hand to answer questions. ⊠ *Bay and George Sts., Nassau* ☎ *242/356–0495* ⊕ *www.*

The Cloisters in Versailles Gardens is possibly the most peaceful spot on the island.

ammcbahamas.com ✉ *$5* ⊙ *Mon.–Wed., Fri., and Sat. 9:30-4:30; Thurs. 9:30–1.*

FAMILY **Pompey Square.** This open space at the western end of Bay Street overlooks the busy Nassau Harbour and is the spot to catch local festivals and events, live music, and Bahamian craft shows. With 24-hour security, public restrooms, an interactive water feature that delights kids of all ages, and a host of small restaurants and bars nearby, this square, which pays tribute to a slave who fought for his freedom, is the start of a strategic redevelopment of downtown Nassau. ⊠ *Bay St., Nassau* ✉ *Free.*

Prince George Wharf. The wharf that leads into Rawson Square is the first view that cruise passengers encounter after they tumble off their ships. Up to a dozen gigantic cruise ships call on Nassau at any one time, and passengers spill out onto downtown, giving Nassau an instant, and constantly replenished, surge of life. Even if you're not visiting via cruise ship, it's worth heading to Festival Place, an outdoor Bahamian village–style shopping emporium. Here you'll find booths for 45 Bahamian artisans; live music; Internet kiosks; vendors selling diving, fishing, and day trips; scooter rentals; and an information desk offering maps, directions, and suggestions for sightseeing. You can also arrange walking tours of historic Nassau here. ⊠ *Waterfront at Rawson Sq., Nassau.*

Queen's Staircase. A popular early-morning exercise regime for locals, the "66 Steps" (as Bahamians call them) are thought to have been carved out of a solid limestone cliff by slaves in the 1790s. The staircase was later named to honor Queen Victoria's reign. Pick up some souvenirs at the ad hoc straw market along the narrow road that leads to the site.

✉ *Top of Elizabeth Ave. hill, south of Shirley St., Nassau.*

Rawson Square. This shady square connects Bay Street to Prince George Wharf. As you enter off Bay Street, note the statue of Sir Milo Butler, the first postindependence (and first native Bahamian) governor general. Horse-drawn surreys wait for passengers along Prince George Wharf (expect to pay about $30 for a half-hour ride through Nassau's streets). Between Rawson Square and Festival Place, check out (or perhaps stop inside) the open-air **hair-braiding pavilion,** where women work their magic at prices ranging from $2 for a single strand to $100 for an elaborate do. An often-overlooked pleasure near the pavilion is Randolph W. Johnston's lovely bronze statue, *Tribute to Bahamian Women.* The prime minister meets with his cabinet every Tuesday in the building that lines the eastern side of the square. ✉ *Bay St., Nassau.*

> **KEEP LEFT**
>
> Driving on the left is one of the many leftovers from colonial British rule. As history goes, the Brits kept to the left so they could easily draw and use their sword on the right if an enemy approached. These days, most of the cars driven in the Bahamas are imported from the United States and are designed for right-hand driving, yet islanders still keep to the other side.

PARADISE ISLAND

The graceful, arched Paradise Island bridges ($1 round-trip toll for cars and motorbikes; free for bicyclists and pedestrians) lead to and from the extravagant world of Paradise Island. Until 1962 the island was largely undeveloped and known as Hog Island. A&P heir Huntington Hartford changed the name when he built the island's first resort complex. In 1994 South African developer Sol Kerzner transformed the existing high-rise hotel into the first phase of Atlantis. Many years, a number of new hotels, a water park, and more than $1 billion later, Atlantis has taken over the island. From the ultra-exclusive Cove to the acclaimed golf course, it's easy to forget there's more to Paradise Island. It's home to multimillion-dollar homes and condominiums and a handful of independent resort properties. Despite the hustle and bustle of the megaresorts, you can still find yourself a quiet spot on Cabbage Beach, which lines the northern side of the island, or on the more secluded Paradise Beach west of Atlantis. Aptly renamed, the island *is* a paradise for beach lovers, boaters, and fun seekers.

FAMILY

Fodor's Choice

★

Aquaventure. From near-vertical slides that plunge through shark tanks to a quarter-mile-long lazy-river ride, this 141-acre water park has something to suit every kind of thrill seeker. Spend the day going from ride to ride, or pick the perfect chair and umbrella on the white sand of three unique but beautiful beaches or any of the 11 swimming pools to unwind. Three pools are designed especially for the youngest of guests, including Splashers, a Mayan-themed water playground. In 2015, Atlantis implemented a policy restricting Aquaventure and beach day passes to local residents and cruise visitors and others affiliated with Atlantis partners, so if you want to play, you're going to have to stay on-property for at least one night. ⊠ *Atlantis Paradise Island, Paradise Island* ☎ *242/363–3000* ⊕ *www.atlantisbahamas.com* ✉ *Day pass $150 high season, $135 low season; beach pass $75* ⊗ *Daily 10–7 during Daylight Saving Time; 9–5 rest of the year (hours can vary during busy or slow periods).*

FAMILY

Fodor'sChoice

★

Atlantis Paradise Island. The unmistakable sight of this pink fantasia comes into view long before you cross one of the Paradise Island bridges. The towering sunstruck visage is Royal Towers, the largest wing of the Atlantis resort. With luxury shops, a glitzy casino, and seemingly unlimited choices for dining and drinks (40 restaurants, bars, and lounges), Atlantis is as much a tourist attraction as a resort hotel. At Dolphin Cay you can interact with dolphins, sea lions, and stingrays. Aquaventure, a 63-acre waterscape, provides thrilling waterslides and high-intensity rapids as well as a lazy-river tube ride through the sprawling grounds. Celebrity sightings are frequent at both Nobu restaurant and Aura nightclub. The Atlantis Live concert series has featured the likes of Taylor Swift, Jerry Seinfeld, and Lady Gaga, and the on-site comedy club Joker's Wild brings top comedians to the stage. Many of the resort's facilities, including the restaurants and casino, are open to nonguests, but the leisure and sports facilities are open only to resort guests and cruise passengers who book a ship-sponsored tour. Atlantis has the world's largest man-made marine habitat, consisting of 11 lagoons. To see it, cruise passengers can take the guided Discover Atlantis tour, which begins near the main lobby at an exhibition called "The Dig." This wonderful series of walk-through aquariums, themed around the lost continent and its re-created ruins, brings you face to face with sharks, manta rays, and innumerable forms of exotic sea life. The rest of the tour tempts you with a walk through the many waterslides and pools inaccessible to nonguests. If you're vacationing in Nassau and want to play at Atlantis, you now have to actually stay at one of the Atlantis hotel properties. The Discover Atlantis Tour, Aquaventure, and beach day passes are available exclusively to cruise-ship visitors or Atlantis-affiliated partners only. ⊠ *Casino Dr., Paradise Island* ☎ *888/528–7155, 242/363–3000* ✉ *Discover Atlantis tour $42; Aquaventure day pass $150 high season, $135 rest of year; beach day pass $75; lockers $10–$15 per day; casino free* ⊗ *Tours daily 9–4, casino daily 24 hrs.*

Potter's Cay. Walk the road beneath the Paradise Island bridges to Potter's Cay to watch sloops bringing in and selling loads of fish and conch—pronounced *konk.* Along the road to the cay are dozens of stands where you can watch the conch, straight from the sea, being extracted from its glistening pink shell. If you don't have the know-how to handle the tasty conch's preparation—getting the diffident creature out of its shell requires boring a hole at the right spot to sever the muscle that keeps it entrenched—you can enjoy a conch salad on the spot, as fresh as it comes, and take notes for future attempts. Empty shells are sold as souvenirs. Many locals and hotel chefs come here to purchase the fresh catches; you can also find vegetables, herbs, and such condiments as fiery Bahamian peppers preserved in lime juice, and locally grown pineapples, papayas, and bananas. Join in on a raucous game of dominoes outside many of the stalls. Some stalls are closed on Sunday. There's also a police station and dockmaster's office, where you can book an inexpensive trip on a mail boat headed to the Out Islands. Be aware that these boats are built for cargo, not passenger comfort, and it's a rough ride even on calm seas. ✉ *Nassau.*

Versailles Gardens. Fountains and statues of luminaries and legends (such as Napoléon and Josephine, Franklin Delano Roosevelt, David Livingstone, Hercules, and Mephistopheles) adorn Versailles Gardens, the terraced lawn at the One & Only Ocean Club, once the private hideaway of Huntington Hartford. At the top of the gardens stand the **Cloisters,** the remains of a stone monastery built by Augustinian monks in France in the 13th century. They were imported to the United States in the 1920s by newspaper baron William Randolph Hearst. (The cloister is one of four to have ever been removed from French soil.) Forty years later, Hartford bought the Cloisters and had them rebuilt on their present commanding site. At the center is a graceful, contemporary white marble statue called *Silence,* by U.S. sculptor Dick Reid. Nearly every day, tourists take or renew wedding vows under the delicately wrought gazebo overlooking Nassau Harbour. Although the garden is owned by the One & Only Ocean Club, visitors are welcome so long as they check in at the security gate. ✉ *One & Only Ocean Club, Paradise Island Dr., Paradise Island* ☎ *242/363–2501.*

CABLE BEACH

From downtown Nassau, West Bay Street follows the coast west past Arawak Cay to the Cable Beach strip. If you're not driving, catch the No. 10 jitney for a direct ride from downtown. This main drag runs the length of the new Baha Mar resort development, which was not yet open at this writing, separating the golf course and green space from the resorts and beach. Walk or drive west of the megaresort for a smattering of smaller restaurants and local neighborhoods.

WORTH NOTING

The Caves. These large limestone caverns that the waves sculpted over the eons are said to have sheltered the early Arawak Indians. An oddity perched right beside the road, they're worth a glance—although in truth, there's not much to see, as the dark interior doesn't lend itself to exploration. Across the street is a concrete viewing platform overlooking the ocean. Just a short drive west beyond the caves, on an island between traffic lanes, is **Conference Corner,** where U.S. president John F. Kennedy, Canadian prime minister John Diefenbaker, and British prime minister Harold Macmillan planted trees on the occasion of their 1962 summit in Nassau. ✉ *W. Bay St. and Blake Rd., Cable Beach.*

WESTERN NEW PROVIDENCE

Immediately west of Cable Beach, the hotel strip gives way to residential neighborhoods interspersed with shops, restaurants, and cafés. Homes become more and more posh the farther west you go; Lyford Cay—the

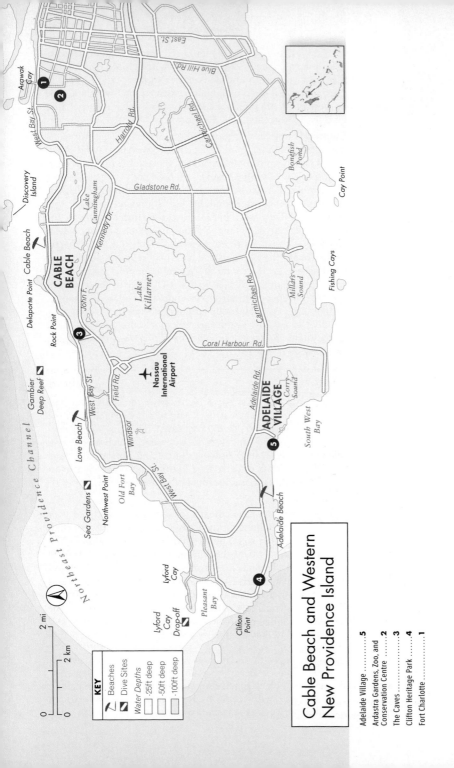

Cable Beach and Western
New Providence Island

KEY

Beaches

Dive Sites

Water Depths

-25ft deep

-50ft deep

-100ft deep

2 mi

2 km

CABLE
BEACH

ADELAIDE
VILLAGE

Northeast Providence Channel

Nassau
International
Airport

Lake
Killarney

Lake
Cunningham

Bonefish
Pond

Millars
Sound

Corn
Sound

South West
Bay

Fishing Cays

Cay Point

Arawak
Cay

Discovery
Island

Cable Beach

Delaporte Point

Rock Point

Gambier
Deep Reef

Love Beach

Sea Gardens

Northwest Point

Old Fort
Bay

Lyford
Cay

Lyford
Cay
Drop-off

Pleasant
Bay

Clifton
Point

Adelaide Beach

West Bay St.

Blue Hill Rd.

East St.

Harrold Rd.

Carmichael Rd.

Gladstone Rd.

Kennedy Dr.

John F.

Coral Harbour Rd.

Carmichael Rd.

Adelaide Rd.

Field Rd.

Windsor

West Bay St.

Cable Beach is the busiest island beach west of Nassau and Paradise Island. It's home to the upcoming Baha Mar resort, as well as several other resorts.

island's original gated community—is home to the original 007, Sean Connery. Hang a left at the Lyford Cay roundabout, and eventually you'll come across the historic Clifton Heritage Park, the local brewery where Kalik and Heineken are brewed and bottled, a new upscale resort development whose financiers include golfers Ernie Els and Tiger Woods, and eventually the sleepy settlement of Adelaide.

The loop around the island's west and south coasts can be done in a couple of hours by car or scooter, but take some time for lunch and a swim along the way. Unless you're being taken around by a taxi or local, it's best to return along the same route, as internal roads can get confusing.

WORTH NOTING

Adelaide Village. The small community on New Providence's southwestern coast sits placidly, like a remnant of another era, between busy Adelaide Road and the ocean. It was first settled during the early 1830s by Africans who had been captured and loaded aboard slave ships bound for the New World. They were rescued on the high seas by the British Royal Navy, and the first group of liberated slaves reached Nassau in 1832. Today, there are two sides to Adelaide—the few-dozen families who grow vegetables, raise chickens, and inhabit well-worn, pastel-painted wooden houses, shaded by casuarina, mahogany, and palm trees; and the more upscale beach cottages that are mostly used as weekend getaways. The village has a primary school, some little grocery stores, and a few small restaurants serving native food. ⊠ *Adelaide*.

FAMILY **Ardastra Gardens, Zoo, and Conservation Centre.** Marching flamingos? These national birds give a parading performance at Ardastra daily at 11, 1:30, and 3:30. The brilliant pink birds are a delight—especially for children, who can walk among the flamingos after the show. The zoo, with more than 5 acres of tropical greenery and ponds, also has an aviary of rare tropical birds including the bright-green Bahama parrot, native Bahamian creatures such as rock iguanas and the little (and harmless) Bahamian boa constrictors, and a global collection of small animals. ⊠ *Chippingham Rd., south of W. Bay St., Nassau* ☎ *242/323–5806* ⊕ *www.ardastra. com* ⊠ *$18* ⊘ *Daily 9–5.*

SNAKES ALIVE!

The Bahamas has five types of snakes, none poisonous, but the most interesting is the Bahamian boa constrictor, threatened with extinction because Bahamians kill them on sight. The Bahamian boa is extremely unusual in that it has remnants of legs, called spurs. The male uses his spurs to tickle the female. Ask one of the trainers at Ardastra Gardens and Zoo to show you the boa, so you can see the tiny legs.

Clifton Heritage Park. It's quite a distance from just about any hotel you could stay at, but for history and nature buffs, this national park, rescued from the hands of developers, is worth the drive. Situated on a prehistoric Lucayan Village dating back to AD 1000–1500, Clifton Heritage Park allows you to walk through the ruins of slave quarters from an 18th-century plantation. The site can claim ties to pop culture as well since a number of hit movies have been filmed on land and sea here. There's still much work to be done to really develop this site; call ahead to arrange a tour guide for the best experience. Be sure to walk the path from the main parking lot toward the west, where you can enjoy the peace and quiet of the Sacred Space and admire the African women carved out of dead casuarina trees by local artist Antonius Roberts. Naturalists will enjoy walking along the paths lined with native flora and fauna that lead to wooden decks overlooking mangrove swamps. ⊠ *Clifton Pier, W. Bay St., Clifton* ☎ *242/362–4368* ⊕ *www.cliftonheritage.org* ⊘ *Weekdays 9–5, weekends and holidays by appointment only.*

FAMILY **Fort Charlotte.** Built in 1788, this imposing fort comes complete with a waterless moat, drawbridge, ramparts, and a dungeon, where children love to see the torture device where prisoners were "stretched." Young local guides bring the fort to life. (Tips are expected.) Lord Dunmore, who built it, named the massive structure in honor of George III's wife. At the time, some called it Dunmore's Folly because of the staggering expense of its construction. It cost eight times more than was originally planned. (Dunmore's superiors in London were less than ecstatic with the high costs, but he managed to survive unscathed.) Ironically, no shots were ever fired in battle from the fort. The fort and its surrounding 100 acres offer a wonderful view of the cricket grounds, the beach, and the ocean beyond. On Wednesday and Friday enjoy fully regaled actors reenacting life as it was in the Bahamas in the 18th and 19th centuries. An historic military parade and canon firing takes place daily at noon. ⊠ *W. Bay St. at Chippingham Rd., Nassau* ✛ *Opposite Arawak Cay* ⊠ *$1* ⊘ *Mon.–Sat. 9–5, Sun. 8–4.*

BEACHES

New Providence is the Bahamas' most urban island, but that doesn't mean you won't find beautiful beaches. Powdery white sand, aquamarine waves, and shade-bearing palm trees are easy to come by, regardless how populated you like your beach to be. Whether you crave solitude or want to be in the middle of the action, there's a sand spot that's just right for you.

Cable Beach and the beaches near Atlantis are where you'll typically find loud music, bars serving tropical drinks, and vendors peddling everything from parasailing and Jet Ski rides to T-shirts and hair braiding. Downtown Nassau only has man-made beaches, the best being Junkanoo Beach just west of the British Colonial Hilton. But the capital city's beaches can't compare to the real thing. For a more relaxed environment, drive out of the main tourist areas. You'll likely find stretches of sand populated by locals only, or, chances are, no one at all.

> ## OFFSHORE ADVENTURES
>
> For a true beach getaway, head to one of the tiny islands just off the coast of Paradise Island. A 20-minute boat ride from Nassau, Blue Lagoon Island has a number of beaches, including one in a tranquil cove lined with hammocks suspended by palm trees. Enjoy a grilled lunch and then rent a kayak or water bike if you're feeling ambitious.

NASSAU

Junkanoo Beach. Right in downtown Nassau, this beach is spring-break central from late February through April. The man-made beach isn't the prettiest on the island, but it's conveniently located if you only have a few quick hours to catch a tan. Music is provided by bands, DJs, and guys with boom boxes; a growing number of bars keep the drinks flowing. **Amenities:** food and drink; parking (no fee); toilets; water sports. **Best for:** partiers; swimming. ⊠ *Immediately west of the British Colonial Hilton, Nassau.*

PARADISE ISLAND

FAMILY **Cabbage Beach.** At this beach you'll find 3 miles of white sand lined
Fodor's Choice with shady casuarina trees, sand dunes, and sun worshippers. This is
★ the place to go to rent Jet Skis or get a bird's-eye view of Paradise Island while parasailing. Hair braiders and T-shirt vendors stroll the beach, and hotel guests crowd the areas surrounding the resorts, including Atlantis. For peace and quiet, stroll east. **Amenities:** food and drink; lifeguards; parking (fee); water sports. **Best for:** solitude; partiers; swimming; walking. ⊠ *Paradise Island.*

CABLE BEACH AND WESTERN NEW PROVIDENCE

FAMILY **Adelaide Beach.** Time your visit to this far-flung beach on the island's southwestern shore to catch low tide, when the ocean recedes, leaving behind sandbanks and seashells. It's a perfect place to take the kids for a shallow-water dip in the sea, or for a truly private rendezvous. Popular with locals, you'll likely have the miles-long stretch all to yourself unless it's a public holiday. **Amenities:** none. **Best for:** solitude; swimming; walking. ✉ *Adelaide.*

Cable Beach. Hotels, including the massive Baha Mar resort development, dot the length of this 3-mile beach, so don't expect isolation. Music from hotel pool decks wafts out onto the sand, Jet Skis race up and down the waves, and vendors sell everything from shell jewelry to coconut drinks right from the shell. If you get tired of lounging around, join a game of beach volleyball. Access via new hotels may be limited, but join the locals and park at Goodman's Bay park on the eastern end of the beach. **Amenities:** parking (no fee); water sports. **Best for:** partiers; sunset; swimming; walking. ✉ *Cable Beach.*

Love Beach. If you're looking for great snorkeling and some privacy, drive about 20 minutes west of Cable Beach. White sand shimmers in the sun and the azure waves gently roll ashore. About a mile offshore are 40 acres of coral reef known as the Sea Gardens. Access is not marked, just look for a vacant lot. **Amenities:** none. **Best for:** solitude; snorkeling; sunset ✉ *Gambier.*

WHERE TO EAT

NASSAU

$$ GREEK
🍴 **Athena Café and Bar.** Gregarious owner Peter Mousis greets his guests with a bellowing "Opa!" and he and his family serve tasty fare at moderate prices seven days a week. This Greek restaurant provides a break from the Nassau culinary routine. Sit on the second floor among Grecian statuary, or on the balcony overlooking the action below. Enjoy souvlaki, moussaka, or a hearty Greek gyro in a relaxed and friendly establishment. Dinner is an option only if you eat very early; it closes by 6 pm (4 on Sunday). [$] *Average main: $20* ✉ *Bay St. at Charlotte St., Nassau* ☎ *242/326–1296* 🌐 *www.athenacafebar.com* 🕒 *No dinner Sun.*

$ BAHAMIAN
Fodor's Choice ★
🍴 **Bahamian Cookin' Kitchen.** Three generations of Bahamian women treat patrons as if they were welcoming them into their own home. And the Bahamian food whipped up in the kitchen is as close to homemade as you can get in a restaurant. This simple locale is bustling with local professionals during the week and has also become a popular "off the beaten path" spot for cruise-ship passengers. Grandmother Mena swears their conch fritters are the "conchiest" you'll find. [$] *Average main: $13* ✉ *Trinity Pl., Nassau* ✣ *Turn left off Bay St. onto Market St. towards Central Bank, then left onto Trinity Pl.* ☎ *242/328–0334* 🕒 *Closed Sun. No dinner Mon.–Wed.*

$$$
ITALIAN
Fodor's Choice
★

✕ Café Matisse. Low-slung settees, stucco arches, and reproductions of the eponymous artist's works set a casually refined tone at this restaurant owned by a husband-and-wife team—he's Bahamian, she's Northern Italian. Sit in the ground-floor garden under large white umbrellas or dine inside the century-old house for lunch or dinner. Start with the warm Parmesan terrine, then dive into freshly made pasta with crabmeat, garlic, hot pepper, cherry tomatoes, and shrimp in a spicy red-curry sauce, or such delights as pizza *frutti di mare* (topped with fresh local seafood). Be sure to save room for dessert and the delicious handmade cookies that come with coffee. Ⓢ *Average main: $36* ✉ *Bank La. and Bay St., behind Parliament Sq., Nassau* ☎ *242/356–7012* ⊕ *cafe-matisse.com* ☾ *Closed Sun., Mon., and Sept.*

> ### POP THE BUBBLY
>
> A meandering maze underneath historic Graycliff's sprawling kitchen and dining area houses more than 200,000 bottles of wine and champagne. Graycliff's wine cellar is one of the most extensive and impressive in the world. It costs $1,000 to book the elegant private cellar dining room, but tours are free.

$$$
CHINESE

✕ East Villa Restaurant and Lounge. In a converted Bahamian home, this is one of the most popular Chinese restaurants in town. The Chinese-Continental menu includes entrées such as conch with black-bean sauce, *hung shew* (walnut chicken), and steak *kew* (cubed prime fillet served with baby corn, snow peas, water chestnuts, and vegetables). The New York strip steak is nirvana. A short taxi ride from Paradise Island or downtown Nassau, this is the perfect spot if you're seeking something a little different from the typical area restaurants. Dress is casual elegance. Ⓢ *Average main: $33* ✉ *E. Bay St. near Nassau Yacht Club, Nassau* ☎ *242/393–3377* ⊕ *www.eastvillabahamas.com* ☾ *No lunch Sat.*

$$$$
EUROPEAN
Fodor's Choice
★

✕ Graycliff Restaurant. A meal at this hillside mansion's formal restaurant begins in the elegant parlor, where, over live piano music, drinks are served and orders are taken. It's a rarefied world, where waiters wear tuxedos, and Cuban cigars and cognac are served after dinner. Graycliff's signature dishes include Kobe beef, Kurobuta pork, and Nassau grouper. The wine cellar contains more than 200,000 bottles that have been hand-picked by owner Enrico Garzaroli, some running into the tens of thousands of dollars. There are plenty of less expensive bottles, but you'll find the markup on better vintages to be much less than what you'd find in a big-city restaurant almost anywhere in the world. You can even buy the world's oldest bottle of wine, a German vintage 1727, for $200,000. Mere mortals can settle for the weekday wine luncheons. For an extra-special dining experience, you can book the wine cellar's private dining room. Ⓢ *Average main: $55* ✉ *Graycliff, W. Hill St. at Cumberland Rd., across from Government House, Nassau* ☎ *242/322–2796* ⊕ *www.graycliff.com* ⬥ *Reservations essential* ⌂ *Jacket required.*

$$
AMERICAN

✕ The Green Parrot. Two locations—Green Parrot Harbourfront and Green Parrot Hurricane Hole—mean you get incomparable views of Nassau Harbour and a fresh breeze, whichever way the wind is blowing. The large Works Burger is a favorite at these casual, all-outdoor restaurants and bars. The menu includes burgers, wraps, quesadillas, and other simple but tasty dishes. The conch po'boy is a new favorite. The weekday happy hour from 5 to 9 and a DJ on Friday nights draw a lively local crowd. $ *Average main: $20* ⊠ *E. Bay St., west of the bridges to Paradise Island, Nassau* ☎ 242/322–9248, 242/363–3633 ⊕ *greenparrotbar.com.*

$$$$

BRAZILIAN

✕ **Humidor Churrascaria Restaurant.** The salad bar at this casual restaurant offers everything from simple salad fixings to scrumptious seafood salads and soups. And that is just the start. Each table setting includes a coaster that's red on one side and green on the other. Just like a stoplight, green means go and red means stop. Waiters serve a never-ending selection of delicious skewered meats and fresh fish until you turn your coaster to red and declare uncle. Another option is the wood-fired pizza served on the terrace out back. The $20 pizza and a bucket of three beers during Friday happy hour is a great deal. When you're done, stop by the smoking lounge to see the cigar rollers in action, or stroll along the garden terraces and fountains out back. $ *Average main: $50* ⊠ *W. Hill St. off Cumberland Rd., next to Graycliff Hotel, Nassau* ☎ 242/328–7050 ⊕ *www.graycliff.com* ☾ *No lunch.*

$$$

ITALIAN

✕ **Luciano's of Chicago.** Green Roofs, the sprawling former residence of the late Sir Roland Symonette (the country's first premier), houses this harborside restaurant. The mansion's mahogany woodwork, gardens, and terraces create a romantic setting for dining on Tuscan fare that features local seafood, including the fisherman's soup, grouper, and homemade pastas—including a delicious frutti di mare over linguine. The lamb, osso bucco, and veal are also popular options. The sweeping view of Paradise Island and the towers of Atlantis is particularly lovely at sunset. Reservations are essential for waterside tables. $ *Average main: $38* ⊠ *E. Bay St., 2 blocks west of Paradise Island bridges, Nassau* ☎ 242/323–7770 ⊕ *www.lucianosnassau.com* ☾ *No lunch weekends.*

$$

BAHAMIAN

Fodor's Choice

★

✕ **Lukka Kairi.** Lukka Kairi means "people of the Islands," and at this hot new restaurant you can experience the food, live music, and hospitality the Bahamian people are known for. The tapas-style menu lets you sample a variety of traditional Bahamian dishes with a twist. The crispy broccoli is a surprising favorite, and the conch fritters are among the best around. The long bar serves up local libations until midnight—Sky Juice with bits of toasted coconut is a must try. If you get tired of the stunning view of Nassau Harbour, take in the larger-than-life mural depicting the history of the Bahamas. Been struggling to understand the Bahamian accents? Listen carefully as you enter the restrooms for a fun lesson in the island vernacular. $ *Average main: $22* ⊠ *Woodes Rodgers Walk, Nassau* ☎ 242/427–8886 ⊕ *www.lukkakairi.com.*

$$

SEAFOOD

✕ **Montagu Gardens.** Angus beef and fresh native seafood—flame-grilled and seasoned with home-mixed spices—are the specialties at this romantic restaurant in an old Bahamian mansion on Lake Waterloo. The dining room opens to a walled courtyard niched with Roman-style statues and gardens that lead to a waterside balustrade. Besides seafood and steak (carnivores should try the filet mignon smothered in mushrooms), menu selections include chicken, lamb, pasta, ribs, and several Bahamian-inspired dishes such as conch fritters and cracked coconut conch. A favorite dessert is Fort Montagu Mud Pie. They offer a free ride both to and from Paradise Island and Cable Beach; just call to make a reservation. $ *Average main: $25* ✉ *E. Bay St., Nassau* ☎ *242/394–6347* ⊕ *stenigh8.wix.com/montagugardens* ⊗ *Closed Sun.*

$ ✕ **Pepper Pot Grill and Juice Bar.** Jamaican transplant Keron Williams
JAMAICAN   takes his role of cooking and serving up the most authentic Jamaican food in Nassau very seriously. His small, simple restaurant draws an international crowd of cruise-ship workers and immigrants from the Caribbean diaspora. Awaken your taste buds with ackee and codfish, oxtail and beans, or escoviche fish with a side of rice and beans infused with coconut milk, then take the edge off the spiciness with a tall glass of freshly made carrot, mango, or soursop juice. Peak lunchtime gets very busy, so be prepared to wait for a table; the restaurant is only open until 6 pm. $ *Average main: $12* ✉ *King St., Nassau* ✛ *From Bay St., turn south onto Market St., then right onto King St.* ☎ *242/323–8177* ⊗ *Closed Sun. No dinner.*

$$$ ✕ **The Poop Deck.** Just east of the bridges from Paradise Island and a
BAHAMIAN   quick cab ride from the center of town is this favorite local haunt. There's usually a wait for a table, and it's worth waiting a little longer for one overlooking the marina and Nassau Harbour. The restaurant's popularity has resulted in a second Poop Deck on Cable Beach's west end, but, for residents, this is still the place. Expect spicy dishes with names such as Mama Mary's Fish; there's also an extensive wine list. Start with Paula's Conch Fritters and then select a fresh, whole-hog snapper or lobster tail for the chef to prepare exactly how you want it. The fish is usually served head to tail, so if you're squeamish, ask your waiter to have the head cut off before it comes out on your plate. Save room for guava duff and a calypso coffee spiked with secret ingredients. $ *Average main: $35* ✉ *E. Bay St. at Nassau Yacht Haven Marina, Nassau* ✛ *East of bridges from Paradise Island* ☎ *242/393–8175* ⊕ *www. thepoopdeck.com.*

$$ ✕ **Seafront Sushi.** One of Nassau's hot spots, this simple sushi restaurant
SUSHI   has an extensive menu including traditional rolls, sushi, and sashimi
Fodor's Choice   as well as more innovative options that incorporate local delicacies
★   like conch. The Volcano Roll topped with their special conch sauce is a favorite. There are enough non-seafood options on the menu to satisfy anyone in your group. Friday and Saturday nights are really busy (and there are no reservations), so be prepared to wait for a table and to be served. $ *Average main: $20* ✉ *E. Bay St., Nassau* ☎ *242/394– 1706* ⊕ *www.seafrontsushibahamas.com* ⊗ *Closed Sun. No lunch Sat.* ⌦ *Reservations not accepted.*

$$ ✕ **Sharkeez Bar & Grill.** If you arrive in Nassau aboard a cruise ship, you
BAHAMIAN   won't miss the sign for this second-floor, hot-spot bar and grill emblazoned atop its thatched roof. You may have a hard time picking your drink from the extensive menu of frozen concoctions. The Sneaky Tiki with seven types of rum is a favorite, as is the Sharkeez Volcano (which is set ablaze), and the Nassau Iced Tea, a twist on the "Long Island" traditional. Sit indoors or enjoy the fresh air and a fantastic harbor view on the long wraparound balcony and enjoy some good Bahamian food like fresh conch salad or lobster poppers followed by the tender cracked

conch or a Caribbean jerk burger. Finish up with guava duff for dessert. No matter what your sport, this is also a good spot to catch your team in action on one of 10 big screen TVs. ⓢ *Average main: $20* ✉ *Woodes Rodgers Walk, Nassau* ☎ *242/601–5325* ⊕ *sharkeezcaribbean.com.*

$$$ ✗ **Van Breugel's Restaurant & Bistro.** Dutch owner Freddy Van Breugel is
MODERN   enough of a character that a chance meeting with him is almost enough
EUROPEAN   to make a visit to this hip spot just off Bay Street worth the effort. The Coconut Curry Conch Chowder—a delicious blend of the Bahamian staple and a Thai coconut chicken soup—is another reason. This is a popular spot for locals to grab a working lunch or catch up during Friday happy hour at the bar that runs the length of the converted Bahamian home. ⓢ *Average main: $33* ✉ *Charlotte St. South, Nassau* ☎ *242/322–2484* ⊕ *www.vanbreugels.com* ⊘ *Closed Sun. No dinner Mon. or Tues.*

PARADISE ISLAND

Restaurants at Atlantis Paradise Island tend to close one or two nights a week, but they don't always close on consistent nights, and their schedules vary with the resort's occupancy levels. Check with the reservations desk at Atlantis if you want to dine there. Reservations are essential at most of the upscale spots and a good idea at all restaurants that accept them.

$$$ ✗ **Anthony's.** This lively, casual spot is one of the most affordable spots
AMERICAN   for breakfast, lunch, or dinner this side of Nassau Harbour, but it's still not cheap. The baby back ribs with a homemade barbecue sauce are among the most popular on this Bahamian and American fare menu. The extensive menu (60+ items to choose from) includes seafood pasta, grilled-to-order shrimp, grouper and salmon brochettes, steaks, burgers, ribs, and salads. The take-out menu features pizzas and a few pasta dishes. ⓢ *Average main: $30* ✉ *Paradise Village Shopping Plaza, Paradise Island* ☎ *242/363–3152* ⊕ *www.anthonysparadiseisland.com.*

$$$$ ✗ **Bahamian Club.** Reminiscent of a British country club, this handsome
EUROPEAN   restaurant has walls lined with dark oak, overstuffed chairs, and leather banquettes. Meat is the house specialty—rib-eye steak, veal chop, lamb loin, and chateaubriand for two—but grilled swordfish steak, Bahamian lobster, salmon fillet, and other fresh seafood dishes are all prepared with finesse. ⓢ *Average main: $55* ✉ *Atlantis Paradise Island, Coral Towers, Paradise Island* ☎ *242/363–3000* ⊕ *www.atlantisbahamas.com* ⊘ *No lunch* ⚅ *Reservations essential.*

$$$$ ✗ **Blue Lagoon Seafood Restaurant.** The interior tends toward the nautical,
SEAFOOD   with hurricane lamps and brass rails, in this narrow third-floor dining room looking out to Nassau on one side and Atlantis on the other. You'll be serenaded by a one-man band most evenings, or head there Thursday night for the sounds of a jazz quartet. Choose from simply prepared dishes such as crepes filled with seafood, stuffed grouper au gratin, lobster, or stoned crab claws. It's also one of the few places where you can still get a traditional Caesar salad. ⓢ *Average main: $44* ✉ *Club Land'Or, Paradise Island* ☎ *242/363–2400* ⊕ *www.bluelagoonseafood. com* ⊘ *Closed Sun. No lunch* ⚅ *Reservations essential.*

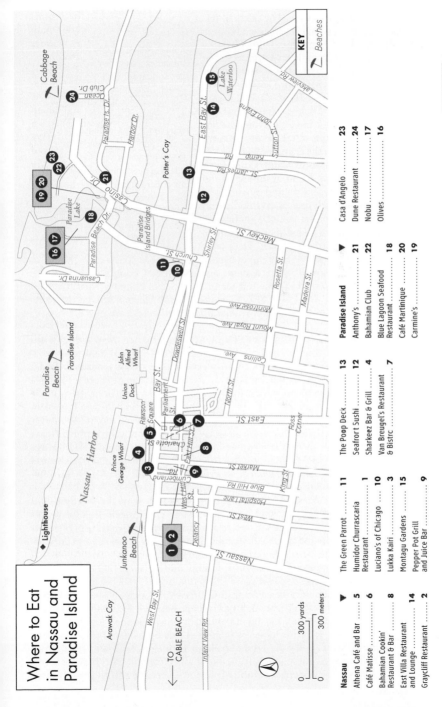

Where to Eat in Nassau and Paradise Island

KEY

↗ Beaches

0 — 300 yards
0 — 300 meters

TO CABLE BEACH ←

Nassau   ▼
Athena Café and Bar **5**
Café Matisse **6**
Bahamian Cookin'
Restaurant & Bar **8**
East Villa Restaurant
and Lounge **14**
Graycliff Restaurant **2**

The Green Parrot **11**
Humidor Churrascaria
Restaurant **1**
Luciano's of Chicago **10**
Lukka Kairi **3**
Montagu Gardens **15**
Pepper Pot Grill
and Juice Bar **9**

The Poop Deck **13**
Seafront Sushi **12**
Sharkeez Bar & Grill **4**
Van Breugel's Restaurant
& Bistrc **7**

Paradise Island   ▼
Anthony's **21**
Bahamian Club **22**
Blue Lagoon Seafood
Restaurant **18**
Café Martinique **20**
Carmine's **19**

Casa d'Angelo **23**
Dune Restaurant **24**
Nobu **17**
Olives **16**

$$$$
FRENCH
Fodor's Choice
★

✕ **Café Martinique.** The original restaurant, which was made famous in the 1965 James Bond film *Thunderball*, has long been bulldozed, but with the help of renowned international chef Jean-Georges Vongerichten and New York designer Adam D. Tihany, Atlantis has resurrected a classic that remains one of the hottest tables at Atlantis. Nestled in the center of Marina Village on Paradise Island, Café Martinique is the height of sophistication in design, service, and cuisine. The decor includes a wrought-iron birdcage elevator and a mahogany staircase; a grand piano helps create a refined experience. The classic

French menu offers simple, classic dishes made spectacular thanks to the highest-quality ingredients and chef Jean-George's influence. The seven-course chef's tasting menu is a special culinary treat. $ *Average main: $60* ✉ *Atlantis Paradise Island, Marina Village, Paradise Island* ☎ *242/363–3000* ⊕ *www.atlantisbahamas.com* ⌕ *Reservations essential.*

$$$$
ITALIAN
FAMILY
Fodor's Choice
★

✕ **Carmine's.** This Italian restaurant is a great place to go with a small group—so long as you can all agree on what to have for dinner. Appetizers, entrées, and desserts come in extra-large portions meant to feed a crowd and are served family style, so the prices can be more affordable (by Paradise Island standards, at least) than they seem at first, especially if you share among several people. The waiters can help you figure out how many dishes you should order without overdoing it. Whatever you choose, save room for dessert—the chocolate cake and ice cream concoction called the "Titanic" requires all hands on deck. $ *Average main: $55* ✉ *Atlantis Paradise Island, Marina Village, Paradise Island* ☎ *242/363–3000* ⊕ *www.atlantisbahamas.com* ☾ *No lunch* ⌕ *Reservations essential.*

$$$$
ITALIAN

✕ **Casa D'Angelo.** At this restaurant, an outpost of the wildly popular Casa d'Angelo chain in south Florida, chef Angelo Elia brings his famous Tuscan-style cuisine to Paradise. The antipasti display whets the appetite for succulent seafood, hearty pasta dishes, and prime cuts of beef. The dessert pastries are delectable. $ *Average main: $50* ✉ *Atlantis Paradise Island, Coral Towers, Paradise Island* ☎ *242/363–3000* ⊕ *www.atlantisbahamas.com* ☾ *No lunch.*

$$$$
MODERN FRENCH

✕ **Dune Restaurant.** Feast on Jean-Georges Vongerichten's intricately prepared dishes while overlooking Cabbage Beach at the renowned One & Only Ocean Club. Go for breakfast or lunch for the most reasonable prices (well, "affordable" is relative at this upscale and pricey resort). For breakfast, try the Dune Breakfast with eggs Benedict, french toast with mango and passion fruit, and smoked salmon. For dinner, share a Black Plate appetizer sampler featuring everything from shrimp satay to quail to start, then end with the White Plate sampler for dessert, an indulgent medley of warm chocolate cake, passion fruit soufflé, and all sorts of other treats. In between, try the unique French-Asian twists on classic entrées like lobster, duck, beef, or mahimahi. It's a great place to unwind amid ocean breezes. $ *Average main: $46* ✉ *One & Only Ocean Club, Ocean Club Dr., Paradise Island* ☎ *242/363–2501* ⊕ *oceanclub.oneandonlyresorts.com* ⌂ *Reservations essential.*

$$$$ ✗**Nobu.** Sushi connoisseurs, celebrities, and tourists pack this Atlantis
SUSHI restaurant night after night. The rock shrimp tempura, and yellowtail sashimi with jalapeño, and miso-glazed black cod are Nobu favorites, but this restaurant also takes advantage of fresh Bahamian seafood—try the lobster shiitake salad or the cold conch shabu-shabu with Nobu sauces. The central dining room is surrounded by a Japanese pagoda, and guests seated at a long, communal sushi bar can watch chefs work. $ *Average main: $60* ✉ *Atlantis Paradise Island, Royal Towers, Paradise Island* ☎ *242/363–3000* ⊕ *www.atlantisbahamas.com* ☽ *No lunch* ⌂ *Reservations essential.*

$$$$ ✗**Olives.** Todd English has paired up with Atlantis to give his signa-
MEDITERRANEAN ture Mediterranean style a taste of the Caribbean. Enjoy the shellfish, clams, and oysters from the Raw Bar, pick the fish you want to see on your plate, or satisfy your meat craving with the huge Tomahawk rib eye—all steaks are 100% Akaushi Wagyu beef. Situated right inside the lively Atlantis Casino, Olives is one of the few places to grab a late-night bite—the kitchen is open with a limited menu of their flavorful flat breads and other staples until 3 am. $ *Average main: $50* ✉ *Atlantis Paradise Island, Royal Towers, Paradise Island* ✛ *In the casino* ☎ *242/363–3000* ⊕ *www.atlantisbahamas.com.*

CABLE BEACH

$$$$ ✗**Black Angus Steakhouse & Grill.** This steak house offers some of the best
STEAKHOUSE certified Angus beef on the island. Bring your appetite if you're going to try the gigantic Cowboy steak (28 or 32 ounces), which is carved right in front of you. It's not all about the beef, though. The grilled sea bass and tuna steak are delightful seafood alternatives. Whichever you go with, select from the array of sauces including a guava glaze. $ *Average main: $50* ✉ *Meliá Nassau Beach Resort, W. Bay St., Cable Beach* ☎ *242/327–6200* ⊕ *www.melia.com* ☽ *No lunch* ⌂ *Reservations essential.*

$$ ✗**Nesbitt's Delaporte Restaurant & Lounge.** The vibe in this hole-in-the-wall
BAHAMIAN restaurant is set by whomever controls the jukebox, which contains everything from current hits to old school R&B love songs to local Rake 'n' Scrape. Feel free to get up and dance if the mood strikes. The food is basic but good, and the lounge is a great place to meet some locals. The cracked conch and grouper (which you can have steamed, fried, or sautéed), are popular for dinner. Breakfast is standard Bahamian fare, but there are omelets for the less adventurous. Late-night revelers head here to ward off a hangover with a plate of greasy, fried "cut-up chicken, pork chop, or conch bites." There is no sign, but you'll know you've found the right spot by the steady stream of local cars pulling into the lot next door. Look for the two-story blue building opposite

Mother Lousie Sweeting Park. Ⓢ *Average main: $20* ⊠ *Cable Beach* ✛ *West of BTC Delaporte phone tower* ☎ *242/327–6036.*

$$$
ASIAN FUSION

✗ **Nikkei.** The menu at this Japanese-Peruvian restaurant is small but interesting; there's even a recommendable sushi bar in the main dining room. But book ahead to reserve a space in the real draw, the Teppanyaki Experience room, where your main course will be prepared right in front of you. Select from lime-and-garlic shrimp, chicken, teriyaki salmon, or beef tenderloin. The conch ceviche, and chaufa rice with a mixture of seafood are delicious. Ⓢ *Average main: $35* ⊠ *Meliá Nassau Beach Resort, W. Bay St., Cable Beach* ☎ *242/327–6000* ☾ *No lunch.*

$$$
MEDITERRANEAN

✗ **Olive's Meze Grill.** Hip and trendy, this restaurant puts a fresh twist on Mediterranean classics. The fare is simple, but locally grown greens and fish caught in nearby waters make the meals special. It's popular with locals for both lunch and dinner, and the bar is hopping most nights. Be sure to save room for desserts—the owners have taken special pains to come up with unique sweet creations. Ⓢ *Average main: $30* ⊠ *W. Bay St., Cable Beach* ☎ *242/327–6393* ⊕ *www.olivesgrill.com.*

$$$
SEAFOOD

✗ **The Poop Deck at Sandyport.** A more upscale version of the other Poop Deck in Nassau, this waterside restaurant has soaring ceilings, a cool-pink-and-aqua color scheme, and a dazzling view of the ocean. Seafood is the star on the menu here. Try the "Thunderball" paella or the zarazuela (a clay pot of all sorts of seafood and shellfish cooked in a tomato broth). Ribs, chicken, and steak are available for the seafood-phobic. Whatever your selection, pair it with a bottle from the extensive wine list. Ⓢ *Average main: $36* ⊠ *W. Bay St., Cable Beach* ☎ *242/327–3325* ⊕ *www.thepoopdeckrestaurants.com* ☾ *Closed Mon.*

$$
NORTHERN
ITALIAN
FAMILY

✗ **Spritz Restaurant and Bar.** This casual, open-air restaurant and bar overlooks the Sandyport Canal and the pedestrian-only streets of the Old Towne at Sandyport. Seating is limited, so reservations are recommended, especially for weekend dining. The wood-fired pizzas are a local favorite, and Northern Italian chef "Ciccio" brings a taste of his hometown with a wide selection of pasta dishes. Ⓢ *Average main: $28* ⊠ *Sandyport Olde Towne Marina Plaza, Cable Beach* ☎ *242/327–0761* ⊕ *www.spritzrestaurant.com* ☾ *No lunch Mon.*

$$
AMERICAN

✗ **Twisted Lime.** This busy sports bar has something for everyone. Indoors, the dining room and bar feature the latest games playing on 18 flat-screen TVs. Outdoors, casual canal-front dining and drinks are available at high-tops or on plush sofas. On big game nights, it's boys' night out, but otherwise it's become a popular option on Nassau's social scene. The menu is quite extensive: fish tacos or nachos fiesta are good options for starters with local flair. For a main course, try the tamarind glazed barbecue ribs or select something from the hot dog, burger, or flat-bread menus. Ⓢ *Average main: $28* ⊠ *Sandyport Marina Village, Cable Beach* ☎ *242/327–0061* ⊕ *www.twistedlimebar.com.*

WESTERN NEW PROVIDENCE

$$$
AMERICAN

✗ **Compass Point.** This friendly restaurant and bar is one of the best sunset-watching spots on the island. Sit indoors or out on the terrace overlooking the ocean and enjoy the simple but tasty Bahamian and island-style American fare for breakfast, lunch, and dinner. The kitchen is open daily until midnight, so it's a great stop for a late-night meal or snack. The long outdoor bar stays open until the last guest leaves, and there's live music every other Saturday. $ *Average main: $35* ✉ *W. Bay St., Gambier* ☎ *242/327–4500* ⊕ *www.compasspointbeachresort.com.*

$
BAHAMIAN
Fodor's Choice
★

✕ **Dino's Gourmet Conch Salad.** Be prepared to grab a stool, order a refreshing (albeit intoxicating) gin and coconut water and wait at least a half hour for your conch salad at this popular roadside joint. You can call ahead to try and cut down on the wait if you're in a hurry. The crowds of tourists and locals who gather here are proof, though, that it's well worth the wait. Dino's is credited with being the first to put a twist on the Bahamian staple, adding apple, mango, and pineapple to create the "tropical" conch salad. The vantage point across the road is a great spot for photos. But it's cash-only here. $ *Average main: $12* ✉ *Gambier* ☎ *242/377–7798* ▬ *No credit cards.*

$
ECLECTIC
FAMILY

✕ **Goodfellow Farms.** This unique treat is well worth the long drive to the western end of the island. The vegetable farm has a country store and small restaurant with outdoor dining under shady trees and umbrellas. Lunch is simple but delicious and changes daily, but one staple is the side salad made from vegetables picked from the farm earlier in the day. $ *Average main: $16* ✉ *Nelson Rd., off Western Rd., Mount Pleasant* ✢ *Take left at Lyford Cay roundabout, go over the hill, entrance to farm road is signposted* ☎ *242/377–5000* ⊕ *goodfellowfarms.com* ⊘ *No dinner.*

$$$$
ECLECTIC

✕ **Mahogany House.** A favorite with the upscale Lyford Cay crowd, Mahogany House is sophisticated simplicity at its best. Whether you're dressed to the nines or sporting flip-flops, you're bound to feel both comfortable and welcome here. Specialty ingredients like quail, foie gras, and buffalo pork belly keep things interesting, but the wood-fired pizzas (including one topped with crawfish, yellow pepper, red onion, avocado, and mozzarella) and the vast selection of cured meats and cheeses can make this a very simple yet satisfying dining experience. The waitstaff can help make the perfect wine pairing for whatever you select from the extensive wine list on offer. Save room for le grand tour: a selection of all the rich desserts to share. $ *Average main: $45* ✉ *Western Rd., Clifton* ☎ *242/362–6669* ⊕ *mahogany-house.com* ⊘ *No lunch weekends.*

WHERE TO STAY

NASSAU

$$$$
HOTEL

🖼 **British Colonial Hilton Nassau.** This landmark hotel is the social heart of Nassau, the setting for political meetings and the city's most important events. **Pros:** right on Bay Street; quiet but trendy beach and pool area; centrally located. **Cons:** busy with local meetings and events; man-made beach; hard to access at peak traffic times. $ *Rooms from: $479* ✉ *1 Bay St., Nassau* ☎ *242/322–3301* ⊕ *www.bchiltonnassauhotel.com* ⇆ *265 rooms, 23 suites* ⦿ *No meals.*

$
HOTEL

🖼 **Grand Central Hotel.** If you're looking for somewhere clean, safe, and cheap to stay in the heart of downtown Nassau, the four-story Grand

Humidor Churrascaria Restaurant is in the Graycliff Hotel.

Central is worth considering. **Pros:** in the heart of downtown Nassau; guesthouse quality; friendly staff who get to know their guests. **Cons:** on busy street; no pool or beach; extremely basic. $ *Rooms from: $90* ✉ *Charlotte St., Nassau* ☎ *242/322–8356* ⤳ *35 rooms* ⅼ◎ⅼ *No meals.*

$$$$
HOTEL
Fodor'sChoice
★

⊞ Graycliff Hotel. The old-world flavor of this Georgian colonial landmark—built in the 1720s by ship captain Howard Graysmith—has made it a perennial favorite among both the rich and the famous. **Pros:** one of the most luxurious accommodations on the island; lush tropical gardens; large rooms. **Cons:** centered around the busy restaurant and bar area; not easily accessible for handicapped; no beach. $ *Rooms from: $435* ✉ *W. Hill St., Nassau* ☎ *242/322–2796, 800/476–0446* ⊕ *www.graycliff.com* ⤳ *10 rooms, 10 suites* ⅼ◎ⅼ *No meals.*

PARADISE ISLAND

You'll find several hotels (and apartment buildings) on Paradise Island, but the sprawling Atlantis resort is the king. It's a bustling fantasy world—part water park, entertainment complex, megaresort, and beach oasis. Other than the new Baha Mar resort complex in Cable Beach, which wasn't yet open at this writing, it's the largest resort in the country. The public areas are lavish, with fountains, glass sculptures, and gleaming shopping arcades. There is plenty of nightlife on the premises; the casino, ringed by restaurants, is one of the largest in the Bahamas and the Caribbean. Some of these facilities can be visited by nonguests (restaurants, shops, the casino, and nightspots), but the famed Aquaventure Water Park is limited to guests of Atlantis, a handful of affiliated hotels, and cruise passengers only.

2

$$ ☷ **Atlantis Paradise Island Beach Towers.** Located at the easternmost edge
RESORT of Atlantis, the Beach Towers offer a bit of a reprieve from the hustle
FAMILY and bustle of the rest of the megaresort. Pros: less congestion at beach
and pools; close to kids' activities; best value for Atlantis Resort. Cons:
far from the main attractions of Atlantis; oldest part of the property;
only one restaurant in this section. $ *Rooms from: $239* ☒ *Atlantis
Paradise Island, Paradise Island* ☎ *242/363–3000, 888/877–7525 res-
ervations* ⊕ *www.atlantisbahamas.com* ⊷ *423 rooms* ⦿ *No meals.*

$$ ☷ **Atlantis Paradise Island Coral Towers.** The Coral Towers is at the heart of
RESORT the Atlantis Resort, giving you the good access to all the top amenities—
FAMILY including the casino and Aquaventure—at a moderate price point. Pros:
good access to restaurants and amenities; close to the casino; Marina
Village steps away. Cons: always busy lobby area; guest rooms lack
some of the pizazz you might expect at Atlantis. $ *Rooms from: $279*
☒ *Atlantis Paradise Island, Paradise Island* ☎ *242/363–3000, 888/877–
7525 reservations* ⊕ *www.atlantisbahamas.com* ⊷ *652 rooms, 41
suites* ⦿ *No meals.*

$$$ ☷ **Atlantis Paradise Island Royal Towers.** If you plan on spending your
RESORT days riding the slides at Aquaventure and nights in the casino and the
FAMILY nightclub, then centrally located Royal Towers is the Atlantis hotel
Fodor'sChoice for you. Pros: best access to top Atlantis amenities, including the spa
★ and Aquaventure water park; larger rooms than other Atlantis tow-
ers; you'll never run out of things to do. Cons: only suites have real
balconies that you can sit on; hard to find peace and quiet; eating on
property gets expensive, and the cheapest fast-food options aren't very
good. $ *Rooms from: $349* ☒ *Atlantis Paradise Island, Paradise Island*
☎ *242/363–3000, 888/877–7525 reservations* ⊕ *www.atlantisbahamas.
com* ⊷ *1,081 rooms, 120 suites* ⦿ *No meals.*

$$ ☷ **Best Western Bay View Suites.** This 4-acre condominium resort has
HOTEL a lush, intimate character. Pros: children 12 and under stay free; pri-
FAMILY vate "at-home" vibe; free Wi-Fi in pool area. Cons: long walk from
beach; no restaurant serving dinner on property; no organized activities on-site. $ *Rooms from: $240* ☒ *Bay View Dr., Paradise Island*
☎ *242/363–2555, 800/757–1357* ⊕ *www.bwbayviewsuites.com* ⊷ *25
suites, 2 villas, 3 town houses* ⦿ *No meals.*

$$ ☷ **Club Land'Or.** In Atlantis's shadow just over the bridges from Nas-
RENTAL sau, this friendly time-share property has one-bedroom villas with full
kitchens, bathrooms, living rooms, desks, and patios or balconies that
overlook the lagoon, the gardens, or the pool. Pros: everything you
need for an extended vacation; walking distance to Marina Village
and Atlantis. Cons: surrounded by Atlantis resort; beach is quite a
walk away. $ *Rooms from: $265* ☒ *Paradise Beach Dr., Paradise Island*
☎ *242/363–2400* ⊕ *www.clublandor.com* ⊷ *72 villas* ⦿ *No meals.*

$$$ ☷ **Comfort Suites Paradise Island.** This all-suites, three-story pink-and-
HOTEL white hotel has a unique arrangement with Atlantis that allows its
FAMILY guests to use the megaresort's facilities, which are just next door (closer
than rooms in Atlantis's own Beach Towers, in fact) for no fee. Pros:
full access to Atlantis amenities; near shops and restaurants; full cooked
breakfast included. Cons: not located on a beach; in the midst of busy
traffic; lots of extra fees, though they are clearly spelled out. $ *Rooms*

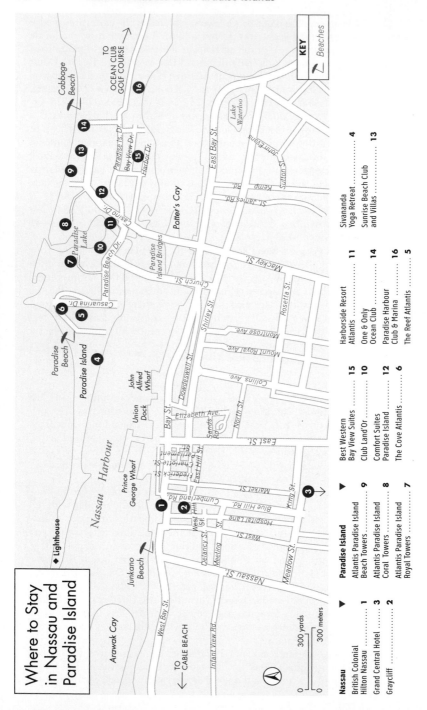

Where to Stay in Nassau and Paradise Island

KEY

Beaches

Nassau

British Colonial Hilton Nassau **1**
Grand Central Hotel **3**
Graycliff **2**

Paradise Island

Atlantis Paradise Island Beach Towers **9**
Atlantis Paradise Island Coral Towers **8**
Atlantis Paradise Island Royal Towers **7**

Best Western Bay View Suites **15**
Club Land'Or **10**
Comfort Suites Paradise Island **12**
The Cove Atlantis **6**

Harborside Resort Atlantis **11**
One & Only Ocean Club **14**
Paradise Harbour Club & Marina **16**
The Reef Atlantis **5**

Sivananda Yoga Retreat **4**
Sunrise Beach Club and Villas **13**

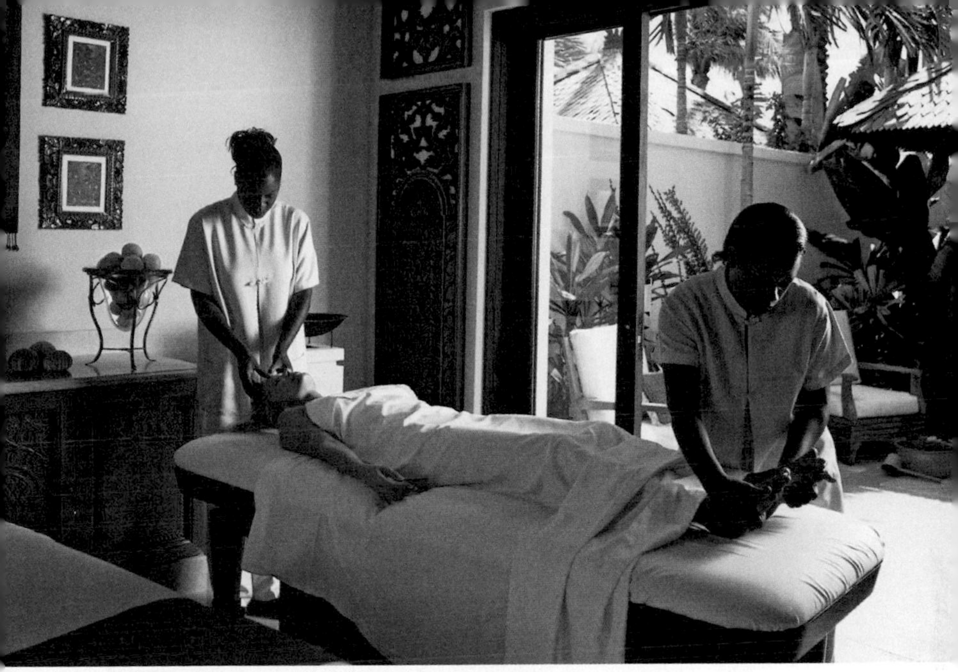

The spa at the One & Only Ocean Club offers indulgent massages.

from: $350 ✉ Paradise Island Dr., Paradise Island ☎ 242/363–3680, 800/424–6423 🌐 www.comfortsuitespi.com 🛏 229 suites 🍴 Breakfast.

$$$$ RESORT Fodor's Choice ★ 🏨 **The Cove Atlantis.** Worlds away from the other properties within the Atlantis Resort in terms of overall look, experience, and sophistication, this high-rise overlooking two stunning white-sand beaches is a true grown-ups' getaway. **Pros:** adult-only pool option; incredible private beaches; amenities of Atlantis, but separated from the hustle and bustle. **Cons:** a long walk to Atlantis amenities; limited dining and bar options on-site. [$] *Rooms from: $545 ✉ Atlantis Paradise Island, Paradise Island ☎ 242/363–3000, 888/877–7525 reservations 🌐 www.atlantisbahamas.com 🛏 600 suites 🍴 No meals.*

$$$$ RENTAL FAMILY 🏨 **Harborside Resort Atlantis.** It you want more space to stretch out during your Paradise Island vacation, consider these one-, two-, and three-bedroom town-house-style villas that can accommodate up to nine guests and are fully equipped with separate living/dining areas, kitchens, and private laundry facilities. **Pros:** lots of space to stretch out; pool area is less crowded than Aquaventure; right next door to Nassau water taxi dock. **Cons:** Wi-Fi is extra; long walk to Atlantis restaurants and amenities; no room service. [$] *Rooms from: $470 ✉ Paradise Beach Dr., Paradise Island ☎ 242/363–3000 🌐 www.atlantisbahamas.com 🛏 392 villas 🍴 No meals.*

$$$$ RESORT Fodor's Choice ★ 🏨 **One & Only Ocean Club.** Once the private hideaway of A&P heir Huntington Hartford, this exclusive resort on magnificent Cabbage Beach's quietest stretch provides the ultimate in understated—and decidedly posh—elegance. **Pros:** ultraexclusive; lovely beach; top-rated amenities. **Cons:** not within walking distance of Atlantis; limited (and very expensive) on-site dining; free Wi-Fi only in certain public areas. [$] *Rooms*

CLOSE UP

Bond in the Bahamas

In *Casino Royale*, the 21st James Bond installment, Bond took on the bad guys at an embassy, which was, in reality, the lovely Buena Vista Restaurant and Hotel in Nassau, which closed shortly after filming and is now home to the John Watling's Distillery. The ruggedly handsome new Bond, Daniel Craig, also had the glamorous background of the One & Only Ocean Club resort on Paradise Island, where another Bond, Pierce Brosnan, frequently stays.

Bond and the Bahamas have a long relationship. Six Bond films have used the Bahamas as a backdrop, including *Thunderball*, filmed in 1965 with the original 007, Sean Connery. Connery loved the Bahamas so much he has chosen to live here year-round in the luxury gated community of Lyford Cay.

Thunderball was filmed at the Café Martinique, which, after being closed for more than a decade, reopened at Atlantis resort on Paradise Island in 2006. Scenes were also shot at the Mediterranean Renaissance–style British Colonial, built in the 1920s.

You can swim and snorkel in Thunderball Cave in the Exumas, site of the pivotal chase scene in the 1965 Sean Connery film. The ceiling of this huge, dome-shaped cave is about 30 feet above the water, which is filled with yellowtails, parrots, blue chromes, and yellow-and-black striped sergeant majors. Swimming into the cave is the easy part—the tide draws you in—but paddling back out can be strenuous, especially because if you stop moving, the tide will pull you back.

The Rock Point house, better known to 007 fans as Palmyra, the villain Emilio Largo's estate, was another Bond location, and Bay Street, where Bond and his beautiful sidekick Domino attended a Junkanoo carnival, is still the location of Junkanoo twice a year. The *Thunderball* remake, *Never Say Never Again*, was also shot in the Bahamas, using many of the same locations as the original.

Underwater shots for many of the Bond flicks were filmed in the Bahamas, including Thunderball Grotto, while Nassau's offshore reefs were the underwater locations for the 1983 film *Never Say Never Again*, the 1967 film *You Only Live Twice*, the 1977 film *The Spy Who Loved Me*, and *For Your Eyes Only*, released in 1981.

—Cheryl Blackerby

from: $1,945 ✉ *Ocean Club Dr., Paradise Island* ☎ *242/363–2501, 866/552–0001* 🌐 *oceanclub.oneandonlyresorts.com* 🛏 *105 rooms and suites, 3 villas, 2 cottages.*

$$ HOTEL FAMILY 🏨 **Paradise Harbour Club & Marina.** With a marina and an enviable location, this collection of oversized, comfortable apartments is a great choice for those who want the freedom of a private residence with the facilities of a large resort. **Pros:** quiet location; cooking facilities; scheduled beach and grocery store shuttle. **Cons:** need to walk or be shuttled to and from the beach; condo built nearby towers over property; no restaurant on-site. [$] *Rooms from: $200* ✉ *Paradise Island Dr., Paradise Island* ☎ *242/363–2992* 🌐 *www.festiva-paradise.com* 🛏 *23 units* 🍴 *No meals.*

$$$$ RESORT FAMILY 🏨 **The Reef Atlantis.** This 497-suite tower has exquisitely outfitted studios or one- and two-bedroom condominium-style accommodations. **Pros:** fully equipped units; quiet; cost-effective option with Atlantis benefits. **Cons:** no restaurants or bars on property; a long walk to Atlantis amenities; units have kitchens, but there are no grocery stores nearby. [$] *Rooms from: $850* ✉ *Atlantis Paradise Island, Paradise Island* ☎ *242/363–3000, 888/877–7525 reservations* 🌐 *www.atlantisbahamas.com* 🛏 *497 apartments* 🍴 *No meals.*

$ B&B/INN 🏨 **Sivananda Yoga Retreat.** Accessible only by boat, this resort is the antithesis of the high-rollers' Atlantis down the road. **Pros:** ideal for peace and quiet; inexpensive accommodations; free shuttle to and from Nassau. **Cons:** strict regulations; basic accommodations; no road access. [$] *Rooms from: $140* ✉ *Paradise Island* ☎ *242/363–2902, 866/559–5167* 🌐 *www.sivanandabahamas.org* 🛏 *48 rooms, 36 dorm beds, 16 tent huts, 90 tent sites* 🍴 *All meals.*

$$$ HOTEL FAMILY 🏨 **Sunrise Beach Club and Villas.** Lushly landscaped with crotons, coconut palms, bougainvillea, and hibiscus, this low-rise, family-run resort on Cabbage Beach has a tropical wonderland feel. **Pros:** on one of the best beaches on the island; lively bar on property; great for families. **Cons:** no activities; lots of walking to get to rooms. [$] *Rooms from: $365* ✉ *Casino Dr., Paradise Island* ☎ *242/363–2234, 800/451–6078* 🌐 *www.sunrisebeachclub.com* 🛏 *26 suites* 🍴 *No meals.*

CABLE BEACH

$$$ HOTEL FAMILY 🏨 **Bluewater Resort.** These simply decorated time-share and short-term rental accommodations are perfect for young families or groups of friends traveling together. **Pros:** spring breakers not allowed; great for families; small, but private beach. **Cons:** minimum two-night stay; need car to go into town; housekeeping costs extra. [$] *Rooms from: $400* ✉ *W. Bay St., Cable Beach* ☎ *242/327–7568* 🌐 *www.bluewaterresortbahamas.com* 🛏 *35 units* 🍴 *No meals.*

$$$ RESORT FAMILY 🏨 **Meliá Nassau Beach Resort.** Although the Meliá is not technically part of the Baha Mar resort, the property has embarked on a series of upgrades to keep pace with the changes to the neighborhood. **Pros:** guests get preferred rates at Baha Mar; lots of activities included. **Cons:** rooms have yet to be upgraded; hotel immediately to east will remain closed for foreseeable future; no private beach. [$] *Rooms from: $360* ✉ *Cable Beach* ☎ *242/327–6000* 🌐 *www.melia.com* 🛏 *662 rooms, 32 suites* 🍴 *All-inclusive.*

$$$$ RESORT 🏨 **Sandals Royal Bahamian Resort & Spa.** Cable Beach's most expensive resort has elegantly furnished rooms with views of the ocean, pool, or grounds replete with pillars and faux-Roman statuary, as well as personal butler service and a room that opens up to a private pool for the ultimate indulgence. **Pros:** no children; lovely setting; private offshore cay. **Cons:** couples only; need car or taxi to go into town; convention center popular for local functions. [$] *Rooms from: $750* ✉ *W. Bay St., Cable Beach* ☎ *242/327–6400, 800/726–3257* 🌐 *www.sandals.com* 🛏 *404 rooms* 🍴 *All-inclusive.*

$$ RESORT 🏨 **SuperClub Breezes Bahamas.** This affordable all-inclusive is ideally situated right on beautiful Cable Beach and next door to the sprawling

CLOSE UP

Baha Mar

The Cable Beach strip has been completely transformed by the sprawling, multibillion dollar Baha Mar resort. New hotels, which include a Grand Hyatt, Rosewood, SLS Lux, and Baha Mar Casino Hotel, have altered the skyline and can be seen from across the island of New Providence. However, long after it was first scheduled to open in December 2014—and with construction reportedly 97% complete—the property has yet to welcome its first guest. From the perimeter, the resort looks ready, but just days before its second scheduled opening in March 2015, the developer announced the property still needed work and suggested that all hotels would be ready for their first guests in May 2015. The third scheduled opening date came and went, after which construction came to a grinding halt. Since then, the developer, the contractor, and the Bahamian government have become embroiled in a very public dispute resulting in court actions in the United States, England, and the Bahamas. At this writing, in August 2015, there is no fourth scheduled opening date, and the hotel companies are also starting to promise legal action. When Baha Mar does open, the resort—which includes four hotels, a TPA golf course, the largest casino in the Caribbean, an ESPA spa, more than 40 planned restaurants, bars, and clubs, and a vast pool complex (all set on a beautiful white-sand beach)—will be an exciting playground catering mainly to an adult clientele and should rival the scope of the Atlantis resort.

Baha Mar resort complex. **Pros:** no kids under 14 allowed; walking distance to Baha Mar casino; lots of activities. **Cons:** not family friendly; need car or taxi to access town; packed with spring breakers during March and April. [$] *Rooms from: $206* ✉ *W. Bay St., Cable Beach* ☎ *242/327–5356, 800/467–8737* 🌐 *www.breezes.com* 🛏 *387 rooms, 5 suites* 🍴 *All-inclusive.*

$$ RESORT FAMILY 🏨 **West Wind II.** Privacy is the lure of these cozy time-share villas on Cable Beach's west end, 6 miles from downtown. **Pros:** great for families; condos sleep six; right on Cable Beach. **Cons:** no major activities; need car or taxi to go downtown; housekeeping, beach towels, and toiletries additional. [$] *Rooms from: $300* ✉ *W. Bay St., Cable Beach* ☎ *242/327–7211, 242/327–7019* 🌐 *www.westwindii.com* 🛏 *54 villas* 🍴 *No meals.*

WESTERN NEW PROVIDENCE

$$ B&B/INN 🏨 **A Stone's Throw Away.** Featuring seaside comfort in fashionable surroundings, this "gourmet bed-and-breakfast" is actually a luxurious hideaway. **Pros:** serene; secluded public-beach access; friendly staff. **Cons:** in flight path; long distance from anything else; hotel access up a steep staircase cut out of the limestone hill. [$] *Rooms from:* ✉ *Tropical Garden Rd. and W. Bay St., Gambier* ☎ *242/327–7030* 🌐 *www.astonesthrowaway.com* 🛏 *8 rooms, 2 suites* 🍴 *Breakfast.*

$$$ RESORT 🏨 **Compass Point.** This whimsical-looking hotel made up of brightly colored one- and two-story cottages offers a relaxing alternative to

Restaurants ▼

Black Angus Grille **6**
Nesbitt's Delaporte Restaurant & Lounge **7**
Nikkei **5**
Olive's Meze Grill **4**
The Poop Deck at Sandyport **3**
Spritz Restaurant and Bar **1**
Twisted Lime ... **2**

Hotels ▼

Bluewater Resort........... **3**
Meliá Nassau Beach Resort ... **4**
Sandals Royal Bahamian Resort & Spa **1**
SuperClub Breezes Bahamas........ **5**
West Wind II **2**

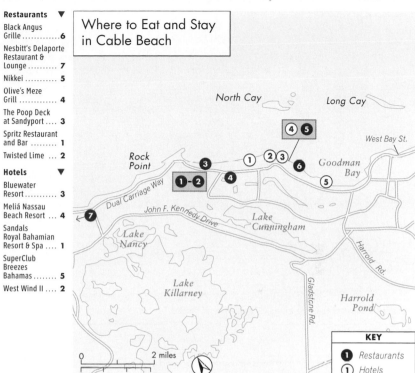

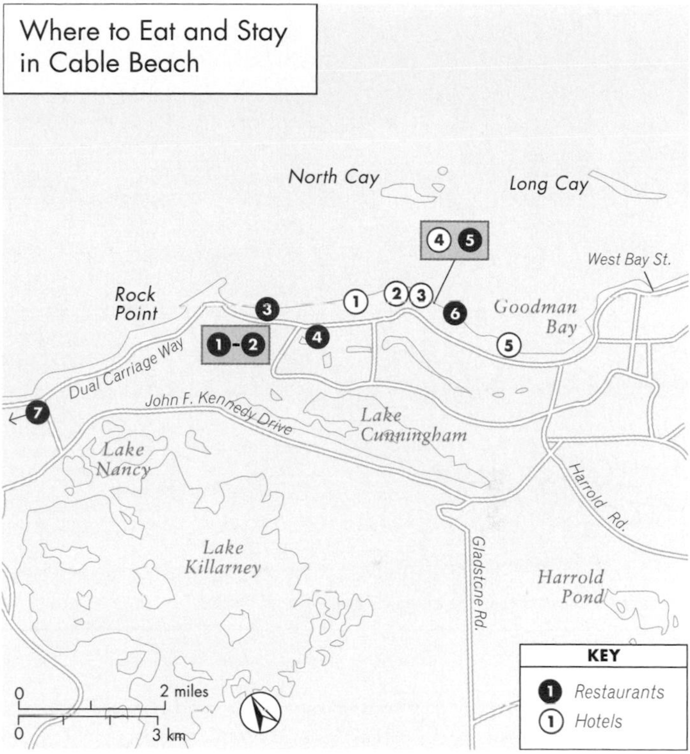
Where to Eat and Stay in Cable Beach
North Cay
Long Cay
West Bay St.
Rock Point
Goodman Bay
Dual Carriage Way
John F. Kennedy Drive
Lake Cunningham
Lake Nancy
Harrold Rd.
Lake Killarney
Gladstone Rd.
Harrold Pond
KEY
Restaurants
Hotels
0
2 miles
0
3 km

many of the area's major resorts. **Pros:** best view on the island; access to incredible private beach. **Cons:** in flight path; not ideal for children; expensive taxi ride to town. [$] *Rooms from: $325* ✉ *W. Bay St., Gambier* ☎ *242/327–4500* 🌐 *www.compasspointbeachresort.com* 🛏 *18 cottages* 🍴 *Breakfast.*

$$$$ **B&B/INN** 🏨 **The Island House.** The antithesis of the big resorts typically found in New Providence, The Island House delivers casual sophistication with high-end, yet understated, amenities and features at every turn. **Pros:** tranquil; near the airport; variety of amenities for sports and wellness enthusiasts. **Cons:** far from just about everything but the airport; no beach nearby. [$] *Rooms from: $650* ✉ *Mahogany Hill, Western Rd., Clifton* ☎ *242/698–6300* 🌐 *www.the-island-house.com* 🛏 *30 suites* 🍴 *No meals.*

$ **B&B/INN** 🏨 **Orange Hill Beach Inn.** If you prefer down-home coziness over slick glamour, then this basic hotel—on the site of a former orange plantation perched on a hilltop overlooking the ocean—is the place to stay. **Pros:** across the road from a nice beach; small; family-style service. **Cons:** long distance from town; not much by way of activities; basic accommodations. [$] *Rooms from: $140* ✉ *W. Bay St., Gambier* ☎ *242/327–7157* 🌐 *orangehill.com* 🛏 *30 rooms, 2 cottages* 🍴 *No meals.*

The cottages at Compass Point are known for their whimsical colors.

NIGHTLIFE

NASSAU

BARS AND CLUBS

Bambu. Pop into this open-air club overlooking Nassau Harbour and you may find the DJ playing the latest Top 40 dance tune. Wait a few moments and Europe's sexiest house beats will change the vibe entirely. It's popular with hip young locals and cruise passengers and staff. The club is open on Tuesday, Friday, and Saturday nights from 9 pm to 5 am and has a $20 cover. ✉ *Upstairs Prince George Plaza, Bay St., Nassau.*

Sharkeez Bar & Grill. Every night brings a different theme—and different vibe—at this popular restaurant and gathering spot. Some nights it's a live band, others it's a DJ. Music ranges from Top 40 to reggae, soca, calypso, and even Latin flavor for rumba night. Trivia and rock 'n' roll bingo nights are also on the lineup. The drinks menu is extensive, including Nassau's largest offering of frozen cocktails in a variety of sizes—all the way up to the 70-ounce monster. And it's open every day. ✉ *Woodes Rodgers Walk, Nassau* ☎ *242/601–5325* ⊕ *www. sharkeezcaribbean.com.*

Via Caffe. This lively restaurant and café is transformed most nights (every night but Sunday, really) into a lively locale for late-night entertainment with no cover charge. Depending on the night, you might find yourself learning salsa techniques while sipping a margarita, dancing to the hottest tunes spun by the house DJ, listening to a live band, or wowing the crowd at karaoke. For a late bite, the kitchen is open until the early morning hours. ✉ *Scotiabank Bldg., corner of Parliament St. and Woodes Rogers Walk, Nassau* 🕾 *242/322–7203.*

PARADISE ISLAND

BARS AND CLUBS

Aura. This is the country's hottest nightclub, located upstairs from the Atlantis Casino. It's the place to see and be seen in Paradise Island, though many of the celebrities who frequent the club opt for the ultra-exclusive private lounge. Dancing goes on all night, and the handsome bartenders dazzle the crowd with their mixing techniques. The music varies, depending on the night. The steep cover charge ranges from $20 to $100 but is free for Atlantis guests from Tuesday through Thursday nights (even they pay on weekends). It's closed Monday nights. ✉ *Atlantis Paradise Island Royal Towers, Paradise Island* 🕾 *242/363–3000* ⊕ *www.atlantisbahamas.com.*

Oasis Lounge. There's live piano or vocal music here every night except Sunday from 7:30 to midnight. Go early to get a good seat and take advantage of one of the best drink deals on Paradise Island—buy one, get one free and complimentary hors d'oeuvres from 5 to 7 pm. The lounge is open until midnight every night. ✉ *Club Land'Or, Paradise Island* 🕾 *242/363–2400* ⊕ *www.clublandor.com.*

CASINOS

PARADISE ISLAND

Atlantis Casino. Featuring a spectacularly open and airy design, the 50,000-square-foot (100,000 if you include the dining and drinking areas) casino is ringed with restaurants and offers more than 1,100 slot machines, baccarat, blackjack, roulette, craps tables, and such local specialties as Caribbean stud poker. There's also a high-limit table area, and most of the eateries have additional games. The casino is always open, with gaming tables open from 10 am to 4 am daily. ✉ *Atlantis Paradise Island Royal Towers, Paradise Island* 🕾 *242/363–3000* ⊕ *www.atlantis.com.*

PERFORMING ARTS

THEATER

Dundas Centre for the Performing Arts. Plays, concerts, ballets, and musicals by local artists are staged here throughout the year. The box office is open from 10 am to 4 pm. ✉ *Mackey St.* 🕾 *242/393–3728.*

SHOPPING AND SPAS

Most of Nassau's shops are on Bay Street between Rawson Square and the British Colonial Hotel, and on the side streets leading off Bay Street. Some stores are popping up on the main shopping thoroughfare's eastern end and just west of the Cable Beach strip. Bargains abound between Bay Street and the waterfront. Upscale stores can also be found in Marina Village, in the Crystal Court at Atlantis, and at Baha Mar on Cable Beach.

You'll find duty-free prices—sometimes as much as 25% to 50% less than U.S. prices—on imported items such as crystal, linens, watches, cameras, jewelry, leather goods, and perfumes, but you really need to know the prices before you buy. Not everything is a bargain.

NASSAU

SHOPS

CIGARS

Be aware that some merchants on Bay Street and elsewhere in the islands are selling counterfeit Cuban cigars—sometimes unwittingly. If the price seems too good to be true, chances are it is. Check the wrappers and feel to ensure that there's a consistent fill before you make your purchase.

Graycliff Hotel. Graycliff carries one of Nassau's finest selections of hand-rolled cigars, featuring leaves from throughout Central and South America. Graycliff's operation is so popular that it has been expanded by the hotel to include an entire cigar factory, which is open to the public for tours and purchases. A dozen Cuban men and women roll the cigars; they live on the premises and work here through a special arrangement with the Cuban government. True cigar buffs will seek out Graycliff's owner, Enrico Garzaroli. In addition to the shop in the hotel, there's another Graycliff boutique at Lynden Pindling International Airport. ⊠ *W. Hill St., Nassau* ☎ *242/302–9150* ⊕ *www.graycliff.com.*

CLOTHING AND ACCESSORIES

Brass and Leather. Here you can find leather goods for men and women, including bags, shoes, and belts. Pick up one of the unique soft leather passport covers that come in an array of colors emblazoned with your country's coat of arms. ⊠ *Charlotte St., off Bay St., Nassau* ☎ *242/322–3806.*

Cole's of Nassau. This is a top choice for everything from ball gowns and cocktail dresses to resort wear and bathing suits with all the shoes and accessories for every look. ⊠ *Parliament St., Nassau* ☎ *242/322–8393* ⊕ *www.colesofnassau.com.*

La Casita. This cute boutique offers high-end straw bags and purses, as well as costume jewelry. ⊠ *Bay St., near the Straw Market, Nassau* ☎ *242/328–5988* ☉ *Closed Sun.*

FOOD

Bahamas Rum Cake Factory. At the Bahamas Rum Cake Factory, delicious Bahamian rum-soaked cakes are made and packaged in tins right on the premises (peek into the bakery) and make a great souvenir. Just make sure you take one home for yourself! ⊠ *E. Bay St., Nassau* ☎ *242/328–3750.*

Model Bakery. Be sure to try the cinnamon twists or the gingerbread sticks at this great local bakery not far from downtown or Paradise Island. ⊠ *Dowdeswell St., Nassau* ☎ *242/322–2595.*

Continued on page 90

JUNKANOO IN THE BAHAMAS

by Jessica Robertson

It's after midnight, and the only noise in downtown Nassau is a steady buzz of anticipation. Suddenly the streets erupt in a kaleidoscope of sights and sounds—Junkanoo groups are parading down Bay Street. Vibrant costumes sparkle in the light of the street lamps, and the revelers bang on goatskin drums and clang cowbells, hammering out a steady celebratory beat. It's Junkanoo time!

Junkanoo is an important part of the Bahamas' Christmas season. Parades begin after midnight and last until midday on Boxing Day (December 26), and there are more on New Year's Day. What appears to be a random, wild expression of joy is actually a well-choreographed event. Large groups (often as many as 500 to 1,000 people) compete for prize money and bragging rights. Teams choose a different theme each year and keep it a closely guarded secret until they hit Bay Street. They spend most of the year preparing for the big day at their "shacks," which are tucked away in neighborhoods across the island. They practice dance steps and music, and they design intricate costumes. During the parade, judges award prizes for best music, best costumes, and best overall presentation.

Junkanoo costume, Grand Bahama

JUNKANOO HISTORY

MUSIC'S ROLE

Junkanoo holds an important place in the history and culture of the Bahamas, but the origin of the word *junkanoo* remains a mystery. Many believe it comes from John Canoe, an African tribal chief who was brought to the West Indies as a slave and then fought for the right to celebrate with his people. Others believe the word stems from the French *gens inconnus*, which means "the unknown people"—significant because Junkanoo revelers wear costumes that mask their identities.

The origin of the festival itself is more certain. Though its roots can be traced back to West Africa, it began in the Bahamas during the 16TH or 17TH century when Bahamian slaves were given a few days off around Christmas to celebrate with their families. They left the plantations and had elaborate costume parties at which they danced and played homemade musical instruments. They wore large, often scary-looking masks, which gave them the freedom of anonymity, so they could let loose without inhibition.

Over the years, Junkanoo has evolved. Costumes once decorated with shredded newspaper are now elaborate, vibrant creations incorporating imported crepe paper, glitter, gemstones, and feathers.

There's something mesmerizing about the simple yet powerful beat of the goatskin drum. Couple that steady pounding with the "kalik-kalik" clanging of thousands of cowbells and a hundreds-strong brass band, and Junkanoo music becomes downright infectious.

Music is the foundation of Junkanoo. It provides a rhythm for both the costumed revelers and crowds of spectators who jump up and down on rickety bleacher seats. The heavy percussion sound is created by metal cowbells, whistles, and oil barrel drums with fiery sternos inside to keep the animal skin coverings pliant. In the late 1970s, Junkanoo music evolved with the addition of brass instruments, adding melodies from Christmas carols, sacred religious hymns, and contemporary hits.

If you're in Nassau anytime from September through the actual festival, stand out on your hotel balcony and listen carefully. Somewhere, someone is bound to be beating out a rhythm as groups practice for the big parade.

DRESS TO IMPRESS

Each year, talented artists and builders transform chicken wire, cardboard, Styrofoam, and crepe paper into magnificent costumes that are worn, pushed, or carried along the Junkanoo parade route. Dancers and musicians tend to wear elaborate head dresses or off-the-shoulder pieces and cardboard skirts completely covered in finely fringed, brightly colored crepe paper—applied a single strip at a time until every inch is covered. Gemstones, referred to as "tricks" in the Junkanoo world, are painstakingly glued onto costumes to add sparkle. In recent years, feathers have been incorporated, giving the cardboard covered creations an added level of movement and flair.

In order to wow the crowd, and more importantly, win the competition, every member of the group must be in full costume when they hit Bay Street. Even their shoes are completely decorated. Massive banner pieces so big they graze the power lines and take up the entire width of the street are carried along the route by men who take turns. Every element, from the smallest costume to the lead banner, as well as the entire color scheme, is meticulously planned out months in advance.

EXPERIENCE JUNKANOO

SECURE YOUR SEATS

■ Junkanoo bleacher seat tickets ($10–$50) can be hard to come by as the parade date approaches. Contact your hotel concierge ahead of time to arrange for tickets or visit ⊕ www.tajiz.com, the official online retailer.

■ Rawson Square bleachers are the best seats. This is where groups perform the longest and put on their best show.

■ If you don't mind standing, make your way to Shirley Street or the eastern end of Bay Street, where the route is lined with barricades. Judges are positioned all along the way so you'll see a good performance no matter where you end up.

■ Junkanoo groups make two laps around the parade route. Each lap can take a few hours to complete, and there are many groups in the lineup, so most spectators stay only for the first round. Head to Bay Street just before dawn, and you'll be sure to score a vacant seat.

BEHIND THE SCENES

■ During the parade, head east along Bay Street and turn onto Elizabeth Avenue to the rest area. Groups take a break in the parking lot here before they start round two. Costume builders frantically repair any pieces damaged during the first rush (Bahamian slang for parading), revelers refuel at barbeque stands, goatskin drums are placed next to a giant bonfire to keep them supple,

and in the midst of all the noise and hubbub, you'll find any number of people taking a nap to ensure they make it through a long and physically demanding night.

■ If star-stalking is your thing, scour the crowds in the VIP section in Parliament Square or look across the street on the balcony of the Scotiabank building. This is where celebrities usually watch the parades. Some who've been spotted include Michael Jordan, Rick Fox, and former New York City mayor Rudy Giuliani.

■ When the parade ends, wander along the route and surrounding streets to score a one-of-a-kind souvenir. Despite the many hours Junkanoo participants spend slaving over their costumes, by the time they're done rushing the last thing they want to do is carry it home. Finders keepers.

■ If you're in Nassau in early December, watch the Junior Junkanoo parade. School groups compete for prizes in various age categories. The littlest ones are usually offbeat and egged on by teachers and parents, but are oh-so-cute in their costumes. The high school groups put on a show just as impressive as the groups in the senior parade.

JUNKANOO TRIVIA

■ Kalik beer, brewed in the Bahamas, gets its name from the sound of clanking cowbells.

■ An average costume requires 3,000 to 5,000 strips of fringed crepe paper to completely cover its cardboard frame.

■ Junkanoo widows are women whose husbands spend every waking moment working on their costumes or practicing music routines the weeks before the parade.

■ During the height of sponge farming in the Bahamas, a major industry in the early 1900s, many Junkanoo participants used natural sponge to create their costumes.

Junkanoo parade in Nassau

JUNKANOO ON OTHER ISLANDS

Nassau's Junkanoo parade is by far the biggest and most elaborate, but most other islands hold their own celebrations on New Year's Day. Nassau's parades are strictly a spectator sport unless you are officially in a group, but Out Island parades are more relaxed and allow visitors to join the rush.

JUNKANOO YEAR-ROUND

Not satisfied with limiting Junkanoo to Christmastime, the Bahamas Ministry of Tourism hosts an annual **Junkanoo Summer Festival**. In addition to the traditional Junkanoo rush, these festivals offer arts and crafts demonstrations, conch cracking, crab catching, coconut-husking competitions, concerts featuring top Bahamian artists, and of course, lots of good Bahamian food. Bay Street in Nassau is transformed every Saturday night in July. ⊕ *www.bahamas.com/summerfestivals*.

Marina Village on Paradise Island hosts **Junkanoo rushouts** on Wednesday (9 pm) and Saturday (9:30 pm). There are no big stand-alone pieces, but dancers and musicians wear color-coordinated cos-

tumes and headpieces. The parade is much less formal, so feel free to jump in and dance along.

The **Educulture Museum and Workshop** in Nassau gives a behind-the-scenes look at Junkanoo. Some of each year's best costumes are on display, as well as costumes from years gone by when newspaper and sponges were used as decoration. The diehard Junkanoo staff will help you make your own Junkanoo creations. Be sure to arrange your visit ahead of time. ☎ *242/328–3786* ⊕ *www.educulturebahamas.com*.

Mortimer Candies. Mortimer Candies whips up batches of uniquely Bahamian sweet treats daily. Pop in for a sno-cone on a hot day, or buy some bags of bennie cake, coconut-cream candy, or their signature Paradise Sweets in a swirl of the Bahamian flag colors. ⊠ *E. St. Hill, Nassau* ☎ *242/322–5230* ⊕ *www.mortimercandies.com.*

GIFTS

Bahama Handprints. Bahama Handprints fabrics emphasize local artists' sophisticated tropical prints in an array of colors. Also look for leather handbags, a wide range of women's clothing, housewares, and bolts of fabric. Ask for a free tour of the factory in back. ⊠ *Island Traders Bldg. Annex, off Mackey St., Nassau* ☎ *242/394–4111* ⊕ *www.bahamahandprints.com* ◷ *Closed Sun.*

The Craft Cottage. This small shop situated in a traditional wooden structure is a great place to buy locally made souvenirs and gifts including soaps and oils, hand-painted glassware, jewelry, straw bags, and textiles. The artists and artisans are often on-site. ⊠ *20 Village Rd., Nassau* ☎ *242/446–7373* ⊕ *www.craftcottagebahamas.com.*

Doongalik Studios Art Gallery. This gallery, housed in a traditional Bahamian style building, features a large exhibition gallery showcasing local artists. On Saturday mornings a bustling farmers' market takes place here. ⊠ *18 Village Rd., Nassau* ☎ *242/394–1886* ⊕ *www.doongalik.com.*

Linen Shop. This shop sells fine embroidered Irish linens and lace and has a delightful Christmas corner. ⊠ *Bay St., Nassau* ☎ *242/322–4266.*

My Ocean. Here you can find candles, soaps, salt scrubs, and lotions in island- and ocean-inspired scents and colors, all locally made. A second location is found at Festival Place. ⊠ *Prince George Plaza, Nassau* ☎ *242/328–6167* ⊕ *www.myocean-bahamas.com* ◷ *Closed Sun.*

JEWELRY, WATCHES, AND CLOCKS

Coin of the Realm. Coin of the Realm has Bahamian coins, stamps, native conch pearls, tanzanite, and semiprecious stone jewelry. ⊠ *Charlotte St. off Bay St., Nassau* ☎ *242/322–4862, 242/322–4497* ⊕ *www.coinrealm.net.*

Colombian Emeralds International. Colombian Emeralds International is the local branch of this well-known jeweler; its stores carry a variety of fine jewelry in addition to its signature gem. In addition to a location in downtown Nassau, there are also branches in Marina Village and at the Atlantis Paradise Island Royal Towers and Beach Towers. ⊠ *Bay St. near Rawson Sq., Nassau* ☎ *242/326–1661.*

John Bull. Established in 1929 and magnificently decorated in its Bay Street incarnation behind a Georgian-style facade, John Bull fills its complex with wares from Tiffany & Co., Cartier, Mikimoto, Nina Ricci, and Yves Saint Laurent. The company has 12 locations throughout Nassau and Paradise Island. ⊠ *284 Bay St., Nassau* ☎ *242/302–2800* ⊕ *www.johnbull.com.*

LIQUOR

Pirate Republic Brewing Company. When you spot a pirate hanging out on Woodes Rogers Walk, you know you've found the home of the Bahamas' only craft brewery. Inside the shop is Pirate Republic beer to sample—Long John Pilsner, Gold and Haze of Piracy, and the Island Pirate Ale—as well as lots of logo gear for sale. ⊠ *Woodes Rodgers Walk, Nassau* ⊕ *www.piraterepublicbahamas.com.*

MARKETS AND ARCADES

International Bazaar. This collection of shops under a huge, spreading bougainvillea, sells linens, jewelry, souvenirs, and offbeat items. There's usually a small band playing all sort of music along this funky shopping row. ⊠ *Bay St. at Charlotte St., Nassau.*

Prince George Plaza. Prince George Plaza, which leads from Bay Street to Woodes Rogers Walk near the cruise-ship docks, just east of the International Bazaar, has about two-dozen shops with varied wares. ⊠ *Bay St., Nassau.*

Straw Market. Years after the original burned to the ground, vendors finally have a new permanent structure from which to sell their wares. Situated on the original site on Bay Street is a towering colonial-style marketplace housing hundreds of straw vendors selling straw bags, T-shirts, and other souvenirs. The Straw Market is one place in the Bahamas where bartering is accepted, so it's best to wander around and price similar items at different stalls before sealing a deal. ⊠ *Bay St., Nassau.*

PERFUMES AND COSMETICS

The Cosmetic Boutique. This shop has beauty experts on hand to demonstrate the latest cosmetics offerings, including M.A.C., Clinique, Bobbi Brown, and La Mer. ⊠ *Bay St. near Charlotte St., Nassau* ☎ *242/323–2731.*

Perfume Bar. This shop carries the best-selling French fragrance Boucheron and the Clarins line of skin-care products, as well as scents by Givenchy, Fendi, and other well-known designers. ⊠ *Bay St., Nassau* ☎ *242/325–1258.*

The Perfume Shop & The Beauty Spot. This is a landmark perfumery that has the broadest selection of imported perfumes and fragrances in the Bahamas. Experienced makeup artists are on hand to help pick out the perfect foundation or blush from a wide array of lines including Lancôme, Clinique, and Chanel. ⊠ *Bay and Frederick Sts., Nassau* ☎ *242/322–2375.*

SPAS

Baha-Retreat. This spa, situated in an old wooden two-story Bahamian home, is popular with locals and offers a full range of spa and salon services seven days a week. Reservations are suggested, but walk-ins are welcome. Specialties include body sugaring and threading for hair removal, but massages are also good here. Book a Couples Spa Day for a complete pampering treat: aromatherapy body polish, aromatherapy massage, spa manicure and pedicure, and gourmet lunch with a glass of wine each. ⊠ *E. Bay St., Nassau* ☎ *242/323–6711* ⊕ *www.baharetreat.com.*

Windermere Day Spa at Harbour Bay. This day spa offers a variety of spa treatments—such as hydrotherapy and salt glows—as well as top-quality facials, massages, manicures, and pedicures. Get to the Lynden Pindling International Airport early for a final massage or manicure at their nail and massage bar in the departure lounge. ⊠ *E. Bay St.* ☎ *242/393–8788* ⊕ *www.windermeredayspa.com.*

PARADISE ISLAND

SHOPS

ARTS AND CRAFTS

Bahamacraft Centre. Bahamacraft Centre offers some top-level Bahamian crafts, including a selection of authentic straw work. Dozens of vendors sell everything from baskets to shell collages inside this vibrantly colored building. You can catch a shuttle bus from Atlantis to the center. ⊠ *Paradise Island Dr., Paradise Island.*

CIGARS

Havana Humidor. Havana Humidor has the largest selection of authentic Cuban cigars in the Bahamas. Watch cigars being made, or browse through the cigar and pipe accessories. ⊠ *Atlantis Paradise Island Crystal Court, Paradise Island* ☎ *242/363–5809.*

SPAS

FodorśChoice ★ **Mandara Spa at Atlantis.** Located at Atlantis but open to the public, the expansive, multistory Indonesian-inspired Mandara Spa has treatments utilizing traditions from around the world. Plan to spend more time than your treatment or service requires to enjoy the unisex relaxation lounge, hot and cold plunge pools, and the sauna and steam room. Use of the 15,000-square-foot fitness center is complimentary for a day when you spend more than $99 on spa or salon services. The full-service salon offers hair and nail treatments as well as tooth whitening, hair extensions, and waxing. Men can get the works at the barbershop. Both the spa and fitness center are open until 9 pm daily. ⊠ *Atlantis Paradise Island Royal Towers, Casino Dr.* ☎ *242/363–3000* ⊕ *www.mandaraspa.com.*

FodorśChoice ★ **One & Only Spa.** Paradise Island's One & Only Ocean Club has one of the island's most luxurious and indulgent spa retreats. The space is so lovely, be sure to allow additional time just to lounge and relax. For the ultimate indulgence, treat yourself to the signature One & Only Massage—two therapists perform a perfectly choreographed blend of five styles of massage; finish it up with the Frangipani Conditioning Hair and Scalp ritual. Take your break from reality a step further and book a treatment for two in a private Bali-inspired villa with private courtyard, canopied daybed, and open-air hydrotherapy bath; this romantic spot is designed for shared treatments, but you can book individually. With just eight villas and two cabanas overlooking the ocean, it's a good idea to book well in advance, particularly during high season. ⊠ *Paradise Island* ☎ *242/363–2501* ⊕ *www.oneandonlyoceanclub.com* ☉ *Daily 9 am–7 pm.*

CABLE BEACH

SPAS

Red Lane Spa. If you're not a guest at Sandals Royal Bahamian, you can still enjoy pampering services at the Red Lane day spa on the outskirts of the all-inclusive property. Facials, massages, wraps, and scrubs utilize an array of tropical scents and ingredients from coffee to frangipani, sugarcane, and even seaweed to guarantee relaxation. To indulge at the full spa or have a massage in a private hut overlooking the ocean on a private island, consider booking a Sandals day pass for access. ⊠ *Sandals Royal Bahamian, W. Bay St., Cable Beach* ☎ *242/327–6400* ⊕ *www.sandals.com.*

WESTERN NEW PROVIDENCE

SHOPS

Pasión Tea & Coffee Company. Pop into this hilltop shop to purchase locally made souvenirs or to grab a spot of tea ($3) or coffee ($3.50) on the breezy deck. The Pasión tea line is made locally in a nearby warehouse. The shop has a great array of teas, coffees, and spices as well as trinkets and soaps, lotions, and scrubs. On a hot day, enjoy a scoop of homemade soursop ice cream. Local bush medicine plants adorn the garden where roosters roam around. ⊠ *Plantation Hill, Caves Rd., off W. Bay St., Gambier* ☎ *242/327–7011* ⊕ *www.pasionteas.com.*

SPORTS AND THE OUTDOORS

BOATING

From Chub Cay—one of the Berry Islands 35 miles north of New Providence—to Nassau, the sailing route goes across the mile-deep Tongue of the Ocean. The Paradise Island Lighthouse welcomes yachters to Nassau Harbour, which is open at both ends. The harbor can handle the world's largest cruise liners; sometimes as many as eight tie up at one time. Two looming bridges bisect the harbor connecting Paradise Island to Nassau. Sailboats with masts taller than the high-water clearance of 72 feet must enter the harbor from the east end to reach marinas east of the bridges.

Atlantis Marina. The marina at Atlantis has 63 megayacht slips and room for yachts up to 240 feet. Stay here and you can enjoy all the amenities at Atlantis, including Aquaventure. ⊠ *Atlantis Paradise Island, Paradise Island* ☎ *242/363–6068.*

Bay Street Marina. With 89 slips accommodating yachts up to 150 feet, this new centrally located marina on the Nassau side of the harbor has all the amenities you might need. The marine is within walking distance to Paradise Island as well as downtown Nassau. ⊠ *E. Bay St., Nassau* ☎ *242/676–7000* ⊕ *www.baystreetmarina.com.*

Paradise Island's One & Only Ocean Club has a scenic golf course.

Brown's Boat Basin. On the Nassau side, Brown's Boat Basin offers a place to tie up your boat, as well as on-site engine repairs. ⊠ *E. Bay St., Nassau* ☎ *242/393–3331.*

Hurricane Hole Marina. Ninety-slip Hurricane Hole Marina is on the Paradise Island side of the harbor and accommodates yachts over 200 feet. ⊠ *Paradise Island* ☎ *242/363–3600* ⊕ *www.hurricaneholemarina.com.*

Lyford Cay. At the western end of New Providence, Lyford Cay, a posh development for the rich and famous, has an excellent 74-slip marina, but there is limited availability for the humble masses. ⊠ *Clifton* ☎ *242/362–4131.*

Nassau Yacht Haven. On the Nassau side of the harbor, Nassau Yacht Haven is a 150-berth marina that also arranges fishing charters. ⊠ *E. Bay St., Nassau* ☎ *242/393–8173* ⊕ *www.nassauyachthaven.com.*

Palm Cay Marina. The easternmost marina on New Providence offers 194 slips and all the amenities, including a full restaurant, pool, and beach. ⊠ *Palm Cay, Yamacraw Hill Rd., Nassau* ☎ *242/676–8554* ⊕ *www. palmcay.com.*

FISHING

The waters here are generally smooth and alive with many species of game fish, which is one of the reasons why the Bahamas has more than 20 fishing tournaments open to visitors every year. A favorite spot just west of Nassau is the Tongue of the Ocean, so called because it looks like that part of the body when viewed from the air. The channel stretches for 100 miles. For boat rental, parties of two to six will pay $600 or so for a half day, $1,600 for a full day.

Born Free Charters. This charter company has three boats and guarantees a catch on full-day charters—if you don't get a fish, you don't pay. Pickup is included from various locations, and the company will make the arrangements for you. ⊠ *Nassau* ☎ *242/698–1770* ⊕ *www. bornfreefishing.com.*

Charter Boat Association. The Charter Boat Association has 15 boats available for fishing charters. Pickup is from Paradise Island Ferry Terminal or Nassau Harbour in front of the Straw Market. ☎ *242/393–3739.*

Chubasco Charters. This charter company has four boats for deep-sea and light tackle sportfishing. Half- and full-day charters are available. Pickup is from Paradise Island Ferry Terminal or Nassau Harbour in front of the Straw Market. ☎ *242/324–3474* ⊕ *www.chubasco charters.com.*

Nassau Yacht Haven. Nassau Yacht Haven can put you in touch with one of the private fishing charter captains operating out of its 150-slip marina. ⊠ *Nassau Yacht Haven, E. Bay St., Nassau* ☎ *242/393–8173* ⊕ *www.nassauyachthaven.com.*

GOLF

Ocean Club Golf Course. Designed by Tom Weiskopf, the Ocean Club Golf Course is a championship course surrounded by the ocean on three sides, which means that the views are incredible, but the winds can get stiff. Call to check on current availability and up-to-date prices (those not staying at Atlantis or the One & Only Ocean Club can play at management's discretion, and at a higher rate). The course is open daily from 6 am to sunset. ⊠ *One & Only Ocean Club, Paradise Island Dr., Paradise Island* ☎ *242/363–6682* ⊕ *oceanclub.oneandonlyresorts. com* ▣ *$225–$295 for 18 holes (discounted after 1 pm); $70 club rentals* 🏌 *18 holes, 6805 yards, par 72.*

HORSEBACK RIDING

Happy Trails Stables. Happy Trails Stables gives guided 90-minute trail rides, including basic riding instruction, through remote wooded areas and beaches on New Providence's southwestern coast. Two morning group rides are offered, but private rides can be arranged at any time. Courtesy round-trip bus transportation from hotels is provided (about an hour each way). Tours are limited to eight people. There's a 200-pound weight limit, and children must be at least 12 years old. Reservations are required. ⊠ *Coral Harbour* ☎ *242/362–1820* ⊕ *www.bahama horse.com* ▣ *$150 per person* ☉ *Mon.–Sat. by appointment.*

PADDLEBOARDING

FAMILY **Pappasurf.** There's no better way to explore the crystal clear blue Bahamian ocean than gliding along the surface. Experienced paddlers can rent boards from this outfitter, or you can sign up for lessons. For a truly unique experience, book a sunset ($85) or nightglow ($65) tour. Both last for about 90 minutes and include all equipment and experienced guides. ⊠ *Henrea Carlette Bldg., W. Bay St., Cable Beach* ✛ *For tours, lessons, and rental drop-offs head to Goodman's Bay Beach opposite Goodman's Bay Corporate Center; the office is across the road and just east of Sandals* ☏ *242/327–3853* ⊕ *www.pappasurf.com.*

SCUBA DIVING AND SNORKELING

DIVE SITES

Coral Reef Sculpture Garden. Created by the Bahamas Reef Environment Education Foundation (BREEF), this underwater art gallery is suitable for SCUBA divers and snorkelers. The highlight is the 17-foot-tall "Ocean Atlas" crouching on the ocean floor. The site is situated just off Clifton Heritage Park on southwestern New Providence and is accessible from land or boat. Be sure to take an underwater camera for a spectacular photographic souvenir.

Lost Ocean Hole. The elusive (and thus exclusive) Lost Ocean Hole (east of Nassau, 40–195 feet) is aptly named because it's difficult to find. The rim of the 80-foot opening in 40 feet of water is studded with coral heads and teeming with small fish—grunts, margate, and jacks—as well as larger pompano, amberjack, and sometimes nurse sharks. Divers will find a thermocline at 80 feet, a large cave at 100 feet, and a sand ledge at 185 feet that slopes down to 195 feet.

Rose Island Reefs. The series of shallow reefs along the 14 miles of Rose Island is known as Rose Island Reefs (Nassau, 5–35 feet). The coral is varied, although the reefs are showing the effects of the heavy traffic. Still, plenty of tropical fish live here, and the wreck of the steel-hulled ship *Mahoney* is just outside the harbor.

Gambier Deep Reef. Off Gambier Village about 15 minutes west of Cable Beach, Gambier Deep Reef goes to a depth of 80 feet.

Sea Gardens. This site is off Love Beach on the northwestern shore beyond Gambier.

Lyford Cay Drop-Off. Lyford Cay Drop-Off (west of Nassau, 40–200-plus feet) is a cliff that plummets from a 40-foot plateau almost straight into the inky blue mile-deep Tongue of the Ocean. The wall has endless varieties of sponges, black coral, and wire coral. Along the wall, grunts, grouper, hogfish, snapper, and rockfish abound. Off the wall are pelagic game fish such as tuna, bonito, wahoo, and kingfish.

DIVE OPERATORS

All recommended New Providence dive shops are PADI-affiliated (Professional Association of Diving Instructors) facilities. Expect to pay about $65 to $99 for a two-tank dive or beginner's course. Shark dives run $100 to $125, and certification costs $450 and up.

Bahama Divers Ltd. The largest and most experienced dive operation in the Bahamas offers two-tank morning dives, single-tank afternoon dives, and twice-daily snorkeling excursions. Introduction to SCUBA and PADI certification courses are available, and there's a full line of scuba equipment for rent. Destinations are drop-off sites, wrecks, coral reefs and gardens, and an ocean blue hole. Bus pickup is scheduled twice daily from hotels throughout New Providence. ⊠ *Nassau* ☎ *242/393–5644, 866/234–8322, 954/602–7731* ⊕ *www.bahamadivers.com.*

Stuart Cove's. This dive operator, on the island's south shore, is considered by aficionados to be the island's leading dive shop. Although they're pros at teaching beginners (scuba instruction and guided snorkel tours are available), experienced thrill-seekers flock to Stuart Cove's for the famous shark dives. The company runs dive trips to the south-shore reefs twice a day, weather permitting. The mini-sub adventure, which requires no experience, is $129; snorkeling expeditions cost $75 for adults and $35 for kids 11 and under. The shark dives are $170 for a three-hour dive. Complimentary shuttle service from all major hotels is included. ⊠ *Clifton* ☎ *242/362–4171, 800/879–9832* ⊕ *www.stuart cove.com.*

TOURS

DAY SAILS

Barefoot Sailing Cruises. The company offers regularly scheduled half-day snorkeling trips, full-day sailing tours of New Providence, and sunset Champagne trips, not to mention private charters. ⊠ *Bayshore Marina, E. Bay St.* ☎ *242/393–5817* ⊕ *www.barefootsailingcruises.com* ⊠ *Half-day sail and snorkel $90; half-day sail, snorkel, and beach $115; full day $140.*

Flying Cloud. This 57-foot catamaran based at the Paradise Island Ferry Terminal offers half-day sailing and snorkeling tours, full-day cruises on some Sundays, as well as sunset sails. Private charters can also be arranged. Price includes round-trip ground transportation from your hotel. ⊠ *Paradise Island Ferry Terminal, Paradise Island* ☎ *242/394–5067* ⊕ *www.flyingcloud.com* ⊠ *Half day (Mon.–Sat.) $80; Sun. full day $95; evening cruise $70.*

OUT ISLANDS TRIPS

You can visit a number of islands and cays on a day trip by boat from Nassau. Bahamas Ferries does a day trip to Harbour Island: 2½ hours in an air-conditioned ferry (or with the ocean breeze blowing through your hair on the upper deck) and enough time onshore to explore the quaint island via golf cart, have lunch, and stroll the beautiful pink-sand beach. A number of operators offer daily powerboat trips to the upper cays in the Exuma chain where you can see wild iguanas, stingrays, and sharks up close and enjoy their private islands for the day, and there are also excursions to Blue Lagoon Island and Rose Island—both a short boat ride away from Nassau. If you want to get up close to the world-famous swimming pigs, you'll need to plan a day or two in George Town or Staniel Cay farther south in the Exumas *(see Island Hopping Itineraries in the Experience chapter).*

Bahamas Fast Ferries. This isn't just a transportation company. Bahamas Fast Ferries also offers day trips from Nassau to Harbour Island, including lunch and pickups at major hotels. ⊠ *Potter's Cay, Nassau* ☎ *242/323–2166* ⊕ *www.bahamasferries.com* ⊠ *$225.*

Island World Adventures. The company, which operates two 45-foot speed boats, offers regularly scheduled full-day or private-charter tours to the northern Exumas from the Paradise Island Ferry Terminal. ⊠ *Paradise Island Ferry Terminal, Paradise Island* ☎ *242/363–3333* ⊕ *www.islandworldadventures.com* ▱ *$200.*

Fodor'sChoice **Powerboat Adventures.** The company offers speed-filled day trips to the
★ Exuma Cays on two custom-made powerboats. You can feed wild iguanas and stingrays, go on a snorkeling safari where you are pushed along by the ocean currents, and watch the daily shark feeding. Overnights on the company's private island, Ship Channel Cay, can also be arranged. ⊠ *Paradise Island* ☎ *242/363–2265* ⊕ *www.powerboatadventures.com* ▱ *$192.53.*

SPECIAL-INTEREST TOURS

Bahamas Outdoors Ecoventures. This outfitter offers half- and full-day birding and nature tours through some of the national parks on New Providence Island. Charters can be arranged to Andros or even Eleuthera. There's a two-person minimum for tours. ☎ *242/362–1574* ⊕ *www.bahamasoutdoors.com* ▱ *$79–$129.*

FAMILY **Dolphin Encounters.** On Blue Lagoon Island, the company offers dolphin and sea lion interactions. Three of their dolphins starred in the movie *Flipper*. Ferry transportation is offered from the Paradise Island Ferry Terminal. Make a day of it by adding a Beach Day on the island before or after your animal encounter. ⊠ *Paradise Island* ☎ *242/363–1003* ⊕ *www.dolphinencounters.com* ▱ *Dolphin Swim $185; Dolphin Encounter $115; Sea Lion Encounter $109; Blue Lagoon Day $32–$59.*

Seaworld Explorer. These trips include both a short harbor cruise as well as a trip on the company's semisubmersible, which allows you to view the underwater world without going into a full-fledged submarine. The boat is docked in Nassau Harbour opposite the Straw Market. ☎ *242/356–2548* ⊕ *www.seaworldtours.com* ▱ *$45.*

WALKING TOURS

Fodor'sChoice **Tru Bahamian Food Tours.** If you have three hours in Nassau, this is a
★ great way to spend it. The eco-friendly walking tour combines the food, history, and culture of the Bahamas in a way that's sure to leave you satisfied. The six tasting stops include some popular hot spots as well as some off-the-beaten-path gems. ⊠ *George St. and King St., Nassau* ✛ *Meet outside Christ Church Cathedral* ☎ *800/656–0713, 242/601–1725* ⊕ *www.trubahamianfoodtours.com* ▱ *$69* ☉ *Mon.–Sat. 11–2* ☞ *Not suitable for visitors in wheelchairs.*

GRAND BAHAMA ISLAND

WELCOME TO GRAND BAHAMA ISLAND

TOP REASONS TO GO

★ **Take endless strolls on your own private beach.** Sprawling, reef-protected shoreline and cays offer more than 50 miles of secluded white-sand beaches along the southern shore.

★ **Go down under.** Between the shipwrecks, caves, coral reefs, and abundant marine life are some of the country's most varied and vivid snorkeling and diving.

★ **Get your green on.** Learn about the island's ecology underwater and among the mangroves where you can feed stingrays or catch sight of spotted dolphins and their calves.

★ **Party at the weekly fish fry or a beach bonfire.** Head to Smith Point to feast and party with locals, or dance around the bonfire at Taino by the Sea with all-you-can-eat authentic Bahamian cuisine and Bahama Mama cocktails.

★ **Swim with the dolphins or feed the sharks.** Several professional dive shops stand ready to introduce you to some of the ocean's most interesting characters.

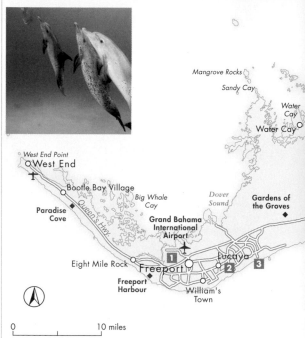

1 Freeport. The working end of Grand Bahama, Freeport is convenient to the airport and harbor for visitors in transit. Rand Nature Centre and The Bahamian Brewery make the area worth a visit, although downtown looks depressed and forlorn as developers await economic recovery.

2 Port Lucaya. Freeport's beachfront counterpart is more tourism-oriented, dominated by three of the island's largest hotels and resorts and Port Lucaya Marketplace (the island's best shopping). It also claims the only casino and the finest concentration of restaurants and bars.

3 Greater Lucaya. Lucayan Beach along Port Lucaya can get crowded, but Taino Beach, Coral Beach, and Fortune Beach are nearby for those who prefer more space and solitude; you'll find additional hotels and restaurants here as well.

3

LITTLE BAHAMA

Halls
Point

Riding
Point

Rocky
Creek

McLean's
Town

August Cay

B A N K

Lucayan
National
Park
◆

Grand Bahama Hwy.

Pelican
Point

Deep Water
Cay

Sweetings
Cay

O Sweeting's Cay

Bevans High Rock
Town

Freetown

Lighthouse Cay

Big Cross Cay

Michael's
Cay

Long Cay

4

Northwest Providence
Channel

GETTING ORIENTED

Only 52 miles off Palm Beach, Florida, 96-mile-long Grand Bahama is one of the chain's northernmost islands. Freeport and Lucaya, which more or less melt into one another, are its main cities, comprising the second-largest metropolitan area in the Bahamas. Lucaya sees the most action, as Freeport struggles to regain ground lost in the hurricanes and financial setbacks of the

last decade. The town of West End is a quiet, colorful fishing village that gathers small crowds on Sunday evenings at local bars and conch shacks. Its upscale Old Bahama Bay Resort and marina are the extent of tourism on this end of the island. East of Freeport-Lucaya, small fishing settlements, secluded beaches, and undeveloped forest stretch for 60 miles to the outlying cays, and luxury bonefishing lodge, Deep Water Cay.

4 **Greater Grand Bahama.** The bulk of the island lies on either side of the neighboring metropolitan duo of Freeport and Lucaya. Escaping town means discovering treasures such as Paradise Cove and Lucayan National Park, in addition to remote beaches, time-stilled fishing villages, and wooded land the locals refer to as the "bush."

LUCAYAN NATIONAL PARK

In this extraordinary 40-acre land preserve, trails and elevated walkways wind through a natural forest of wild tamarind and gumbo-limbo trees, past an observation platform, over a mangrove swamp, along a postcard-worthy beach, and in and around one of the world's largest explored underwater cave systems (more than 6 miles long).

Twenty-five miles east of Lucaya, the park contains examples of the island's five ecosystems: beach, hardwood forest, mangroves, rocky coppice, and pine forest. From the designated parking lot, you can enter the caves at two access points; one is closed in June and July for the bat-nursing season. Across the highway from the caves, two trails form a loop. Creek Trail's boardwalk showcases impressive interpretive signage, and crosses a mangrove-clotted tidal creek to Gold Rock Beach, claimed by Grand Bahama's Ministry of Tourism to be the island's "welcome mat." A narrow strand of white sand at high tide, and an expansive white-sand playground at low

tide, this lightly visited beach is edged by some of the island's highest dunes and a picturesque jewel-tone sea.

Visitors will find subtle treasures no matter what time of year they explore. Summer can be overbearingly hot for walking. However, that's also when certain orchids and other plants flower. Migrating birds and cooler temperatures make October–April optimal, especially mornings and low tide, when birds are most plentiful.

BEST WAYS TO EXPLORE
By Kayak. A kayak launch, near a beach where parts of the *Pirates of the Caribbean* movies were filmed, lies just east of

3

the park's parking lot on the south side. From here paddlers can work their way through mangrove forest to the beach and Gold Rock Creek.

Underwater. Snorkeling around Gold Rock Beach and its eponymous offshore Gold Rock is good. Certified cave divers can explore the intricate underwater network with Underwater Explorers Society (UNEXSO).

On Foot. Trails come in two parts. On the north side of the highway at the parking lot, one trail takes you into Ben's Cave and the Burial Mound Cave, where ancient Lucayan remains and artifacts have been discovered. A tricky spiral staircase descends into the dark depths of the former, and an easier wooden staircase to the latter. At both, observation platforms accommodate visitors who want to peer into the caves' clear depths. Across the highway, two flat, easy trails form a loop to the beach. Creek Trail (0.2 mile) is the easiest because its boardwalk is newer and more elevated. Birds are more abundant here in the tidal creek with its low forest of mangroves at your feet. Mangrove Swamp Trail (0.3 mile) tends to be wet at high tide, and its boardwalk more difficult to negotiate (especially for small feet). Take one to the beach and the other to return to see the full range of environment here.

PETERSON CAY NATIONAL PARK
Only accessible by boat or a long swim, Peterson Cay National Park, one of the Bahamas' smallest national parks, takes up 1½ acres 1 mile offshore from Barbary Beach. Its gorgeous, usually deserted beach and lively marine life make it worth the effort of snorkeling the reef or enjoying a quiet picnic. However, vegetation on the cay is salt-stunted and scrubby, so shade is scarce, but lively hermit crabs are abundant. All wildlife is protected in the park by the Bahamas National Trust, including a quarter mile of surrounding marine environment. Local ecotour operators lead kayak and snorkel excursions.

FUN FACT
A species of crustacean labeled *Speleonectes lucayensis* was discovered here and exists exclusively in the caverns of Lucayan National Park, where its population is protected. The rare, cave-dwelling Remipedia has no eyes or pigmentation.

Updated by
Jamie Werner

Natural beauty conspires with resort vitality to make Grand Bahama Island one of the Bahamas' most well-rounded, diverse destinations. In its two main towns, Freeport and Lucaya, visitors can find what the more bustling Nassau has to offer: resort hotels, a variety of restaurants, golfing, duty-free shopping, and gambling. But unlike New Providence, the touristy spots take up only a small portion of an island that, on the whole, consists of uninhabited stretches of sand and forest.

Prior to the development of Freeport, West End (the capital of Grand Bahama Island) was the epicenter of the Bahamas' logging industry and a playground for the wealthy in the 1920s. The fate of Grand Bahama changed in the 1950s when American financier Wallace Groves envisioned Grand Bahama's grandiose future as a tax-free shipping port. The Bahamian government signed an agreement that set in motion the development of a planned city, an airport, roads, waterways, and utilities as well as the port. From that agreement, the city of Freeport—and later, Lucaya—evolved. The past decade's hurricanes and economic downfall have demolished Freeport's resort glamour, and the tourism center has shifted to Lucaya, now home to the island's largest resorts.

Not much else on the island has changed since the early days, however. Outside of the Freeport-Lucaya commercial-and-resort area, fishing settlements remain, albeit now with electricity and good roads. The East End is Grand Bahama's "back-to-nature" side, where Caribbean yellow pine–and-palmetto forest stretches for 60 miles, interrupted by the occasional small settlement. Little seaside villages with white churches and concrete-block houses painted in bright pastels fill in the landscape between Freeport and West End. Many of these settlements are more than 100 years old.

PLANNING

WHEN TO GO

As one of the northernmost Bahama Islands, Grand Bahama experiences temperatures dipping into the 60s with highs in the mid-70s in January and February, so you may need a jacket and wet suit. On the upside, the migrant bird population swells and diversifies during that time of year. The other timing considerations are seasonal crowds and the subsequent increase in room rates. High tourist season runs from Christmas to Easter, peaking during spring break (late February to mid-April), when the weather is the most agreeable, but October through mid-December is also a good time to visit for weather.

Summers can get oppressively hot (into the mid and high 90s) and muggy, however; unless you're planning on doing a lot of snorkeling, diving, and other water sports, you may want to schedule your trip for cooler months. Afternoon thunderstorms and occasional tropical storms and hurricanes also make summer less attractive weather-wise. The island averages around 20 days of rain per month from June to September, but it usually falls briefly in the afternoon. The good news is that hotel rates plummet and diving and fishing conditions are great.

TOP FESTIVALS

WINTER **Festival Noel,** an annual holiday fest featuring music, crafts, wine tastings, and food at the Rand Nature Centre, takes place in early December.

New Year's Day Junkanoo Parade. Junkanoo is the National Festival of the Bahamas, named after an African tribal chief named "John Canoe," who demanded the right to celebrate with his people after being brought to the West Indies in slavery. Starting in the evening on January 1, and into the early morning hours, the downtown streets of Freeport come alive with larger-than-life costumed dancers jumping to the sounds of drums, whistles, and cowbells. At the end of January, watch local primary and secondary students take to the streets in the same colorful, cultural garb for Junior Junkanoo.

SPRING **Pelican Point Coconut Festival.** Experience coconut in more ways than you can count! This homecoming celebration on the East End of the island includes live music, coconut food sampling, coconut crafts, coconut bowling, and other contests and activities held annually on Easter Monday.

Extreme Kayak Fishing Tournament. Called "an open ocean tournament with no boundaries," these competing anglers rely on sheer man-powered paddling instead of motorized boats, in an effort to protect fragile coral reefs. The "extreme" part is reeling in a catch half the size of your kayak or SUP board! The two-day "Battle in the Bahamas" tournament has quickly gained popularity and is open to international anglers. ⊕ *www.extremekayakfishingtournament.org.*

SUMMER **BASRA's Bernie Butler Swim Race and Beach Party.** Every summer a party crowd gathers for the Bahamas Air Sea Rescue Association's annual swim race and daylong beach bash. Grand Bahama residents of all ages swim the sea in honor and support of BASRA's volunteer force, who in conjunction with the Bahamas Defense Force and the U.S. Coast Guard help people in distress. Live music, food and drink tents, and a bikini-clad, end-of-summer party atmosphere make this a memorable event. ✉ *Coral Beach, behind the Coral Beach Bar, just off Royal Palm Way and Coral Rd.* ⊕ *basragrandbahama.com.*

Grand Bahama Regatta and Heritage Festival. Sailing sloops from throughout the country meet in July for various sailing races and crowd-pleasing favorite, the sculling competition. Onshore festivities take place at Taino Beach and include Junkanoo parades, dancing, live music, and food and drinks. ✉ *Taino Beach.*

FALL **Conchman Triathlon.** The annual Conchman Triathlon at Taino Beach in November is a swimming-running-bicycling competition for amateurs of all ages that raises funds for local charities. International applicants welcome. ⊕ *www.conchman.com.*

McLean's Town Conch Cracking Festival. McLean's Town's annual homecoming event on the East End began in 1972 and includes conch-cracking competitions, games, live music, crafts, and various conch dishes for sample. The best conch-cracker goes home with an authentically Bahamian designed conch trophy. ✉ *East End, McClean's Town* ☎ *242/350–8600.*

GETTING HERE AND AROUND
AIR TRAVEL
Grand Bahama International Airport (FPO) is about 6 minutes from downtown Freeport and about 10 minutes from Port Lucaya. Several international carriers offer direct service to Grand Bahama from various U.S. gateways, but you can also connect in Nassau on regional carriers, including Bahamasair. No bus service is available between the airport and hotels. Metered taxis meet all incoming flights. Rides cost about $15 for two to Freeport, $22 to Lucaya; see posted signs for fixed rates. The price drops to $4 per person with larger groups. There's also an airport in **West End (WTD)**, but it's strictly for private planes and charters.

Contacts Grand Bahama Airport Company (MYGF). ✉ *Grand Bahama International Airport* ☎ *242/350–4233, 242/350–4277* ⊕ *www.freeportcontainerport.com.* **West End Airport (MYGW).** ✉ *West End* ☎ *242/727–1335.*

BOAT AND FERRY TRAVEL
Balearia Bahamas Express sails from Fort Lauderdale's Port Everglades and provides fast-ferry service, making a day trip possible, while Bahamas Paradise Cruise Line sails overnight from West Palm Beach, offering a more traditional cruise-ship experience, with two-night Grand Bahama hotel packages available. Taxis meet all ships.

BUS TRAVEL
Buses (usually minivans) are an inexpensive way to travel the 4 miles between downtown Freeport and Port Lucaya Marketplace daily until 8 pm. The fare is $1. Buses from Freeport to the West End cost $5 each way; to the East End, $15. Exact change is required.

CAR TRAVEL
If you plan to drive around the island, it's cheaper and easier to rent a car than to hire a taxi. You can rent vehicles from local and major U.S. agencies at the airport. Calling ahead to reserve a car is recommended.

Cars can range from $40/day to $125/day depending on the agency and length of rental.

Contacts AVIS. ✉ *Grand Bahama International Airport* ☎ *242/351–2847, 800/331–1084* ⊕ *www.avis.com.bs.* **Brad's Car Rental.** ✉ *Grand Bahama International Airport* ☎ *242/352–7930, 954/703–5246* ⌫ *bradscarrental@gmail.com* ⊕ *www.bradscarrental.com.* **Hertz Rent-a-Car.** ✉ *Grand Bahama International Airport* ☎ *242/352–3297* ⊕ *www.hertz.com.* **KSR Car Rental.** ✉ *Grand Bahama International Airport* ☎ *242/351–5737, 954/703–5819* ⌫ *ksr@ksrrentacar.biz* ⊕ *www.ksrrentacar.com.*

SCOOTER TRAVEL

Contacts Island Jeep and Car Rentals. ✉ *Island Seas Resort* ☎ *242/373–4001, 242/727–2207* ⊕ *www.islandjeepcarrental.com.*

TAXI TRAVEL

Taxi fares are fixed (but generally you're charged a flat fee for routine trips; see posted trip fares at the airport) at $3 for the first ¼ mile and 40¢ for each additional ¼ mile. Additional passengers over two are $3 each. Taxis are available outside of the big resorts or you can call the Grand Bahama Taxi Union for pickup.

Contacts Grand Bahama Taxi Union. ☎ *242/352–7101.*

HOTELS

Grand Bahama accommodations remain some of the Bahamas' most affordable, especially those away from the beach. The majority of these provide free shuttle service to the nearest stretch of sand. The island's more expensive hotels are beachfront, with the exception of Pelican Bay. These include the sprawling Grand Lucayan Resort; the all-inclusive Memories Grand Bahama Beach & Casino Resort; Viva Wyndham Fortuna Beach, an all-inclusive east of Port Lucaya; West End's elegant Old Bahama Bay Resort & Yacht Harbour; and the east-end luxury bonefishing resort, Deep Water Cay. Small apartment complexes and time-share rentals are economical alternatives, especially if you're planning to stay for more than a few days.

Rates post-Easter through December 14 tend to be 25%–30% lower than those charged during the rest of the year.

RESTAURANTS

The Grand Bahama dining scene stretches well beyond traditional Bahamian cuisine. The resorts and shopping centers have eateries that serve up everything from West Indian rotis to fine Continental and creative Pacific Rim specialties. For a true Bahamian dining experience, look for restaurants named after the owner or cook—such as Billy Joe's, Geneva's, or Mary Ann's.

A native fish fry takes place every Wednesday evening at Smith's Point, east of Port Lucaya (taxi drivers know the way). Here you can sample fresh fish, sweet-potato bread, conch salad, and all the fixings cooked outdoors at the beach. It's a great opportunity to meet local residents and taste real Bahamian cuisine—and there's no better place than seaside under the pines and palms.

Note: A gratuity or "service charge" (15%) is often added to the bill automatically; be sure to check your total before adding an additional tip.

Restaurant prices are based on the median main course price at dinner, excluding gratuity, typically 15% and VAT, which is often automatically added to the bill. Hotel prices are for two people in a standard double room in high season, excluding service and 6%–12% of various taxes.

WHAT IT COSTS IN DOLLARS			
$	$$	$$$	$$$$
Restaurants under $20	$20–$30	$31–$40	over $40
Hotels under $200	$200–$300	$301–$400	over $400

VISITOR INFORMATION

Tourist information centers are open Monday–Friday at the Grand Bahama International Airport (9–5), Freeport Harbour (according to cruise ship arrivals), and Port Lucaya Marketplace (10–6). The People-to-People Program matches your family with hospitable locals who share like interests.

Contacts Ministry of Tourism Grand Bahama Office. ☎ *800/224–2627* ⊕ *www.grandbahama.bahamas.com.* **People-to-People Program.** ☎ *242/302–2000* ⊕ *www.bahamas.com/people-to-people.*

EXPLORING

FREEPORT

Freeport, once an attractive, planned city of modern shopping centers, resorts, and other convenient tourist facilities, took a bad hit from the 2004 and 2005 hurricanes and subsequent economy downturn; its main resort and casino have not reopened. An Irish firm purchased the former Royal Oasis Resort & Casino but no plans have been made to rebuild or renovate. The International Bazaar next door is currently an abandoned ghost town with only a few crafts vendors and shops. Despite all this, Freeport's native restaurants, Rand Nature Centre, Bahamian Brewery, and beaches make it worth the visit. It's close to Lucaya (a 15-minute drive), and the airport and harbor are just a few minutes from downtown.

The Bahamian Brewery. One hundred percent Bahamian owned, this 20-acre brewery opened in 2007, bringing to the Bahamian islands five new beers including Sands, High Rock Lager, Bush Crack, and Strong Back Stout. The brewery even makes a signature red ale served exclusively at the Atlantis Resort on Paradise Island. The brewery does everything on-site including bottling and labeling, and offers 15- to 20-minute tours that take you along each step in the brewing process. The tour ends in the tasting room where you can belly up to the bar or cocktail tables to sample each beer. Weekday tours are $5 and walk-ins

GREAT ITINERARIES

IF YOU HAVE 3 DAYS

Rent a car for easy island touring at your own pace and schedule. Have breakfast and book tomorrow's dolphin or shark excursion at **UNEXSO**. Drive east along Grand Bahama Highway for a day's worth of adventures: Stop at **Owl's Hole** for a quick cliff jump and cool off in the natural pool. Stop and wander around **Lucayan National Park** through the caves and along the boardwalks to **Gold Rock Beach** for swimming and beach time. Continue east to Bishop's Place in High Rock for a late lunch and cold drink. End the night back in Lucaya with a fish fry or beach bonfire. On Day 2, after your morning UNEXSO experience, head to Banana Bay on **Fortune Beach** to have lunch and unwind. For your evening's entertainment, stroll through **Port Lucaya Marketplace**, have drinks at Pelican Bay's Bones Bar, then dine on the dock at Flying Fish Modern Seafood. On Day 3, drive to **West End** for the day, stopping at Lover's Beach for sea glass, **Paradise Cove** for a good snorkel around Deadman's Reef,

and on to West End's northeastern water's edge to sample a variety of fresh, made-in-front-of-you conch salads and fritters. End the night with dinner at East Sushi at Pier One to watch the sunset and the sharks.

IF YOU HAVE 5 DAYS

Book ecotours on Days 4 and 5 to kayak through the mangroves, bicycle from Garden of the Groves, snorkel around Peterson Cay, or feed stingrays around Sandy Cay. Reserve one night's dinner at Cappuccino's Italian Restaurant and the other aboard the *Bahama Mama* for a sunset dinner cruise.

IF YOU HAVE 7 DAYS

Save your last two days for more private, quiet relaxation away from the tourist crowds at one of Grand Bahama's far-end resorts: Old Bahama Bay at the West End, or Deep Water Cay on the East End. If two day's time on a beach lounger or hammock is too slow for you, these two resorts have access to some of the best fishing on the island, along with the best fishing guides, too.

3

are accepted. Beer and liquor can be purchased in the retail store; Bahamian Brewery souvenirs are available in the gift shop. ✉ *Just off Queen's Hwy., east of the turn to West End, Freeport* ☎ *242/352–4070* ⊕ *www. bahamianbrewery.com.*

Bahamas National Trust Rand Nature Centre. Established in 1939 on 100 acres just minutes from downtown Freeport, a half mile of self-guided botanical trails shows off 130 types of native plants, including many plants known for their use in bush medicine. The remaining tracts of land are left natural and undisturbed to serve as wildlife habitat. The center is also one of the island's birding hot spots, where you might spy a red-tailed hawk or a Cuban emerald hummingbird. Visit Donni, the caged one-eyed Bahama parrot the center has adopted, and the two Bahamian boas, a species that inhabits most Bahamian islands, but not Grand Bahama. On Tuesday and Thursday, free (with admission) guided tours depart at 10 am. The visitor center also hosts changing local art exhibits. The center survives on admissions, gift shop purchases, and donations alone, but has high hopes and plans for a future face-lift and new exhibits, ⊠ *E. Settlers Way, Freeport* 🕾 *242/352–5438* ⊕ *www. bnt.bs* 🖅 *$5* ⊙ *Weekdays 8:30–4, Sat. 9–1; guided nature walk by advance reservation.*

The Perfume Factory. Behind the now nearly defunct International Bazaar, the quiet and elegant Perfume Factory occupies a replica 19th-century Bahamian mansion—the kind built by Loyalists who settled in the Bahamas after the American Revolution. The pink interior resembles an old-world tasteful drawing room. This is the home of Fragrance of the Bahamas, where you can find a large variety of perfumes, lotions, and colognes. Its biggest-selling Pink Pearl cologne actually contains conch pearls, and Sand cologne for men has a little sterilized Grand Bahama island sand in each bottle. Take a free 10-minute tour of the mixology laboratory and bottling area and get a free sample. For $30 an ounce, you can blend your own perfume using any of the 35 scents ($15 for 1½ ounces of blend-it-yourself body lotion). Sniff mixtures until they hit the right combination, then bottle, name, and take home the personalized potion. ⊠ *On the north side of the International Bazaar, W. Sunrise Hwy. and Mall Dr., Freeport* 🕾 *242/352–9391, 800/628–9033* ⊕ *www.perfumefactory.com* 🖅 *Free* ⊙ *Weekdays 9:30–5, Sat. 11–3.*

LUCAYA

On Grand Bahama's southern coast, Lucaya was developed after western neighbor Freeport as another resort center, this one on the beach and harbor. Colorful Port Lucaya Marketplace grew up along the safe harbor, known for its duty-free shops, bars, restaurants, straw market, and outdoor bandstand. This is also the home of UNEXSO, the island's famous diving and dolphin-encounter attraction. Surrounding the port are the island's biggest hotels: Grand Lucayan, Memories Beach and Casino Resort, and Pelican Bay.

PORT LUCAYA

FAMILY

Fodor's Choice
★

The Dolphin Experience. Encounter Atlantic bottlenose dolphins in Sanctuary Bay at one of the world's first and largest dolphin facilities, about 2 miles east of Port Lucaya. A ferry takes you from Port Lucaya to the bay to observe and photograph the animals. If you don't mind getting wet, you can sit on a partially submerged dock or stand waist deep in the water and one of these friendly creatures will swim up to you. You can also engage in one of two swim-with-the-dolphins programs, but participants must be 55 inches or taller. The Dolphin Experience began in 1987, when it trained five dolphins to interact with people. Later, the animals learned to head out to sea and swim with scuba divers on the open reef. A two-hour dive program is available. You can buy tickets for the Dolphin Experience at UNEXSO in Port Lucaya but be sure to make reservations as early as possible. ⊠ *Port Lucaya, next to Pelican Bay Hotel, Port Lucaya Marketplace* 🕾 *242/373–1244, 800/992–3483*

More than 300 bird species call the Bahamas home, including this Bananaquit.

⊕ *www.unexso.com* ✉ *Dolphin Encounter $85, Dolphin Swim $179, Dolphin Dive $219* ⊙ *Daily 8–6.*

Port Lucaya Marketplace. Lucaya's capacious and lively shopping complex is on the waterfront across the street from the Grand Lucayan and Memories Beach Resort and Casino. The outdoor shopping center, whose walkways are lined with hibiscus, bougainvillea, and croton, has more than 100 well-kept, colorfully painted establishments, among them waterfront restaurants and bars, water-sports operators, and shops that sell clothes, silver, jewelry, perfumes, and local arts and crafts. The marketplace's centerpiece is **Count Basie Square,** where live entertainment featuring Bahamian bands appeals to joyful nighttime crowds every weekend. Lively outdoor watering holes line the square, which is also *the* place to celebrate the holidays: a tree-lighting ceremony takes place in the festively decorated spot at the beginning of December and fireworks highlight New Year's Eve, the Fourth of July, and Bahamian Independence Day, July 10th. In February 2015, Port Lucaya Marketplace changed owners and began implementing $2 million of renovations and upgrades, including a lineup of new restaurants and shops. ✉ *Across from Grand Lucayan and Memories Resort & Casino, Sea Horse Rd., Port Lucaya Marketplace* ☎ *242/373–8446* ⊕ *www.portlucaya.com* ⊙ *Daily 10–6. Restaurants, bars ,and some shops remain open at night.*

GREATER LUCAYA

The lion's share of restaurants and resorts in Lucaya are located around Port Lucaya. But if you go a bit farther than you can travel easily on foot, there are also a handful of interesting establishments and

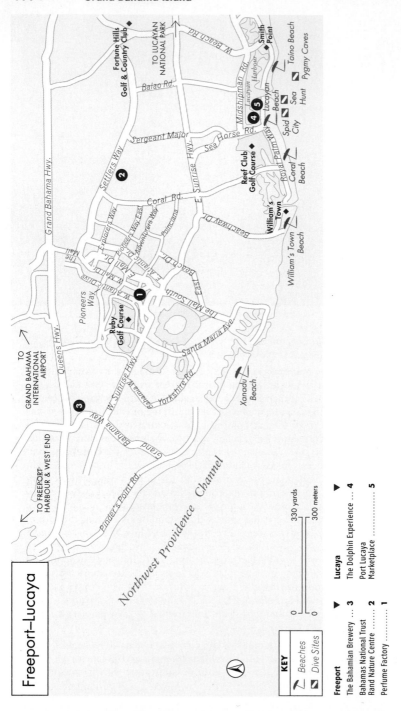

Freeport–Lucaya

KEY

🏖 *Beaches*

🤿 *Dive Sites*

Freeport

The Bahamian Brewery ... **3**

Bahamas National Trust
Rand Nature Centre **2**

Perfume Factory **1**

Lucaya

The Dolphin Experience ... **4**

Port Lucaya
Marketplace **5**

attractions, including places to eat and stay that are away from the crush of tourists.

The Garden of the Groves. This vibrant 12-acre garden and certified wildlife habitat, featuring a trademark chapel and waterfalls, is filled with native Bahamian flora, butterflies, birds, and turtles. Interpretative signage identifies plant and animal species. First opened in 1973, the park was renovated and reopened in 2008; additions include a labyrinth modeled after the one at France's Chartres Cathedral, colorful shops and galleries with local arts and crafts, a playground, and a multideck indoor and outdoor café and bar. Explore on your own or take an hour-long guided tour at 10 am (Monday–Saturday). Enjoy the garden under twinkling lights on Friday nights only, with dinner specials and live music. ⊠ *Midshipman Rd. and Magellan Dr.* ☎ *242/374–7778, 242/374–7779 Fri.-night dinner reservations* ⊕ *www.thegardenofthegroves.com* ✉ *$15* ☼ *Daily 9–5; guided tours Mon.–Sat. at 10.*

> **DID YOU KNOW?**
>
> The term "Lucayan" is derived from the Arawak Indian word Lukka-Cairi, or "Island People." The early tribespeople gave the Bahama Islands its first name, the Lucayas.

GREATER GRAND BAHAMA

Farther out on either side of the Freeport–Lucaya development, the island reverts to natural pine forest, fishing settlements, and quiet secluded beaches. Heading west from Freeport, travelers pass the harbor area, a cluster of shacks selling fresh conch and seafood at Fishing Hole, a series of small villages, and Deadman's Reef at Paradise Cove before reaching the historic fishing town of West End and its upscale resort at the island's very tip. East of Lucaya lie long stretches of forest interrupted by the occasional small village, the Lucayan National Park, myriad bonefishing flats along the eastern end up to McClean's Town, and the outer Grand Bahama cays: Sweetings, Deep Water, and Lightbourne.

High Rock. About 45 miles east of Lucaya and 8 miles from Lucayan National Park, it's worth the extra drive to visit an authentic, old-time island settlement affected only lightly by tourism. Its beach spreads a lovely white blanket of plump sand, with two beach bars for food and drink, including Bishop's Place. Time spent at the bar with Bishop himself (aka Ruben "Bishop" Roberts) and his dog, will make you feel local. Take a walk along the beach and its parallel road (rock outcroppings interrupt the sand in places) past the cemetery to the faux lighthouse that makes a nice photographic punctuation. Although the welcome sign identifies the village as "Home of Hospitality," it holds just two small lodges and offers only simple fried Bahamian fare, albeit the service is friendly and the beer is cold. ⊠ *Eastern Grand Bahama.*

Lucayan National Park. In this extraordinary 40-acre land preserve, trails and elevated walkways wind through a natural forest of wild tamarind and gumbo-limbo trees, past an observation platform, over a mangrove swamp, along a postcard-worthy beach, and in and around one of the

Grand Bahama Island

Key

- Beaches
- Dive Sites

Water Depths
- 25ft deep
- 50ft deep
- 100ft deep

BANK

Hawksbill Cays

Fish Cays
Upper Cay

LITTLE ABACO ISLAND

Fox Town

Sponge Cay

Little Cave Cay

LITTLE BAHAMA BANK

Cross Cays

Riding Point

Halls Point

Great Sale Cay

Noss Mangrove

Sandy Harbour

Little Water Cay

Water Cay

Water Cay

Mangrove Rocks

Sandy Cays

Mangrove Cay

Dover Sound

GRAND BAHAMA ISLAND

Lucayan National Park

Owl's Hole ♦

Gardens of the Groves

Grand Bahama International Airport

August Cay

McLean's Town

Sweeting's Cay

Deep Water Cay

Sweetings Cay

Lighthouse Cay

Big Cross Cay

Michael's Cay

Long Cay

Rocky Creek

Pelican Point

Grand Bahama Hwy.

Bevens Town

Freetown

High Rock

Gold Rock Beach

Ol' Freetown Farm

Freetown Beach

Old Freetown Beach

Ben's Blue Hole ♦

Fortune Beach

Smith's Point

Theo's Wreck

Taino Beach

Midshipman Rd.

Lucayan Beach

Shark Junction

Coral Beach

Sea Horse Rd.

Lucaya

William's Town

Xanadu Beach

William's Town Beach

The Bahamian Brewery

Freeport
see detail map

Freeport Harbour

Lover's Beach

Queen's Hwy.

Bootle Bay Village

Big Whale Cay

Paradise Cove

Deadman's Reef

West End

West End Point

Northwest Providence Channel

10 mi

10 km

0

0

largest explored underwater cave systems in the world (more than 6 miles long). Twenty-five miles east of Lucaya, the park contains examples of the island's five ecosystems: beach, hardwood forest, mangroves, rocky coppice, and pine forest. From the designated parking lot, you can enter the caves at two access points; one is closed in June and July for bat-nursing season. Across the highway from the caves, two trails form a loop. The

> ### RUN DOGGIE RUN
>
> Island dogs, known as "potcakes"—a reference to the bottom of the rice pans they clean up—run wild, so be careful when driving. Efforts in recent years by the active Grand Bahama Humane Society have raised awareness of the need for neutering and spaying.

easier (0.2-mile) Creek Trail's boardwalk showcases impressive interpretive signage, and crosses a mangrove-clotted tidal creek to Gold Rock Beach, claimed by Grand Bahama's Ministry of Tourism to be the island's "welcome mat." This beach is a great place for a swim or picnic at low tide, but at high tide the beach all but disappears. ⊠ *Grand Bahama Hwy., Freetown* ☎ *242/353–4149, 242/352–5438* ⊕ *www.bnt. bs* ⊠ *$5* ⊗ *Daily 9–5.*

FAMILY **Ol' Freetown Farm.** This family-owned-and-operated farm offers farm tours to meet, greet, feed, and pet the resident animals, including horses, ponies, Abaco wild hogs, peacocks, turkeys, goats, sheep, rabbits, guinea pigs, and the biggest personality of them all, Patches the potbelly pig, among others. The farm also grows its own fruit and vegetables, available for purchase at their farm stand along with fresh-pressed sugarcane juice and eggs straight from the chicken coop. A weekend BBQ is available on Saturdays where visitors gather around picnic benches to listen to the parrots squawk and watch the various horse and cart rides for guests of all ages, including horseback lessons. Opening hours change with the seasons and daily weather, so call ahead before you visit. ⊠ *Grand Bahama Hwy., 6 miles east of College of the Bahamas, before Lucayan National Park, Freetown* ☎ *242/441–8611, 242/375–6301.*

Owl's Hole. Named for the mama owl who nests here every year, this vertical freshwater cave (a limestone sinkhole formed by the collapse of a section of a cavern's roof) is a popular local swimming hole. It's rimmed by a 24-foot cliff if you're up for taking a plunge. The less adventuresome can climb down a ladder into the cool but refreshing water. Take snorkel gear down with you to experience the beauty at its full potential, and if you're a certified cavern diver you can join local scuba diving excursions to explore even deeper. If your timing is right, you will see a nest full of fuzzy owlets (April–May) tucked under the ledge as you descend the ladder. The drive here feels a bit like a ride on a Bahamian bush roller coaster but it's worth it—finding the hole is half the adventure. ⊠ *Off Grand Bahama Hwy.* ⌖ *From Grand Bahama Hwy., turn right on last dirt road before the "Dangerous Curve" sign (before Lucayan National Park). Drive 1.6 miles to tiny parking area on left. You've gone too far if you reach beach.*

West End. Once a rowdy, good-time resort area, West End still attracts small crowds on Sunday evenings for friendly, casual street gatherings. Today's reputation, however, rests more firmly on its charter fishing. Afternoon visitors stop at Paradise Cove for snorkeling, and farther west at the bay-front conch shacks for conch salad straight from the shell (try Shebo's or Ian's on the Bay) or at other tiny eateries along the way like Chicken's Nest, touted to have the best conch fritters on island. Overnighters stay at Old Bahama Bay Resort & Yacht Harbour, an upscale gated Guy Harvey Outpost resort. Nonguests are welcome at the hotel's beachside Tiki Bar for breakfast and lunch, or at the Dockside Grill for dinner. ⊠ *Western Grand Bahama.*

BEACHES

Fluffy white-sand-carpets in-your-dream beaches, where water sparkles like sapphires, lapis, tanzanite, emeralds, aquamarines... you get the picture. Grand Bahama Island has more than its share of beautiful beaches fringing the south coast of its 96-mile length, and even a few remote ones along the west coast, too. Some are bustling with watersports activities, while others lie so far off the beaten path it takes a four-wheel-drive vehicle and local knowledge to find them.

FREEPORT

William's Town Beach. When the tide is high, this 1.9-mile slice of relatively hidden beach (from East Sunrise Highway, take Coral Road south, turn right onto Bahama Reef Boulevard, then left on Beachway Drive) can get a little narrow, but there's a wide area at its East End near Island Seas Resort, where a food stand called Michele's does business. A sidewalk runs the length of the beach along the road and at low tide the beach expands far and wide for easy walking on the shore. Across the road, a number of forlorn roadside beach bars have names such as Gone Le-Git and Toad's on the Bay. Island Seas Resort has its own modern interpretation of the local beach shack, called CoCoNuts Grog & Grub. **Amenities:** food and drink; parking (no fee); water sports. **Best for:** solitude; swimming; walking. ⊠ *Next to Island Seas Resort, Silver Point Dr. at Beachway Dr., Williams Town.*

Xanadu Beach. The old Xanadu Resort of Howard Hughes fame has been abandoned and is all but crumbling and even the surrounding buildings look depressed, but there is local talk that the day will come when the area will be restored and renovated. There are no longer amenities nor flocks of tourists on this beach. However, the mile-long stretch of sand is still serene and worth a walk at sunset, especially when cruise ships depart into the twilight. **Amenities:** parking (no fee). **Best for:** solitude; sunset; walking. ⊠ *Freeport.*

LUCAYA

PORT LUCAYA

Lucayan Beach and Coral Beach. This single, long stretch of white sand divides into separately named beaches at the intersection of Sea Horse Road and Royal Palm Way. The eastern end is Lucayan Beach, heavily monopolized by the broad spread of the Grand Lucaya and Memories resorts, where nonguests can purchase day passes from either hotel which, in addition to the beach, include use of pools, non-motorized water equipment, and restaurants. Cruise-ship excursions can add to the crowds on this end.

FLYING TEETH

Known in some parts as no-see-ums, the practically invisible sand fleas called "flying teeth" in the Bahamas are a force to be reckoned with, especially at the West End and in the summer months. At and after sunset they come out in force on still nights, and their bites can result in itchy red welts. Dress in long sleeves and pants or apply a repellent. Baby oil is also a generally accepted deterrent.

This end of the beach is also interrupted by rocky protrusions at places, so it's not great for strolling. Instead, spend the day swimming, people-watching, feeding jack fish, or doing multiple water sports including snorkel trips out to Rainbow Reef, parasailing, or WaveRunner tours. Near a long-standing conch shack, Billy Joe's and Ocean Motion Watersports, there is no admission fee for the beach. Go west from here along Coral Beach, where the shore widens for easier strolling and the crowds thin considerably on the way to Coral Beach Bar. **Amenities:** food and drink; lifeguards; parking (no fee); water sports. **Best for:** partiers; snorkeling; sunrise; swimming; walking. ⊠ *Sea Horse Dr., Royal Palm Way, behind Grand Lucaya, Memories Beach Resort and Casino, and Coral Beach Bar, Freeport.*

GREATER LUCAYA

FAMILY **Fortune Beach.** The clean white sand of Fortune Beach lies between two canal channels, and in the middle sits the Wyndham Viva Fortuna all-inclusive resort, where visitors can purchase day passes to use water-sports equipment and resort facilities. Just steps either way from the resort, however, the beach becomes quiet and secluded and offers an endless expanse both ways for exceptional strolling, easy off-shore snorkeling, and great swimming. The western end backs the Margarita Villa Sand Bar and the private homes along Spanish Main Drive, what locals refer to as "Millionaire Row." The eastern end is home to Banana Bay Restaurant, where at low tide a shallow lagoon forms alongside a drawn-out sandbar, allowing you to walk yards out to sea with cold drink in hand. **Amenities:** food and drink; parking near east end only (no fee). **Best for:** solitude; snorkeling; sunrise; swimming; walking. ⊠ *Fortune Bay Dr., Greater Lucaya.*

FAMILY **Taino Beach.** Taino Beach is just far enough removed from Port Lucaya to thin the crowds some, although cruise-ship passengers often make their way here on group excursions. Junkanoo Beach Club has a small food menu (compared to its long menu of 34 drinks) and water-sports operators are on hand. With lapping water that puts gemstones to shame, this fluffy-sand beach begs for exploration. A short walk down the long, gently coved beach takes you to Tony Macaroni's Conch Experience where music plays and an all-welcome volleyball game is usually in session. A few steps farther and you arrive at Outriggers Beach Club, home to the always-popular fish fry held every Wednesday night. Plenty of green space edges the beach and there's a playground for families. **Amenities:** food and drink; parking (no fee); water sports. **Best for:** partiers; sunset; swimming; walking. ⊠ *W. Beach Rd., near Smith's Point, Greater Lucaya.*

GREATER GRAND BAHAMA

Fodor's Choice
★ **Gold Rock Beach.** Located just off the Grand Bahama Highway 26 miles outside town, this secluded stretch of sand is accessible via a lovely 10-minute walk through the Lucayan National Park, and is both wide and spectacular, spanning for yards into the sea when the tide is low. The turquoise water is exceptionally clear, calm, and shallow, making it a perfect play place for families with young children. Occasional cruise-ship tours visit for a couple of hours around midday, but there is enough space that you will never feel crowded. Note however, that the white sandy beach is almost nonexistent when the tide is high and shade is sparse, so time your visit appropriately. **Amenities:** none. **Best for:** solitude; swimming, walking. ⊠ *Grand Bahama Hwy., Freetown.*

Lover's Beach. This beach on the island's west side is relatively unknown and rarely visited by tourists, and its sand is far less fine and powdery than what's found along the southern shores. However, it's the only spot on Grand Bahama to find sea glass. Adding to its uniqueness is its view of the large tanker and container ships anchored at sea for the island's industrial businesses, and the pastel-painted heavy-equipment tires planted in the sand for seating. **Amenities:** parking (free). **Best for:** walking. ⊠ *Hepburn Town in Eight Mile Rock, across the channel from Freeport Harbour, West End.*

Old Freetown Beach. This lightly visited beach will take you far from the tourist crowds and resorts. Airplane parts in the water from a long-ago crash are visible from shore and easy to see at low tide on a calm day. Local island sip-sip (gossip) is that the prop and fuselage pieces belonged to a wayward drug-smuggling plane, but no official word has ever confirmed. Considered one of the prettiest beaches on the island, with a wide scattering of sea biscuits, blinding white sand, and shallow turquoise water, the best part here is that you will most likely have the whole stretch of sand to yourself! **Amenities:** none. **Best for:** solitude; swimming; walking. ⊠ *Off Grand Bahama Hwy., just west of Ol' Freetown Farm ✛ Turn south on the dirt road that lies just east of Grand Bahama Hwy.'s "Dangerous Curve" sign. The road to Owl's Hole will also land you at this beach.*

Paradise Cove Beach. A 20-minute drive from Freeport, this beach's spectacular swim-to reef (called Deadman's Reef) is its best asset, with marine life that includes various rays, sea turtles, and barracudas. Paradise Cove is a small native-owned resort that will bus you out if you call ahead. The beach is short but wide with scrubby vegetation and swaying palm trees. Snorkel equipment and kayaks are available to rent, and refreshments flow at the Red Bar. There is a $3/person fee just to hang at the beach. **Amenities:** food and drink; parking (no fee); showers; toilets; water sports. **Best for:** snorkeling. ✉ *Warren J. Levarity Hwy., between Eight Mile Rock and West End, West End* 🌐 *www.deadmansreef.com* 🎫 *$3* ⏲ *Daily 9:30–5:30.*

3

WHERE TO EAT

FREEPORT

$$ SUSHI Fodor's Choice ★

🍴 **East Sushi at Pier One.** Pier One has one of the most unique settings of any restaurant in Grand Bahama. Built on stilts above the ocean near Freeport Harbour, it offers one-of-a-kind views of magnificent sunsets, larger-than-life cruise ships departing, and sharks swimming for chum. Pier one has two levels and two menus, the best one being East's. Their menu is both creative and extensive including Japanese favorites such as miso soup, seaweed salads, tempura, and a variety of rolls—try the Bahama Mama with tempura conch, avocado, mango, and chili-lime mayo for a tropical twist. Diners can eat inside either upstairs or downstairs, but the large tables on the balcony offer the best views of the shark feedings, done every hour on the hour starting at 7 pm. For those who prefer their fish cooked or Continental fare, the other menu includes grilled fish, vegetable pasta, steaks, and chicken. [$] *Average main: $25* ✉ *Next to Freeport Harbour, Freeport* ☎ *242/352–6674* 🌐 *pieroneandeast.com* ⏲ *No lunch Sun.*

$ VEGETARIAN

🍴 **Livity Vegetarian Juice Bar & Take-Out.** Offering the healthiest food on the island, this little shop (located in a shabby strip mall) doesn't look like much, but the quality of the food says differently. Livity blends up fresh fruit and vegetable juices and smoothies with names like Flu Shot, Pressure Reliever, and Incredible Hulk, with the idea that you should "Eat Smarter." Lunch includes daily specials such as chickpea stew, sautéed green beans, and mushrooms served on quinoa or wild rice, in addition to barbecued tofu and Rasta pasta. Fruit and vegetable salads, veggie fritters, soups, veggie burgers, and salmon burgers are staples on the menu. Check out their new location at Port Lucaya Marketplace, opening in the spring of 2015. [$] *Average main: $8* ✉ *West Atlantic Dr., in Rolle's Furniture Plaza, Freeport* ☎ *242/352–1855* 💳 *No credit cards* ⏲ *Closed weekends. No dinner.*

$ BAHAMIAN

🍴 **Mary Ann's Restaurant and Lounge.** This native restaurant tucked in a Freeport strip mall attracts a steady local clientele for it's home-cooked Bahamian cuisine. Named after owner Mary Ann Ward, who runs the place with her husband, the little diner is known for its cracked or curried lobster, along with traditional favorites like chicken souse, tuna and grits, peas 'n' rice, johnnycake, and a slightly spicy baked mac 'n cheese. The dining room is warm and inviting and the walls are adorned with framed newspaper clippings and Bahamian art. The outside deck opens for happy hour. [$] *Average main: $12* ✉ *West Settler's Way, Elite Plaza, Freeport* ☎ *242/352–8875, 242/477–8040.*

$ MEXICAN

🍴 **Senor Frog's Restaurant Bar & Souvenir Shop.** Opened in October 2012, this party place fills with cruise-ship passengers when docked for the day, and sends them back to the boat happy, fed, and full of rum drinks. The location at the Freeport Harbour is open-air and full of life, complete with a dance stage, large flat-screen TVs, a wraparound bar, and seating for more than 100 people. The music is loud, the crowd is lively, especially around spring break months, and the Mexican menu has fun Bahamian and tropical twists. Watch out for waiters who run around blowing whistles and pouring tequila down your throat, and if your party endurance is ready for a challenge, try your luck at a musical chairs game that includes two shots with every circle! [$] *Average main: $17* ✉ *Freeport Harbour, Freeport* ☎ *242/351–3764* 🌐 *www.senorfrogs.com* ⏲ *Closed when there are no docked cruise ships.*

DID YOU KNOW?

Sands Beer made its first appearance with the opening of The Bahamian Brewery in 2008 and is now a favorite local brew, available throughout the Bahamas. Subsequently, the brewery and its logo of a man sculling in a boat, have been a catalyst in bringing back one of the country's oldest pastimes. "Man in the Boat" sculling races are now part of sailing regattas all over the Bahamas, after a 20+ year absence.

LUCAYA

Most of the dining in Lucaya is in or around the Port Lucaya Marina or Port Lucaya Marketplace, which means that all the restaurants are within walking distance of each other and of the hotels in the immediate vicinity.

$ CARIBBEAN FAMILY Fodor's Choice ★

🍴 **Banana Bay Restaurant.** Directly on Fortune Beach, Banana Bay is a great place for lunch or daytime cocktails, whether you sit on the restaurant's shaded deck or on a lounger in the sand. As the tide rolls out the beach grows, creating a wonderful shallow lagoon and sandbar, perfect for wading and for frolicking kids. In addition to daily fresh-fish specials, the kitchen serves up homemade warm banana bread loaves along with salads, sandwiches, wraps, and seafood appetizers like conch fritters and crab cakes. On windy days, you will have a front-row seat to kite surfers in action. A few times a week, cruise ships drop off tourists en masse, so you can expect service to get a little slow . . . which will give you more time to enjoy your piña colada. [$] *Average main: $12* ✉ *Fortune Beach, Fortune Bay Dr., Lucaya* ☎ *242/373–2960* ⏲ *No dinner.*

$ ITALIAN Fodor's Choice ★

🍴 **Cappuccino's Italian Restaurant.** This Italian family-run cozy restaurant offers consistently good food and great service. Traditional comfort pasta dishes adorn the menu, like pesto gnocchi and seafood linguine, in addition to steaks and daily fresh-fish specials. The dining room and outside patio are both small and intimate, which makes this restaurant the most charming and romantic choice in Port Lucaya. [$] *Average main: $18* ✉ *Port Lucaya Marketplace, Sea Horse Rd., Lucaya* ☎ *242/373–1584* ⏲ *Closed Wed. No lunch* ✍ *Reservations essential.*

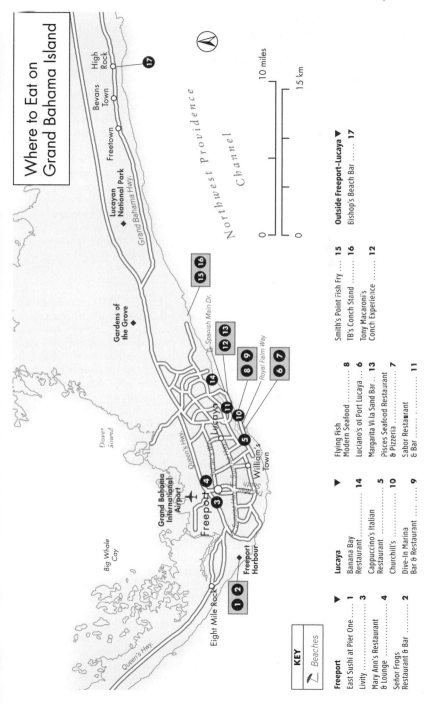

Where to Eat on Grand Bahama Island

KEY

⬧ *Beaches*

Freeport ▶

East Sushi at Pier One **1**
Livity **3**
Mary Ann's Restaurant
& Lounge **4**
Señor Frogs
Restaurant & Bar **2**

Lucaya ▶

Banana Bay
Restaurant **14**
Cappuccino's Italian
Restaurant **5**
Churchill's **10**
Dive-In Marina
Bar & Restaurant **9**

Flying Fish
Modern Seafood **8**
Luciano's of Port Lucaya ... **6**
Margarita Vila Sand Bar .. **13**
Pisces Seafood Restaurant
& Pizzeria **7**
Sabor Restaurant
& Bar **11**

Smith's Point Fish Fry **15**
TB's Conch Stand **16**
Tony Macaroni's
Conch Experience **12**

Outside Freeport–Lucaya ▼
Bishop's Beach Bar **17**

3

$$$ STEAKHOUSE 🍴 **Churchill's.** Unwind in the handsome wood piano bar before enjoying a four-course dinner in the dining room, surrounded by white wainscoting and French windows. The atrium ceiling over the circular room illuminates Bahamian life with mural scenes and heavy chandeliers, and the character evokes the plantation era. The menu is Mediterranean inspired, with house specialties such as lobster and wild mushroom risotto and veal marsala, but also includes create-your-own pasta dishes, steaks, and seafoods. No shorts, tank tops, or baseball caps allowed. [$] *Average main: $30* ✉ *Grand Lucayan Resort, Lucaya* ☎ *242/373–1333* 🌐 *www.grandlucayan.com* 🕒 *Closed Tues.–Thurs. No lunch* ✍ *Reservations essential.*

CONCHING OUT

Conch harvesting is illegal in the United States and closely regulated in other tropical locations to guard against overfishing. Currently, conch harvesting is limited to six per vessel in the Bahamas, but populations, while still plentiful, are slowly becoming depleted. The Bahamas National Trust launched a Conchservation Campaign in 2013 in an effort to educate and preserve Queen Conch fishing in the Bahamas. For more information, visit 🌐 *www.bnt.bs/conchservation.*

$ CARIBBEAN FAMILY 🍴 **Dive-In Marina Bar & Restaurant.** This relaxing poolside bar and grill at UNEXSO is great for lunch and weekend brunch, with delicious and creative items such as hot *antojitos* (Mexican small plates), banana bread French toast, veggie wraps, and the heaping spinach-and-bacon salad. Kids can splash in the pool (which has underwater windows to the marina, so bring goggles!) while adults sip spicy Bloody Marys and tropical drinks. [$] *Average main: $15* ✉ *UNEXSO, Lucaya* ✥ *Next to Pelican Bay Hotel* ☎ *242/373–1244* 💳 *No credit cards.*

$$$ SEAFOOD Fodor's Choice ★ 🍴 **Flying Fish Modern Seafood.** At Flying Fish, you'll find quality service with an eclectic collection of seafood and Bahamian favorites, made with local ingredients and done with a gourmet and artistic twist. Since its opening in February 2012, the restaurant has gained national popularity and international critical acclaim. The owners, originally from Canada, are local couple Tim and Rebecca Tibbits—Tim being the genius behind the food, Rebecca the genius behind the wine. Ask Rebecca for a pairing, and she will find something to both delight and surprise you (sake or tequila may be her choice). The restaurant is on the canal front and has an ambience that is both romantic and contemporary. But don't let all the gourmet reviews fool you; the upscale pub grub served outside attracts regulars as well. Sit on the patio or on the floating dock and choose from the bar menu that includes chef Tim's own homemade bacon served on the BLT paired with shoestring fries. Happy hour on the dock is nightly from 5 to 7 pm, weather permitting, and Sunday nights on the dock, chef Tim himself sings and plays guitar. Check their website for weekly culinary events. [$] *Average main: $38* ✉ *1 Sea Horse Rd., Lucaya* ✥ *Next to Pelican Bay Hotel* ☎ *242/373–4363* ✉ *reservations@flyingfishbahamas.com* 🌐 *www.flyingfishbahamas.com* 🕒 *Closed all public holidays. No lunch Mon. and Tues.* ✍ *Reservations essential* ☞ *Docking facilities for boaters.*

This sailboat is in front of Grand Lucayan.

$$$ EUROPEAN 🍴 **Luciano's of Port Lucaya.** Linens, soft candlelight, and a twinkling view of the harbor add to the glamour and romance of this second-story Port Lucaya restaurant. Interior renovations have given this long-standing establishment new life, but the original menu still speaks French with English subtitles, including such specialties as *coquilles St. Jacques florentine* (scallops on spinach with hollandaise) , *filet au poivre vert* (tenderloin fillet with green peppercorn sauce), scampi flambé, Dover sole, stuffed quail, and chateaubriand for two. Dinner is served in the formal dining room or on the veranda overlooking the marina, and service can be slow, so plan to make a night of it or be frustrated. [$] *Average main: $38* ✉ *Port Lucaya Marketplace, Lucaya* ☎ *242/373–9100* 🌐 *www.lucianosofportlucaya.com* 🕐 *No lunch.*

$ AMERICAN 🍴 **Margarita Villa Sand Bar.** There is no flooring in this cozy little beach bar, just sand, along with a few bar-top tables and some stools along the bar. You'll feel like an old friend talking to the bartender. Party photos adorn the walls along with velvet paintings of Elvis. It's the place to be for Sunday football games (especially Miami Dolphin fans), and they also offer up free Wi-Fi, live music, and outdoor seating right on the beach. Favorites on the menu include fish-and-chips, conch burgers and fries, Greek salads, and Philly cheesesteaks, among other Bahamian and American favorites. [$] *Average main: $12* ✉ *Fortune Beach, off Spanish Main Rd., Mather Town, Lucaya* ☎ *242/373–4525* 🌐 *www.sandbarbahamas.com.*

$ PIZZA 🍴 **Pisces Seafood Restaurant & Pizzeria.** Run by the owners of Neptune's Cocktail Lounge across the walkway, as noted by the similar and plentiful statues in front of both places, this well-established restaurant is known for its seafood, curry, and pizza. Twenty-nine different thin-crust

pizzas and 10 different curries are on the menu! The inside dining room is small but decorative with Tiffany lamps and shell-studded mirrors, and the winding, circular staircase up to the restrooms is an adventure in itself. However, the outside patio has more tables, and given its location at the main entrance of Port Lucaya Marketplace, an outside seat makes for great people-watching. $ *Average main: $15* ✉ *Port Lucaya Marketplace, Sea Horse Rd., Lucaya* ☎ *242/373–5192* ⊕ *www. piscesportlucaya.com* ◐ *Closed Sun. and Sept. No lunch* ⌂ *Reservations not accepted.*

3

$ ✕ **Sabor Restaurant and Bar.** The setting makes this restaurant the per-
ECLECTIC   fect place for an evening cocktail whether you sit overlooking the Port Lucaya Marina or nestled among the twinkling lights and palm trees around the pool deck. The lunch and dinner menu is a fun fusion of Bahamian and American favorites with tropical twists, such as O.M.G. Jalapeno Shrimps, Grand Cay Cracked Conch, fresh Hog Snapper, seared tuna, and steaks and burgers to boot. Be warned that service can be slow, so it's a good thing the view is superb! Happy hour is nightly from 5 to 7. $ *Average main: $17* ✉ *Pelican Bay Hotel, Lucaya* ☎ *242/373–5588* ⊕ *www.sabor-bahamas.com.*

$ ✕ **Smith's Point Fish Fry.** For Bahamian food fixed by Bahamians, head
BAHAMIAN   to Smith Point for the famous weekly fish fry. Every Wednesday night this little settlement by Taino Beach comes to life with both locals and tourists, when the open-air beach shacks along the street serve up fried fish (with the head and tail still on), cracked conch (pounded and fried), lobster tail, fried grouper, and barbecue chicken down-home style. Out-riggers Beach Club is the generational property of an old island family, and the most popular of them all, but you'll often find long lines there. Try any of the other stands including Da Bus Stop, Gully Wash Beach Bar, Snapper Shoal, and Penny's Fish Fry for similar menus. Expect the restaurants to start serving at 6 pm. Come early for the food, stay late for the party. Occasional beach bonfires add to the fun and festive atmosphere. $ *Average main: $10* ✉ *Smith's Point, off W. Beach Rd., Lucaya* ✛ *Next to Taino Beach* ⊕ *www.outriggersbeachclub.com* ▭ *No credit cards.*

$ ✕ **TB's Conch Stand.** For conch salad straight from the shell, complete
BAHAMIAN   with a relaxed and quiet view of the sea, head to TB's Conch Stand. A hidden gem at the end of Smith Point, and nestled next door to a quaint neighborhood church, this conch stand is off the beaten path from the touristy, publicized conch shacks, and gathers an easygoing local crowd. $ *Average main: $8* ✉ *Smith Point, Lucaya* ✛ *Next to St. Jude's Anglican church at the eastern end of Taino Beach* ☎ *242/443–0932* ▭ *No credit cards.*

$ ✕ **Tony Macaroni's Conch Experience.** For a taste of the local beach scene,
BAHAMIAN   follow the music to this weathered, thatch-roof shack at Taino Beach
FAMILY   and get your fill of roast conch, the specialty of the "house." Operated by local personality Anthony "Macaroni" Hanna, the popular eatery also sells conch salad, roast lobster and shrimp, and Gully Wash cock-tails (green coconut water, sweetened condensed milk, and gin) for noshing en plein air on a stilted deck overlooking pristine sands and

sea. [$] *Average main: $11* ✉ *Taino Beach, Lucaya* ☎ *242/533–6766* 💳 *No credit cards.*

GREATER GRAND BAHAMA

$ BAHAMIAN 🍴 **Bishop's Place.** A longtime favorite of locals and visitors who venture out to Lucayan National Park (about 6 miles away) and into the East End's settlements, Bishop's serves all the fried Bahamian favorites with a view of the sea. The beach bar itself doesn't sell food, so you'll have to make the short walk across the parking lot to order in the restaurant and they will bring it out to you. Conch fritters, cracked conch, fish fingers, burgers, and crab salad are a few of the menu choices, but the food isn't what makes this place special. Bishop himself mans this kick-back beach bar along with his dog, and plays great music that adds to the ambience. Come for a cold drink and stay for the beach. [$] *Average main: $15* ✉ *High Rock* ☎ *242/353–5485* 🌐 *www.bishopsresort.net* 💳 *No credit cards.*

WHERE TO STAY

Grand Bahama has a selection of time-shares in addition to regular hotels and resorts. For more information about time-share houses, apartments, and condominiums, contact the Ministry of Tourism Grand Bahama Office (☎ *800/224–2627* 🌐 *www.bahamas.com*).

FREEPORT

$$ RESORT FAMILY 🏨 **Island Seas Resort.** This time-share property also accommodates nonmembers looking for fun on the beach away from urban traffic. **Pros:** on-site restaurant; fun pool and bar area; great beach. **Cons:** fitness center is below par; other resort guests use property; property is worn and room decor is outdated. [$] *Rooms from: $249* ✉ *123 Silver Point Dr., Williams Town* ☎ *242/373–1271, 800/801–6884* 🌐 *www.islandseas.com* 🛏 *190 rooms* 🍽 *No meals.*

LUCAYA

$ HOTEL 🏨 **Bell Channel Inn.** Right on the water and a short walk from Port Lucaya Marketplace, this charming family-run (through three generations) inn with simple spacious rooms has quick and easy access to the island's best down-under sites, making it perfect for scuba-oriented and budget travelers. **Pros:** friendly, longtime staff; clean, affordable rooms; on the water. **Cons:** no beach; 10-minute walk from shopping and restaurant scene; rooms are dated but well maintained. [$] *Rooms from: $128* ✉ *Kings Rd., just off of Midshipman, Lucaya* ☎ *242/373–1053, 242/373–9111 dive shop* 🌐 *bellchannelinn.com* 🛏 *32 rooms* 🍽 *No meals.*

$ RESORT FAMILY 🏨 **Grand Lucayan.** One of Lucaya's biggest resorts (with three pools, golf, tennis, and nonmotorized water sports) boasts art deco elegance with Bahamian charm on more than 5 acres of soft-sand beach. **Pros:** across the street from Port Lucaya Marketplace; great beach front

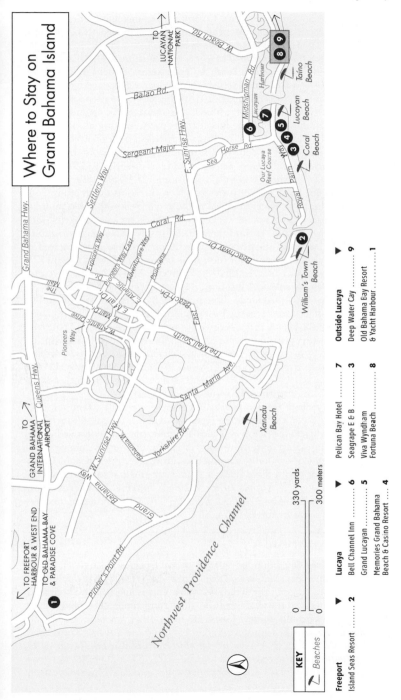

Where to Stay on Grand Bahama Island

Freeport ▸
Island Seas Resort **2**

Lucaya ▸
Bell Channel Inn **6**
Grand Lucayan **5**
Memories Grand Bahama
Beach & Casino Resort **4**

Pelican Bay Hotel **7**
Seagrape E & B **3**
Viva Wyndham
Fortuna Beach **8**

Outside Lucaya ▸
Deep Water Cay **9**
Old Bahama Bay Resort
& Yacht Harbour **1**

KEY
~ Beaches

0 ⌶ 330 yards
0 ⌶ 300 meters

activities; babysitting services. **Cons:** some rooms and bathrooms are tired and dated; all-inclusive meals are average and repetetive. [$] *Rooms from: $151* ✉ *Sea Horse Rd., Lucaya* ☎ *242/373–1333, 855/708–6671* 🌐 *www.grandlucayan.com* 🛏 *540 rooms, 26 suites* 🍴 *All meals.*

$$ RESORT FAMILY 🏨 **Memories Grand Bahama Beach & Casino Resort.** Bought by Blue Diamond resorts in 2013, this refurbished property reopened its doors as an all-inclusive resort in January 2014, with renovated rooms and decor. **Pros:** water park; alll-inclusive food is average; optional upgrades. **Cons:** resort was refurbished from an older property, and not all areas were updated; beachfront can be rocky and crowded. [$] *Rooms from: $295* ✉ *Sea Horse La., next door to Grand Lucayan, across the street from Port Lucaya Marketplace, Lucaya* ☎ *242/373–2583, 855/744–8372* 🌐 *www.memoriesresorts.com* 🛏 *492 rooms* 🍴 *All-inclusive.*

$ HOTEL Fodor's Choice ★ 🏨 **Pelican Bay Hotel.** Close to the beach, with rooms overlooking Port Lucaya Marina or waterfront along the canal, Pelican Bay has a funky modern appeal, and suites overflow with character and decorative elements collected from around the world. **Pros:** stylish and comfortable; water views; trendy on-site bars and restaurants. **Cons:** no beach; fee for Wi-Fi; poolside/marina-front rooms can be noisy. [$] *Rooms from: $175* ✉ *Sea Horse Rd., Lucaya* ☎ *242/373–9550, 800/852–3702* 🌐 *www.pelicanbayhotel.com* 🛏 *90 rooms, 96 waterside suites* 🍴 *Breakfast.*

$ B&B/INN 🏨 **Seagrape Bed & Breakfast.** This quiet B&B offers tourists something more intimate, away from the hustle and bustle of Port Lucaya, yet mere steps from the beach and a short walk from everything else. **Pros:** free airport pickup; central location to beach and amenities; insider tips to seeing the "less traveled" sights on the island. **Cons:** only two rooms; fee for return trip to airport. [$] *Rooms from: $95* ✉ *Off Royal Palm Way, Lucaya* ☎ *954/234–2387, 242/373–1769* 🌐 *www.seagrapehouse.com* 💳 *No credit cards* 🛏 *2 rooms* 🍴 *Breakfast.*

$$ RESORT 🏨 **Viva Wyndham Fortuna Beach.** Popular with couples, families, and spring breakers, this secluded resort provides a casual, all-inclusive getaway where one price covers meals, drinks, tips, nonmotorized water sports, and nightly entertainment. **Pros:** family-friendly; dining variety (though food is only average); beautiful, secluded beach. **Cons:** need a car or taxi to Port Lucaya; rooms are small; resort bustles with spring breakers. [$] *Rooms from: $220* ✉ *Churchill Dr. at Doubloon Rd., Lucaya* ☎ *242/373–4000, 800/996–3426 in U.S.* 🌐 *vivaresorts.com* 🛏 *276 rooms* 🍴 *All-inclusive.*

GREATER GRAND BAHAMA

$$$$ RESORT Fodor's Choice ★ 🏨 **Deep Water Cay.** Founded in 1958 by Gil Drake and iconic *Field and Stream* editor A.J. McClane, Deep Water Cay is the longest established bonefishing lodge in the Bahamas. **Pros:** Out Island feel and seclusion from commercial tourism; great on-site dining; unmatched bonefishing and expert fishing guides. **Cons:** far from other amenities on Grand Bahama; pricey. [$] *Rooms from: 630* ✉ *Off Grand Bahama's East End, Deep Water Cay* ✥ *A 5-min boat ride from McClean's Town, with reservations at the resort* ☎ *242/353–3073, 888/420–6202* 🌐 *www.deepwatercay.com* 🛏 *7 oceanfront cottages, 6 villas* 🍴 *Some meals.*

These handwoven souvenirs can be purchased at Port Lucaya Marketplace.

$$ RESORT FAMILY Fodor's Choice ★ **Old Bahama Bay Resort & Yacht Harbour.** Fishing enthusiasts, yachters, and families can relax in relative seclusion at this West End, Guy Harvey Expedition Resort, comprised of colorful beachfront and poolside suites decorated with island charm. **Pros:** top-shelf marina; close to local color; out island feel; many on-site activities, including tennis and basketball courts. **Cons:** limited dining choices; far from main airport, shopping, and other restaurants; need a car to explore the rest of the island. [$] *Rooms from: $245* ✉ *West End* ☎ *242/350–6500, 888/800–8959* 🌐 *www.oldbahamabay.com* 🛏 *67 rooms, 6 suites* 🍴 *No meals.*

NIGHTLIFE

For evening and late-night entertainment, Port Lucaya is filled with restaurants and bars, and there's live entertainment in the middle square throughout the week, but specifically on Friday and Saturday nights. Other options include bonfire beach parties at Taino by the Sea, the Wednesday-night fish fry at Smith's Point, or taking a sunset cruise through the canals.

LUCAYA

BARS

***Bahama Mama* Dinner and Sunset Cruises.** The *Bahama Mama*, which is owned and operated by Superior Watersports, hosts some of the most unique nightlife in Grand Bahama. In addition to the popular sunset "booze cruises" during the month of March for spring breakers, the *Bahama Mama* offers a surf-and-turf dinner with a colorful "native" show (a local term used to indicate entertainment with a traditional cultural flair); both wine and Bahama Mama rum punch are unlimited all night. The Sunset Cruise and Show is for adults only. Reservations are essential. Both cruises are offered Wednesday and Friday. ⊠ *Port Lucaya Marketplace, Lucaya* ☎ *242/373–7863* ⊕ *www.superior watersports.com.*

Fodor's Choice
★

Bones Bar. Opened in 2014, this trendy spot on the waterfront at Pelican Bay Hotel is a cool and classy fishermen's clubhouse, with swim-up seating at the adjacent pool. Owned by the guys who run H2O Bonefishing, this little bar serves up high-end tasting rums with fancy ice cube spheres and fresh-squeezed cocktails like the Silver Fox (lime juice, homemade simple syrup, and vodka), in addition to fishing gear and bonefish stories. Bones is not a restaurant, so no food is served outside of chips or pretzels at the bar. ⊠ *Pelican Bay Hotel, Sea Horse Rd., on the canal next to Flying Fish Modern Seafood, Lucaya* ☎ *242/374–4899* ⊕ *www. h2obonefishing.com/clubhouse.html.*

Club Neptune's Lounge and Nightclub. Adorned with Tiffany lamps, couch seating, and a swanky bar, all circling the dance floor, this place is *the* place to get your groove on at night. Hostesses and waitresses are decked out in bustier tops and add plenty of character, even though the place is not "R" rated. You can find respite from the rocking DJ tunes upstairs in the small lounge on your way to the restrooms. Happy hour is nightly from 7 to 9, and other events, including karaoke and Ladies Nights, grace a changing weekly schedule. ⊠ *Port Lucaya Marketplace, Lucaya* ☎ *242/374–1221* ⊕ *neptunesportlucaya.com* ⊘ *Tues.–Sat. 7 pm–2 am* ⊘ *Closed Sun. and Mon.*

Coral Beach Bar and Restaurant. At the popular and long-standing condominium property Coral Beach Hotel, this spacious, open-air bar bustles with visitors and locals, too. Bartenders serve up tropical drinks and cold beer to a lively crowd with music in the background. The menu boasts Bahamian favorites like conch fritters along with burgers and sweet-potato fries. Situated poolside and beachfront to Coral Beach, this spot is fun for lunch and a daytime drink, too. ⊠ *Coral Rd., off Royal Palm Way, Lucaya* ☎ *242/373–2468* ⊕ *www.coralbeach online.com.*

FAMILY
Count Basie Square. The stage at Count Basie Square at the center of the Port Lucaya Marketplace becomes lively after dark, with live or piped-in island music and other performances (made all the more festive by surrounding popular watering holes: the Corner Bar, Sparky's, and Rum Runners). Entertainment includes live Bahamian bands on weekend evenings, fire dancers, fashion shows, classic movie showings, and special holiday events. ⊠ *Port Lucaya Marketplace, Sea Horse Rd., Lucaya* ☎ *242/373–8446* ⊕ *www.portlucaya.com.*

Rum Runners. This busy outdoor bar in Count Basie Square specializes in keeping barhoppers young and old supplied with free Wi-Fi, tropical frozen drinks and punches, and pina coladas served in coconuts. Their sign says it all: "If you're drinking to forget, pay in advance." ⊠ *Port Lucaya Marketplace, Lucaya* ☎ *242/373–7233.*

FAMILY **Taino by the Sea Restaurant and Beach Bonfire.** This restaurant hosts one of the island's most popular tourist events—an authentic island party around a beach bonfire. The night includes a Bahamian dinner buffet with local specialties like coconut johnnycakes, conch and baked chicken with peas 'n rice, all you can drink Bahama Mamas, Kamakazes, and fruit punch; games and activities; and a bonfire in the sand—all this in addition to the beautiful sunset on Taino Beach. Bonfires start at 6 pm every Tuesday, Thursday, and Sunday and every other Friday. Kids are welcome! Get tickets at the restaurant upon arrival, or ahead of time at your hotel. ⊠ *Taino Beach Resort, Jolly Roger Dr., Lucaya* ☎ *242/350–2215.*

CASINOS

Treasure Bay Casino. Located at Memories Resort, this 17,000-square-foot, tropically decorated adult playland has more than 320 slot machines and 33 game tables consisting of minibaccarat, Caribbean stud and three-card poker, craps, blackjack, and roulette. The casino is open from 9 am until 2 am Sunday through Thursday and 9 am to 4 am Friday and Saturday (or at the manager's discretion). Bathing suits, bare feet, and children are not permitted. In recent years the casino has been slow and quiet, with few tables open at a time. At this writing, the casino was undergoing a change in management and possible re-branding under a new name. ⊠ *Memories Grand Bahama Beach & Casino Resort, Lucaya* ✛ *Next door to Grand Lucayana, cross the street from Port Lucaya Marketplace* ☎ *242/350–2000.*

SHOPPING AND SPAS

In the stores, shops, and boutiques in Port Lucaya Marketplace you can find duty-free goods costing up to 40% less than what you might pay back home. At the numerous perfume shops, fragrances are often sold at a sweet-smelling 25% below U.S. prices. Be sure to limit your haggling to the straw markets.

Shops in Lucaya are open Monday–Saturday from 9 or 10 to 6. Stores may stay open later at the Port Lucaya Marketplace. Straw markets, grocery stores, some boutiques, and drugstores are open on Sunday.

FREEPORT

SHOPS

ART

Treasure Nest. In addition to displaying original artwork by well-known local watercolorist Sheldon Saint, this shop sells reproductions of his paintings on posters, postcards, and greeting cards. Treasure Nest also carries clothing, shoes, handbags, and accessories for ladies. ⊠ *Bullard's Plaza, W. Atlantic Dr., Freeport* ☎ *242/352–1230* ⊕ *www.sheldonsaint. com* ۞ *Closed Sun. and Mon.*

SPAS

La Belle Spa & Boutique. This small but charming luxury day spa offers top-of-the-line treatments and specialty services such as gel manicures and pedicures, advanced facials and enzyme peels, microdermabrasion, reflexology, and hot stone massages. The technicians are knowledgeable and friendly, and you can relax with provided refreshments to the sounds of trickling water and meditative music. La Belle Spa uses and sells retail brands such as Eminence Organics, OPI, and Essie. ⊠ *W. Atlantic Blvd., Freeport* ☎ *242/351–3565* ⊘ *Tues.–Sat. 9:30–5:30* ⊘ *Closed Sun. and Mon.*

Renu Day Spa. New in 2013, this simple, yet elegant, spa, situated in the bright blue, statuesque Millenium House, offers many general spa services including nail treatments, waxing, facials, body wraps and scrubs, massage, and Reiki. They use Essie and OPI nail products and Guinot skin products, in addition to several other organic lines. However, what makes them unique to other spas on island are the various half-day workshops they offer, such as Feng Shui Basics and Meditation Training. ⊠ *Millenium House, E. Mall Dr., Freeport* ☎ *242/352–7368* ⊕ *www.renudayspabahamas.com* ⊘ *Closed Sun. and Mon., except by appointment.*

LUCAYA

SHOPS
ART
The Grand Gallery. Rotating exhibitions and events showcase and sell work by local artists in a variety of mediums, including mixed media, watercolor, oil on canvas, acrylic paintings, oil paintings, wood carvings, acrylic on plywood, acrylic on paper, postcards, greeting cards, fine art prints, and clay pottery. One of the gallery's goals is to promote special, one-of-a-kind pieces to the tourist looking to bring home a souvenir. ⊠ *Retail St., Lucaya* ✛ *Across from Port Lucaya Market between Grand Lucayan and Memories Resort, next to Iries Restaurant* ☎ *242/373–6111* ⊘ *Closed Sun.*

Leo's Art Gallery. This little shop showcases the expressive Haitian-style paintings and Bahamian impressionism of famed local artist Leo Brown, each piece with its own story. This storefront is both his studio and his showroom. ⊠ *Port Lucaya Marketplace, across from Zorba's, Lucaya* ☎ *242/373–1758.*

FASHION
Animale. This long-standing shop is known for the wild appeal of its fine ladies' clothing and jewelry. ⊠ *Port Lucaya Marketplace, Lucaya* ☎ *242/374–2066.*

Bandolera. Bandolera sells European-style women's fashions, bags, jewelry, and swimwear. ⊠ *Port Lucaya Marketplace, Lucaya* ☎ *242/373–7691.*

DID YOU KNOW?

Most dive operations in the Bahamas offer certification programs. If you are simply looking to try scuba on your vacation, opt for a resort course that provides enough instruction to get you into the water with equipment. If you find scuba is your new favorite adventure, get a full open-water certification. Initial certification in the Bahamas costs about $600. To save valuable vacation and bottom time, you can often begin your instruction at home or online.

JEWELRY AND WATCHES

Colombian Emeralds. Colombian Emeralds purveys a line of Colombia's famed gems plus other jewelry and crystal. ⊠ *Port Lucaya Marketplace, Lucaya* ☏ *242/373–8400* ⊕ *www.colombianemeralds.com.*

John Bull. With locations throughout the Bahamas, this 85-year-old family business sells high-end items including gemstones; gold and designer jewelry like David Yurman and Antica Murrina; fine leather bags and accessories such as Dooney & Bourke and Michael Kors; and designer sunglasses by Maui Jim, Guccis, and Ray-Ban. John Bull has also been the official Rolex retailer in the Bahamas since 1955. ⊠ *Port Lucaya Marketplace, Lucaya* ☏ *242/374–6614* ⊕ *www.johnbull.com.*

MARKETS AND ARCADES

Port Lucaya Crafts Center. This independent collection of 27 small shops and booths on the west side of the Port Lucaya Marketplace is comprised of individual Bahamian artisans, each selling unique arts and homemade handicrafts, many customized on request. Items for sale include sea-shell ornaments, candles, soaps, straw goods, dolls, and more. Don't miss seeing Mrs. Goldsmith's fun and fanciful paper hats, made from recycled cardboard. Stop by Ms. Ferguson's fruit stand for fresh coconut water or a daiquiri served up in a coconut shell. ⊠ *Port Lucaya Marketplace, across from Dominos Pizza, Lucaya* ⊕ *www.port lucaya.com.*

FAMILY   **Port Lucaya Marketplace.** In February 2015, Port Lucaya Marketplace changed hands, and the new owners immediately implemented renovations to create a new upscale shopping and entertainment experience. With $2 million worth of changes in the works, visitors can expect not just a face-lift, but a handful of new restaurants and cuisines, including a gourmet burger joint, Spanish tapas, a chocolate factory, and a new coffee shop, as well as new retail stores. This marketplace already has more than 100 boutiques and restaurants in a harbor-side locale, plus an extensive straw market and 20-plus local crafts vendors. Live music and entertainment brings the center bandstand to life at night on the weekends. ⊠ *Sea Horse Rd., across from Grand Lucayan and Memories Resort, Lucaya* ☏ *242/373–8446* ⊕ *www.portlucaya.com* ☉ *Daily 9–6.*

Port Lucaya Straw Markets. Come to this collection of 100 wooden stalls at Port Lucaya Marketplace's East and West ends to bargain for straw goods, T-shirts, and souvenirs. ⊠ *Port Lucaya Marketplace, Sea Horse Rd., Lucaya* ⊕ *www.portlucaya.com.*

MISCELLANEOUS

Photo Specialist. Photo Specialist carries photo and video equipment, memory cards, rechargeable batteries, cell phone chargers, and any other electronic accessory you may have forgotten to bring with you. ⊠ *Port Lucaya Marketplace, Lucaya* ☏ *242/373–7858.*

Sun & Sea Outfitters at UNEXSO. This retail shop at UNEXSO offers the biggest shopping selection in Lucaya, including water-sports equipment, toys, jewelry and accessories, brand-name apparel and swimsuits, island-style housewares, and books by local authors. ⊠ *UNEXSO, next to Pelican Bay Hotel, Lucaya* ☏ *242/373–1244, 800/992–3483* ⊕ *www. unexso.com* ☉ *Sun. and Mon. 8 am–6 pm, Thurs.–Sat. 8 am–7 pm.*

SPAS

Senses Spa at Grand Lucayan. This three-level spa offers a variety of luxury services including body wraps and scrubs, facials, various massage techniques, and manicures and pedicures, in addition to a full-service salon. On the top floor you will find state-of-the-art exercise equipment, including free weights and elliptical machines, a Spinning studio, and daily exercise classes for every interest. The fee is $25 per day for nonguests, which includes use of the locker room, lap pool, hot tubs, and sauna facilities. All spa services are by appointment. ⊠ *Grand Lucayan, Lighthouse Point, Lucaya* ☎ *242/350–5281* ⊕ *www.grandlucayan.com.*

SPORTS AND THE OUTDOORS

BIKING

By virtue of its flat terrain, broad avenues, and long straight stretches of highway, Grand Bahama is perfect for bicycling. There's a designated biking lane on Midshipman Road.

When biking, wear sunblock, carry a bottle of water, and keep left when riding on the road. Inexpensive bicycle rentals are available from some resorts, and the Viva Wyndham Fortuna Beach allows guests free use of bicycles. In addition to its other ecotouring options, Grand Bahama Nature Tours offers 10-mile biking excursions that include a visit to a native settlement and Garden of the Groves.

CocoNutz Cruisers. CocoNutz is locally owned and operated and offers the only motorized bicycle experience on the island—the bicycles pedal themselves! Alfredo Bridgewater takes tourists along the southern shores of the island, offering island history and stops along the way for unique Grand Bahamian experiences. The 5½-hour ride can take up to 12 bikers, and includes bottled water and lunch. They'll even take photos along the way to email you. Find them behind the Port Lucaya Marketplace parking lot at the water's edge. ⊠ *Port Lucaya Marketplace, Lucaya* ☎ *242/374-6889, 954/354–6889* ✉ *info@coconutzcruisers.com* ⊕ *www.coconutzcruisers.com.*

BOATING AND FISHING

CHARTERS

Private boat charters for up to four people cost $100 per person and up for a half day. Bahamian law limits the catching of game fish to six each of dolphinfish, kingfish, tuna, and wahoo per vessel.

Bonefish Folley & Sons. Committed to giving you the best fishing experience possible, Bonefish Folley & Sons will take you deep-sea fishing or through the flats for bonefish and permit. The late "Bonefish Folley" is a legend in these parts and delighted in taking people on bonefish tours for more than 60 years. He passed away in 2012 at the age of 91, but his two sons, Tommy and Carl, are continuing on in his footsteps. ⊠ *Blue Marlin Cove, West End* ☎ *242/646–9504, 242/349–4101,* ⊕ *www.bluemarlincove.com.*

Captain Phil & Mel's Bonefishing Guide Service. This independent bonefishing group provides a colorful and expert foray into the specialized world of bonefishing around the East End of Grand Bahama. A whole day (eight hours) for up to two people will run you $450, transportation included; a half day costs $350. ☒ *East End, McClean's Town* ☏ *242/353–3960* ⊕ *www.bahamasbonefishing.net.*

H2O Bonefishing. Clients of this professional saltwater fly-fishing outfitter book well ahead of their arrival on island. H2O's fleet of flats boats and professional guides are available as part of a prearranged multiday package that typically includes three to six days of fishing. They cater exclusively to their anglers both on and off the water for the length of their stay, including waterfront lodging at one of Grand Bahama's finest hotels. Fly-fish year-round for trophy-sized bonefish and permit as well as seasonal tarpon, or fish offshore for yellowfin tuna and mahimahi spring through summer. Light tackle and conventional fishing is also available. Check out their trendy clubhouse, Bones Bar. ☒ *Lucaya* ☏ *242/359–4958, 954/364–7590* ⊕ *www.h2obonefishing.com.*

Reef Tours. This family-owned company has been offering various tours on Grand Bahama since 1969. Deep-sea and bottom reef fishing tours are three to four hours in duration. Full-day trips are also available, as are paddleboard and kayak rentals, bottom-fishing excursions, glass-bottom-boat tours, snorkeling trips, wine-and-cheese evening cruises, parasailing, and guided Segway tours. Reservations are essential. ☒ *Port Lucaya Marketplace, Lucaya* ☏ *242/373–5880, 242/373–5891* ⊕ *www. reeftoursfreeport.com.*

West End Ecology Tours. "Ecology and fishing to benefit humanity" is the motto for husband-and-wife ecotour guides Keith and Linda Cooper, who provide educational fishing experiences, focused on Grand Bahama's historical West End and the conservation and preservation of the area and its marine life. With them, you'll fish, feed stingrays, learn about birds, and more. Their company started as a community organization initiative, to educate young people about the island's ecology, but it has evolved into much more. Their clients leave saying, "Thank you," not just for the fun, but for bettering the environment. Ask about their complete eco-vacation packages. ☒ *West End* ☏ *242/602–0641, 561/370–7583* ✎ *weefca@gmail.com* ⊕ *www.weefca.com.*

CRICKET

Lucaya Cricket Club. For a taste of true Bahamian sports, visit the Lucaya Cricket Club. If you feel like joining in, visit a training session on Sunday. Visitors can use equipment free of charge and are welcome to train, play a round, or just watch. The clubhouse has a bar, gym, and changing rooms. Tournaments take place at Easter and Thanksgiving, and teams visit for various scheduled matches throughout the year. ☒ *Baloa Rd., Lucaya* ☏ *242/373–1460* ⊕ *www.cricketbahamas.com.*

Pinetree Stables can take you horseback riding on the beach.

GOLF

Fortune Hills Golf & Country Club. On 17 acres of some of the highest ground in Freeport, Fortune Hills Golf & Country Club is a 3453-yard, 9-hole, par-36 course—a Dick Wilson and Joe Lee design—with a restaurant, bar, and pro shop. This is the least expensive of the three golf courses open on Grand Bahama and is usually quiet, so you'll most often have the course to yourself. The staff is friendly but both the course and the equipment are poorly maintained. ⌧ *E. Sunrise Hwy., Freeport* ☎ *242/373–2222,* ☎ *$35 for 9 holes, $50 to play it twice. Admission includes cart* ⚐ *9 holes, 3453 yards, par 36* ☼ *Restaurant closed Mon.*

Reef Club Golf Course. The Reef Course is a par-72, 6930-yard links-style course. Designed by Robert Trent Jones Jr., it features lots of water (on 13 of the holes), wide fairways flanked by strategically placed bunkers, and a tricky dogleg left on the 18th. While it is the most expensive and nicest of the three golf courses on the island, budget constraints have left it comparable to an average municipal course in the States. Club rentals are available. ⌧ *Sea Horse Rd., Lucaya* ☎ *242/373–2002, 866/870–7148* ⊕ *www.grandlucayan.com* ☎ *$99 plus tax for resort guests, $115 plus tax for nonguests. Admission includes shared golf cart* ⚐ *18 holes, 6930 yards, par 72* ☼ *Daily 10–6.*

Ruby Golf Course. This course reopened in 2008 with renovated landscaping but basically the same 18-hole, par-72 Jim Fazio design. It features a lot of sand traps and challenges on holes 7, 9, 10, and 18—especially playing from the blue tees. Hole 10 requires a tee shot onto a dogleg right fairway around a pond. This course is very tight and is more of a parkland-style course. Popular with locals, there is also a small restaurant-bar and pro shop. ✉ *Wentworth Ave., off W. Sunrise Hwy., behind Ruby Swiss Restaurant, Freeport* ☎ *242/352–1851* ⊕ *www. rubygolfcoursebahamas.com* ✆ *From $65 (fees are higher during the winter season)* ⤫ *18 holes, 7000 yards, par 72* ⊙ *Daily 7:30–5.*

HORSEBACK RIDING

Pinetree Stables. Horseback rides are offered on eco-trails and the beach twice a day, starting at 9 am. All two-hour rides are accompanied by a guide—no previous riding experience is necessary, but riders must be at least eight years old. Plan to bring a waterproof camera because you will get wet! Reservations are essential and drinks are available for purchase. Pinetree Stables offers free shuttles from hotels and the harbor. ✉ *N. Beachway Dr., Freeport* ☎ *242/602–2122* ⊕ *www.pinetree-stables.com.*

KAYAKING

FAMILY **Calabash Eco Adventures.** This tour company, run by a Grand Bahama local and avid diver, Shamie Rolle, offers a variety of eco-excursions to areas all over Grand Bahama for sport, history, and education. Options include kayaking, snorkeling, birding, bicycling, and cavern diving into some of the island's famous inland blue holes. All tours include pickup and drop-off at your lodging. ☎ *242/727–1974* ⊕ *www.calabasheco adventures.com.*

Fodor'sChoice **Grand Bahama Nature Tours.** One of the most well-known ecotour opera-
★ tors on the island for more than 20 years, Grand Bahama Nature tours is continually updating and adding to their wide variety of excursions, run mostly by Grand Bahama natives who are both entertaining and full of educational information. Popular adventures include snorkeling around Peterson Cay, kayaking through the mangroves at Lucayan National Park, jeep safaris, off-road ATV tours, and birding through the Garden of the Groves. All tour prices include air-conditioned pick-ups at your lodging and any necessary equipment. A zip line is in the works. ☎ *242/373–2485, 866/440–4542* ⊕ *www.grandbahamanature tours.com.*

SCUBA DIVING

An extensive reef system runs along Little Bahama Bank's edge; sea gardens, caves, and colorful reefs rim the bank all the way from the West End to Freeport–Lucaya and beyond. The variety of dive sites suits everyone from the novice to the advanced diver, and ranges from 10 to 100-plus feet deep. Many dive operators offer a "discover" or "resort" course where first-timers can try out open-water scuba diving with a short pool course and an instructor at their side.

SITES

A horseshoe-shaped ledge overlooks **Ben's Blue Hole**, which lies in 40 to 60 feet of water. Certified cavern divers can further explore the depths of the cave with guided groups from UNEXSO or Calabash Adventure

Tours. Otherwise, interested visitors can view it aboveground when visiting the Lucayan National Park. For moderately experienced divers, **Pygmy Caves** provides a formation of overgrown ledges that cut into the reef. The high- profile corals here form small caves, but one would have to be as small as a pygmy to swim through them!

One of Grand Bahama Island's signature dive sites, made famous by the UNEXSO dive operation, **Shark Junction** is a 45-foot dive where 4- to 6-foot reef sharks hang out, along with moray eels, stingrays, nurse sharks, and grouper. UNEXSO provides orientation and a shark feeding with its dives here.

HERE'S WHERE

The last time locals spotted pirates on Grand Bahama Island was in 2005 when Johnny Depp and his crew were filming the second and third movies in the *Pirates of the Caribbean* series. They used a special device in Gold Rock Creek at one of the world's largest open-water filming tanks to give the illusion that the pirate ship was pitching and yawing. You can view the set near Gold Rock Beach.

Spid City has an aircraft wreck, dramatic coral formations, blue parrot fish, and an occasional shark. You'll dive about 40 to 60 feet down.

For divers with some experience, **Theo's Wreck,** a 228-foot cement hauler, was sunk in 1982 in100 feet of water, and was the site for the 1993 Imax film *Flight of the Aquanaut.*

OPERATORS

Caribbean Divers. This family-owned-and-operated dive shop offers personalized and uncrowded trips to coral reefs, wrecks, tunnels, and caverns, as well as shark dives. They also rent equipment and offer NAUI, PADI, and SSI instruction. A resort course allows you to use equipment in a pool and then in a closely supervised open dive. The professionally trained dive staff has more than 30 years of experience and the boat resides right on the channel leading out to the sea, so rides to most major sites are about 5–10 minutes. Lodging packages with Bell Channel Inn are available, in addition to snorkeling trips and private charters. ✉ *Bell Channel Inn, King Rd., Lucaya* ☎ *242/373–9111, 242/373–9112* ⊕ *www.bellchannelinn.com* ☉ *Daily 8–5.*

Sunn Odyssey Divers. This family-run shop has been on island for more than 20 years. You'll dive with the owner himself, who caters to smaller dive groups for a more personalized experience. Full PADI certifications available. ✉ *Beach Way Dr., Williams Town* ✛ *Near Island Seas Resort and Williams Town Beach* ☎ *242/373–4014, 866/652–3483* ⊕ *www.sunnodysseydivers.com.*

UNEXSO (*Underwater Explorers Society*). This world-renowned scuba-diving facility provides rental equipment, guides, and boats. Facilities include a 17-foot-deep training pool with windows that look out on the harbor, changing rooms and showers, docks, an outdoor bar and grill, and an air-tank filling station. Daily dive excursions range from one-day discovery courses and dives, to specialty shark, dolphin, and cave diving. Both the facility and its dive masters have been featured in international and American magazines for their work with sharks and cave exploration. UNEXSO and its sister company, the Dolphin Experience, are known for their work with Atlantic bottlenose dolphins. ✉ *Port Lucaya, Lucaya ✛ Next to Pelican Bay Hotel* ☎ *242/373–1244, 800/992–3483* ⊕ *www.unexso.com* ☞ *One-tank reef dives $59, Discover Scuba course $109, night dives $79, dolphin dives $219, shark dives $109, equipment included.*

Viva Dive Shop, a Reef Oasis Diving Center. Part of the Reef Oasis Dive Club, this shop offers daily dives and snorkels to various reefs and wrecks on a large boat seating 21 divers straight off of Fortune Beach at Viva Wyndham Fortuna Resort. This professional PADI-licensed shop also offers certifications for all levels (all equipment is included). ✉ *Viva Wyndham Fortuna Resort, Churchill and Doubloon Rd., Lucaya* ☎ *242/441–6254* ⊕ *www.reefoasisdiveclub.com.*

SNORKELING

FAMILY **Pat & Diane Tours.** This company offers two snorkel trip options aboard a fun-boat catamaran with a 30-foot rock-climbing wall and slide into the water. One tour goes to the vibrant 1-mile-long Rainbow Reef; the other is a longer tour to a private beach and includes lunch. Free pickup and return to all hotels is included. ✉ *Port Lucaya Marina, Lucaya* ☎ *242/373–8681, 888/439–3959, 954/323–1975* ⊕ *www.snorkeling bahamas.com.*

WATER SPORTS

Fodor's Choice **Ocean Motion Water Sports.** In business since 1990, Ocean Motion Water
★ Sports is one of the largest water-sports companies on Grand Bahama and operates all water sports at the Grand Lucayan Resort. Located next to Billy Joe's, they offer everything from a water trampoline and Banana Boat rides, to guided Waverunner tours through the canals and to Peterson Cay. For $70, you can parasail high above the beach and the water—kids and adults alike. In addition, Ocean Motion offers kayaks, Hobie Cat sailboats, waterskiing, and windsurfing instruction. If you'd rather keep it simple, rent snorkel equipment for the day ($40), and regular ferries will take you to Rainbow Reef and back so you get plenty of beach time, too. ✉ *Lucayan Beach, Lucaya* ☎ *242/373–2139, 242/373–9603* ⊕ *www.oceanmotionwatersportsbahamas.com* ☉ *Daily 9–6.*

Paradise Watersports. This company offers a variety of tours and sports excursions from two locations, including glass-bottom boats, Waverunner tours, snorkeling cruises, and fishing trips. There's another location at Taino Beach Resort. ✉ *Island Seas Resort, Lucaya* ☎ *242/373–4001, 954/237–6660 in U.S., 905/231–1689 in Canada* ⊕ *www.the-bahamas-watersports.com/paradisewatersports.*

THE ABACOS

WELCOME TO THE ABACOS

TOP REASONS TO GO

★ **Bonefish the Marls:** One of the most spectacular bonefishing flats anywhere, the Marls is an endless maze of lush mangrove creeks, hidden bays, and sandy cays. Hire a professional guide to show you the best spots.

★ **Cay-hop:** Rent a boat and spend a day (or more) skipping among 150 cays. Settle onto your own private strip of beach and enjoy.

★ **Beach bash:** When the Gully Roosters play on Green Turtle Cay, the island rocks. Stop in at Miss Emily's Blue Bee Bar first for a mind-altering rum, pineapple juice, and apricot brandy Goombay Smash; it's where the popular drink was born. On Great Guana Cay, Nippers's Sunday pig roast is the best beach party of the year—and it happens every week.

★ **Swim with the fishies:** With clear shallow waters and a series of colorful coral reefs extending for miles, the Abacos provide both the novice and the experienced underwater explorer plenty of visual stimulation.

GETTING ORIENTED

The Abacos, 200 miles east of Palm Beach, Florida, are the northernmost chain of cays in the Bahamas. Covering 120 miles, this mini-archipelago offers both historic settlements and uninhabited islands. Great Abaco is the main island, the chain's largest and its most populated. Up north on Little Abaco, a smaller cay connected by bridge, tourism is less prominent and locals live as they have for the last hundred years. Running parallel 5 miles off the east coast of these islands are the Abaco Cays, including Green Turtle, Great Guana, Man-O-War, and Elbow. The majority of the other 146 cays are uninhabited.

1 Great Abaco Island. The Abacos' commercial center still boasts fishing and farming communities, blue holes, caves, wild parrots, and pine forests. Marsh Harbour, the island's main hub, has great restaurants and bustling nightlife. Treasure Cay has a large marina, the only public golf course, and one of the best beaches in the world. Other communities are quiet and tucked away, each with its own personality that makes them worthy day trips.

2 Elbow Cay. Home of the famous candy cane–striped Hope Town Lighthouse, this cay balances a historic getaway with modern conveniences. Hope Town, the main settlement, is known for neat clapboard cottages painted in pastel hues.

3 Man-O-War Cay. Proud of its stance as a dry island (no liquor sold), this community holds fast to its history. It's famous for its boatbuilding, which can still be seen here daily on the waterfront, where men work by hand.

4 Great Guana Cay. A real getaway island, here you'll find modern luxuries or empty beaches. Guana also has Nippers, a restaurant–bar with the best party scene in Abaco.

Grand Cay

Carter's Cay

Great Sale Cay

Fish Cays

Upper Cay

Umbrella Cay

Hawksbill Cays

Pensacola Cays

Sponge Cay

Fox Town

Cedar Harbour

Cooper's Town

Powells Cay

Grand Bahama Island

Rocky Creek

McLean's Town

Sweetings Cay

Lighthouse Cay

Michael's Cay

Little Abaco Island

Nun Jack Cay

Crab Cay

Green Turtle Cay 5

New Plymouth

No Name Cay

Whale Cay

Northwest Providence Channel

LITTLE BAHAMA BANK

Big Joe Downer Cay

Treasure Cay

Sea of Abaco

Great Guana Cay 4

Man-O-War Cay 3

Dundas Town

Marsh Harbour

Marsh Harbor Airport

Hope Town

Elbow Cay 2

Tilloo Cay

Hard Bargain

Moore's Island

Top Cay

Southern Cay

Great Abaco Island 1

Wilson City

Lynyard Cay

Casuarina Point

Little Harbour

Cherokee Sound

Eight Mile Bay

Castaway Cay

Disney Cruise Ship Dock

Crossing Rocks

Sandy Point

◆ **Saw Mill Sink Blue Hole**

◆ **Abaco National Park**

◆ **Hole-in-the-Wall**

5 Green Turtle Cay. This idyllic island, with homes still built with Loyalist architecture and painted in pastels, is quiet by day but bumping at night when the local band plays.

0   10 mi

ABACO NATIONAL PARK

The Abaco National Park was established in 1994 as a sanctuary for the endangered Abaco parrot, of which there are fewer than 3,000. Many other birds call the park home, including the Bahama yellow-throat and pine warbler.

A 15-mile dirt track passes through the 20,500 protected acres, ending at the Hole-in-the-Wall lighthouse, a starkly beautiful and desolate location overlooking the ocean. The drive from the paved highway all the way to the lighthouse takes about 1½ hours, and can only be done in a 4x4 vehicle. The lighthouse is not technically open to visitors, but people still do climb the rickety stairs to the top where views of the island and the sea are mesmerizing. *South end of Great Abaco Island, before you make the final turn on the main road leading to Sandy Point* ☎ 242/367–3067.

BEST TIME TO GO
Berries ripen in fall and spring, and the parrots become active. The best time to spot the birds is early morning, when they move out of the forest to feed. Temperatures then are also ideal, in the 70s and 80s. The annual bird counts in North and South Abaco held at the beginning of each year are a good opportunity to work with other bird-watchers to gather information on the parrots, which is sent to the Audubon Society.

BEST WAYS TO EXPLORE
By Car on Your Own. Take the 15-mile, 1½-hour drive along a dirt trail out to the lighthouse. This is the only part of

the park you can drive. This lighthouse has spectacular views of the coast. Take a packed lunch and have a picnic on a ledge overlooking the ocean.

By Guided Tour. For the best experience, arrange a guided tour with the tourist office. A knowledgeable guide will walk or drive you through the park, pointing out plant and animal species. If you're an early riser, join a bird-watching tour to find the endangered Abaco parrot, as well as other avian beauties that reside here. Walking the park alone is not recommended, as poisonous wood saplings are a problem if you don't know how to identify them.

Note: *Friends of the Environment (☎ 242/367–2721) is a local education organization that offers more information on the park and the parrots.*

FUN FACT
The park's pine forest is prone to summer lightning fires, but the Abaco pine is extremely resistant and actually depends on the fires to remove dense underbrush that would otherwise smother it. The Abaco parrots nest in holes in the limestone floor to escape the flames. Unfortunately, this makes them vulnerable to feral cats and raccoons that threaten their population.

FOWL CAY NATIONAL RESERVE
This quarter-mile reef located on the ocean side of Fowl Cay is a great

snorkeling and dive spot. It's well known among divers for its tunnels and wide variety of fish. On the opposite side of Fowl Cay is a small sand spit, which makes a great spot to reconvene for a sun-soaked picnic.

PELICAN CAYS LAND AND SEA PARK
This 2,000-acre land and marine park is protected and maintained by the Bahamas National Trust. The park's preserved reef is only 25 feet underwater, making it an easy snorkel excursion. It's also a great dive site, as the variety of life here is astounding. Nearby is an incredibly soft beach, great for a postswim picnic.

(above) Abaco parrot (lower left) Hole-in-the-Wall Lighthouse

Updated
by Jessica
Robertson

The attitude of the Abacos might best be expressed by the sign posted in the window of Vernon's Grocery in Hope Town: "If you're looking for Wal-Mart—it's 200 miles to the right." In other words, the residents of this chain of more than 100 islands know that there's another world out there, but don't necessarily care to abandon theirs, which is a little more traditional, slow-paced, and out of the way than most alternatives.

Here you'll feel content in an uncrowded environment, yet still have access to whatever level of accommodations and services you desire. Ecotourism is popular, and aficionados have revitalized exploration of Abacos' Caribbean pine forests, which are home to wild boar, wild horses, the rare Abaco parrot, and myriad other bird and plant life. Hiking and biking through these forests and along abandoned beaches at the forest's edges are popular activities. Sea kayaking in pristine protected areas also provides a rewarding sense of adventure, and more conventional activities such as golf, tennis, and beach volleyball are available, too. But if you don't feel like doing anything at all, that's also a highly rated activity.

Of course, this is the Bahamas, so you shouldn't neglect activities happening in one of its most magnificent assets—the water. Snorkeling and diving have long been staple activities for visitors. Abaconians are proud of their marine environment and have worked with the government to protect some of the more vibrant reefs. The islands' calm, naturally protected waters, long admired for their beauty, have also helped the area become the Bahamas' sailing capital. Man-O-War Cay remains the Bahamas' boatbuilding center; its residents turn out traditionally crafted wood dinghies as well as high-tech fiberglass craft. The Abacos play host annually to internationally famous regattas and to a half-dozen game-fish tournaments.

From island-long stretches to strips as short as your boat, with powder-white to pink to warm-cream sand, the roar of the surf or the silence of a slow-rising tide, the Abacos have a beach suited to everyone's liking. And most likely, you'll find a secluded spot to call your own.

Oceanside beaches are long expanses of white powder that change their form throughout the year depending on the surge brought in by weather. Beaches sheltered from strong winds, on the lee sides of islands, are small, narrow, and stable. Trees are taller on the lee sides of the islands and provide shaded areas for picnics. On the outer cays beaches make popular surf spots and snorkel sites, with the barrier reef running along the shore. Most Abaco beaches are secluded, but if you're looking for a beach party, head to Great Guana Cay for the Nippers's Sunday pig roast.

PLANNING

WHEN TO GO

June, July, and early August are the best months for sailing, boating, and swimming, precisely why the most popular regatta and fishing tournaments are held during this time. Afternoon thunderstorms are common but usually clear quickly. Temperatures often reach the 90s.

December through May is a pleasant time to visit, with temperatures in the 70s and 80s, though sometimes dropping into the 50s at night when cold fronts blow through. Fishing, particularly deep-sea fishing, is good during this time of year.

In September and October, typically the peak of hurricane season, visitors drop to a trickle and many hotels and restaurants shut down for two weeks to two months. If you're willing to take a chance on getting hit by a storm, this can still be a great time to explore, with discounts of as much as 50% at the hotels that remain open.

TOP FESTIVALS

WINTER **Junkanoo.** Many Abaco communities have their own Junkanoo celebrations; Hope Town has a New Year's Eve children's rushout for locals and visitors to join in. Parades in the Abacos are much smaller and more intimate than in Nassau, and far less competitive. ⊠ *Hope Town.*

SPRING **Heritage Day.** Hope Town's annual Heritage Day in March celebrates the Loyalist settlement's history with traditional songs, speeches, and exhibits on historical topics, and a boat parade. ⊠ *Hope Town.*

Island Roots Festival. The Island Roots Festival celebrates Bahamian traditions with an outdoor party on tiny Green Turtle Cay the first weekend in May. ⊕ *www.islandrootsheritagefestival.com.*

SUMMER **Junkanoo Summer Festival.** Junkanoo Summer Festival—traditional summertime parties with dance troupes and musical groups—take place in Marsh Harbour. ⊠ *Marsh Harbour.*

Regatta Time. Regatta Time in Abaco, the first week of July, stretches over several islands, with races and plenty of onshore parties. ⊕ *www. regattatimeinabaco.com.*

Treasure Cay Billfish Championship. There are big cash prizes that increase with the number of registered boats at the Treasure Cay Billfish Championship in June. The final day includes a Lionfish Tournament designed to help save the Bahamas indigenous marine life from this relatively new predator. ⊠ *Treasure Cay* ⊕ *treasurecay.com.*

GETTING HERE AND AROUND

AIR TRAVEL

Most flights land at the international airports in **Marsh Harbour (MHH)** or **Treasure Cay (TCB)**. Taxis wait at the main airports, and the fare to most resorts is between $15 and $30 for the first two passengers and $3 for each additional person. Cab fare between Marsh Harbour and Treasure Cay or the ferry dock is $85 each way.

Contacts Marsh Harbour Airport. ⊠ *Marsh Harbour* ☎ *242/367–5500.* **Treasure Cay Airport.** ⊠ *Treasure Cay* ☎ *242/365–8602.*

BOAT AND FERRY TRAVEL

The *Legacy* mail boat leaves Potter's Cay, Nassau, on Tuesday for Marsh Harbour and Green Turtle Cay, returning to Nassau on Thursday. Each one-way journey takes about 10 hours and costs $60 per person. The *Sealink* leaves Nassau on Friday and Sunday mornings for Sandy Point, at the southern tip of Great Abaco, and returns to Nassau on Friday and Sunday. For details, call the **Dockmaster's Office.**

A good system of public ferries allows you to reach even the most remote cays. *(See Getting Here and Around within the island sections.)*

If you don't want to be bound by the somewhat limited ferry schedule, rent a small boat. The best selections are at Marsh Harbour, Treasure Cay, Hope Town, and Green Turtle Cay.

Contacts Dockmaster's Office. ⊠ *Nassau* ☎ *242/393–1064.*

CAR TRAVEL

On Great Abaco, renting a car is the best option if you plan on exploring outside Marsh Harbour or Treasure Cay. Rentals start at $70 a day, and gasoline costs about $6 per gallon. Cars are not necessary on most of the smaller cays in the Abacos; in fact, rental cars aren't even available in most locations.

Contacts A & P Auto Rentals. ⊠ *Marsh Harbour* ☎ *242/367–2655* ⊕ *www. aandpautorentals.com.* **Bargain Car Rentals.** ⊠ *Marsh Harbour* ☎ *242/367–0500.* **Cornish Car Rentals.** ⊠ *Treasure Cay* ☎ *242/365–8623.* **Rental Wheels of Abaco.** ⊠ *Marsh Harbour* ☎ *242/367–4643* ⊕ *www.rentalwheels.com.*

GOLF CART TRAVEL

Golf carts are the vehicle of choice on the majority of the smaller cays, including Elbow Cay, Green Turtle Cay, Great Guana Cay, and Man-O-War Cay, as well as in Treasure Cay on Great Abaco. Rates are $40 to $50 per day, or $245 per week. Reservations are essential from April to July. See specific islands sections for rental recommendations.

Contacts Blue Marlin Rentals. ⊠ *Treasure Cay* ☎ *242/365–8687.*

TAXI TRAVEL

Taxi service is available on Great Abaco in Marsh Harbour and Treasure Cay. Hotels will arrange for taxis to take you on short trips and to the airport. Fares are generally $1.50 per mile. A 15% tip is customary.

HOTELS

Intimate hotels, cottage-style resorts, and rental homes are the rule in the Abacos. There are a few full-scale resorts in Marsh Harbour, Treasure Cay, Green Turtle Cay, and Hope Town—with multiple restaurants, bars, pools, and activities—but most accommodations are more homey. What you might give up in modern amenities you'll gain in privacy and beauty. Many hotels have water views, and with a cottage or private house you may even get your own stretch of beach. Air-conditioning is a standard feature, and more places are adding luxuries like cable TV and wireless Internet. Small and remote doesn't equate with inexpensive, however; it's almost impossible to find lodging for less than $100 a night, and not uncommon to pay more than $300 a night for beachside accommodations with all the conveniences.

4

RESTAURANTS

Fish, conch, land crabs, and rock lobster—called crawfish by the locals—have long been the bedrock of local cuisine. Although a few menus, mostly in upscale resorts, feature dishes with international influences, most restaurants in the Abacos still serve simple Bahamian fare, with a few nods to American tastes. There are some fancier restaurants in Marsh Harbour, Treasure Cay, and Hope Town, but most restaurants are relaxed about attire and reasonably priced. Some offer live music, and shape the nightlife scene on weekends.

HOTEL AND RESTAURANT PRICES

Restaurant prices are based on the median main course price at dinner, excluding gratuity, typically 15%, which is often automatically added to the bill. Hotel prices are for two people in a standard double room in high season, excluding service and 6%–12% tax. Both restaurant meals and hotel rooms as well as just about every other goods or service you purchase also now incur an additional 7.5% government VAT.

WHAT IT COSTS IN DOLLARS			
$	**$$**	**$$$**	**$$$$**
Restaurants	under $20	$20–$30	$31–$40	over $40
Hotels	under $200	$200–$300	$301–$400	over $400

SHIPPING

GPS Bahamas. Renting a beach house for a week or longer? Maybe you can't take everything with you, but GPS Bahamas has air-freight service for everything from perishable foods to electronics and computers. It beats the mail boat. ⊠ *Marsh Harbour* ☎ *242/475–5480, 954/689–6761* ⊕ *gpsbahamas.com.*

VISITOR INFORMATION

Contacts Abaco Tourist Office & Information Center. ⊠ *Harbor Place Bldg., Queen Elizabeth Dr., Marsh Harbour* ☎ *242/367-3067* ⊕ *www.bahamas.com.*

GREAT ABACO ISLAND

If arriving by air, your trip will begin on Great Abaco, the main island. It's bordered on its eastern side by a chain of cays that extend from the north to about midway down the island, and on the western side by a fishing flat called the Marls, a shallow-water area of mangrove creeks and islands. Great Abaco was once logged for its pine trees, and traveling by car allows you to access many old logging trails that will lead you to secluded beaches along the coast. The island is home to wild horses, cows, and boars, and the endangered Abaco parrots, who make their homes in the pine forests.

Marsh Harbour is the main hub of activity on the island, and where most visitors stay. Heading north on the S.C. Bootle Highway will take you to **Treasure Cay** peninsula, a resort development. There's another, smaller, airport here. Farther north are **Cooper's Town** and the small communities of **Little Abaco**, which don't provide much for visitors besides nearly total seclusion. South of Marsh Harbour off the Ernest Dean Highway are artists' retreat **Little Harbour,** and **Cherokee Sound** and **Sandy Point**, both small fishing communities. Also there is the quaint yet upscale second home and vacation community **Schooner Bay.**

GETTING HERE AND AROUND

To travel around Great Abaco you'll need a vehicle. Renting a car is the most convenient and economical option. If you plan on staying in one town or only making short, one-time, or one-way trips you can hire a taxi. Taxis will take you all over the island, but the farther you travel from Marsh Harbour, the more extreme rates get, sometimes in excess of a hundred dollars. The closest settlement worth a visit out of Marsh Harbour is Little Harbour, about 30 minutes away.

Golf carts are used locally in Treasure Cay and Cherokee Sound. From Marsh Harbour you can boat to Little Harbour and Cherokee Sound to the south and Treasure Cay in the north.

MARSH HARBOUR

Most visitors to the Abacos make their first stop in Marsh Harbour, the Bahamas' third-largest city and the Abacos' commercial center. Besides having the Abacos' largest international airport, it offers what boaters consider to be one of the easiest harbors to enter. It has several full-service marinas, including the 190-slip Boat Harbour Marina and the 80-slip Conch Inn Marina.

Marsh Harbour has a more diverse variety of restaurants, shops, and grocery items than other communities. **Maxwell's Supermarket** and one of the larger liquor stores to stock up on supplies are standard stops on the way to other settlements or islands. The downtown area has several other supermarkets, as well as a few department and hardware stores. If you need cash, this is the place to get it; banks here are open every day and have ATMs, neither of which you will find on the smaller, more remote settlements or cays.

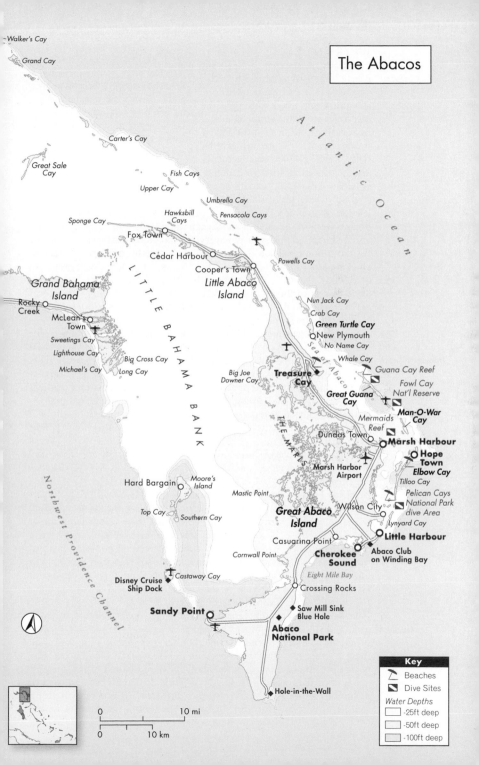

WHERE TO EAT

$$$
BAHAMIAN

✕**Angler's Restaurant.** Dine on roasted rack of lamb with garlic mashed potatoes or a broiled lobster tail while overlooking gleaming rows of yachts moored in the Boat Harbour Marina at the Abaco Beach Resort. White tablecloths with fresh orchid arrangements and sea-blue napkins folded like seashells create an experience a step up from typical island dining.

It's not uncommon to see guests dressed in sport coats and cocktail dresses fresh off a stunning megayacht alongside other guests in shorts and T-shirts with kids in tow. Everyone can enjoy fresh grilled catch of the day—don't pass up the grilled wahoo—seafood pastas, Bahamian chicken, or charbroiled steaks. For dessert try the calorie-drenched guava duff. Angler's is also the only place to get a cooked breakfast along the main tourist drag in Marsh Harbour. $ *Average main: $35* ✉ *Abaco Beach Resort, off Bay St.* ☎ *242/367–2158, 800/468–4799* ⊕ *abacobeachresort.com.*

$$$
BAHAMIAN
Fodor's Choice
★

✕**Curly Tails Restaurant and Bar.** Enjoy kick-back harborside dining for lunch and dinner at the Conch Inn Hotel and Marina. Savor your meal outside on the open-air deck. At lunch, salads, burgers, cracked conch, and grouper fillets go great with a cold Kalik. For dinner, go casual at the large bar upstairs, or opt for something more upscale in the downstairs air-conditioned dining room. Chicken stuffed with local johnnycake or blackened grouper, snapper, mahimahi, or tuna are traditional favorites. If you're into sunsets, don't miss the daily happy hour. Sample a frozen Tail Curler or a Curlytini to go with your conch fritters. There's also live music every Thursday and Saturday night. $ *Average main: $30* ✉ *Conch Inn Hotel and Marina, Bay St.* ☎ *242/367–4444* ⊕ *www. abacocurlytails.com* ⊗ *Closed Tues.*

$
BAHAMIAN

✕**Jamie's Place.** There's nothing fancy about this clean, bright, diner-style eatery, but the welcome is warm, the Bahamian dishes are well executed, and the prices are right, with most meals clocking in under $15. Choose fried chicken, cracked conch, or fresh-caught dolphin (also called mahimahi), with a side of mashed or roasted potatoes, peas 'n' rice, macaroni and cheese, or coleslaw. Jamie's is also an ice-cream parlor, with a dozen flavors. Locals love this place, and it has stayed one of Great Abaco Island's best-kept secrets. $ *Average main: $14* ✉ *Queen Elizabeth Dr.* ☎ *242/367–2880* ⊟ *No credit cards.*

$$
BAHAMIAN

✕**Jib Room.** Expect casual lunches of hot wings, conch burgers, fish nuggets, and steak wraps in this harbor-view restaurant and bar, located inside the Marsh Harbour Marina. Dinner is served twice a week, and these "barbecue nights" are especially popular; on Wednesday it's baby back ribs, fish, chicken, potato salad, slaw, and baked beans. On Saturday it's grilled steak, featuring New York strip, with fish and chicken as options along with baked potatoes and salad. If you're dying for a steak after a steady fish diet, these are the best in the Abacos. Unless you're staying on this side of the harbor, you'll need a car or taxi to get here, or expect a long walk from the main street. $ *Average main: $25 ⊠ Pelican Shores ☏ 242/367–2700 ⊕ www.jibroom.com ☯ Closed Sun.–Tues. No dinner Thurs. and Fri. ⚓ Reservations essential.*

$
BAHAMIAN
Fodor'sChoice
★

✕ **Junovia's Diner.** A steady stream of locals flow in and out of this unassuming diner to either dine in or grab breakfast or lunch on the run. Chicken souse is usually on the menu board. Oftentimes it's also a good place to grab boil' or stew' fish served up with a chunk of fresh-baked johnnycake and a bowl of steaming yellow grits—this is the way locals do breakfast. Not ready for fish for breakfast? The western omelet is stuffed and delicious. Junovia's closes early on weekdays at 5 pm, and on weekends it's only open for breakfast. $ *Average main: $14 ⊠ Don Mackay Blvd. ☏ 242/367–1271 ☯ No dinner. No lunch weekends.*

$
BAHAMIAN

✕ **Meke's Snack Shack.** If you're looking for a simple but tasty lunch at a great price, check out this octagonal wooden takeout-only restaurant on the western end of Bay Street. The burgers are hand-formed and served up on homemade buns—the spicy bacon cheeseburger is a local favorite. Grab a box of their fried chicken if you're headed out in the boat for a day of exploring, and on a hot day, their homemade ice cream in an array of tropical flavors including coconut, guava, pineapple, and mango is delicious and refreshing. The only seating is on a handful of park benches nearby. $ *Average main: $9 ⊠ Bay St. ☏ 242/367–4005 ☯ Closed Sun. ⚓ Reservations not accepted ▭ No credit cards.*

$
BAHAMIAN

✕ **Show-Boo's Conch Salad Stand.** Look along the harbor for this ramshackle stand between the Harbour View and Conch Inn marinas for what Show-Boo himself claims to be "the world's best conch salad," often diced and mixed while you watch. Hours are erratic, especially during the September–November off-season. To find out if Show-Boo showed up for business, just swing by around lunchtime and see if there's a line forming in front of his stand. Call ahead to place your order for a chance at reducing your wait time. $ *Average main: $12 ⊠ Bay St., between Conch Inn and Harbour View ☏ 242/458–7114 ▭ No credit cards ☯ No dinner.*

$$
BAHAMIAN

✕ **Snappas.** Savvy boat people and in-the-know locals hang out here in the Harbour View Marina. The wood bar is the center of gravity around which the dining room sprawls outward toward the open-air waterside deck. Killer appetizers include grilled shrimp, chicken kebabs, and sizzling onion rings. For lunch the grilled-fish Caesar salad and the Snappa Filly are hard to beat. Fresh-grilled catch of the day and grilled conch are crossover items that always hit the spot. When the sun goes down—the sunsets are dazzling—order a New York steak or grilled lobster with a garden salad. Want more? Party on with live music Wednesday and Saturday nights. Happy hour lasts from 5 to 7:30 daily except Wednesday when it goes on until 11 pm. $ *Average main: $25 ⊠ Harbour View Marina, Bay St. ☏ 242/367–2278 ⊕ www.snappasbar.com.*

$$$
BAHAMIAN
Fodor'sChoice
★

✕ **Wally's.** This two-story, pink colonial villa sits across Bay Street from the marina, fronted by green lawns, hibiscus, and white-railed verandas. This is the Abacos' most popular restaurant—*the* place to go for good food, potent rum cocktails, and serious people-watching. Lunch is a scene, especially if you sit outside, where you'll find a mix of locals,

4

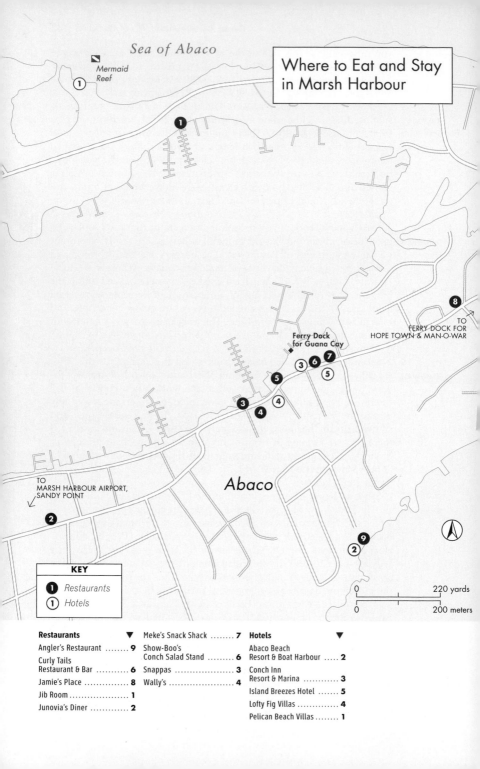

Where to Eat and Stay in Marsh Harbour

Sea of Abaco

Mermaid Reef

Ferry Dock for Guana Cay

TO FERRY DOCK FOR HOPE TOWN & MAN-O-WAR

TO MARSH HARBOUR AIRPORT, SANDY POINT

Abaco

KEY
- ● Restaurants
- ① Hotels

0 — 220 yards
0 — 200 meters

tourists, and boat people munching on Greek or Caesar salads, spicy grouper, and mahimahi burgers. Inside there's a stylish bar, a boutique, and three dining rooms, all adorned with Haitian-style paintings. Dinner is served every night except Sunday and the menu includes creamy curried shrimp, mahimahi Provençal, or a filet mignon smothered in a mushroom sauce, as well as a daily sashimi. Save room for the irresistible key lime pie or Bahamian bread pudding with coconut and raisins, drenched in a brandy sauce. $ *Average main: $30* ⊠ *E. Bay St.* ☎ *242/367–2074* ☉ *Closed Sun.* ☖ *Reservations essential.*

WHERE TO STAY

$$$
RESORT
FAMILY
Abaco Beach Resort and Boat Harbour. The largest hotel in Marsh Harbour is lively at spring break and during fishing tournaments throughout the year, but can also be very quiet outside the high season. **Pros:** ideal location for all water-related activities; easy access to town shops and restaurants; one of the best marinas in the Abacos. **Cons:** can be crowded and noisy during fishing tournaments; pricey accommodations; long walk from car to rooms. $ *Rooms from: $368* ⊠ *East of Conch Sound Marina* ☎ *242/367–2158, 800/468–4799* ⊕ *abacobeach resort.com* ⤳ *78 rooms, 4 suites* ⏉ *No meals.*

$
HOTEL
Conch Inn Resort and Marina. This low-key, one-level marina hotel is a good choice for budget or business travelers, but make reservations well in advance. **Pros:** smack dab in the middle of everything in Marsh Harbour—marina, shops, and restaurants; easy to arrange boat rentals and diving; good value for comfortable rooms. **Cons:** far from beaches; small pool area. $ *Rooms from: $165* ⊠ *E. Bay St.* ☎ *242/367–4000* ⊕ *www.conchinn.com* ⤳ *10 rooms.*

$
HOTEL
Fodor'sChoice
★
Island Breezes Hotel. This simple, no-frills motel is ideal if you plan to spend your days exploring the mainland by car or the surrounding cays by ferry or boat and just need a place for a cold shower and a good sleep before starting all over the next day. **Pros:** lowest rates in Marsh Harbour; large rooms; right in the midst of the main tourist area. **Cons:** very simple accommodations; no indoor common area; no pool. $ *Rooms from: $127.50* ⊠ *Bay St.* ☎ *242/367–3776* ⊕ *islandbreezes hotel.com* ⤳ *8 rooms.*

$$
HOTEL
Lofty Fig Villas. The hotel owners envelop guests with exceptional hospitality, as does the superfriendly staff. **Pros:** location, location, location; good pool area for hanging out; excellent value with warm and friendly service. **Cons:** room furnishings are dated; no place to tie up a rental boat. $ *Rooms from: $198* ⊠ *Marsh Harbour* ☎ *242/367–2681* ⊕ *www.loftyfig.com* ⤳ *6 villas.*

$$
RENTAL
Pelican Beach Villas. On a quiet private peninsula opposite the main settlement of Marsh Harbour sit seven waterfront clapboard cottages cheerily painted in pale pink, yellow, blue, and green. **Pros:** tranquil beach location; near some of the best snorkeling in the Abacos; many repeat guests. **Cons:** no restaurant; need to rent a car or boat; on the expensive side for less than full-service accommodations. $ *Rooms from: $250* ⊠ *Northwest of Marsh Harbour Marina* ☎ *877/367–3600* ⊕ *www.pelicanbeachvillas.com* ⤳ *7 cottages.*

$$$$
RESORT
The Residences at Abaco Beach Resort. Lots of room, contemporary upscale island decor, and large balconies where you can sit and enjoy

amazing views of the Sea of Abaco make these two- and three-bedroom condos a popular choice. **Pros:** lots of room for a family; upscale accommodations; restaurant on property. **Cons:** no elevator to upstairs condos; noise from marina below. [$] *Rooms from: $900* ✉ *Abaco Beach Resort & Marina, Bay St.* ☎ *242/367–2158, 800/468–4799* 🌐 *abacobeachresort.com* 🛏 *9 2- and 3-bedroom condos.*

PLAN AHEAD

Even though you're going to the laid-back islands, you need to reserve your boats, cars, and golf carts in advance. You can save time and money by having your boat-rental company meet you at the airport or the ferry dock nearest to your offshore cay.

NIGHTLIFE

Curly Tails. Stop by for live music Thursday and Saturday nights. ✉ *Conch Inn Hotel and Marina, Bay St.* ☎ *242/367–4444* 🌐 *www.abacocurlytails.com* 🕒 *Closed Tues.*

Snappas. Thursday through Saturday nights feature live music. ✉ *Harbour View Marina, Bay St.* ☎ *242/367–2278* 🌐 *www.snappasbar.com.*

SHOPPING

Abaco Neem. More than 30 different products are made using locally grown Neem trees at this shop and production plant. Salves, soaps, and lotions are organic and in many cases claim to offer medicinal benefits against skin conditions, arthritis, and even hypertension. Abaco Neem also produces an entire range of pet products. Call or email in advance to arrange a tour of the production facility and nearby farm. Tours take about 1½ hours and are free, although a $10 per person donation is welcomed. ✉ *Don Mackay Blvd.* ☎ *242/367–4117* 🌐 *www.abaconeem.com* 🕒 *Mon.–Sat. 9–5.*

Abaco Treasures. At Marsh Harbour's traffic light, look for the turquoise awnings of Abaco Treasures, purveyors of fine china, crystal, perfumes, Bahamian books, and gifts. ✉ *Don Mackay Blvd.* ☎ *242/367–3460.*

Iggy Biggy. This store, inside a bright peach-and-turquoise building, is your best bet for hats, sandals, tropical jewelry, sportswear, and souvenirs. If you are looking for gifts to take back home, you should be able to find something cool here. ✉ *E. Bay St.* ☎ *242/367–3596.*

Java in Abaco. Sip an iced latte or a strong mug of Hope Town Roasted joe while admiring the smattering of ceramics, paintings, carved wooden boats, and other locally produced creations at Java in Abaco. ✉ *E. Bay St.* ☎ *242/367–5523.*

Sand Dollar Shoppe. This shop sells resort wear and jewelry. Look for the locally made Abaco gold necklaces and earrings. ✉ *E. Bay St.* ☎ *242/367–4405.*

SPORTS AND THE OUTDOORS

BIKING

Rental Wheels of Abaco. You can rent bicycles for $10 a day or $45 a week here. It's located on the main strip between Conch Inn Marina and the turnoff to Boat Harbour Marina. ✉ *E. Bay St.* ☎ *242/367–4643* 🌐 *www.rentalwheels.com.*

The Abacos are the sailing capital of the Bahamas.

BOATING

Boat Harbour Marina. The marina has 198 fully protected slips and a slew of amenities, including on-site customs and immigration clearance and accommodations at the Abaco Beach Resort. ⊠ *Bay St.* ☎ *242/367–2158* ⊕ *www.abacobeachresort.com.*

Conch Inn Marina. This is one of the busiest marinas and has 80 slips, with accommodations available at the Conch Inn. ⊠ *Bay St.* ☎ *242/367–4000* ⊕ *www.conchinn.com.*

Harbour View Marina. The first marina on the west end of Bay Street, across from Wally's Restaurant, has extra-wide slips and 100-foot piers to accommodate boats with unlimited beam size, a private heated swimming pool, wireless Internet, and Snappas Restaurant. ⊠ *Bay St.* ☎ *242/367–3910* ⊕ *www.harbourviewmarina.com.*

Mangoes Marina. This marina has 29 slips and a full range of amenities, including onshore showers, a pool, and a small cabana where you can grill your day's catch. ⊠ *Bay St.* ☎ *242/367–4996* ⊕ *www.mangoes inabaco.com.*

Marsh Harbour Marina. Marsh Harbour Marina has 68 slips and is the only full-service marina on the left side of the harbor, near Pelican Shores. It is a 10-minute drive from most shops and restaurants. ⊠ *Marsh Harbour* ☎ *242/367–2700* ⊕ *www.jibroom.com.*

BOAT RENTALS

The best way to explore the Abacos is by renting a small boat from one of the many rental companies in Marsh Harbour.

Bluewave Boat Rentals. Boats range from 21 to 33 feet, and rental includes access to the pool and other marina facilities. You may wish to opt for the luxury *Regal* that comes with a sound system and a captain. ⊠ *At Harbour View Marina, Bay St.* ☎ *242/367–3910.*

The Moorings. What better way to truly enjoy the beautiful waters and islands of the Abacos than on board your own private yacht? The Moorings rents single- and double-hull boats with up to four cabins. You can set sail on your own or hire a skipper and even a private chef, or you can simply arrange full provisioning. ⊠ *Marsh Harbour* ☎ *242/367–4000* ⊕ *www.moorings.com.*

> ## PLAY THE TIDES
>
> If you're going bonefishing, tide pooling, or snorkeling, you'll want up-to-date tide information for the best results. A low incoming tide is usually best for bonefishing, though the last of the falling is good, too. Low tides are best for beachcombing and tide pools, although higher tides can give better coverage to your favorite reef. Ask at your hotel or a local dive shop for current tide information.

Rainbow Rentals. Single- and twin-engine boats are available for rental from this outfitter. You'll have to get special written approval to head out for deep-sea fishing, but there are plenty of spots in shallow waters to explore. ⊠ *Marsh Harbour* ☎ *242/367–4602* ⊕ *www.rainbow rentals.com.*

FISHING

You can find bonefish on the flats, yellowtail and grouper on the reefs, or marlin and tuna in the deeps of the Abacos.

Justin Sands. Premier fly-fishing guide Justin Sands works out of a state-of-the-art Hell's Bay flats skiff that will put you in the shallowest of water. Justin was the Abacos bonefish champ for two years running, and he will guide you in the Marls or around Snake Cay, Little Harbour, and Cherokee Sound. Advance reservations are a must. ⊠ *Marsh Harbour* ☎ *242/367–3526* ⊕ *www.bahamasvacationguide.com/justfish.html.*

Pinder's Bone Fishing. Buddy Pinder has more than 20 years' experience in the local waters, and professional Pinder's Bone Fishing provides year-round excursions in the Marls, a maze of mangroves and flats on the western side of Abaco. Advance reservations are essential. ⊠ *Marsh Harbour* ☎ *242/366–2163.*

SCUBA DIVING AND SNORKELING

There's excellent diving throughout the Abacos. Many sites are clustered around Marsh Harbour, including the reef behind **Guana Cay,** which is filled with little cavelike catacombs, and **Fowl Cay National Reserve,** which contains wide tunnels and a variety of fish. **Pelican Cays National Park** is a popular dive area south of Marsh Harbour. This shallow, 25-foot dive is filled with sea life; turtles are often sighted, as are spotted eagle rays and tarpon. The park is a 2,000-acre land and marine park protected and maintained by the Bahamas National Trust. Hook up your own boat to one of the moorings, or check with the local dive shops to see when trips to the park are scheduled. All of these sights can be easily snorkeled. Snorkelers will also want to visit **Mermaid Beach,** just off Pelican Shores Road in Marsh Harbour, where live reefs and green moray eels make for some of the Abacos' best snorkeling.

Dive Abaco. Located at the Conch Inn, Dive Abaco offers scuba and snorkeling trips on custom dive boats. Sites explored include reefs, tunnels, caverns, and wreck dives. ⊠ *Marsh Harbour* ☎ *800/247–5338, 242/367–2787, 800/247–5338* ⊕ *www.diveabaco.com.*

Rainbow Rentals. This outfit rents catamarans and snorkeling gear. ⊠ *Marsh Harbour* ☎ *242/367–4602* ⊕ *www.rainbowrentals.com.*

TENNIS

Abaco Beach Resort. The two lighted courts here are open to visitors. A tennis pro is on hand for clinics and private lessons for adults and children, and there are round-robin tournaments for guests. ⊠ *Marsh Harbour* ☎ *242/367–2158.*

TOURS

Abaco Eco Kayak Tours and Rentals. Get up close and personal with Abaco's amazing ecosystem while on a kayak tour with this environmentally sensitive operator. If you want to go it alone, rent a kayak for half a day or up to a week. ⊠ *Hope Town* ☎ *242/366–0398* ⊕ *www.abacoeco.com.*

Brendal's Dive Center. Whether you're looking for a close encounter with a shark, a dolphin, or a turtle, this dive operator has a tour designed just for you, plus they offer scuba courses, island-hopping adventures, and sunset cruises. ⊠ *New Plymouth* ☎ *242/365–4411,* ⊕ *www.brendal.com.*

Froggies Out Island Adventures. Take a day trip to one of the Bahamas' protected national parks, or, on a Sunday, catch a ride to the infamous Nippers pig roast on neighboring Guana Cay. This operator offers a variety of snorkeling and scuba combination tours and also certifies divers. ⊠ *Hope Town* ☎ *242/366–0431* ⊕ *www.froggiesabaco.com.*

WINDSURFING

Abaco Beach Resort. Small sailboats and sea kayaks are available free of charge to hotel and marina guests at the Abaco Beach Resort. ⊠ *Marsh Harbour* ☎ *242/367–2158* ⊕ *www.abacobeachresort.com.*

TREASURE CAY

Twenty miles north of Marsh Harbour is Treasure Cay, technically not an island but a large peninsula connected to Great Abaco by a narrow spit of land. This was once the site of the first Loyalist settlement in Abaco, called Carleton.

While Treasure Cay is a large-scale real-estate development project, it's also a wonderful small community where expatriate residents share the laid-back, sun-and-sea vibe with longtime locals. The development's centerpiece is the Treasure Cay Hotel Resort and Marina, with its Dick Wilson–designed golf course and a 150-slip marina that has boat rentals, a dive shop, pool, restaurant, and lively bar. Treasure Cay's commercial center consists of two rows of shops near the resort as well as a post office, self-service laundries, restaurants, a couple of well-stocked

Treasure Cay Beach is one of the most beautiful beaches on Great Abaco Island.

grocery stores, and BTC, the Bahamian telephone company. You'll also find car-, scooter-, and bicycle-rental offices here.

EXPLORING

Carleton Settlement Ruins. Tucked away toward the northwestern end of the Treasure Cay development are the ruins of the very first settlement in Abaco, founded by the Loyalists that left the Carolinas during the American Revolutionary War. The sight is not well marked, but ask a local for directions. ⊠ *Treasure Cay.*

Treasure Cay Blue Hole. You'll need a car or at least a bicycle to visit this natural wonder, but it's worth the trek. Scientists believe the Treasure Cay Blue Hole is 200 feet deep, but feel free to dip your toes into the crystal clear blue waters or make a splash swinging from one of the rope swings tied to surrounding pine trees. The water is both salt and fresh and there is no known marine life in the blue hole. ⊠ *Off S.C. Bootle Hwy.* ✛ *Turn left off S.C. Bootle Hwy. just before entrance to Green Turtle Cay Ferry Dock. Take wide dirt road about 2½ miles and follow narrow dirt road at left 500 ft to blue hole.*

BEACHES

FAMILY
Fodor's Choice
★

Treasure Cay Beach. This beach is world famous for its expanse of truly powderlike sand and breathtaking turquoise water. In front of the handful of hotels lining the beach are bar and grill spots with a couple of shade-bearing huts. The rest of the beach is clear from development, since the land is privately owned, and almost clear of footprints. With a top-notch marina across the road and lunch a short stroll away, you have luxury; a walk farther down the beach gives you a quiet escape.

Amenities: food and drink; parking (no fee); toilets; water sports. **Best for:** sunrise; sunset; swimming; walking. ✉ *Treasure Cay.*

WHERE TO EAT

$ BAKERY Fodor's Choice ★ 🍴 **Café La Florence.** Stop off at this bakery-café in the Treasure Cay resort's main shopping strip for just-made muffins and the best cinnamon rolls in the universe. There's no sign, but you'll know you've found it by the smell of those fresh-baked treats and the line of people waiting to indulge. Or go for a light lunch of lobster quiche, conch chowder, or a spicy, Jamaican-style meat patty. Anglers can order picnic lunches to go. You can also arrange for the chef to cater private dinners of lobster, steak, and the like in your rented condo or cottage. [$] *Average main: $10* ✉ *Treasure Cay* ☎ *242/365–8185* 💳 *No credit cards* 🕒 *No lunch, dinner Sun.*

$ BAHAMIAN FAMILY 🍴 **Coco Beach Bar.** Enjoy the stunning scenery of one of the world's top-rated beaches while enjoying lunch or a cocktail at this casual, laid-back spot. Sit at the bar or on the open deck, or, for the best views, enjoy your meal under one of the thatched shades right on the beach. Eggs, done pretty much any way, and fluffy pancakes are popular for breakfast. A Bahamian dinner is served complete with a beach bonfire Tuesday nights during the high season. [$] *Average main: $15* ✉ *Treasure Cay* ☎ *242/365–8470* 🌐 *www.treasurecay.com* 💳 *No credit cards* 🕒 *No dinner Wed.–Mon.*

$$$ BAHAMIAN 🍴 **Spinnaker Restaurant and Lounge.** Ceramic-tiled floors, rattan furniture, and floral-print tablecloths accent this large resort restaurant—250 guests fit in the air-conditioned main dining area and the adjacent screened-in outdoor patio—and bar at the Treasure Cay Marina. Dinner boasts an international flair and each night there's a special theme: Sunday is Italian Pasta Night; Monday and Saturday choose from prime rib, duck, lamb, steaks, and lobster on the Deluxe menu; Wednesday is Caribbean Delights; and Friday is the popular Bahamian Buffet. Even with reservations you often have to wait, but you can relax in the lounge and enjoy an array of cocktails and frozen rum drinks. [$] *Average main: $35* ✉ *Treasure Cay Marina* ☎ *242/365–8801* 🌐 *www.treasurecay.com* 🕒 *No lunch.*

$$ BAHAMIAN 🍴 **Touch of Class.** Ten minutes north of Treasure Cay Resort, this locals'-favorite, no-frills restaurant serves traditional Bahamian dishes such as grilled freshly caught grouper and minced local lobster stewed with tomatoes, onions, and spices. Reasonably priced appetizers, such as conch chowder and conch fritters, and a full bar make this a nice option for a night out. Be sure to save room for their homemade banana or coconut cream pies. Free shuttle service is available from the parking lot in front of the Treasure Cay Marina. [$] *Average main: $28* ✉ *Queen's Hwy. at Treasure Cay Rd.* ☎ *242/365–8195* 🕒 *No lunch.*

$$$ BAHAMIAN Fodor's Choice ★ 🍴 **Treasure Sands Club.** Be sure to make a reservation for a Friday or Saturday night dinner especially during the season, as this recent addition to the Treasure Cay dining scene draws locals and snowbirds from all over the Abacos. If it's not too cool, the sides are up and you're right on the world-famous Treasure Cay Beach. A large pool surrounded by lounge chairs and a sound system give this spot a very South Beach vibe. For lunch, enjoy a lobster club or top the already decadent TSC

Premium Burger with fried lobster and avocado. For dinner, select from the pastas, seafood, duck, lamb, short ribs, or steak Diane. Finish it up with a Grand Marnier souflé and an "adult" coffee. Sunday brunch is a mix of Continental, American, and Bahamian classics. [$] *Average main: $35* ✉ *Treasure Cay* ☎ *242/365–9385* 🌐 *www.treasuresandsclub.com.*

WHERE TO STAY

$$ HOTEL Fodor's Choice ★ 🏨 **Bahama Beach Club.** Ideal for families and small groups, these two- to four-bedroom condos are right on the famous Treasure Cay beach. **Pros:** luxury accommodations on one of the most sublime beaches in the world; large pool area with Jacuzzi; walking distance to the marina, restaurants, and shops. **Cons:** check-in can be slow; housekeeping is separate cost. [$] *Rooms from: $250* ✉ *Treasure Cay* ☎ *800/284–0382, 242/365–8500* 🌐 *www.bahamabeachclub.com* 🛏 *87 condos* 🍴 *No meals.*

$ HOTEL FAMILY 🏨 **Treasure Cay Hotel Resort & Marina.** Treasure Cay is known for its 18-hole golf course, one of the few open to the public in Abaco; its first-class 150-slip marina; and its location across the street from one of the most beautiful beaches in the world. **Pros:** most convenient location in Treasure Cay; multiple on-site restaurants and bar; Dick Wilson championship golf course. **Cons:** restaurant reservations essential in high season; pool area can get crowded with boat people and happy-hour patrons at the Tipsy Seagull Bar; rooms need updating. [$] *Rooms from: $130* ✉ *Treasure Cay Marina* ☎ *242/365–8801, 800/327–1584* 🌐 *www.treasurecay.com* 🛏 *32 suites, 32 town houses* 🍴 *Breakfast.*

NIGHTLIFE

Tipsy Seagull. This outside bar and grill is a fun happy-hour spot. There's usually live music on the weekend and Thursday night's Pizza Night is a big hit with locals and visitors alike. ✉ *Treasure Cay Marina* ☎ *242/365–8814* 🌐 *www.treasurecay.com.*

SHOPPING

Fodor's Choice ★ **Abaco Ceramics.** Near Treasure Cay Resort is Abaco Ceramics, which offers its signature white-clay pottery with a variety of designs. The Royal fish pattern remains a favorite. ✉ *Treasure Cay* ☎ *242/365–8489* 🌐 *www.abacoceramics.com* 🕒 *Closed weekends.*

SPORTS AND THE OUTDOORS

BIKING

Wendell's Bicycle Rentals. Rent mountain bikes by the half day, day, or week. ✉ *Treasure Cay* ☎ *242/365–8687.*

BOATING

Treasure Cay marina has 150 slips and can accommodate large yachts. It's a great base for jaunting to outer uninhabited cays for day fishing or diving trips, or to Green Turtle Cay.

Contacts J.I.C. Boat Rentals. ✉ *Treasure Cay* ☎ *242/365–8582* 🌐 *www.jicboatrentals.com.*

FISHING

Justin Sands. Reservations are a must to fish with Justin Sands, the Abacos' two-time bonefishing champ. ✉ *Marsh Harbour* ☎ *242/367–3526* 🌐 *www.bahamasvacationguide.com/justfish.html.*

O'Donald Macintosh. Top professional bonefishing guide O'Donald Macintosh meets clients each day at the Treasure Cay Marina for full or half days of guided bonefishing in the northern Marls or outside Coopers Town. In more than 20 years of guiding, O'D has built up a large loyal base of repeat clients, so you'll need to book him well in advance—especially in the prime months of April, May, and June. ⊠ *Treasure Cay* ☎ *242/365–0126.*

Treasure Cay Hotel Resort & Marina. Arrange for local deep-sea fishing or bonefishing guides through Treasure Cay Hotel Resort & Marina. ⊠ *Treasure Cay* ☎ *242/365–8250* ⊕ *www.treasurecay.com/fishing.*

GOLF

Treasure Cay Hotel Resort & Marina. A half mile from the Treasure Cay Hotel Resort & Marina is the property's par-72, Dick Wilson–designed course, with carts available. There's no need to reserve tee times, and the course is usually delightfully uncrowded—ideal for a leisurely round. A driving range, putting green, and small pro shop are also on-site. ⊠ *Treasure Cay* ☎ *242/365–8045* ⊕ *www.treasurecay.com/golf* ⊠ *$85–$105* ⅃. *18 holes, 6985 yards, par 72.*

SCUBA DIVING AND SNORKELING

No Name Cay, Whale Cay, and the **Fowl Cay Preserve** are popular marine-life sites. The 1865 wreck of the steamship freighter *San Jacinto* also affords scenic diving and a chance to feed the resident green moray eel.

Treasure Divers. In the Treasure Cay Marina, Treasure Divers rents scuba and snorkeling equipment and takes divers and snorkelers out to a variety of sites. ⊠ *Treasure Cay* ☎ *242/365–8571* ⊕ *www.treasure-divers. com.*

TENNIS

Treasure Cay Hotel Resort & Marina. The tennis courts here are six of the best courts in the Abacos, four of which are lighted for night play. Make your reservations at the resort reception desk. ⊠ *Treasure Cay* ☎ *242/577–6779* ⊕ *www.treasurecaytennis.org* ⊠ *$25 per hr* ☉ *Daily 7 am–8 pm.*

WINDSURFING

Treasure Cay Hotel Resort & Marina. Windsurfers and a complete line of nonmotorized watercraft are available for rent at the Treasure Cay Hotel Resort & Marina. ⊠ *Treasure Cay* ☎ *242/365–8250* ⊕ *www. treasurecay.com.*

SOUTH OF MARSH HARBOUR

Thirty minutes south of Marsh Harbour, the small, eclectic artists' colony of **Little Harbour** was settled by the Johnston family more than 50 years ago. Randolph Johnston moved his family here to escape the consumerist, hectic lifestyle he felt in the United States and to pursue a simple life where he and his wife could focus on their art. The family is well known for their bronze sculptures, some commissioned nationally.

Just to the south of Little Harbour is the seaside settlement of **Cherokee Sound,** home to fewer than 100 families. Most of the residents make their living catching crawfish or working in the growing tourism industry; many lead offshore fishing and bonefishing expeditions. The deserted Atlantic beaches and serene salt marshes in this area are breathtaking, and though development at Winding Bay and Little Harbour are progressing, the slow-paced, tranquil feel of daily life here hasn't changed. **Schooner Bay** is a new, by-design village just a bit farther south. Initially intended as a living, breathing community, it has turned into more of a second home and vacation destination, but it maintains that quaint island village feel. **Sandy Point,** a "takin' it easy, mon" fishing village with miles of beckoning beaches and a couple of bonefishing lodges, is slightly more than 50 miles southwest of Marsh Harbour, about a 40-minute drive from Cherokee.

EXPLORING

Abaco Club on Winding Bay. Twenty-five minutes south of Marsh Harbour this glamorous private golf and sporting club is set on 534 acres of stunning oceanfront property. The clubhouse, restaurant, and pool, which sit on 65-foot-high white limestone bluffs, offer guests and members a mesmerizing view of the purple-blue Atlantic Ocean, and the bay has more than 2 miles of sugar-sand beaches. Amenities and activities at the club include an 18-hole tropical links golf course, a luxurious European-style spa and fitness center, scuba diving, snorkeling, tennis, bonefishing, and offshore fishing. This is a private club whose members have bought property; nonmembers can stay in the hotel-style cabanas and cottages and use all facilities one time while evaluating membership and real-estate options. ✉ *Cherokee Sound turnoff, Cherokee Sound* ☎ *242/366–3820, 800/593–8613* ⊕ *www.theabacoclub.com.*

Abaco National Park. The Abaco National Park was established in 1994 as a sanctuary for the endangered Abaco parrot, of which there are fewer than 3,000. Many other birds call the park home, including the Bahama yellowthroat and pine warbler.

A 15-mile dirt track passes through the 20,500 protected acres, ending at the Hole-in-the-Wall lighthouse, a starkly beautiful and desolate location overlooking the ocean. The drive from the paved highway all the way to the lighthouse takes about 1½ hours, and can only be done in a 4x4 vehicle. The lighthouse is technically not open to visitors, but people still do climb the rickety stairs to the top where views of the island and the sea are mesmerizing. ✉ *South end of Great Abaco* ✛ *The turn-off for the park is just before you make the final turn on the main road leading to Sandy Point* ☎ *242/367–6310 Bahamas National Trust Abaco Office* ⊕ *www.bnt.bs/_m1731/The-National-Parks-of-The-Bahamas.*

Hole-in-the-Wall. Off the Great Abaco Highway at the turn in the road that takes you to Sandy Point, a rugged, single-lane dirt track leads you to this navigational lighthouse that stands on Great Abaco's southern tip. The lighthouse was constructed in 1838 against local opposition from islanders who depended on salvaging shipwrecks for their livelihood. Over the years the lighthouse has survived sabotage and hurricanes, and was automated in 1995 to continue serving maritime interests. The Bahamas Marine Mammal Research Organisation has leased the site to monitor whale movements and conduct other ocean studies. ✉ *South of Sandy Point.*

Fodor's Choice ★ **Johnston Studios Art Gallery and Foundry.** Sculptor Pete Johnston and his sons and acolytes cast magnificent lifelike bronze figures using the age-old lost-wax method at the only bronze foundry in the Bahamas. You can purchase the art in the gallery. Tours are available by appointment for $50 per person. ⊠ *Little Harbour* 🕾 *242/577–5487* ⊕ *www.petespubandgallery.com* ⊠ *$50 for tours.*

Sawmill Sink Blue Hole. A half-hour drive south of Marsh Harbour is a crudely marked electric pole directing you to turn right onto an old logging trail. A short drive down this road takes you to an incredible blue hole. It was featured by *National Geographic* in 2010 for the fossils found deep within it. Though you cannot dive this hole, you can swim in it. ⊠ *Great Abaco Hwy.*

4

BEACHES

Pelican Cay Beach. In a protected park, this is a great spot for snorkeling and diving on nearby Sandy Cay reef. The cay is small and between two ocean cuts, so the water drops off quickly but its location is also what nurtures the beach's pure white sand. If you get restless, ruins of an old house are hidden in overgrowth at the top of the cay, and offer fantastic views of the park. **Amenities:** none. **Best for:** snorkeling. ⊠ *8 miles north of Cherokee Sound, Cherokee Sound.*

Sandy Point Beach. If shelling and solitude are your thing, venture 50 miles southwest of Marsh Harbour to the sleepy fishing village of Sandy Point. Large shells wash up on the sandy beaches, making it great for a stroll and shelling. The best spot for picking up one of nature's souvenirs is between the picnic site and Rocky Point. Well offshore is the private island Castaway Cay, where Disney Cruise Line guests spend a day. **Amenities:** none. **Best for:** solitude; walking. ⊠ *Sandy Point.*

WHERE TO EAT

$$ BAHAMIAN **Fodor's Choice** ★ ✗ **Pete's Pub.** Next door to Pete's Gallery is an outdoor tiki-hut restaurant and bar where you can wiggle your toes in the sand while you chow down on fresh seafood, burgers, and cold tropical drinks. Try the mango-glazed grouper, lemon-pepper mahimahi, or coconut cracked conch while you kick back and enjoy the view of the harbor. If you want to be part of the local scene, don't miss the wild-pig roasts, which happen whenever big events take place. It's a long drive, so in the slow season, it's best to call ahead to make sure they're open. ⓢ *Average main: $20* 🕾 *242/577–5487* ⊕ *www.petespubandgallery.com.*

WHERE TO STAY

$$$$ B&B/INN **Fodor's Choice** ★ 🏨 **Black Fly Lodge.** Make your reservations well in advance if you want to stay at what has very quickly become one of the most popular bonefishing lodges around. **Pros:** world-class fishing lodge; excellent meals; lovely location. **Cons:** often booked far in advance; near, but not on the beach; not much for nonfishing guests to do. ⓢ *Rooms from: $870* ⊠ *Bay St., Schooner Bay Village* 🕾 *242/376–0321* ⊕ *www.blackflylodge.com* ⊘ *Closed mid Aug.–early Sept. and Christmas eve until just after New Year's* 🔁 *10 rooms* ⦿ *All-inclusive.*

$$$$ B&B/INN Fodor's Choice ★ 🏨 **Delphi Club.** Although Delphi Club is billed as a bonefishing lodge, it really is a great middle-of-nowhere bed-and-breakfast perfect for anyone looking to get away from it all but not willing to give up on style and comfort. **Pros:** private and secluded; great bonefishing; situated on a beautiful private beach. **Cons:** very remote; lots of stairs. [$] *Rooms from: $1130* ✣ *Leaving Marsh Harbour, head south 24 miles along Great Abaco Hwy; turn left when you see a large white rock on the right-hand side, and follow the signs to the Delphi Club along the unpaved road.* ☎ *242/366–2222* 🌐 *www.delphi-bahamas.com* 🛏 *8 rooms.*

$$$$ B&B/INN 🏨 **Rickmon Bonefish Lodge.** Well-regarded fishing guide Ricardo Burrows operates this comfortable waterside lodge at the end of the road in Sandy Point. **Pros:** perfect location for bonefishing; some of the best professional fly-fishing guides in the Abacos; comfortable for nonfishing companions. **Cons:** average restaurant; intermittent Internet; 3-night min. [$] *Rooms from: $650* ✉ *Sandy Point* ☎ *800/628–1447* 🌐 *www.angleradventures.com/rickmon* 💳 *No credit cards* 🛏 *11 rooms* 🍴 *All-inclusive.*

$$ B&B/INN Fodor's Choice ★ 🏨 **Sandpiper Inn.** With harbor views, luxuriously decorated rooms and suites, and the only restaurant and swimming pool in Schooner Bay right downstairs, this quaint bed-and-breakfast inn is the perfect spot for visitors who want to be taken care of. **Pros:** personalized service; only public pool in area; small and intimate. **Cons:** ongoing construction; no organized activites; limited dining options. [$] *Rooms from: $250* ✉ *Schooner Bay Village* ☎ *242/376–9858* 🌐 *www.sandpiperabaco.com* 🛏 *4 rooms, 3 suites.*

$$$$ RENTAL FAMILY 🏨 **Schooner Bay.** Most of the homes and cottages in this designer community are available for rent. **Pros:** homes are completely turnkey; a selection of beaches; sense of community. **Cons:** no organized activities; just one full restaurant in the village; long way from other communities. [$] *Rooms from: $425* ✉ *Schooner Bay Village* ☎ *242/366–2048* 🌐 *schoonerbaybahamas.com* 🛏 *19 homes* 🍴 *No meals.*

SHOPPING

Johnston Studios Art Gallery. The gallery displays original bronzes by the Johnstons, as well as unique gold jewelry, prints, and gifts. ✉ *Little Harbour* ☎ *242/577–5487* 🌐 *www.petespubandgallery.com.*

SPORTS AND THE OUTDOORS

TOURS

Destination Schooner Bay. There is so much to see and do in southern Abaco—particularly for nature buffs and fitness enthusiasts. The problem is that the area is so undeveloped and off the beaten path it's hard for a visitor to head out alone. DSB has curated a selection of tours with a range of difficulty levels to ensure you can truly explore this pristine part of the island. Explore blue holes, kayak through mangroves, visit untouched beaches, or ride bikes through the forest. If you don't see an itinerary that suits your needs, customize your own. All excursions are led by top local guides and range from two to six hours and can accommodate two to six people. ✉ *Schooner Bay Village* ☎ *242/376–9858* 🌐 *www.dsbbahamas.com.*

ELBOW CAY

Five-mile-long Elbow Cay's main attraction is the charming village of **Hope Town**. The saltbox cottages—painted in bright colors—with their white picket fences, flowering gardens, and porches and sills decorated with conch shells, will remind you of a New England seaside community, Bahamian style. Most of the 300-odd residents' families have lived here for several generations, in some cases as many as 10. For an interesting walking or bicycling tour of Hope Town, follow the two narrow lanes that circle the village and harbor. (Most of the village is closed to motor vehicles.)

Although modern conveniences like high-speed Internet and satellite TV are becoming more common, they are a relatively new development. In fact, most residents remember the day the island first got telephone service—back in 1988. Before that, everyone called each other the way many still do here and in the other Out Islands: by VHF, the party line for boaters. If you are boating, want to communicate with the locals, or would like to make a dinner reservation on one of the cays, you should carry a VHF radio and have it tuned to channel 16.

GETTING HERE AND AROUND

FERRY TRAVEL Elbow Cay is 4 miles southeast of Marsh Harbour. Every day except Sunday and holidays, **Albury's Ferry Service** (☎ *242/367–0290* ⊕ *www. alburysferry.com*) leaves Marsh Harbour for the 20-minute ride to Hope Town at 7:15, 9, 10:30, 12:15 (unavailable August-October), 2, 4, and 5:45; ferries make the return trip at 8, 9:45, 11:30 (unavailable August–October), 1:30, 3, 4, 5, and 6:30. A same-day round-trip costs $27. One-way tickets cost $17. Children 6–11 are half price and under age 5 free.

GOLF CART TRAVEL Once in Hope Town you can walk everywhere. In fact, only local work vehicles are permitted through town. To visit other areas you can rent a bicycle or a golf cart.

Contacts Hope Town Cart Rentals. ⊠ *Hope Town* ☎ *242/366–0064* ⊕ *www. hopetowncartrentals.com.* **Island Cart Rentals.** ⊠ *Hope Town* ☎ *242/366–0448* ⊕ *www.islandcartrentals.com.* **T&N Cart Rentals.** ⊠ *Hope Town* ☎ *242/366– 0069* ⊕ *www.tandncarts.com.*

EXPLORING

Hope Town Lighthouse. Upon arrival in Hope Town Harbour you'll first see a much-photographed Bahamas landmark, an 89-foot-tall, peppermint-stripe lighthouse built in 1838. The light's construction was delayed for several years by acts of vandalism; then-residents feared it would end their profitable wrecking practice. Today the lighthouse is the last hand-turned, kerosene-fueled beacon in operation. Monday through Saturday from 9 to 5 and Sunday from 10 to 2 you can climb up the spiral staircase to the top for a superb view of the sea and the nearby cays. There are 101 steps in all and there is no graceful way for an adult to crawl through the small door onto the viewing platform that goes all the way around the top. The lighthouse keepers and their families live in the small cottages at its base, so keep noise to a minimum as one of them is resting up for his nonstop night shift. There's no road between the lighthouse and the town proper. You can use your own boat to cross the harbor or catch a ride on the ferry before it leaves to go back to Marsh Harbour, but if you take a ferry it probably won't be back for at least an hour. 🎟 *Free*

Wyannie Malone Historical Museum. This volunteer-run museum houses Hope Town memorabilia and photographs. Exhibits highlight Lucayan and pirate artifacts found on the island. Many descendants of Mrs. Malone, who settled here with her children in 1875, still live on Elbow Cay. ✉ *Queen's Hwy., Hope Town* ☎ *242/366–0293* 🌐 *www.hopetownmuseum.com* 🎟 *$5 adults, $2 children* 🕒 *Nov.–Aug., Mon.–Sat. 10–4.*

BEACHES

Tahiti Beach. This small beach at the southern tip of Elbow Cay is a popular boater's stop. The soft white sand is well protected from the close ocean cut by thick vegetation, a few barrier cays, and shallow water. This shallow area is popular for shelling, and of course simply relaxing and watching the tide rise. At low tide, the true beauty of this beach is revealed when a long sand spit emerges, perfect for picnics. It's great for young children, as the water on one side of the spit is ankle deep, stays calm, and remains warm. During peak season the beach can become a bit crowded. **Amenities:** none. **Best for:** surfing; swimming.

WHERE TO EAT

$$$
BAHAMIAN
Fodor's Choice ★

🍴 **Abaco Inn Restaurant.** Set in the country-club-style main lodge splashed with lively Bahamian colors and floor-to-ceiling windows that provide an incredible view of the ocean, the restaurant serves breakfast, lunch, and dinner to guests and visitors in classic island style. Fresh-baked bread, fruit, and egg dishes are breakfast highlights. But where the restaurant really shines is in its servings of the freshest seafood on the island. At lunch, sample the grilled grouper or spicy cracked conch. For dinner, grilled wahoo, hog snapper, or mahimahi can be prepared to your liking. There's also crawfish in season-blackened, grilled, fried, or coconut fried, as well as escargot. When you make your reservation, ask for a table on the enclosed patio overlooking the ocean. [$] *Average main: $38* ✉ *2 miles south of Hope Town, Hope Town* ☎ *242/366–-0133* 🌐 *www.abacoinn.com.*

$$
CARIBBEAN

🍴 **Bridget's Rum Bar.** Catch the Hope Town Inn & Marina's free boat shuttle from any of the docks across the harbor in Hope Town and pull up a chair under the open octagonal restaurant or hop in and place your order at the swim-up bar. The Caribbean-inspired menu features lots of seafood for lunch and dinner as well as some fun twists on Bahamian staples like the Bahamian cheese sticks—fried macaroni and cheese. The chili lime mussels are drowned in local beer and the crunchy Parmesan lobster is a top seller. [$] *Average main: $30* ✉ *Across the harbor, Hope Town* ☎ *242/366–0003* 🌐 *www.hopetownmarina.com.*

$
BAHAMIAN

🍴 **Cap'n Jack's Restaurant and Bar.** There are a handful of booths and a small rowdy bar, but most of this casual eatery's seating is out on the pink-and-white-striped dock–patio. Locals, boat people, and land-based tourists gather here every day for value-priced eats and drinks. The menu is nothing fancy, but provides reliable grouper burgers, pork chops, fresh fish catch-of-the-day, and cracked conch. When it's in season, there's sometimes a lobster special. Cap'n Jack's serves three meals a day, offers a full bar, and has live music Friday nights and a DJ Wednesday and Saturday nights. There are nightly drink specials and a different event each night, from trivia to bingo and a Saturday-morning mimosa special. [$] *Average main: $17* ✉ *Hope Town* ☎ *242/366–0247* 🌐 *www.capnjackshopetown.com* ⏲ *Closed Sun. and mid-Aug.–Sept.*

$$ BAHAMIAN Fodor's Choice ★ 🍴 **Firefly Bar & Grill.** Ask anyone in the Abacos where you must eat during your stay and there's a good chance this is it. Whether you pull in by golf cart or tie up by boat, it's worth the trip. Owned by the developers of Firefly Vodkas, this bar carries the full line along with the Mo-Tea-To, their take on the mojito, and the Fly Swatter, a delicious mixture that's a closely guarded secret. Seafood is their speciality and the extensive menu makes choosing just one dish a challenge. Locals travel from throughout the Abaco island chain to enjoy lunch or dinner here and catch one of the best views of the Sea of Abaco. [$] *Average main: $30* ✉ *Hope Town* ☎ *242/366–0145* 🌐 *www.fireflysunsetresort.com* 💳 *No credit cards* ⏲ *Closed Wed.*

$$$ BAHAMIAN 🍴 **Great Harbour Room.** While casual attire is fine, this restaurant overlooking the harbor feels like an upscale establishment with dimmed lighting, quiet music, and especially attentive service. Start off with a creamy white conch chowder. From there it's anything from lamb chops, lobster, duck breast, or even the Seafood Supreme—a medley of sautéed lobster, shrimp, and scallops in a white- wine-cream-and-Parmesan sauce. The wine list is one of the most extensive on the island and Prime Rib Sunday is a special treat that requires a reservation. [$] *Average main: $34* ✉ *Upper Rd., Hope Town* ☎ *242/366–0095* 🌐 *www.hopetownlodge.com* ⏲ *No lunch.*

$$ BAHAMIAN 🍴 **Harbour's Edge.** Hope Town's happening hangout for locals and tourists, this bar and restaurant's deck is the best place to watch the goings-on in the busy harbor; you can tie your boat up right in front. The bar opens at 10 am, so kick back and have an icy Kalik or the Scattered Shower or Dark & Stormy cocktail concoctions. For lunch, try the tender conch burgers, white caps, or lobster salad. For dinner, the fresh grilled seafood and pasta dishes are some of the best in the islands. A band plays on Thursday and Saturday nights during high season. [$] *Average main: $25* ✉ *Lower Rd., Hope Town* ☎ *242/366–0087* 🌐 *www.harboursedge.net* ⏲ *Closed Tues.*

$ BAKERY 🍴 **Hope Town Coffee House.** Overlooking Hope Town Harbour, this upscale coffeehouse, bakery, boutique, and hot-spot café features coffees roasted right in the historic settlement, the first roastery in the Bahamas. It's a must for java drinks, smoothies, homemade pastries and gelato, quiches, and tapas-size savories. If you're headed out in a boat for the day, grab a shake and salad or pasta to go. [$] *Average main: $10* ✉ *Queen's Hwy., Hope Town* ☎ *242/366–0760* 🌐 *hopetowncoffeehouse.com* ⏲ *Closed Sun. and late-Aug.–early-Nov.*

4

$ BAHAMIAN 🍴 **On Da Beach Bar and Grill.** Burgers, grilled kebabs, sandwiches, conch, fish, and icy rum drinks are served up with a terrific Atlantic view at this open-air bar and grill perched high on the beach dunes across the road from the small Turtle Hill resort. It closes at sunset because all seating is open to the elements, and a gully washer of a storm can shut the place down. Go in your bathing suit and enjoy the beach and snorkeling right out front. [$] *Average main: $15* ✉ *Queens Hwy. between Hope Town and White Sound, Hope Town* ☎ *242/366–0557* 🌐 *www.turtlehill.com* 🕑 *Closed Mon.* ✍ *Reservations not accepted.*

$ BAHAMIAN 🍴 **The Reef Bar & Grill.** Pull up a chair by the pool or on the open-air deck overlooking the beach and enjoy salads, burgers, and wraps all served up with signature dressings and sauces like Pineapple Ginger Aioli, Creamy Caribbean Petal Dressing, and Guava BBQ Sauce. Try a classic Bahamian Chicken or Conch in a Bag—fried and served with french fries and smothered in ketchup and hot sauce. Breakfast is as light or hearty as you want it. Sunday brunch features a number of different takes on classic eggs Benedict along with complimentary mimosas. [$] *Average main: $15* ✉ *Hope Town Harbour Lodge, Hope Town* ☎ *242/366–0095* 🌐 *www.hopetownlodge.com* 💳 *No credit cards.*

$ DELI 🍴 **Sugar Shack.** This cute shack is an ice-cream parlor (14 flavors!), deli, and T-shirt shop all tied into one. Located at the end of Hope Town, it's a worthwhile walk or ride for a cool treat or a fresh sandwich. Unique gift items such as Bahama Bee pepper jelly are available, too. [$] *Average main: $7* ✉ *Centerline Rd., White Sound, Hope Town* ☎ *242/366–0788* 🕑 *Closed Aug. and Sept. No dinner Sun.*

WHERE TO STAY

PRIVATE VILLA RENTALS

Elbow Cay Properties. Besides being the most cost-efficient way for a family to stay a week or longer on Elbow Cay, a private house or villa is also likely to be the most comfortable. This long-standing rental agency handles a variety of properties, from cozy two-bedroom, one-bath cottages to a six-bedroom, six-bath villa better described as a mansion. Many of the rental homes are on the water, with a dock or a sandy beach right out front. The owners are set on finding you a place to match your wishes and budget and can arrange any extra services—from boat rental to a personal chef or yoga classes. There are no Sunday check-ins, as the agency is closed, and a three-night minimum is required most weeks; a full week is required during peak holiday seasons. ✉ *Western Harborfront, Hope Town* ☎ *242/366–0569* 🌐 *www.elbowcayrentals.com.*

Hope Town Hideaways. This property-management company rents more than 75 private cottages and houses, including spectacular beachfront retreats at Tahiti Beach on the south end of the cay. Most of these units sleep four or more, and some of the more upscale properties can accurately be described as mansions. The management can also arrange for everything from kayak, boat, and golf-cart rentals to island excursions and fishing guides. All rentals have a four-night minimum stay. ✉ *Hope Town* ☎ *242/366–0224* 🌐 *www.hopetown.com.*

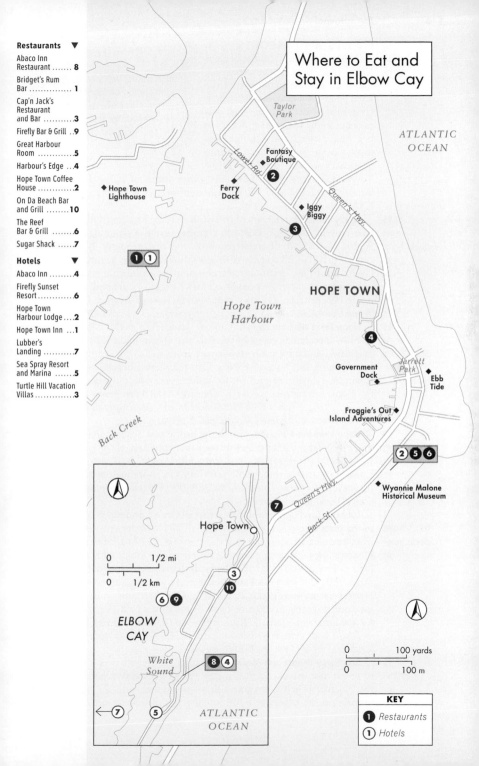

Where to Eat and Stay in Elbow Cay

Taylor Park

ATLANTIC OCEAN

Fantasy Boutique

Ferry Dock

Iggy Biggy

♦ Hope Town Lighthouse

HOPE TOWN

Hope Town Harbour

Back Creek

Government Dock

Jarrett Park

Ebb Tide

Froggie's Out Island Adventures

Wyannie Malone Historical Museum

Queen's Hwy.

Back St.

Hope Town

ELBOW CAY

White Sound

0   1/2 mi
0   1/2 km

ATLANTIC OCEAN

0   100 yards
0   100 m

KEY

① *Restaurants*

① *Hotels*

HOTELS AND RESORTS

$$ | **HOTEL** — ⊞ **Abaco Inn.** The motto here is "Tan your toes in the Abacos," making this beachfront resort the ideal place for a getaway. **Pros:** self-contained resort with the best restaurant on the island; easy access to beaches, surfing, and fishing; hypnotic ocean views. **Cons:** 10-min golf-cart or boat ride to Hope Town. $ *Rooms from: $210* ✉ *2 miles south of Hope Town, Hope Town* ☎ *242/366–0133* ⊕ *www.abacoinn.com* ⤵ *12 rooms, 8 suites* ⦿| *No meals.*

> **SURFS UP, DUDE!**
>
> Though it's not well known, there is good surfing off Elbow Cay. If you want to wake up to the waves, stay at the Abaco Inn or at the Sea Spray Resort, or rent a house at Tahiti Beach.

$$$$ | **HOTEL** | **Fodor's**Choice ★ — ⊞ **Firefly Sunset Resort.** Each of these fully equipped, beautifully appointed two-, three-, and four-bedroom cottages boasts a stunning view of the Sea of Abaco and all are situated on the vast property in a way that creates privacy and a sense of true exclusivity. **Pros:** beautiful settings; large, beautifully decorated accommodations; fantastic restaurant on-site. **Cons:** golf cart or boat is a must for getting around; small man-made beach; three-day stay required. $ *Rooms from: $406* ✉ *Hope Town* ☎ *242/366–0145* ⊕ *www.fireflysunsetresort.com* ⤵ *7 cottages.*

$$ | **HOTEL** | **Fodor's**Choice ★ — ⊞ **Hope Town Harbour Lodge.** You can have it all at this casually classy resort—spectacular views of the Atlantic Ocean and the beach, quality amenities, and a location steps away from the town and harbor. **Pros:** best lodging location on Elbow Cay for views, beach, and access to town; casual patio restaurant for lunch overlooking the ocean; romantic. **Cons:** Internet access can be sporadic. $ *Rooms from: $235* ✉ *Upper Rd., Hope Town* ☎ *242/366–0095* ⊕ *www.hopetownlodge.com* ⤵ *12 rooms, 6 cabanas, 6 cottages, 1 private house.*

$$ | **RESORT** | **Fodor's**Choice ★ — ⊞ **Hope Town Inn & Marina.** Watch the hustle and bustle (relatively speaking, of course) of Hope Town from this spot across the harbor. **Pros:** complimentary shuttle to and from Hopetown; removed from town. **Cons:** across the harbor from everything else; not much to do. $ *Rooms from: $220* ✉ *Hope Town* ☎ *242/366–0003* ⊕ *www.hopetownmarina. com* ⤵ *6 rooms, 3 suites.*

$ | **HOTEL** | **Fodor's**Choice ★ — ⊞ **Lubber's Landing.** You'll come to Lubber's Landing as a guest, and more than likely leave as a friend of the owners Austin and Amy. They're quick to point out that their little piece of paradise on Lubber's Quarters Cay is not for everyone, but if you're looking for something a little different, and like rustic but still demand creature comforts, then this is the place for you. **Pros:** peace and quiet; on-site owners cater to your every need; as green as possible. **Cons:** remote; must rent a boat for your stay; you need to be back by sundown or make arrangements for a shuttle/water taxi. $ *Rooms from: $195* ✉ *Lubber's Quarters Cay* ⊹ *5-min boat ride from Elbow Cay* ☎ *242/577–2000* ⊕ *www.lubbers landing.com* ⤵ *3 rooms* ⦿| *No meals.*

$ | **RESORT** — ⊞ **Sea Spray Resort and Marina.** Consider this resort if you're planning to catch any waves, or you just want to get away from it all. **Pros:** the Atlantic beach is on one side of the resort, and the leeward-side marina on the other; self-contained relaxing retreat near the Abaco

Tahiti Beach on Elbow Cay is a family favorite.

Inn; full-service marina for boaters and guests. **Cons:** restaurant food is just OK; 10-minute golf-cart or boat ride to Hope Town. $ *Rooms from: $164* ✉ *South end of White Sound, Hope Town* ☎ *242/366–0065* ⊕ *www.seasprayresort.com* ⤳ *7 villas.*

$$$
HOTEL

⌗ **Turtle Hill Vacation Villas.** Bougainvillea- and hibiscus-lined walkways encircle the central swimming pools of this cluster of six one- and two-bedroom villas, each with its own private patio. **Pros:** comfortable accommodations for families and small groups; steps away from the beach. **Cons:** you have to golf cart out to restaurants for dinner if you don't want to cook in; extra charge for daily maid service; two night minimum. $ *Rooms from: $380* ✉ *Off Queens Hwy. between Hope Town and White Sound, Hope Town* ☎ *242/366–0557* ⊕ *www. turtlehill.com* ⤳ *6 villas.*

NIGHTLIFE

Cap'n Jack's. Each evening Cap'n Jack's offers a different event, including bingo and trivia, along with drink specials. After 9 pm on Wednesday there is DJ music. This is a popular spot for young adults. ✉ *Hope Town* ☎ *242/366–0247* ⊕ *www.capnjackshopetown.com* ☾ *Closed Sun. and mid Aug.–Sept.*

Harbour's Edge. After 9 pm every Saturday, Harbour's Edge has local bands playing Bahamian and reggae music. They also play Thursday nights during peak seasons. This is a favorite spot for locals. ✉ *Lower Rd., Hope Town* ☎ *242/366–0087* ⊕ *www.harboursedge.net* ☾ *Closed Tues.*

Sea Spray Resort. Local bands perform here quite frequently. This is a popular stop where locals and visitors can mingle and dance to classic rock-and-roll and Bahamian tunes. ⊠ *South end of White Sound, Hope Town* ☎ *242/366–0065* ⊕ *www.seasprayresort.com.*

Wine Down and Sip Sip. Featuring a selection of 50 properly cellared wines, Wine Down and Sip Sip is a classy hangout with a high-end liquor bar, draft beer, and weekly flights and pairings. The aura is sophisticated, and complimented by a lend-and-exchange selection of books. ⊠ *Queen's Hwy., Hope Town* ☎ *242/366–0399.*

SHOPPING

Da Crazy Crab. Here you can find a nice selection of souvenirs, beach wraps, T-shirts, arts and crafts, and Cuban cigars. ⊠ *Front Rd., Hope Town* ☎ *242/366–0537.*

Ebbtide. This shop is on the upper-path road in a renovated Loyalist home. Come here for such Bahamian gifts as batik clothes, original driftwood carvings and prints, and nautical jewelry. Browse through the extensive Bahamian book collection. ⊠ *Hope Town* ☎ *242/366–0088.*

Hummingbird Cottage Art Centre. This quaint gallery, located in a fully restored, century-old home, showcases the works of local artists and offers monthly art workshops overlooking the stunning ocean out back. ⊠ *Hope Town* ☎ *242/366–0272* ⊕ *www.hopetownart.com.*

Iggy Biggy. This is the only shop in Hope Town that carries the lovely Abaco ceramics handmade in Treasure Cay. It also sells home decorations, handmade dishware and glasses, wind chimes, sandals, resort wear, jewelry, and island music. ⊠ *Front Rd., Hope Town* ☎ *242/366–0354.*

SPORTS AND THE OUTDOORS

BOATING

Hope Town Hideaways. Hope Town Hideaways has 12 slips, mostly used for guests staying in its rental cottages and houses. Call well in advance to reserve yours. ⊠ *Hope Town* ☎ *242/366–0224.*

Lighthouse Marina. This marina situated at the base of the Hope Town Lighthouse is relatively small—with just six transient slips that accommodate vessels up to 60 feet, but it has all the expected amenities as well as a few more. There's laundry, fuel, bait and tackle, as well as a nice gift shop and an on-site liquor store. ⊠ *Hope Town* ☎ *242/366–0154* ⊕ *www.htlighthousemarina.com.*

Sea Spray Resort and Marina. This full-service marina has 60 slips accommodating vessels up to 120 feet and all the amenities in a very well protected area. Sail and powerboat rentals are available. ⊠ *Hope Town* ☎ *242/366–0065* ⊕ *www.seasprayresort.com.*

BOAT RENTALS

Island Marine. Island Marine rents 17- to 27-foot boats ideal for exploring the Abaco cays. It's closed early August to early October. ⊠ *Hope Town* ☎ *242/366–0282* ⊕ *www.islandmarine.com.*

Sea Horse Boat Rentals. Captain one of the Albury brothers' boats, which are handcrafted in nearby Man O'War Cay as you explore the islands. Sea Horse also has other makes ranging from 17 feet up to a 26-foot Paramount that can seat up to 10 people. ✉ *Hope Town* ☎ *242/366–0023* ⊕ *www.seahorseboatrentals.com.*

FISHING

A Salt Weapon. This company offers deep-sea-fishing charters at the best price in Hope Town. ✉ *Hope Town* ☎ *242/366–0245* ⊕ *www.asaltweaponcharters.com.*

Local Boy. Deep-sea charters are available with Local Boy Justin Russell—an eighth-generation Bahamian who has been fishing these waters for more than 20 years. ✉ *Hope Town* ☎ *242/366–0528* ⊕ *www.hopetownfishing.com.*

Maitland Lowe. Book well in advance to have "Bonefish Dundee" Maitland Lowe guide you around Snake Cay or Little Harbour. ✉ *Hope Town* ☎ *242/366–0234* ⊕ *www.wildpigeoncharters.com.*

Seagull Charters. This charter company sets up guided deep-sea excursions with Captain Robert Lowe, who has more than 35 years' experience in local waters. ✉ *Hope Town* ☎ *242/366–0266* ⊕ *www.seagullcottages.com/fishing.*

KAYAKING

Abaco Eco. This company offers kayaking tours and rentals of the local area and Snake Cay. ✉ *Hope Town* ☎ *242/475–9616* ⊕ *www.abacoeco.com.*

Froggies Out Island Adventures. Froggies has snorkel and dive trips, scuba and resort courses, full-day adventure tours, island excursions, and dolphin encounters. You can also rent snorkeling and diving gear to venture out on your own. Professional and friendly service has earned Froggies many repeat customers. You need to book your excursions as far in advance as possible. ✉ *Hope Town* ☎ *242/366–0431* ⊕ *www.froggiesabaco.com.*

PADDLEBOARDING

Abaco Paddle Board. Rent a paddle- or surfboard by the hour or by the day or go on a guided nature tour. If you're new to the sports, sign up for private lessons or the three-day surf clinic. ✉ *Hope Town* ☎ *242/475–0954, 242/366–3125* ⊕ *www.abacopaddleboard.com.*

MAN-O-WAR CAY

Fewer than 300 people live on skinny, 2½-mile-long Man-O-War Cay, many of them descendants of early Loyalist settlers who started the tradition of handcrafting boats more than two centuries ago. These residents remain proud of their heritage and continue to build their famous fiberglass boats today. The island is secluded, and the old-fashioned, family-oriented roots show in the local policy toward liquor: it isn't sold anywhere on the island. (But most folks won't mind if you bring your own.) Three churches, a one-room schoolhouse, several boutique shops, small grocery stores, and just one restaurant round out the tiny island's offerings.

A mile north of the island you can dive to the wreck of the USS *Adirondack,* which sank after hitting a reef in 1862. It lies among a host of cannons in 20 feet of water.

GETTING HERE AND AROUND

FERRY TRAVEL Man-O-War Cay is an easy 20-minute ride from Marsh Harbour by water taxi or aboard a small rented outboard runabout. The island has a 28-slip marina. No cars are allowed on the island, but you'll have no problem walking it, or you can rent a golf cart. The two main roads, Queen's Highway and Sea Road, run parallel.

EXPLORING

Hero's Wall. Outside the public library is a wall adorned with plaques honoring residents who have helped to develop the community over the years. Notice that most of them share the same last name, as is often the case in small island communities. In this case, Albury and Sweeting are the most common names. ✉ *Ballfield Rd. and Queen's Hwy.*

Man-O-War Heritage Museum. Historic artifacts from the boatbuilding industry are on display in this small museum. Built in the 1800s, the quaint white wooden building is the former "Church Corner House" commissioned by the patriarch of one of the island's best-known boatbuilding families. ✉ *Queen's Hwy. and Pappy Ben Hill* 🎟 *Free* ⏲ *Thurs. and Sat. 11–1.*

WHERE TO EAT

$ BAHAMIAN 🍴 **Dock & Dine.** The only full-fare restaurant on the island sits on a covered deck overlooking the sheltered harbor. The nautical decor makes for a nice place to eat and enjoy. No liquor is served on this dry island. Food is basic Bahamian and American style with everything from salads to burgers and wraps. Try their twist on a local favorite: "chicken in da bag" is fried chicken served on a pile of fries, doused in ketchup and hot sauce, and wrapped up in foil and a paper bag to soak up the grease. [$] *Average main: $18* ✉ *Waterfront, Sea Rd.* ☎ *242/365–6380* 💳 *No credit cards.*

WHERE TO STAY

Waterways Boat and Cottage Rentals. With no hotels on the island, the only way to stay in this quaint settlement is to rent a condo or a home. Available accommodations range from a tiny dockside cottage at the entrance to the sheltered harbor to Loyalist-era houses nestled among the locals to newly constructed beachfront homes that sleep 10 comfortably and offer all the amenities of home. Most require a week's rental agreement. The company also rents boats and golf carts. ✉ *Sea Rd. and Pappy Ben Hill* ☎ *242/365–6143, 242/357–6540* 🌐 *www.waterwaysrentals.com* 🛏 *18 homes.*

SHOPPING

Albury's Sail Shop. This shop is popular with boaters, who stock up on duffel bags, briefcases, hats, and purses, all made from duck, a colorful, sturdy canvas fabric traditionally used for sails. ✉ *Lover's La. at Sea Rd.* ☎ *242/365–6014.*

Joe's Studio. This store sells paintings by local artists, books, clothing, and other nautically oriented gifts, but the most interesting souvenirs are the half models of sailing dinghies. These mahogany models, which are cut in half and mounted on boards, are meant to be displayed as wall hangings. Artist Joe Albury, one of the store's owners, also crafts full, 3-D boat models. ✉ *Sea Rd.* ☎ *242/365–6082* ⊕ *www.joesstudio abaco.com.*

Sally's Seaside Boutique. Ladies sit in the back of this small shop and sew Bahamian-made Androsia fabric into original shirts, dresses, blouses, and linens for the home. You can also pick up a locally made wooden handicraft or book about the Abacos. ✉ *Sea Rd.* ☎ *242/365–6044.*

SPORTS AND THE OUTDOORS

BOATING

Man-O-War Marina. This marina has 28 slips and also rents golf carts. For people coming from Marsh Harbour or other cays, the Albury Ferry dock is adjacent. ✉ *Front Rd.* ☎ *242/365–6008* ⊕ *www.manowar marina.com.*

SCUBA DIVING

DiveTime. Learn to scuba dive in some of the most beautiful waters around. Seasoned divers can join one of the daily two-tank dives, rent equipment, or book a private charter for a maximum of six divers. Half-day snorkeling trips are also available. ☎ *242/365–6235* ⊕ *www. divetimeabaco.com.*

GREAT GUANA CAY

The essence of Great Guana Cay can be summed up by its unofficial motto, painted on a hand-lettered sign: "It's better in the Bahamas, but it's gooder in Guana." This sliver of an islet just off Great Abaco, accessible by ferry from Marsh Harbour or by private boat, is the kind of place people picture when they dream of running off to disappear on an exotic island, complete with alluring deserted beaches and grassy dunes. Only 100 full-time residents live on 7-mile-long Great Guana Cay, where you're more likely to run into a rooster than a car during your stroll around the tranquil village. Still, there are just enough luxuries here to make your stay comfortable, including a couple of small, laid-back resorts and a restaurant–bar with one of the best party scenes in the Abacos. The island also has easy access to bonefishing flats you can explore on your own.

Nippers Beach Bar & Grill is the best restaurant on Great Guana Cay.

GETTING HERE AND AROUND

The ferry to Great Guana Cay leaves from the Conch Inn Marina in Marsh Harbour. The ride is about 30 minutes. Golf carts are available for rent in Great Guana Cay, though most places are within walking distance.

WHERE TO EAT

$$ BAHAMIAN 🍴 **Kidd's Cove Seafood Bar & Grill.** Perch on a bar stool around the tiki bar or take a seat on one of the rocking chairs on the porch and enjoy the comings and goings of Guana Cay's harbor and main road. While they boast the "conchiest" conch fritters around, it's the sushi that keeps folks coming back. The seasonal fresh lobster dinners and lobster salad are worth the trip. [$] *Average main: $20* ✉ *Front St.* ☎ *242/475–3701.*

$$ BAHAMIAN Fodor's Choice ★ 🍴 **Nippers Beach Bar & Grill.** With awesome ocean views and a snorkeling reef just 10 yards off its perfect beach, this cool bar and restaurant is a must-visit hangout. Linger over a lunch of burgers and sandwiches or a dinner of steak and lobster, then chill out in the two-tiered pool. Nurse a "Nipper Tripper"—a frozen concoction of five rums and two juices. If you down more than one or two of these, you'll be happy to take advantage of the Nippermobile, which provides free transport to and from the cay's public dock. Every Sunday, everybody who is anybody, or not, revels in the all-day party disguised as a pig roast. [$] *Average main: $30* ☎ *242/365–5111* 🌐 *www.nippersbar.com.*

$$ BAHAMIAN 🍴 **Sunsetters.** Sit indoors to soak up the cool air-conditioning or outdoors on the open deck overlooking the Sea of Abaco while enjoying a cool beverage and enjoying some of the best Bahamian food available on

island. The conch and fresh fish are always a hit, and Thursday night's wings special is only beat by the one pound of ribs for $10 on Saturday nights. [$] *Average main: $30* ✉ *Orchid Bay Yacht Club* ☎ *242/365–5175* ⏲ *Closed Mon.* ✍ *Reservations not accepted.*

WHERE TO STAY

$$ 🏨 **Flip Flops on the Beach.** Reserve one of the four one- or two-bedroom
HOTEL beachside bungalows at this casually elegant boutique resort and you can melt into the island lifestyle of sun, sand, serenity, and ocean breezes on arrival. **Pros:** beachfront location; the essence of tranquillity; quality accommodations and in-room amenities. **Cons:** remote location means there is no nightlife, shopping, or larger resort-style activities; no Internet. [$] *Rooms from: $220* ☎ *800/222–2646, 242/365–5137* 🌐 *www.flipflopsonthebeach.com* ⏲ *Closed mid-Aug.–mid-Oct.* 🛏 *4 bungalows* 🍴 *No meals.*

4

NIGHTLIFE

Grabbers Bar and Grill. This is a popular local spot on weekend nights. There's music and the Guana Grabber, a potent frozen drink designed to lighten any mood. ☎ *242/365–5133* 🌐 *www.grabbersatsunset.com.*

SHOPPING

Gone Conchin'. Pick up some island-appropriate outfits for your vacation in this small yellow store right at the foot of the ferry dock. They also sell sea-glass jewelry and other trinkets. It's the only place in Abaco that carries the full range of Bahama Handprints clothing. ☎ *242/365–5215* ⏲ *Daily 10–4.*

SPORTS AND THE OUTDOORS

BOATING

Baker's Bay Golf & Ocean Club. At the northwestern end of the island, Baker's Bay Golf & Ocean Club has 158 slips. ☎ *242/557–0635* 🌐 *www.bakersbayclub.com.*

Orchid Bay Yacht Club and Marina. Orchid Bay Yacht Club and Marina has 66 deepwater slips and full services for boaters at the entrance to the main settlement bay, across from the public docks. The club office rents luxury apartments, cottages, and homes, and prime real estate is for sale. There's also a swimming pool and a restaurant that serves fresh seafood, steaks, and healthy salads on an outdoor deck overlooking the marina. ☎ *242/365–5175.*

SCUBA DIVING

Dive Guana. This dive shop organizes scuba and snorkeling trips and island-hopping boat tours. The shop also rents boats, kayaks, and bicycles. Renting a boat, at least for a day, is the best way to get around and enjoy other nearby cays. ☎ *242/365–5178* 🌐 *www.diveguana.com.*

GREEN TURTLE CAY

This tiny 3-mile-by-½-mile island is steeped in Loyalist history; some residents can trace their heritage back more than 200 years. Dotted with ancestral New England–style cottage homes, the cay is surrounded by several deep bays, sounds, bonefish flats, and irresistible beaches. **New Plymouth**, first settled in 1783, is Green Turtle's main community. Many of its approximately 550 residents earn a living by diving for conch or selling lobster and fish. There are a few grocery and hardware stores, several gift shops, a post office, a bank, a handful of restaurants, and several offices.

GETTING HERE AND AROUND

FERRY TRAVEL Many hotels provide an occasional shuttle from the main ferry dock in Green Turtle Cay to their property, and there are a couple of taxis on the island. Most people travel via golf cart or boat. Don't worry, you won't miss having a car; even in the slowest golf cart you can get from one end of the island to the other in 20 minutes or less.

The **Green Turtle Cay Ferry** (☎ 242/365–4166) leaves the Treasure Cay airport dock at 8:30, 10:30, 11:30, 1:30, 2:30, 3:30, 4:30, and 5, and returns from Green Turtle Cay at 8, 9, 11, 12:15, 1:30, 3, and 4:30. The trip takes 10 minutes, and one-way fares are $12, same-day round-trip fare is $16. The ferry makes several stops in Green Turtle, including New Plymouth, the Green Turtle Club, and the Bluff House Beach Hotel.

GOLF CART   **Contacts KoolKart Rentals.** ⊠ *New Plymouth* ☎ *242/356–4176* ⊕ *www.*
TRAVEL   *koolkartrentals.com.*

EXPLORING

Albert Lowe Museum. New Plymouth's most frequently visited attraction is the Bahamas' oldest historical museum, dedicated to a model-ship builder and direct descendant of the island's original European-American settlers. You can learn island history through local memorabilia from the 1700s, Lowe's model schooners, and old photographs, including one of the aftermath of the 1932 hurricane that nearly flattened New Plymouth. One of the galleries displays paintings of typical Out Island scenes by acclaimed artist Alton Lowe, Albert's son. Christopher Farrington, the museum's curator, enjoys showing visitors around and sharing stories of life in the Out Islands before the days of high-speed Internet and daily airline flights. ⊠ *Parliament St., New Plymouth* ☎ *242/365–4094* 🎟 *$5 adults, $3 children* ☉ *Mon.–Sat. 9–11:45 and 1–4.*

Memorial Sculpture Garden. The past is present in this garden across the street from the New Plymouth Inn. (Note that it's laid out in the pattern of the British flag.) Immortalized in busts perched on pedestals are local residents who have made important contributions to the Bahamas. Plaques detail the accomplishments of British Loyalists, their descendants, and the descendants of those brought as slaves, such as Jeanne I. Thompson, a contemporary playwright and the country's second woman to practice law. This is an open garden, free to the public. ⊠ *Parliament St., New Plymouth.*

WHERE TO EAT

$$ ✕ **Ballyhoo Bar & Grill.** This casual eatery on the water in the Bluff House
AMERICAN Marina offers tasty meals. Sitting under an umbrella on the deck is the best way to enjoy the view of the sailboat-filled harbor, but you can also eat in the air-conditioned pub-style dining room. Menu choices range from standard Bahamian (conch fritters and burgers) to new American (roasted pork tenderloin with salsa, salads with goat cheese and roasted vegetables). Another fun option is to enjoy a rum drink from the bar while catching some rays at the pool. $ *Average main: $25* ⊠ *Between Abaco Sea and White Sound, at Bluff House Beach Hotel Marina, New Plymouth* ☎ *242/365–4200* ⊕ *www.bluffhouse.com.*

$$ ✕ **Green Turtle Club Dining.** Breakfast and lunch are served harborside on
EUROPEAN a covered, screened-in patio, while dinner takes place in the elegant din-
Fodor's Choice ing room. At lunch, treat yourself to a lobster salad, lobster corn chow-
★ der, cheeseburger, or grilled grouper sandwich. Dinner is where the club really shines, transporting you back to the 1920s with elegant dining beneath antique chandeliers. The steaks are among the best around. The jumbo lobster and artichoke ravioli, Coconut Curry Seafood Hotpot, and Stone Crab Souffle are just some of the temptations on the extensive menu. For dessert, try the guava crème brûlée. For those who prefer a casual environment, an à la carte dinner menu is available outside on the enclosed patio. $ *Average main: $30* ⊠ *Green Turtle Club, north end of White Sound, New Plymouth* ☎ *242/365–4271* ⊕ *www.green turtleclub.com* ☾ *Closed mid-Sept.–Oct.*

$$ ✕ **Harvey's Island Grill.** Sit inside and enjoy the cool air-conditioning, or
BAHAMIAN grab one of the brightly painted blue and pink picnic tables on the har-
borside beach across the street to enjoy your lunch or dinner. The menu is a simple mix of American and Bahamian fare. Monday's pizza night is popular as is the Friday-night fish fry. On a hot day, grab a daiquiri or a scoop of homemade coconut or mango ice cream from the stand out-
side. $ *Average main: $20* ⊠ *Bay St., New Plymouth* ☎ *242/365–4389* ▭ *No credit cards.*

$$ ✕ **Lizard Bar & Grill.** Dine poolside overlooking the Leeward Yacht Club
BAHAMIAN marina at this casual bar and grill. The grilled lobster or fresh catch (which can be jerked, blackened, grilled, or fried) are popular menu choices as are the conch burger and conch fritters. Wash it all down with a potent Leaning Lizard. $ *Average main: $20* ⊠ *Leeward Yacht Club, New Plymouth* ☎ *242/365–4191* ⊕ *www.leewardyachtclub.com.*

$$ ✕ **McIntosh Restaurant and Bakery.** At this simple, diner-style restaurant,
BAHAMIAN lunch means excellent renditions of local favorites, such as fried grouper and cracked conch, and sandwiches made with thick slices of slightly sweet Bahamian bread. At dinner, large portions of pork chops, lobster, fish, and shrimp are served with rib-sticking sides like baked macaroni and cheese, peas 'n' rice, and coleslaw. Save room for a piece of rum cake or key lime pie, baked fresh daily and displayed in the glass case up front. Breakfast is also served. $ *Average main: $20* ⊠ *Parliament St., New Plymouth* ☎ *242/365–4625.*

4

$$ BAHAMIAN 🍴 **Pineapples Bar & Grill.** Hang out, take a dip in the saltwater pool, and enjoy Bahamian fare with a flair. In Black Sound, at the entrance to the Other Shore Club and Marina, you'll find this simple open-air restaurant with a canopy-shaded bar and picnic tables next to the pool. Some of the best conch fritters in the islands are served from 11 am on. At lunch, try a fresh salad or spicy jerk chicken; for dinner, grilled daily-caught fish. The jerk-spiced grouper is sensational. Specialty drinks include a Pineapple Smash and a Yellowbird, both capable of mellowing your mood. Piña coladas here are world famous. [$] *Average main: $20* ✉ *Black Sound, New Plymouth* ☎ *242/365–4039* 🌐 *www.othershoreclub.com.*

$ BAHAMIAN 🍴 **The Wrecking Tree.** The wooden deck at this casual restaurant was built around the wrecking tree, a place where 19th-century wrecking vessels brought their salvage. Today it's a cool place to linger over a cold Kalik and a hearty lunch of cracked conch, fish-and-chips, or zesty conch salad. It has great pastries, too—take some back to your hotel. Dinner is served Friday and Saturday, more frequently during "the season." [$] *Average main: $16* ✉ *Bay St., New Plymouth* ☎ *242/365–4263* 🌐 *www.wreckingtree* ⏲ *Closed Sun. Dinner served in the busy season only.*

WHERE TO STAY

PRIVATE VILLA RENTALS

Island Property Management. A five-bedroom, oceanfront mansion with wraparound veranda, full-time staff, and a marble fireplace could be yours. Or rent a two-bedroom cottage in the heart of New Plymouth. This agency has more than 50 cottages and houses for rent to meet different budgets and needs. It can also help arrange excursions and boat and golf-cart rentals. Most homes have water views, and some have docks for your rental boat. The offices in New Plymouth are in a blue two-story building along with Green Turtle Real Estate, just down from the ferry dock. ✉ *Various Green Turtle Cay locations, New Plymouth* ☎ *242/365–4047, 888/405–6054 reservations* 🌐 *www.abacoislandrentals.com.*

HOTELS AND RESORTS

$$ RESORT 🏨 **Bluff House Beach Resort & Marina.** Newly constructed, but full of old-world charm, the first stage of this property's restoration includes eight beautifully appointed suites overlooking the Sea of Abaco. **Pros:** secluded and private; great views; beautiful decor. **Cons:** golf cart or boat required to get into New Plymouth; lots of steps up to all suites. [$] *Rooms from: $250* ✉ *New Plymouth* ☎ *242/365–4247* 🌐 *www.bluffhouse.com* 🛏 *8 rooms* 🍽 *No meals.*

$$ RENTAL 🏨 **Coco Bay Cottages.** Sandwiched between one beach on the Atlantic and another calmer, sandy stretch on the bay are six spacious cottages—including two three-bedroom cottages and a four-bedroom cottage—that all have views of the water. **Pros:** spacious, well-located do-it-yourself accommodations; awesome beaches; Wi-Fi for those who can't totally get away. **Cons:** renting a boat and/or golf cart is essential; if you don't like silence, the peace and quiet will kill you. [$] *Rooms*

from: $250 ✉ *Coco Bay, north of Green Turtle Club, New Plymouth* ☎ *561/202–8149, 800/752–0166* 🌐 *www.cocobaycottages.com* 🛏 *6 cottages* 🍴 *No meals.*

$$ RESORT 🏨 **Green Turtle Club.** The long-standing colonial tradition and tone of casual refinement continues at this well-known resort. **Pros:** excellent on-site restaurants for casual or fine dining; easy access to great beaches; personalized service. **Cons:** if you're looking for Bahamian casual, this isn't it; golf cart or boat is essential to explore the island. [$] *Rooms from: $239* ✉ *North end of White Sound, New Plymouth* ☎ *242/365–4271, 866/528–0539* 🌐 *www.greenturtleclub.com* 🕓 *Closed Labor Day–Oct.* 🛏 *24 rooms, 2 suites, 8 villas.*

$$ RENTAL 🏨 **Linton's Beach and Harbour Cottages.** These three classic Bahamian-style cottages are ideally placed on 22 private acres between Long Bay and Black Sound. **Pros:** well-located do-it-yourself cottages; value priced for families and groups. **Cons:** gathering groceries and supplies can be an adventure; some beach cottages don't have phones or TV. [$] *Rooms from: $230* ✉ *S. Loyalist Rd., Black Sound, New Plymouth* ☎ *772/538–4680* 🌐 *www.lintoncottages.com* 🛏 *3 cottages* 🍴 *No meals.*

4

NIGHTLIFE

Gully Roosters. At night, Green Turtle can be deader than dead or surprisingly lively. Bet on the latter if the local favorites, the Gully Roosters, are playing anywhere on the island. Known locally as just the Roosters, this reggae-calypso band is the most popular in the Abacos. Its mix of original tunes and covers can coax even the most reluctant reveler onto the dance floor. The band's schedule is erratic, but they play every Wednesday at 9 pm under the Buttonwood tree at the **Green Turtle Club** during the high season.

Fodor's Choice ★ **Miss Emily's Blue Bee Bar.** Other nighttime options include a visit to Miss Emily's Blue Bee Bar, where you might find a singing, carousing crowd knocking back the world-famous Goombay Smash. (Or not—many Goombay novices underestimate the drink's potency, and end up making it an early night.) Mrs. Emily Cooper, creator of the popular Goombay Smash drink, passed away in 1997, but her daughter Violet continues to serve up the famous rum, pineapple juice, and apricot brandy concoction. The actual recipe is top secret, and in spite of many imitators throughout the islands, you'll never taste a Goombay this good anywhere else. It's worth a special trip to try one. ✉ *Parliament St., New Plymouth* ☎ *242/365–4181.*

Pineapples Bar & Grill. On the water in front of the Other Shore Club and Marina, this bar has a hopping happy hour from 4 to 6 daily and live music every Friday at 8. ✉ *Brooklyn Rd.* ☎ *242/365–4039* 🌐 *www.othershoreclub.com.*

Sundowner's. Locals hang out at Sundowner's, a waterside sports bar and grill where attractions include a pool table, lots of big-screen TVs, and, on weekend nights, a DJ spinning dance music on the deck under the stars. ✉ *New Plymouth* ☎ *242/365–4060.*

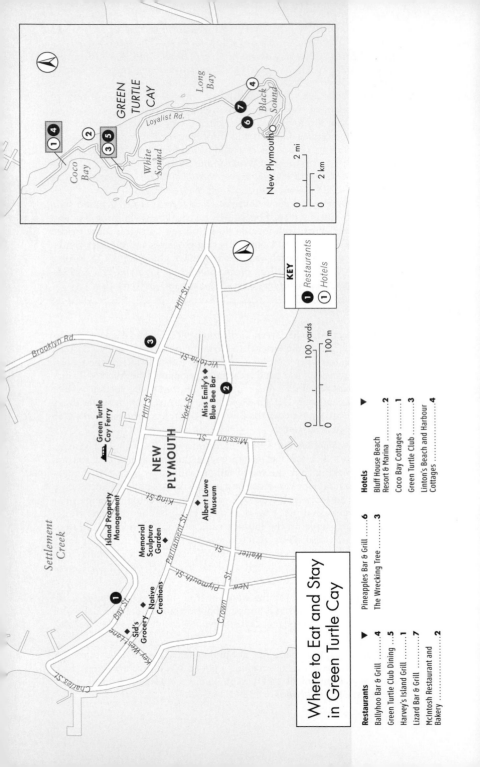

Where to Eat and Stay
in Green Turtle Cay

Restaurants

▶

Ballyhoo Bar & Grill	.....**4**
Green Turtle Club Dining	...**5**
Harvey's Island Grill	.....**1**
Lizard Bar & Grill	.......**7**
McIntosh Restaurant and Bakery	...............**2**
Pineapples Bar & Grill	......**6**
The Wrecking Tree	.........**3**

Hotels

▶

Bluff House Beach Resort & Marina	............**2**
Coco Bay Cottages	.......**1**
Green Turtle Club	.........**3**
Linton's Beach and Harbour Cottages	...............**4**

GREEN TURTLE CAY

Long Bay

Loyalist Rd.

Coco Bay

White Sound

Black Sound

New Plymouth

0   2 mi
0   2 km

KEY

①	*Restaurants*
①	*Hotels*

Brooklyn Rd.

Settlement Creek

Green Turtle Cay Ferry

NEW PLYMOUTH

Island Property Management

Memorial Sculpture Garden

Native Creations

Sid's Grocery

Albert Lowe Museum

Miss Emily's Blue Bee Bar

Hill St.

Victoria St.

York St.

Mission St.

King St.

Parliament St.

Plymouth St.

Crown St.

New St.

Waller St.

Bay St.

Key West Lane

Charles St.

0   100 yards
0   100 m

SHOPPING

Native Creations. This is one of the only places to get a bolt of fabric or clothing made from the bright and whimsical Androsia fabrics. The shop also sells beaded jewelry, local artwork, picture frames, locally made candles, postcards, and books. ⊠ *Parliament St., New Plymouth* ☎ *242/365–4206.*

Plymouth Rock Liquors and Café. This shop sells Cuban cigars and more than 60 kinds of rum. ⊠ *Parliament St., New Plymouth* ☎ *242/365–4234.*

Sid's Grocery. Sid's has the most complete line of groceries on the island, plus a gift section that includes books on local Bahamian subjects— great for souvenirs or for replenishing your stock of reading material. ⊠ *Upper Rd., New Plymouth* ☎ *242/365–4055.*

Vert's Model Ship Shop. Stop here to pick up one of Vert Lowe's hand-crafted two-mast schooners or sloops. Model prices range anywhere from $100 to $1,200. If Vert's shop door is locked—and it often is—knock at the white house with bright pink shutters next door. If you're still unsuccessful, inquire at the Green Turtle Club, where Vert worked for more than 30 years. He recently retired, but still builds his model boats. ⊠ *Corner of Bay St. and Gully Alley, New Plymouth* ☎ *242/365–4170.*

SPORTS AND THE OUTDOORS

BOATING

It's highly recommended that you reserve your boat rental at the same time you book your hotel or cottage. If you're unable to rent a boat on Green Turtle Cay, try nearby Treasure Cay or Marsh Harbour.

BOAT RENTALS

Donny's Boat Rentals. The best way to spend your Abaco vacation is by exploring the cays by boat. Rent a 14-, 17-, or 19-foot Whaler, a 20-foot Wellcraft, or a 23-foot Angler for the day or week and find your own deserted beach or island. Bonefishing and deep sea fishing excursions are also offered. ☎ *242/365–4119* ⊕ *www.donnysboatrentalsgtc.com.*

Reef Boat Rentals. A 17-foot Keywest with a bimini top and 90-hp engine is perfect for up to four people, but you can rent boats in varying sizes, all the way up to the 26-foot Panga with 150 hp, which is perfect for shallow seas and accommodates up to eight people comfortably. ☎ *242/365–4145.*

FISHING

Captain Rick Sawyer. The top recommendation on Green Turtle Cay, Captain Rick Sawyer is one of the best guides in the Abacos. Rick's company, Abaco Flyfish Connection and Charters, offers bonefishing on 17-foot Maverick flats skiffs, and reef and offshore fishing aboard his 33-foot Tiara sportfisher. Book as far in advance as you can. ☎ *242/365–4261* ⊕ *www.abacoflyfish.com.*

Ronnie Sawyer. Considered one of the best in the business, Ronnie Saw-yer has been fishing the Abaco flats professionally for more than a quarter century. ☎ *242/365–4070* ⊕ *www.go-abacos.com/ronnie.*

SCUBA DIVING AND SNORKELING

Brendal's Dive Center. This dive center leads snorkeling and scuba trips, plus wild-dolphin encounters, glass-bottom-boat cruises, and more. Personable owner Brendal Stevens has been featured on the Discovery Channel and CNN, and he knows the surrounding reefs so well that he's named some of the groupers, stingrays, and moray eels that you'll have a chance to hand-feed. Trips can include a seafood lunch, grilled on the beach, and complimentary rum punch. Kayak and canoe rentals are available. ☎ 242/365–4411 ⊕ www.brendal.com.

Lincoln Jones. Rent some snorkel gear or bring your own, and call Lincoln Jones, known affectionately as "the Daniel Boone of the Bahamas," for an unforgettable snorkeling adventure. Lincoln will dive for conch and lobster (in season) or catch fish, then grill a sumptuous lunch on a deserted beach. ✉ New Plymouth ☎ 242/365–4223 ⊕ www. go-abacos.com/lincoln.

ANDROS, BIMINI, AND THE BERRY ISLANDS

ANDROS, BIMINI, AND THE BERRY ISLANDS

WELCOME TO ANDROS, BIMINI, AND THE BERRY ISLANDS

TOP REASONS TO GO

★ **Bonefish:** Andros, Bimini, and the Berry Islands have world-class reputations for bonefishing. Hire a guide to show you how to fly-fish, then hunt the bights of Andros or the shallow flats of Bimini and the Berries in pursuit of the elusive "gray ghost."

★ **Casino cruise:** From Miami, catch the Bimini Superfast cruise ship to Resorts World Bimini for gaming, beaching, and a menu of fun shore excursions.

★ **Dive Andros or Bimini:** Go with the diving experts at Small Hope Bay or Kamalame Cay and drop "over the Andros wall" or at Neal Watson's Bimini Scuba Center to explore magnificent wrecks and reefs.

★ **Fish for big game:** Charter a boat and experience the thrill of catching deep-sea prizes such as marlin, mahimahi, tuna, and wahoo.

1 Andros. Incredible blue holes, vibrant reefs (including the third-largest barrier reef in the world), and the Tongue of the Ocean wall make diving and snorkeling some of the main reasons adventurers travel to Andros year-round. Legendary bonefishing in its creeks and bights is the other. The island is mostly flat, lush with pine forests and mangroves, rimmed with white-sand beaches, and laced with miles of creeks and lakes. Explore North and Central Andros by car to see stunning beaches and quaint settlements.

2 Bimini. Year-round, boaters and tourists from Florida cross the Gulf Stream seeking fish and fun. Most visit North Bimini via the Bimini Superfast cruise ship to enjoy Resorts World Bimini with its new Hilton hotel, casino, dining, and fun excursions. Fishing and

yachting fans frequent Alice Town's quaint hotels, bars, and native food shacks. South Bimini, with the islands' only airport and the Bimini Sands Resort & Marina, appeals more to the nature-minded visitor looking for peace, beach, fishing, and diving.

3 The Berry Islands. For the ultimate remote island getaway, fly and stay on the small capital of Great Harbour Cay in the north or on Chub Cay in the south. In between lies a necklace of beautiful island gems accessible only by boat. Both hubs have clubs, affordable villas, and full-service marinas, and both are celebrated for bone-, deep-sea, and bottom-fishing. On every Berry Island, the beaches and reefs are breathtaking.

Great Stirrup
Cay

Great Harbour
Cay

Hoffman's Cay

Berry   Comfort Cay
Islands   Bond's Cay

3

Chub Cay   Whale
Cay

0 ———————— 20 mi
0 ———————— 30 km

Joulters
Cays

Lowe
Sound   Morgan's Bluff
Red Bays

Nicholl's Town

Mastic Point

San
Andros   *Barrier
Reef*

NASSAU

Staniard
Creek

Fresh Creek

Andros Town

*New
Providence I.*

**Andros
Island**

1

Cargill Creek
Behring Point   *Barrier
Reef*

Big Wood
Cay

T o n g u e   o f   t h e   O c e a n

Moxey Town
Lisbon Creek
Yellow Cay   Mangrove   Driggs Hill
Cay   Congo Town
South Bight   The Bluff
Kemps Bay

*Barrier
Reef*

Deep Creek

Mars Bay

G R A N D   B A H A M A   B A N K

Water Cays   Curley Cut
Cays

GETTING
ORIENTED

The northwestern islands of
Andros, Bimini, and Berry
lie just off the east coast of
Florida. Bimini's three main
islands—North, South,
and East Bimini—are only
50 miles from Miami. The
Berry Islands are a 30-cay
chain about 80 miles east of
Bimini. South of the Berries is
Andros, the Bahamas' largest island occupying about
half of all the Bahamas' total
landmass. North and Central
Andros comprise the largest
of the three major islands,
while Mangrove Cay and
South Andros are separated
from it by North, Middle,
and Southern Bight. On
each of these northwestern
islands you'll find magnificent
remote beaches on one side
and vast mangrove estuar-
ies and flats on the other.

5

Updated by
Bob Bower

Legends loom large (and small) on these northwestern Bahamas islands. On Bimini, you'll hear about the lost underwater city of Atlantis, Ernest Hemingway's visits, and the Fountain of Youth. Tiny birdlike creatures known as chickcharnies are said to inhabit the pine forests of Andros Island. On both islands, along with the Berry Islands, bonefishing has made legends of mere men.

Despite the stories, Andros, Bimini, and the Berries remain a secret mostly known to avid divers, boaters, and fishermen. These islands stash their reputation for superlative bonefishing, diving, blue holes, and other natural phenomena away from the glamour of nearby Nassau, just minutes away by plane but a world apart. Historic for its Hemingway lore and deep-sea fishing records, North Bimini has been transformed into a busier island by Resorts World; its casino and new Hilton hotel are fed with hundreds of golf-carting tourists that buy packages on the Bimini Superfast cruise ship. Although Andros is the largest Bahamas island, it is mostly uninhabitable and largely undiscovered. In fact, it offers only three notable resorts and a dozen or so bonefishing lodges. The 30-some cays of the Berry Islands are less known still, in spite of gorgeous, secluded beaches and superb snorkeling and fishing. None of the islands have traffic lights, movie theaters, or fast-food outlets—let alone water parks or shopping centers.

So, with that in mind, plan your trip here as an adventurer. If you're not into diving, snorkeling, fishing, kayaking, hiking, biking, or secluded beach-vegetating, these are not the islands for you. If you are into any of the above, you will be thrilled and endlessly delighted. All three islands are spoken of synonymously with bone-, deep-sea, and bottom-fishing—focused on lobster, grouper, and snapper, and it is this fishing and commercial diving that sustain the economies of many of the smaller settlements. Andros thrives also on its harvest of land crabs, fruit and vegetable crops, and straw work that it exports to Nassau.

PLANNING

WHEN TO GO

Andros, Bimini, and the Berries have a slightly different high season than most of the other Bahamas islands. Because of their close proximity to Florida, boaters make the crossing in droves from spring break through summer, especially to Bimini. Waters tend to be calmest during these months. All the islands and their resorts peak on the various U.S. holidays: Thanksgiving, mid-December through January 5, Easter, and Labor Day. Generally, February to June are busiest months, and rates are higher at these times and during the Christmas season. Fishing and diving are good throughout the year, although cold fronts in winter can cause rough seas. Temperatures usually remain steady enough to enjoy the beaches year-round, but occasionally drop into the 60s. From November to April the cool, breezy, and drier months mean flying insects are minimal. Hurricane season technically runs from June through November; August and September (the most likely months for hurricanes) can be hot and steamy, and many resorts and restaurants are closed.

5

TOP FESTIVALS

WINTER While Resorts World Bimini is large enough to generate its own unique fun events and concerts (check the website) you can go native and catch a mini-version of the Bahamas' popular **Junkanoo festivities** on New Year's Day in North Andros on Nicholl's Town's beachside park, and on Boxing Day and New Year's Day in Bimini where two groups—the Bimini Tum Tum's and Bimini Stompers—parade down Alice Town's main street. The fishing year starts in January or February with the **Great Harbour Cay Wahoo Tournament** in the Berry Islands. The marina there also hosts a **Winter Fest Street Party** at the end of February.

SPRING In Andros, although bonefishing is the name of the game, in April the town of Red Bays in North Andros hosts a **Snapper Tournament**. Mastic Point, near Margan's Bluff in the north, celebrates the settlements' **Homecoming Festival** around Easter while in South Andros, around the same time is the **Back to the Island Festival** in Long Bay's Park, near Congo Town.

SUMMER Calmer waters bring more fishing tournaments including the **Percy Darville Bottom Fishing Tournament** in early July and the **Lobster Fest & Lion Fish Derby** in early August in Great Harbour Cay. Homecomings are village reunions sometimes combined with native sloop regattas that attract home-born locals from other islands. The biggest regatta is the **All Andros & Berry Islands Regatta** held near July 10 (around the Independence Holiday) at Morgan's Bluff, North Andros. The main homecomings are in Alice Town, in Mangrove Cay (in May with the Mother's Day Regatta) and in Kemp's Bay, South Andros (early June). South Andros also holds a **Seafood Festival** in late August. Dates vary so check with your island's tourist office or website. In Andros, however, nothing is bigger than the **All Andros Crab Fest**, held the second week of June, where you can eat crab cooked 20 (or 100?) different ways. Festivities last two or three days with an atmosphere filled with music from the nations top Rake 'n' Scrape bands, cultural shows, parties, and crab-catching displays. Other festivals held on most islands include the Ministry of Tourism's **Junkanoo Summer Festival**—a series of Saturday nights in June or July—and the festivities held around Independence Day, July 10.

The largest fishing event in these islands is the popular **Bimini Big Game Club Wahoo Smackdown Tournament** in mid-November. In South Andros, in early October is the delicious **Conch Festival** held way down south in Mars Bay, and then, in early November, held in Pleasant Bay village, 3 miles north of the Slavery Wall, is **South Andros's Coconut Festival**—also a tasty festival. Keeping with the food theme, before Thanksgiving, the Ministry of Tourism puts on a **HarvestFest and People-to-People Festival** at the Lighthouse Yacht Club & Marina, in Fresh Creek, Central Andros. This big bash features an Androsia fabrics fashion show, live bands, Junkanoo mini-parade "rush-outs," an arts-and-crafts show, a seafood-and-produce marketplace, fun for the kids, and, of course, lots of food and drink. Expats, snowbirds and, anyone else are invited. Expect to see workers from the U.S. Navy's huge submarine testing base (AUTEC) just south of Fresh Creek.

GETTING HERE AND AROUND
AIR TRAVEL
From the United States, all the islands are served with direct scheduled flights out of Fort Lauderdale; Bimini through SkyBahamas, and Silver Airways which code-shares with United Airlines and JetBlue. Great Harbour Cay is served from Fort Lauderdale by Watermakers Air and Tropic Ocean Airways, and Watermakers also flies to three Andros airports four days a week. For convenience and timing, groups flying in from south Florida should consider chartering a private plane. From Nassau, you can reach Bimini via SkyBahamas, and fly to Great Harbour Cay and four Andros airports via LeAir, Western Air, Glen Air, and Flamingo Air. Choose your Andros airport carefully or you could face a costly taxi ride. Note that you can't drive from North/Central Andros to South Andros or Mangrove Cay: you have to fly back to Nassau. For ultimate fun, charter a private jet, seaplane, or helicopter from Nassau or Florida. Safari Seaplanes flies from Nassau airport, while Miami Seaplane flies from Key Biscayne.

See Travel Smart for airline contact information, or visit your resort's website for more options.

BOAT AND FERRY TRAVEL
For Florida's private boaters, it's just a 50-mile skip to Bimini and another 80 miles to the Berries. Thrice weekly, the entertainment-rich Bimini Superfast cruise ship speeds between Miami and Resorts World on North Bimini. Although the ferry service is aimed primarily at guests of the large Resorts World timeshare complex on Bimini, you can book a one-way trip to avoid paying for a ferry/hotel package for just transportation, with or without a private cabin (port charges are in addition to the fare). Andros, with its daunting barrier reef, is more of a challenge to yachts, yet Fresh Creek Harbour offers a rewarding, tranquil setting and marina. Thrice weekly, Bahamas Ferries offers a three-hour, comfortable ferry with air-conditioning between Fresh Creek and Nassau.

But getting from Nassau to other ports in these islands requires taking a slower local mail boat which, although an authentic experience, is devoid of creature comforts. Owing to weather and breakdowns, mail-boat services are often irregular and can leave you marooned. Check with the Potter's Cay Dockmaster's Office for the latest schedules.

Contacts Potter's Cay Dockmaster's Office. ☎ *242/393–1064* ✉ *curtiscraig220@yahoo.com.*

CAR TRAVEL

While car rentals are best for Andros and Great Harbour Cay in the Berries, golf carts, walking, or hitching a ride (it's safe!) are options on smaller islands. Rentals are done through local micro-enterprises and are often arranged by your hotel or lodge. To have a car or cart ready for your arrival, call in advance. In Bimini, Resorts World runs an hourly tram to Alice Town and offers free buses for getting around the resort.

TAXI TRAVEL

Taxis are readily available to meet incoming scheduled flights and ferries. In Andros, the distances are long and rates can be costly so you may prefer a car rental from the airport—especially if you intend to explore.

HOTELS

In Andros, Bimini, and the Berry Islands, accommodations range from luxurious resorts and rental villas to simpler motel-types and bone-fishing lodges. You'll find luxury in Bimini at Resorts World (with its new Hilton), and in Andros at the stunning Kamalame Cay private island and Tiamo Resort. For casual luxury in the Berries, seek out the Carriearl Boutique Hotel and rental villas around Great Harbour Cay. Central Andros's Small Hope Bay Lodge is much-loved by families and repeat guests, lured by famous bonefishing and scuba diving. Bimini's historic Big Game Club and the quieter, modern Bimini Sands Resort attract bone- and deep-sea fishermen and divers that come to dive with sharks, dolphins, and on famous wrecks. All large resorts have water sports, splendid beaches, and all but one have freshwater pools. Most smaller fishing lodges are ill-suited to activity-needy families and small children. Although most hotel clubhouses have Internet, TVs, and phones, many rooms don't. Also ask about air-conditioning in summer and credit card acceptability.

The highest rates and busiest times vary with each resort, usually occurring around the Thanksgiving, Christmas, and Easter holidays and from February to June. High season is usually February to April, but these islands can also be busy through June.

RESTAURANTS

Dining options range widely between haute cuisine and "down-home" tasty local specialties. For casual sophistication, opt for Kamalame Cay on Andros, Carriearl Restaurant on Great Harbour Cay, and Sabor at Resorts World Bimini. Most others serve Bahamian fare—fresh fish and lobster, grilled chicken, cracked (deep-fried) conch, and BBQ or fried pork with native sides (coleslaw, peas 'n' rice, and mac 'n' cheese). Ask your hotel in advance what place is open when; for dinner, most restaurants require a booking. In the hotter, rainy season, it's best to

5

dine in the cool indoors—away from flies and biting bugs. Colorful roadside bars and conch stands are a treat—and a cool way to mingle with the locals.

HOTEL AND RESTAURANT PRICES

Restaurant prices are based on the median main course price at dinner, excluding gratuity, typically 10% to 15%, coupled with the new Bahamas Valued Added Tax (VAT) of 7.5%—which are usually automatically added to the bill. Hotel prices are for two people in a standard double room in high season, excluding service and 6%–12% tax and 7.5% VAT. Some establishments are by law too small to charge VAT and some, especially in the smaller Out Islands, don't charge gratuities either.

WHAT IT COSTS IN DOLLARS			
	$	**$$**	**$$$**	**$$$$**
Restaurants	under $20	$20–$30	$31–$40	over $40
Hotels	under $200	$200–$300	$301–$400	over $400

VISITOR INFORMATION

Contacts Andros Tourist Offices. ✉ Fresh Creek ☎ 242/368–2286 Central Andros, 242/369–1688 South Andros ⊕ www.bahamas.com/islands/andros. **Bahama Out Islands Promotion Board.** ✉ Nassau ☎ 954/740–8740 U.S. and Canada, 242/322–1140 Nassau office ⊕ www.myoutislands.com. **Berry Islands Tourism Administrator.** ✉ Great Harbour Cay Airport ☎ 242/367–8291 office, 242/451-0404 cell, 242/225–2563 toll free within the Bahamas ⊕ www.bahamas.com/islands/berry. **Bimini Tourist Office.** ✉ Alice Town ☎ 242/347–3529 ⊕ www.bahamas.com/islands/bimini.

ANDROS

The Bahamas' largest island (100 miles long and 40 miles wide) and one of the least explored, Andros's landmass is carved up by myriad channels, creeks, lakes, and mangrove-covered cays. The natural **Northern, Middle,** and **South bights** cut through the width of the island, creating shallow boating access between both coasts. Andros is best known for its bonefishing and diving, and is also a glorious ecotourism spot with snorkeling, blue-hole exploration, sea kayaking, and nature hikes.

The Spaniards who came here in the 16th century called Andros *La Isla del Espíritu Santo*—the Island of the Holy Spirit—and it has retained its eerie mystique. The descendants of Seminole Indians and runaway slaves who left Florida in the mid-19th century settled in the North Andros settlement of **Red Bays** and remained hidden until a few decades ago. They continue to live as a tribal society, making a living by weaving straw goods. The Seminoles originated the myth of the island's legendary (and elusive) chickcharnies—red-eyed, bearded, green-feathered creatures with three fingers and three toes that hang upside down by their tails from pine trees. These mythical characters supposedly wait deep in the forests to wish good luck to the friendly passerby and vent their mischief on the hostile trespasser. The rest of Andros's roughly 8,000 residents live in a dozen settlements on the eastern shore. Farming and commercial fishing sustain the economy, and the island is the country's largest source of freshwater.

Andros's undeveloped **West Side** adjoins the Great Bahama Bank, a vast shallow-water haven for lobster, bonefish, and tarpon. Wild orchids and dense pine and mahogany forests cover the island's lush green interior. The marine life–rich **Andros Barrier Reef**—the world's third largest—is within a mile of the eastern shore and runs for 140 miles. Sheltered waters within the reef average 6 to 15 feet, but on the other side ("over the wall") they plunge to more than 6,000 feet at the **Tongue of the Ocean**.

GETTING HERE

AIR TRAVEL   There are four airports on Andros. San Andros airport (SAQ) is in North Andros, closest to Nichols Town and Stafford Creek. Andros Town airport (ASD) in Central Andros serves Fresh Creek, Small Hope Bay, Staniard Creek, and Kamalame Cay. Thirty miles south is Mangrove Cay airport (MAY) and then a farther 10 miles south lies Congo Town airport (TZN) on South Andros serving Tiamo Resort. From Fort Lauderdale Executive Airport (FXE), Watermakers Air flies four days a week to San Andros, Fresh Creek, and Congo Town. From Nassau (NAS) twice daily, LeAir flies to Andros Town and Mangrove Cay, Western Air flies to San Andros and Congo Town, and Glen Air flies to Congo Town and San Andros. Flamingo Air flies daily from Nassau to Mangrove Cay. For thrills, charter Safari Seaplanes from Nassau or Miami Seaplanes from Key Biscayne. Visit each resort's website for more options.

Contacts Andros Town Airport. ☎ 242/368–2134. **Congo Town Airport.** ☎ 242/369–2270. **Mangrove Cay Airport.** ☎ 242/369–0270. **San Andros Airport.** ☎ 242/329–4401.

FERRY TRAVEL   Andros is divided by water into three parts: Central/North Andros (combined), Mangrove Cay, and South Andros. Only Central/North Andros has a ferry service from Nassau. (Note: ferries and mail boats are different types of vessels. Ferries from Nassau are large, with comfortable air-conditioned lounges and snack bars, can transport cars, and are more regular. Mail boats are smaller, native cargo vessels, only take small cars, and sail mostly once a week and sometimes less frequently.) Bahamas Ferries runs the comfortable Sealink ferry twice or three times a week, depending on season. Check schedules and buy tickets online. They leave Nassau Harbour's Potter's Cay Dock, off East Bay Street, located under the exit bridge from Paradise Island (*see below*). Note that once on Andros, there is no service that connects Central/North Andros to its sister landmasses, Mangrove Cay and South Andros.

For those with more time (and patience) and who want a true Bahamian "down-home" adventure, you can take old-fashioned mail boats from Potter's Cay. Always consult the Dockmaster's Office there for information on mail-boat schedules: many websites have out-of-date sailing days and times. Extraordinary for these times, the office has no Internet or access to email. Note that mail boats sometimes have sporadic service and you may be marooned for days until the next mail boat arrives. To reach Morgan's Bluff, sail on the M/V *Lady Rosalind* that leaves Nassau on Wednesday and returns on Thursday. To reach Driggs Hill in South Andros or Mangrove Cay (Lisbon Creek) sail with either the M/V *Lady Katrina* that leaves Nassau on Wednesday and returns Tuesday, or with the M/V *Captain Moxey* that leaves Nassau on Monday and returns Sunday. Note that both mail boats sail to Driggs Hill, then Mangrove Cay, then back to Driggs Hill, and finally to Nassau. The trip between Nassau and Driggs Hill takes five hours and costs $35 one way. Schedules are subject to change due to weather conditions or occasional dry-docking.

Once on Andros, it's not possible to reach Mangrove Cay or South Andros from Central/North Andros. However, it is possible to cross between Mangrove Cay and South Andros. A free government ferry makes the half-hour trip between Mangrove Cay and South Andros twice daily. It departs from Driggs Hill, South Andros at 8 am and 4 pm and from Lisbon Creek, Mangrove Cay at 8:30 am and 4:30 pm, but schedules are subject to change. Call the Commissioner's Office for information.

Contacts Potter's Cay Dockmaster's Office. ☎ *242/393–1064* ✍ *curtiscraig220@yahoo.com.* **South Andros Tourist Office.** ✉ *Mangrove Cay* ☎ *242/369–1688.*

TAXI TRAVEL   Taxis meet airplanes and ferries and are available for touring around the islands. You can arrange for pickup with your hotel. Rates are around $1.50 a mile, though most fares are set. Always agree on a fare before you set foot in a taxi. Tour rates vary: for five passengers and up they start from $50 per person for a half day and $100 per person for a full day.

NORTH ANDROS

The northern part of Andros spreads from the settlements of **Morgan's Bluff**, **Nicholl's Town**, and **Red Bays** and ends at **Stafford Creek.** North Andros consists of long stretches of pine forests, limestone bluffs, and fields and gardens of ground crops. Seminole Indians, American slaves, and Mennonites settled this land along with the West Indian population. White-sand beaches, mostly deserted, line the island's eastern face, interrupted by creeks, inlets, and rock outcroppings. Logging supported North Andros in the '40s and '50s, and laid the foundation for its roads.

San Andros is home to North Andros's airport, but **Nicholl's Town** is the port and largest settlement here and in all of Andros. Once home to a vogue resort in the 1960s (Andros Beach Hotel), today it is mostly residential, inhabited in part by snowbirds who own the adorable Bahamian-style, brightly painted cottages that were once part of the iconic resort. Visitors driving from Central Andros should expect a bit of a wild ride, as the main highway is riddled with potholes. North of the airport, the road is good. But don't worry about traffic; you'll be lucky if you see more than 20 vehicles on the highway in a single day.

DID YOU KNOW?

Andros is the largest yet one of the most sparsely developed islands in the Bahamas. Putting the first footprints of the day on an empty beach might become your favorite activity.

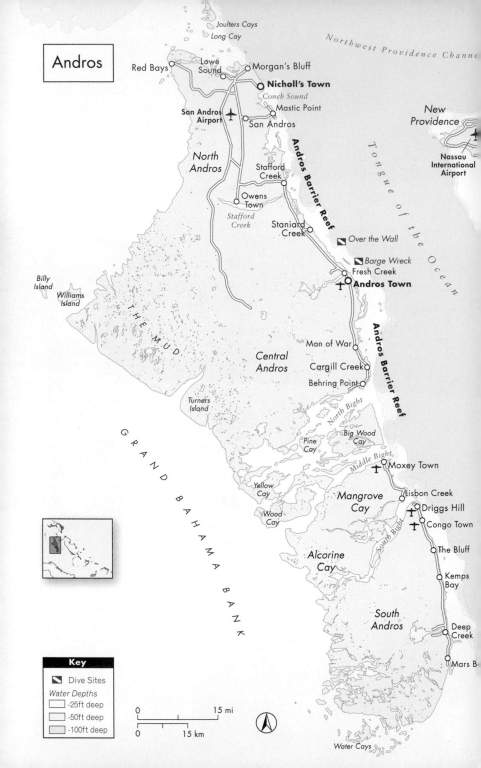

GETTING HERE AND AROUND

The San Andros airport (SAQ) has flights from Fort Lauderdale via Watermakers Air and from Nassau via Le Air, Western Air, and Glen Air. Taxis meet incoming flights. If you want to explore Andros, a car ($70–$90/day), van ($120/day), or a guided group tour by taxi bus (from $50 a half day or $100 a day for a group of five or more), are recommended. Between Fresh Creek and San Andros airport the road is full of potholes, but a repaving project was promised for 2016. Bikes are a good way to get around the closer resort areas and nearby settlements.

Car Rentals Darran's Car Rental. ✉ *Nicholl's Town* ☎ *242/329–1009.* **Executive Car Rental.** ✉ *Nicholl's Town* ☎ *242/471–5259.*

EXPLORING

Morgan's Bluff. Three miles north of Nicholl's Town is a crescent beach, a headland known as Morgan's Bluff, and a set of caves named after the 17th-century pirate Henry Morgan, who allegedly dropped off some of his stolen loot in the area. The beach and park is the site of Regatta Village, a colorful collection of stands and stalls used in July when the big event, the All Andros & Berry Islands Regatta, takes place. Adjacent is the Government Dock and a safe harbor, with a small, popular native bar and restaurant. ✉ *Nicholl's Town.*

Nicholl's Town. Nicholl's Town, on Andros's northeastern corner, lies on a beautiful beach and is the island's largest settlement, with a population of about 600. This friendly community, with its agriculture-based economy, has grocery and supplies stores, a few motels, a public medical clinic, a telephone station (yes these still exist), and more. Adorable cottages, a throwback from the town's big resort era of the '60s, house the island's wintering population from the United States, Canada, and Europe. ✉ *Nicholl's Town.*

Red Bays. Fourteen miles west of Nicholl's Town, Red Bays is the sole west-coast settlement in all of Andros. The town was settled by Seminole Indians and runaway African slaves escaping Florida pre–Civil War and was cut off from the rest of Andros until a highway connected it to Nicholl's Town in the 1980s. Residents are known for their craftsmanship, particularly straw basketry and wood carving. Tightly plaited baskets, some woven with scraps of colorful Androsia batik, have become a signature craft of Andros. Artisans have their wares on display in front of their homes (with fixed prices). Despite opening their homes to buyers, Red Bays locals don't seem very used to visitors. Expect a lot of curious stares and occasional smiles! ✉ *Red Bays.*

Uncle Charlie's Blue Hole. Mystical and mesmerizing, blue holes pock Andros's marine landscape in greater concentration than anywhere else on Earth—an estimated 160-plus—and provide entry into the islands' network of coral-rock caves. Offshore, some holes drop off to 200 feet or more. Inland blue holes reach depths of 120 feet, layered with fresh, brackish, and salt water. Uncle Charlie's Blue Hole is one of Andros's most popular inland blue holes. The hole's perimeter is lined with picnic benches and a ladder leads into the mysterious (and refreshing) blue hole. The hole is 40 feet in diameter and 120 feet deep. ✉ *300 yards off main highway in North Andros after turnoff for Owen Town.*

5

BEACHES

If solitude is what you're searching for, you'll definitely find it on the beaches of North Andros. Long and secluded, you might find each beach with just one small resort or bar close by—and a few reefs for snorkeling.

Conch Sound. South of Nicholl's Town, Conch Sound is a wide protected bay with strands of white sand and tranquil waters. Swimmers and bonefishers can wade on their own on the easily accessible flats. Commercial fishermen bring their catches to a little beach park nearby and you can buy fresh catch. A small offshore blue hole beckons snorkelers a short way off the beach. Be careful if wading in the water not to fall in the blue hole! **Amenities:** none. **Best for:** solitude; snorkeling. ⊠ *Nicholl's Town.*

Morgan's Bluff Beach. This one-third-mile-long crescent beach is a place to relax when touring North Andros. You might see a few locals enjoying it and the adjacent park with its colorful stalls that only come alive in June when the All Andros & Berry Islands Regatta is held. Nearby is the government dock, a public marina, and a bar and restaurant popular with the locals and boat captains. **Amenities:** none. **Best for:** solitude, swimming, walking. ⊠ *Nicholl's Town.*

Nicholl's Town Beach. On the east side of Nicholl's Town is a powdery, white-sand beach over a mile long. It's pretty much deserted except for a few guests at the Andros Island Beach Resort and few snowbirds. In winter and afternoons trees cast shade on the beach. **Amenities:** none. **Best for:** solitude, swimming, walking. ⊠ *Nicholl's Town.*

WHERE TO STAY

$
RESORT
🖼 **Andros Island Beach Resort.** On Nicholl's Town's one-mile-long impressive beach, Andros Island Beach Resort is a small, colorful, and quiet resort of beachfront cottages and villas with life added through its flotsam-festooned tiki bar and restaurant. **Pros:** beautiful beach close to town; well-appointed rooms with kitchens; nice restaurant and bar. **Cons:** breakfast usually self-catered; might be too quiet for some; only kayaks are free. $ *Rooms from: $150* ⊠ *Nicholl's Town* 🕾 *242/329–1009* ⊕ *www.androsislandbeachresorts.com* ↯ *4 villas and 3 suites from 1 to 3 bedrooms* ⁝◯⁝ *No meals.*

$
B&B/INN
🖼 **Love at First Sight.** At the mouth of Stafford Creek, self-sufficient anglers and do-it-yourself vacationers can sit on the sundeck or at the bar, sip a cold local beer or a cocktail, and contemplate the superb fishing and diving in Central Andros. **Pros:** restaurant and bar overlooking creek; quiet and clean. **Cons:** rental car necessary; basic rooms with amenities; not on beach. $ *Rooms from: $130* ⊠ *On the main highway at the mouth of Stafford Creek, Central Andros* 🕾 *242/368–6082* ⊕ *www.loveatfirstsights.com* ↯ *10 rooms.*

$
B&B/INN
🖼 **Pineville Motel.** This truly one-of-a-kind, eye-popping plot of land fits in 16 rooms, a petting zoo, a small disco, a movie theater, a bar, and a DIY gift-shop—made mostly of recycled materials such as tires, reclaimed wood, and seashells. **Pros:** unique experience; cheap rates; enthusiastic owner. **Cons:** not near beach; basic accommodations;

overcrowded petting zoo. $ *Rooms from: $75* ✉ *Nicholl's Town* ☏ *242/329–2788* ⊕ *www.pinevillemotel.com* ↻ *16 rooms* ¶⊙¶ *No meals.*

NIGHTLIFE

Big Shop. Overlooking Nicholl's Town beach, Big Shop is as local as it gets. The 200-year-old building used to be Andros's only trading post for the sponge harvesters. Now, it's North Andros's only nightspot. The bar opens daily from noon til late. On weekends it has DJs and on some holidays, a live band. For lunch or dinner, try Big Shop's native dinners, sandwiches, burgers, and pastas. You might be the only tourists there. ✉ *Nicholl's Town* ☏ *242/225–2947* ⊿ *Free entry.*

CENTRAL ANDROS

Those arriving in **Central Andros** by Bahamas Ferries from Nassau will arrive in the village of **Fresh Creek**; those arriving by plane will arrive in neighboring **Andros Town** (the petite transportation and governmental hub). Both Fresh Creek and Andros Town are found midisland, on the east coast of greater Andros Island.

Heading north from Andros Town and Fresh Creek, Central Andros extends as far north as Stafford Creek, near Kamalame Cay, whereupon the land officially becomes North Andros (though it's debated exactly where Central ends). As you head south from Andros Town airport, scrub pine forests and brush give way to mangroves and hardwood coppice. Long beaches scallop the eastern shoreline and the sole road, Queen's Highway, will bring you to the bonefishing villages of **Cargill Creek** and **Behring Point**. Here, along the bonefish sweet spot of **Northern Bight**, you'll find nice homes with flowering gardens, palm trees, and sea grapes that overlook the wide estuary.

Central Andros accounts for 70% of Andros's entire hotel inventory. Expect no glitz and glamour but, instead, natural beauty. The small resorts range from the luxurious and exclusive private island **Kamalame Cay**, to the family-friendly, all-inclusive **Small Hope Bay Lodge**, and simpler bonefishing lodges and home rentals. All, however, attract many repeat visitors who come to savor Andros's beautiful beaches, reefs, and world-class fishing.

Central Andros's famed and remote **West Side** teems with mangrove estuaries rich with marine life, including lobster and bonefish. However, this uninhabited region is accessible only by private boat.

GETTING HERE AND AROUND

Fly into Andros Town airport (ASD) with LeAir from Nassau or with Watermakers Air from Fort Lauderdale Executive (FXE) or take the three-hour Sealink ferry with Bahamas Ferries from Nassau to Fresh Creek. Taxis meet airplanes and ferries. The fare from the airport to Fresh Creek is $15; to Cargill Creek area, some 20 miles south of the airport, about $40.

Car rentals start at $80 a day. For a guided bus tour of Andros, sign up early at your hotel so they can group you with others to lower the price. In Fresh Creek, you can easily get around to the local restaurants, beaches, and blue holes by bike.

Car Rental Contacts Adderley's Car Rental. ⊠ *Fresh Creek* ☎ *242/357–2149.* **Rooney's Auto Car Rental.** ⊠ *Fresh Creek* ☎ *242/471–0346, 242/368–2021.*

EXPLORING

Androsia Batik Works Factory. The Androsia Batik Works Factory in Andros Town is home to the famous Androsia batik that has been declared the official fabric of the Bahamas. Small Hope Bay Lodge's Birch family established it in 1973 to boost employment in Andros. The brightly colored hand-dyed cotton batik has designs inspired by Andros's flora, fauna, and culture. You can prearrange a batik lesson ($25) and make your own design on a choice of fabric, garment, or bag. Self-tours are free. The unique brand is seen and sold throughout the Bahamas, the Caribbean, and online. The outlet store (with different opening times) offers bargains on shirts, skirts, wraps, fabric, jewelry, books, crafts, and souvenirs. ⊠ *Andros Town* ☎ *242/368–2020* ⊕ *www.androsia.com* ⊗ *Factory: weekdays 7:15–4; shop: weekdays 9:30–4:30, Sat. 9:30–2.*

Andros Lighthouse. If you enter Fresh Creek by boat or ferry, you'll see this old white lighthouse (circa 1892) east of the Andros Lighthouse Yacht Club & Marina. Walk through the marina and you'll see that the tower overlooks two rusty cannons and big shipwreck. To the east lies a quiet beach. ⊠ *Fresh Creek.*

Captain Bill's Blue Hole. One famous Andros sight that nature lovers should catch is Captain Bill's Blue Hole, one of hundreds in Andros. Blue holes are the top of extensive water-filled underground cave systems formed in the ice age. Located northwest of Small Hope Bay, the Bahamas National Trust has made Captain Bill's popular and comfortable with a boardwalk and a shady gazebo. Steps allow you to jump 30 feet down to cool off and there's a nature trail around the hole's 400-foot diameter. Accessible by car or bike, Captain Bill's is included on most guided tours. ⊠ *Fresh Creek* ⊕ *Go 2 miles north from Small Hope Bay, turn left (west) in Love Hill, and take white road 2.7 miles west.*

Fresh Creek. Fresh Creek is an estuary, harbor, and a small hamlet, 3 miles north of Andros Town airport. The village lies north of the estuary and north of the bridge that takes you to Andros Town, the ferry dock, the tourist office, and the Andros Lighthouse, which guards the harbor's southern entrance. Expect smiles and locals to hail you as you bike or walk around the village and harbor front, exploring its few bars, restaurants, and quaint shops. The creek itself cuts over 16 miles into the island, creating tranquil bonefishing flats and inviting mangrove-lined bays that fishermen and sea kayakers can explore. ⊠ *Fresh Creek.*

Staniard Creek. Sand banks that turn gold at low tide lie off the northern tip of Staniard Creek, a small island settlement 9 miles north of Fresh Creek, accessed by a bridge off the main highway. Coconut palms and casuarinas shade the ocean-side beaches, and offshore breezes are pleasantly cooling. Kamalame Cove, part of nearby luxurious resort and private Kamalame Cay, are at the northern end of the settlement. Three creeks snake into the mainland, forming extensive mangrove-lined back bays and flats, good for wading and bonefishing. ⊠ *Staniard Creek.*

Andros has the third-largest barrier reef in the world (behind those of Australia and Belize).

BEACHES

Because they're famous for their off-the-chart fishing and diving, the islands of Andros often get shorted when talk turns to beaches. This is a great injustice, especially in the case of the long, deserted beaches defining Central Andros's east coast and the abandoned white-sand beaches of Central Andros's outlying cays.

Kamalame & The Saddleback Cays. East of Staniard Creek lies a series of serene cays, idyllic for beach drops or consummating the ultimate Robinson Crusoe fantasies. The first is Kamalame Cay, home to the luxurious resort of the same name. Just past Kamalame, uninhabited Big and Little Saddleback Cay boast sparkling, white-sand beaches and crystal clear waters. You'll need a small, private boat to reach either (note that these cays are a regular drop point for guests of Kamalame Cay). Little Saddleback is tiny with no shade; so bring plenty of sunblock. Big Saddleback has a wider crescent beach, and plenty of shade from the pine trees. Also nearby is Rat Cay, which offers excellent snorkeling especially around the adjacent blue hole. **Amenities:** none. **Best for:** solitude; snorkeling; swimming; walking. ⊠ *Central Andros.*

Small Hope Bay Beach. Small Hope Bay Lodge is planted squarely on this long, coved beach where the near-shore snorkeling is excellent and the sand is white. Sign up for a resort course, a dive excursion, or simply enjoy a $55 beachside lunch buffet (with advanced notice). A full day of beach fun with breakfast, lunch, and dinner, and all drinks and water sports included, is $199. **Amenities:** food and drink; showers; toilets; water sports. **Best for:** snorkeling; swimming; walking. ⊠ *Small Hope Bay Lodge.*

Somerset Beach. Two miles south of Andros Town airport, off a long beaten-up bare road through an arch of Australia pines, is Somerset Beach, a stunning, long, and wide beach with offshore sandbars that let you walk offshore for half a mile. The pines offer shade and there's a picnic table built by the workers from AUTEC, the nearby U.S. Navy's submarine testing base. Bring a camera as this is one of the most beautiful beach sights in the Bahamas. **Amenities:** none. **Best for:** solitude; swimming; walking.

WHERE TO EAT

$ BAHAMIAN

🍴 **Hank's Place Restaurant and Bar.** On the north side of Fresh Creek, near the bridge, this restaurant and bar juts out into the harbor and is graced with sweeping views. Locals, visitors, and workers from the U.S. Navy base enjoy Hank's for decent Bahamian dinners (chicken, fish, lobster, and pork), and for the popular dance parties on Saturday nights. Hank's signature cocktail, aptly named "Hanky Panky," is a dynamite frozen rum–and–fruit juice concoction. [$] *Average main: $16* ✉ *Fresh Creek* ☎ *242/368–2447* 🌐 *hanks-place.com* 🕒 *Closed Sun. and Mon.* ✍ *Reservations essential.*

$$$ CARIBBEAN Fodor's Choice ★

🍴 **Kamalame Cay.** If you're not a guest on Kamalame Cay's private island resort you might have to travel miles to enjoy this casual but luxurious dining experience. It's every bit worthwhile. Set on one of the Bahamas' most beautiful beaches, Kamalame's guests gather to enjoy cocktails at the poolside Tiki Bar then spread out in the Big House to enjoy Andros's top cuisine. Choose from a small set menu that varies nightly, with main courses of imported viands and fowl to creatively prepared fresh local seafood. Later, sip gently aged postprandial spirits on the terrace or the beach. Nestled in a grove of palms and kamalame trees, dinner at Kamalame could be your vacation's romantic highlight. [$] *Average main: 33* ✉ *Kamalame Cay Resort, Staniard Creek* ✍ *Reservations essential.*

$$$$ BAHAMIAN

🍴 **Small Hope Bay Lodge.** Unless you're a lucky all-inclusive guest at this resort, famous for its diving and fishing, the best way to enjoy it is to buy an all-inclusive $199 day pass allowing you breakfast, lunch, and dinner and bar drinks with lunch and through the evening. From 7 am to 10 pm you can enjoy all the facilities and equipment on Small Hope's gorgeous beach: kayaks, windsurfers, sailboats, snorkeling, paddleboards, and the fresh whirlpool on the gorgeous beach. Dinner and wine alone is $90 but does not include bar drinks. [$] *Average main: 199* ✉ *Small Hope Bay* ☎ *242/368–2014* 🌐 *www.smallhopebay.com* ✍ *Reservations essential.*

WHERE TO STAY

$$$$ B&B/INN

🏨 **Andros Island Bonefish Club** (*AIBC*). If you're a hard-core bonefisher, AIBC is the place for you—guests have access to 100 square miles of lightly fished flats, including wadable (at low tide) flats, right out front. **Pros:** outdoor deck and bar idyllic for fishing stories; prime location on Cargill Creek. **Cons:** not much for nonanglers other than relaxing waterside; basic accommodations. [$] *Rooms from: $485* ✉ *Cargill Creek* ☎ *242/368–5167* 🌐 *www.androsbonefishing.com* 🛏 *12 rooms* 🍽 *All meals.*

$$$$ B&B/INN [🏨] **Big Charlie's & Fatiha's Fishing Lodge.** On the banks of Cargill Creek, this small and charming bonefishing lodge is run by Charlie Neymour, a bonefishing legend, and his charming wife Fatiha who serves deliciously aromatic Moroccan and Mediterranean cuisine in the dining room—with tasty, fresh seafood Bahamian-style as well. **Pros:** new, clean, and smart; fridges, satellite TV, and Wi-Fi in rooms; unusually good cuisine for a lodge. **Cons:** beach is some distance; only for fishing fans. [$] *Rooms from: $500* ✉ *Cargill Creek* ☎ *242/368–4297* 🌐 *www.bigcharlieandros.net* 🛏 *4 rooms, 8 guests maximum* 🍴 *All-inclusive.*

$$ RESORT Fodor's Choice ★ [🏨] **Kamalame Cay.** Occupying a Bahamian pinnacle in luxury island retreats, the breathtaking 96-acre Kamalame Cay in Central Andros is a well-kept secret and surprisingly affordable. **Pros:** private white-sand beaches; quiet, remote location; discreet pampering; delicious, innovative food; on-site overwater spa. **Cons:** Wi-Fi only in reception area; eye mask needed for sleeping past sunrise; round-trip airport transfers are costly. [$] *Rooms from: $250* ✉ *Staniard Creek* ✥ *At the north end of Staniard Creek* ☎ *242/368–6281, 800/768–9423* 🌐 *www.kamalame.com* ⏲ *Closed Aug. 10–Oct. 7* 🛏 *5 cottages, 5 villas, 9 rooms* 🍴 *All-inclusive.*

$$$$ RENTAL Fodor's Choice ★ [🏨] **Kettlestone Luxury Villa.** Perched on a small bluff overlooking Andros's Barrier Reef, this dreamy newly constructed luxury villa provides a consummate private getaway. **Pros:** customized oceanfront luxury ; very private; near town; freshwater pool and free snorkeling. **Cons:** must drive to beach; self-catered or hired chef. [$] *Rooms from: $750* ✉ *Fresh Creek* ☎ *242/357–2746 cell, 800/827–7048 toll free in U.S. and Canada* 🌐 *www.kettlestoneluxuryvilla.com* 🛏 *3 bedrooms sleeping 8 maximum* 🍴 *No meals.*

$$$$ B&B/INN [🏨] **Mount Pleasant Fishing Lodge.** Mount Pleasant caters to fishermen who care only to be out on the water all day. **Pros:** nice beach; from-shore fishing. **Cons:** small and off-the-beaten-path; far from other restaurants. [$] *Rooms from: $420* ✉ *Cargill Creek* ☎ *242/368–5171* 🌐 *www.mtpleasantfish.com* 🛏 *6 rooms* 🍴 *All meals.*

$$$$ HOTEL FAMILY Fodor's Choice ★ [🏨] **Small Hope Bay Lodge.** This much-loved, beachside all-inclusive resort—over 50 years strong and the Atlantic/Caribbean's first dive resort—has a devoted following of repeat divers, snorkelers, eco-adventurers, anglers, couples, and families. **Pros:** best dive operation on Andros; air-conditioning; free Wi-Fi in public areas; free long-distance calls to the United States and Canada. **Cons:** in summer you'll need insect repellent; hot tub instead of pool. [$] *Rooms from: $570* ✉ *Small Hope Bay* ☎ *242/368–2014, 800/223–6961* 🌐 *www.smallhope.com* 🛏 *21 cottages* 🍴 *All-inclusive.*

$$$ B&B/INN [🏨] **Sunset Point House Boat.** A mile and a quarter west of the bridge on Fresh Creek is the unique Sunset Point House Boat, built on the water with the majestic creek flowing around it. **Pros:** houseboat on wide, flowing creek; private, serene, and eco-immersed; self-catered or cook for hire. **Cons:** no air-conditioning or cable and Wi-Fi only at owner's house 160 feet away; too quiet for some; children must be able to swim and over eight years. [$] *Rooms from: $300* ✉ *Fresh Creek* ✥ *1¼ miles west of Fresh Creek Bridge, on southern side of estuary* ☎ *242/357–2061 cell* 🌐 *http://www.homeaway.com/vacation-rental/p3177425* 🛏 *3*

5

beds, 3 baths, available for 2 to 6 persons ❑ *No meals.*

NIGHTLIFE

Hank's Place. The overwater bar at Hank's Place Restaurant and Bar is *the* place to be on Saturdays and some Fridays. Sunset is more of a relaxed scene; but come late night the music gets louder, people get "happier," and the dancing begins! It's also enjoyed by mostly young workers from the nearby AUTEC U.S. Navy base. It's open from 2 pm

> **DID YOU KNOW?**
>
> In the Bahamas, mail is still delivered by mail boats, as it has been for decades. Mail boats leave Nassau's Potter's Cay carrying mail, cars, produce, consumer goods, and passengers on trips to more than 30 Bahamian islands, including Andros, a four-hour cruise.

to 10 pm Tuesday to Friday, and until 3 am on Saturday. ✉ *Fresh Creek* ☎ *242/368–2447* ⊕ *www.hanks-place.com.*

SHOPPING

Androsia Store. Adjacent to the Androsia Batik Works Factory is the Androsia Store, where you can buy original fabrics, clothing, bags, souvenirs, and stuffed toys. Designed with island-inspired natural and cultural motifs, Androsia is popular nationwide and is the official fabric of the Bahamas. ✉ *Fresh Creek* ☎ *242/368–2080* ⊕ *www.androsia.com* ◔ *Weekdays 9:30–4:30, Sat. 9:30–2* ◔ *Closed Sun.*

SPORTS AND THE OUTDOORS

BOATING AND FISHING

Andros fishermen claim the island is the world's best bonefishing location, and legends at Central Andros's south end are famed for pioneering the field of fly-fishing and island fishing lodges. The four main fishing regions are the hard-to-reach West Side flats, the creeks (Stafford, Staniard, and Fresh Creek), the Joulters Cays north of Andros, and the bights between Central and South Andros. Fishermen will find a wealth of knowledgeable bonefishing guides in the **Cargill Creek–Behring Point** area who will take you into the Northern Bight and West Side for some of the world's best bonefishing. Full-day fishing excursions cost about $500 to $600 for two. Better value are the lodges' guided bonefishing, lodging, and dining packages that work out to range from $400 to $660 per person per day at the half-dozen lodges in the area.

Reef and deep-sea fishing excursions are secondary although you can catch snapper, and in season, grouper, along with game fish mahimahi, wahoo, and tuna.

Andra "Andy" Smith. Based in Central Andros, Andy Smith is highly recommended for guiding anglers through Andros's bights and to the bonefish-rich West Side. Andy guides both novice and professional bonefishers. You can book him through Small Hope Bay Lodge. ✉ *Cargill Creek* ☎ *242/368–4261.*

Andros Island Bonefish Club. Near Behring Point and overlooking beautiful Cargill Creek, Andros Island Bonefish Club is one of the Bahamas' top lodges, with attractive rooms in cottages spread over a large waterfront garden. The air-conditioned dining room lounge and the breezy waterfront bar are perfect for gathering and swapping stories. Expect great native food and pleasant service. Owner Rupert Leadon is an expert fishing guide and has more experts on tap. Fishing-dining-lodging packages run from $500 per night without taxes. An excellent choice for fishing devotees but not suitable for children or those wanting a beachfront stay. ✉ *Cargill Creek* ☎ *242/368–5167.*

Charlie Neymour. Legend and expert guide Charlie Neymour is popular for guided fishing expeditions, and now has, with his wife Fatiha, a cute new bonefishing lodge with excellent cuisine and fishing, dining, and lodging packages. Located in Behring Point near the expansive flats. ✉ *Cargill Creek* ☎ *242/368–4297* ⊕ *www.bigcharlieandros.net.*

Small Hope Bay Lodge. A popular Andros diving and bonefishing resort, Small Hope Bay Lodge has bone-, deep-sea, fly-, and reef fishing, as well as a "West Side Overnight"—a two-night camping and bone- and tarpon-fishing trip to the island's remote western end. Regular rates to fish along Fresh Creek run $290–$400 for a half day and $450–$550 for a full day (full-day trips include all gear and lunch). Small Hope books seven of the top bonefishing guides in Andros including Glaister Wallace, known for his magical casting skills. Book in advance. ✉ *Small Hope Bay* ☎ *242/368–2014, 800/223–6961* ⊕ *www.smallhope.com.*

HIKING

Small Hope Bay Lodge. This lodge offers four self-guided and three guided nature and cultural tours through the beach, mangroves, and blue holes, and into Fresh Creek by bike or on foot. ✉ *Small Hope Bay* ☎ *242/368–2014, 800/223–6961* ⊕ *www.smallhope.com.*

SCUBA DIVING AND SNORKELING

Divers can't get enough of the sprawling **Andros Barrier Reef,** the world's third largest, stretching the length of the island's east coast, ½ to 3 miles offshore. Boats from local lodges and resorts bring guests to beautiful parts of the reef to relish in underwater rapture. Snorkelers can explore such reefs as the Trumpet Reef, where visibility is clear 15 feet to the sandy floor and jungles of elkhorn coral snake up to the surface. Divers can delve into the 60-foot-deep coral caves of the Black Forest, beyond which the wall slopes down to depths of 6,000 feet. Anglers can charter boats to fish offshore or over the reef, and bonefishers can wade the flats on their own. While the marine life is not as rich nor as diverse as one would expect from such a vibrant, healthy reef, the assemblies of coral are breathtaking.

Small Hope Bay Lodge. Andros's top dive center is full-service with resort dives, PADI certification courses, one- and two-tank dives, specialty dives such as shark and night, and snorkeling. One-tank dives are $90, two-tanks are $110, and a day with three dives is $140. Rental equipment is available for Small Hope Bay Lodge excursions only. Lodging-dive packages are offered. Hot showers await after long days at sea! ✉ *Small Hope Bay* ☎ *242/368–2014, 800/223–6961* ⊕ *www. smallhope.com.*

MANGROVE CAY

Remote Mangrove Cay is sandwiched between two sea-green bights that separate it from Central and South Andros, creating an island of shorelines strewn with washed-up black coral and scented ambergris, gleaming deserted beaches, and dense pine forests. **Moxey Town,** known locally as Little Harbour, rests on the northeast corner in a coconut grove. Pink piles of conch shells and mounds of porous sponges dot the small harbor of this commercial fishing and sponging community. Anglers come on a mission, in search of giant bonefish on flats called "the promised land" and "land of the giants." A five-minute boat ride takes fly-fishers to Gibson Cay to wade hard sand flats sprinkled with starfish.

GETTING HERE AND AROUND
Both Le Air and Flamingo Air offer twice-daily flights from Nassau to Mangrove Cay Airport (MAY). The cay's main road runs south from Moxey Town, past the airport, then along coconut-tree-shaded beaches to the settlement of Lisbon Creek. Car rentals are available from B&I Enterprises and PG's Car Rental for exploring Mangrove Cay's 8 miles of roads. They run about $70 to $85 a day. Taxis meet airplanes and ferries (as do many lodges and hotels) and are available for touring around the 7-mile-long cay.

A free government ferry makes the half-hour trip between Mangrove Cay (Lisbon Creek) and South Andros (Driggs Hill) twice daily. It departs from South Andros at 9 am and 5 pm and from Mangrove Cay at 8:30 am and 4:30 pm, but schedules are subject to change. Call the South Andros Tourist Office for information. There's no public transportation from Central Andros to Mangrove Cay.

At this writing, there was no public ferry to Central Andros from Mangrove Cay or from South Andros, but the government was hoping to establish a new round-trip ferry service from Kemp's Bay to Lisbon Creek (Mangrove Cay), and then to Behring Point (Central Andros), where a new concrete dock was built in spring 2015.

Car Rental Contacts B & I Enterprises. ✉ Mangrove Cay ☎ 242/369–0353. **PG's Car Rental.** ✉ Mangrove Cay ☎ 242/471–1126.

EXPLORING
Victoria Point Blue Hole. On an island known for magical blue holes (water-filled caves), the Victoria Point Blue Hole is Mangrove Cay's superlative spot for snorkeling and diving. Just ask the folks at Swain's Cay Lodge, Seascape Inn, or Mangrove Cay Inn—or any local—to point out which of the island's myriad blue holes is the famed Victoria Point. ✉ Mangrove Cay.

WHERE TO EAT
If you stay at one of Mangrove Cay's lodges, you're sure to be served fresh, delicious native fare, usually as part of your lodging and fishing package. You can, however, also explore other lodges. It's a great way to get to know them, so long as you book a day ahead. Swain's Cay Lodge is a wonderful dining spot on the beach, 3 miles south of the airport on the main road. Enjoy fresh catches, conch, lobster, and more native

dishes either alfresco on the beachfront porch or in the cool inside. The island's famous conch stand is Shine's One-Stop Conch Shack north and then west of the airport road, sitting on the edge of Middle Bight. Here, enclosed in air-conditioning and away from flies, enjoy conch and fresh fish myriad ways. Some snowbirds and second-home owners treat themselves to Tiamo Resort's finer dining by taking the Tiamo's free ferry from Lisbon Creek (south Mangrove Cay) to the resort on South Andros. Explore other eateries as you bike, drive or walk around other settlements on the 7-mile-long cay.

$$ ✕ **Seascape Inn's Barefoot Bar and Grill.** Every table has a nice ocean view
BAHAMIAN at this warm and friendly beachfront restaurant and bar at the Seascape Inn. Owners Mickey and Joan McGowan do the baking and cooking themselves. If you are staying elsewhere, make sure to call at least one day ahead, if not more. Grilled chicken salad, burgers, sandwiches on kaiser rolls, and, at times, quesadillas are ample lunch temptations which you can pre-order for daily outings. Chicken in white wine–lime sauce, roast pork loin, grilled steaks, and fresh fish of the day are a few dinner sensations. Even if you're full, the chocolate ganache, Grand Marnier–chocolate cloud, and homemade ice creams should not be missed. $ *Average main: $24* ✉ *Seascape Inn* ☎ *242/369–0342* ⊕ *www. seascapeinn.com* ⌕ *Reservations essential.*

WHERE TO STAY

$$$$ ☷ **Mangrove Cay Club.** Located on the rocky south shore of the Middle
B&B/INN Bight, 1½ miles northwest of Mangrove Cay Airport, is this purely for bonefishing club that only offers fishing-dining-lodging packages normally sold through fishing and hunting agencies. **Pros:** close to prized bonefish areas; great fishing gear and skiffs; superbly trained guides. **Cons:** hard to swim in currrents; no beach; somewhat remote. $ *Rooms from: $740* ✉ *Mangrove Cay* ☎ *242/369–0731 lodge, 402/222–0624 U.S. office* ⊕ *mangrovecayclub.com* ⌕ *8 identical waterfront suites sleeping 16* ⎟◎⎟ *All-inclusive.*

$ ☷ **Mangrove Cay Inn.** In a coconut grove with wild orchid and hibiscus
B&B/INN gardens, the inn caters to hard-core escapists and anglers alike. **Pros:** on-site restaurant and bar; quiet location near the beach; friendly staff. **Cons:** lots of insects; very basic accommodations; mainly for anglers. $ *Rooms from: $140* ✉ *Mangrove Cay* ☎ *242/369–0069* ⊕ *www. mangrovecayinn.net* ▤ *No credit cards* ⌕ *12 rooms, 2 cottages.*

$ ☷ **Seascape Inn.** One of Andros's few lodging options catering to more
B&B/INN than fishermen, Seascape Inn is a small, rustic beachfront gem: five individual, well-maintained cottages with private decks overlook the glass-clear ocean. **Pros:** quiet beachfront location; outstanding food; great snorkeling, kayaking, and bird-watching on-site. **Cons:** no air-conditioning; no TV; insect repellent a must. $ *Rooms from: $159* ✉ *Mangrove Cay* ☎ *242/369–0342* ⊕ *www.seascapeinn.com* ⌕ *5 cottages* ⎟◎⎟ *Breakfast.*

$ ☷ **Swain's Cay Lodge.** This petite, beachfront resort is a gem for bone-
B&B/INN fishing fans and escape artists who want to enjoy Andros's natural beauty in peace and quiet. **Pros:** beachfront; excellent native food; free transfers to airport and tours. **Cons:** sleeps only 22; beach is shallow for swimming. $ *Rooms from: $170* ✉ *Mangrove Cay* ☎ *242/422–5018*

Undersea Adventures in Andros

Andros probably has the largest number of dive sites in the country. With the third-longest barrier reef in the world (behind those of Australia and Belize), the island offers about 100 miles of drop-off diving into the Tongue of the Ocean.

Uncounted numbers of **blue holes** are forming in the area. In some places these constitute vast submarine networks that can extend more than 200 feet down into the coral (Fresh Creek, 40–100 feet; North Andros, 40–200-plus feet; South Bight, 40–200 feet). Blue holes are named for their inky-blue aura when viewed from above and for the light-blue filtered sunlight that is visible from many feet below. Some of the holes have vast cathedral-like interior chambers with stalactites and stalagmites, offshoot tunnels, and seemingly endless corridors. Others have distinct thermoclines (temperature changes) between layers of water and are subject to tidal flow.

The dramatic Fresh Creek site provides an insight into the complex Andros cave system. There isn't much coral growth, but there are plenty of midnight parrot fish, big southern stingrays, and some blacktip sharks. Similar blue holes are all along the barrier reef, including several at Mastic Point in the north and the ones explored and filmed off South Bight.

Undersea adventurers also have the opportunity to investigate wrecks such as the *Potomac*, a steel-hulled freighter that sank in 1952 and lies in 40 feet of water off Nicholl's Town. And off the waters of Fresh Creek, at 70 feet, lies the deteriorated 56-foot-long World War II LCM (landing craft mechanized) known only as the

Barge Wreck, which was sunk in 1963 to create an artificial reef. Newer and more intact, the *Marian* wreck lies in 70 feet. Both are encrusted with coral and are home to a school of groupers and a blizzard of tiny silver-fish. You'll find fish-cleaning stations where miniature cleaning shrimp and yellow gobies clean grouper and rockfish by swimming into their mouths and out their gills, picking up food particles. It's an excellent subject matter for close-up photography.

The multilevel **Over the Wall** dive at Fresh Creek takes novices to depths of 65–80 feet and experienced divers to 120–185 feet. The wall is covered with black coral and all kinds of tube sponges. **Small Hope Bay Lodge** is the most long-respected dive resort on Andros. It's a friendly, informal place where the only thing taken seriously is diving and fishing. There's a fully equipped dive center with a wide variety of specialty dives, including customized family-dive trips with a private dive boat and dive master. If you're not certified, check out the lodge's morning resort course and be ready to explore the depths by afternoon. If you are certified, don't forget to bring your C card.

If you are leery of diving but want to view the spectacular undersea world, try a snorkeling excursion. Shallow reefs, beginning in 6 feet of water, and extending down to 60 feet or more, are ideal locations for spotting myriad brightly colored fish, sea urchins, and starfish. Don't forget your underwater camera!

Winter water temperatures average about 74°F. In summer, water temperatures average about 84°F.

Tiamo Resort is the most luxurious resort in South Andros.

⊕ *www.swainscaylodge.com* ⇌ *3 rooms and one 3-bed apartment with kitchenette* ⎮◯⎮ *Breakfast.*

NIGHTLIFE

Shine's One-Stop Conch Shack. As close to nightlife as you'll get on Mangrove Cay, visit Shine's conch shack and you'll be wall-diving deep into Androsian flavor. Exuberant Shine is a superfriendly host, fishing guide, and lobster catcher (a major industry on Mangrove Cay). He can't wait for you to down one of his stories along with a beer or a pineapple-coconut-flavored Goombay Smash. Smack on the water, this popular local hangout is a place to mix fresh conch salad and seafood with friendly native banter. Shine rivals Mangrove Cay's blue holes as a memorable attraction. Dominoes and backgammon with reggae and calypso tunes add to the upbeat ambience. ⊠ *Mangrove Cay.*

SOUTH ANDROS

South Andros's road stretches 25 miles from **Drigg's Hill**—a small settlement of pastel houses, a tiny church, a grocery store, the government dock, and the Emerald Palms Resort—to Mars Bay. Eight miles farther south, the Bluff settlement sprawls atop a hill overlooking miles of golden beaches, lush cays, and the Tongue of the Ocean. Here skeletons of Arawak natives were found huddled together. A local resident attests that another skeleton was found—this one of a 4-foot-tall, one-eyed owl, which may have given rise to the legend of the mythical, elflike chickcharnie. South Andros is laced with an almost continuous set of beaches on the northwest and east coast, and more than 15 boutique resorts, bonefishing lodges, inns, and rentals are scattered along the island's many small settlements.

GETTING HERE AND AROUND

The Congo Town Airport (TZN) is 4 miles south of Drigg's Hill and receives flights four times a week from Fort Lauderdale Executive Airport (FXE) via Watermakers Air and daily flights from Nassau (NAS) via Western Air. Nassau-based Golden Wings Charters is a respected charter company that can be used to reach South Andros. For the ultimate thrill and the convenience of flying direct to your resort's beach or dock, charter a seaplane either with Miami Seaplane Tours & Charters or Safari Seaplanes from Nassau. Taxis and many lodges and hotels meet incoming flights and ferries.

A free government ferry makes the half-hour trip between Mangrove Cay and South Andros twice daily. It departs from South Andros at 9 am and 5 pm and from Mangrove Cay at 8:30 am and 4:30 pm, but schedules are subject to change. Call the South Andros Tourist Office in Congo Town (☎ 242/369–1688) for information.

At this writing, there was no public ferry to Central Andros from Mangrove Cay or from South Andros but government was hoping to establish a new round-trip ferry service from Kemp's Bay (South Andros) to Lisbon Creek (Mangrove Cay), and then to Behring Point (Central Andros), where a new concrete dock was built in 2015.

Car Rental Contacts Lenglo Car Rental. ⊠ *South Andros, Congo Town* ☎ *242/369–1702.*

WHERE TO STAY

$$
B&B/INN
Fodor's Choice
★
⚏ Andros Beach Club. Andros Beach Club is a beautiful getaway on South Andros's finest beach, a 4-mile secluded strand of powder, mere steps from your room. **Pros:** on 4-mile-long beautiful beach; self-catered or catered; DIY fishing and adventures. **Cons:** aged building over 150 years old; no pool. $ *Rooms from: $200 ⊹ ½ mile north of Kemp's Bay Marina, South Andros* ☎ *242/369–1454 South Andros, 954/681–4818 in U.S. and Canada* ⊕ *www.androsbeachclub.com* ⤴ *5 or more suites/rooms/sleeping areas* ⦿*All meals.*

$
HOTEL
⚏ The Pointe Resort. This modern, smart, two-story resort with six suites, a restaurant, bar, and small marina lies on a breathtaking point south of Kemp's Bay and makes great use of the views. **Pros:** modern, attractive, good condition; popular restaurant and bar; nice, clean suites with kitchenettes, cable, and Wi-Fi. **Cons:** 1¼-mile walk to beach; 16 miles from airport. $ *Rooms from: $175* ⊠ *Johnson's Bay, 200 yards northwest of Deep Creek Bridge* ☎ *242/465–7505 cell, 242/369–4497 hotel* ⊕ *www.thepointeresortsouthandros.com* ⤴ *6 suites.*

$$$$
RESORT
Fodor's Choice
★
⚏ Tiamo Resort & Spa. One of the Atlantic's latest great secrets, Tiamo is a hideaway for jet-setters in-the-know—arrival at this low-key yet sophisticated South Bight resort via private launch is just the start. **Pros:** 1½-to-1 staff-to-guest ratio; spectacular private beachfront location; great cuisine. **Cons:** alcohol not included in rates; insect repellent a must; only accessible by resort's ferry. $ *Rooms from: $850* ⊠ *South Bight, Driggs Hill ⊹ 3-mile boat ride from Driggs Hill or Lisbon Creek (Mangrove Cay)* ☎ *242/225–6871 within Bahamas, 786/374–2442 in*

U.S. and Canada ⊕ *www.tiamoresorts.com* ☾ *Closed Sept. and Oct.* ➴ *2 small rooms, 11 villas (3 large, 8 medium; 9 with pools, 2 without)* ⏀ *All meals.*

SPORTS AND THE OUTDOORS

FISHING

Reel Tight Charters. Often arranged by nearby lodges and resorts, this renowned charter company with its 25-foot 300HP catamaran and 14-foot skiff, offers a variety of excursions, mostly in South Andros but also farther afield, including deep-sea, reef, and spearfishing, plus diving, snorkeling, private island picnics, and blue hole exploring tours. They also rent water sports gear and kayaks. ⊠ *Drigg's Hill Marina, Driggs Hill* ☎ *242/369–1454 Bahamas, 954/681–4818 in U.S. and Canada.*

BIMINI

5

Bimini has long been known as the Bahamas' big game-fishing capital. Bimini's strong tourist season falls from spring through summer, when calmer seas mean the arrival of fishing and pleasure boats from South Florida. The nearest of the Bahamian islands to the U.S. mainland, Bimini consists of two main islands and a few cays just 50 miles east of Miami, across the Gulf Stream that sweeps the area's western shores. Most visitors spend their time on bustling North Bimini; South Bimini is quieter and more eco-oriented. Except for the vast new Resorts World Bimini development that occupies the island's northern third, most of the hotels, restaurants, churches, and stores in Bimini are in capital **Alice Town** and neighboring **Bailey Town** and **Porgy Bay**, along North Bimini's King's and Queen's highways. Along the east coast of North Bimini are long beaches; on the west, the protected harbor, docks, and marinas. Most of the islands' 2,500 inhabitants reside in the southern 2-mile southern built-up area. Although Alice Town is walkable, the preferred (and fun) way to scoot around is by golf cart. Resorts World Bimini has increased North Bimini's bustle and economy. Three times a week, its Superfast Bimini cruise ship brings over between 500 and 1,000 guests from Miami who spread around the island enjoying its beaches, eateries, bars, nightclubs, and casino.

Sparsely populated **South Bimini** is where Juan Ponce de León allegedly looked for the Fountain of Youth in 1513, and a site with a well and natural trail memorialize it. More engaging, however, is the island's biological field station, known as the Sharklab for its study of lemon-, hammerhead-, and nurse-shark behavior and tracking, among other things. The main resort on this island is the modern, marina-based, Bimini Sands Resort & Marina with its South Bimini Beach Club in the south, which both stride a gorgeous mile-long beach and are home to the famous Neal Watson's Bimini Scuba Center. South Bimini is much more low key than North Bimini, a slower pace loved by hundreds of visiting residents (and some visiting boating partiers) who have built nearly 80 homes in Port Royal on the island's southern tip.

Salvagers, gunrunners, rum-runners, and the legendary Ernest Hemingway peopled the history of Bimini. Hemingway wrote much of *To Have and Have Not* and *Islands in the Stream* here between fishing forays and street brawls.

GETTING HERE AND AROUND

AIR TRAVEL South Bimini's teensy airport (BIM) was enlarged and improved in 2015, thanks to help from Resorts World Bimini, to cope with the extra traffic it brings. It services flights from Fort Lauderdale International Airport (FLL) with Skybahamas and Silver Airways (which code shares with United Airlines), from Nassau with Skybahamas and Western Air, and from Freeport, Grand Bahama Island with Flamingo Air and Western Air. More than six charter airlines fly from Fort Lauderdale: Apollo Jets from FLL, Island Air Charters and Tropic Ocean Airways from Sheltair FBO at FLL, and Watermakers Air and Bahamas Express from FXE. Tropic Ocean Airways also flies a floatplane from Miami Seaplane Base. To reach North Bimini, you take a short taxi ride ($3) from the airport and a five-minute ferry ($2). The ferry runs until 10 pm or so for staff and guests who live on South Bimini.

Contacts Bimini Airport. ☏ *242/347–4111.*

BOAT AND From Miami, the Bimini Superfast cruise ship takes 2½–3 hours to
FERRY TRAVEL reach Resorts World's new pier. On board, guests enjoy gaming, restaurants, and bars—or take a nap. You can buy a variety of packages: some include meals and different length stays at a Resorts World villa/condo or the new Hilton hotel. Although rarely chosen, to reach Bimini by old-fashioned mail boat, contact the Dockmaster in Potter's Cay in Nassau at or the Bimini mail boat office at ☏ *242/347–3203* for an up-to-date schedule. M/V *Sherice M* usually leaves Potter's Cay, Nassau, on Thursday afternoons for Chub Cay, North Bimini, and Cat Cay, and returns on Monday morning. The one-way trip takes about 12 hours and costs $50. Going between North and South Bimini requires a five-minute ferry crossing, managed by the local government ($2 each way) which runs from early morning to fairly late at night.

Bimini's eight marinas accommodate private yachts and fishing boats in droves with most crossing the Gulf Stream from Florida, a distance of around 48 nautical miles. As you enter port, fly the yellow quarantine flag. Coming into North Bimini, you have to clear Customs in Alice Town at the Bimini Big Game Club and Immigration in the government buildings in Bailey Town. Coming into South Bimini, dock at Bimini Sands Resort & Marina and take a taxi to clear at Customs and Immigration at the airport, 2 miles away.

Once docked, only the captain can leave the boat in order to clear with local Customs and Immigration. All crew are required to remain on board until the captain returns having cleared. The clearance fee is $150 for boats up to 30 feet in length and $300 for boats over 30 feet, and covers the cruising permit, fishing permit, Customs and Immigration charges, and the $25 per person departure tax for up to three persons. Additional persons over the age of six are charged a $25 departure tax.

Sunsets in Bimini can be otherworldly.

Contacts Bimini Big Game Resort & Marina. ☎ *242/347–3391* ✉ *dockmaster@biminibiggameclub.com* ⊕ *www.biggameclubbimini.com.* **Bimini Customs Office.** ☎ *242/347–3100.* **Nassau Dockmaster's Office.** ☎ *242/393–1064.*

VISITOR INFORMATION
Contacts Bimini Tourist Office. ☎ *242/347–3528, 242/347–3529.*

NORTH BIMINI

Bimini's capital, **Alice Town**, is at North Bimini's southern end. It's colorful, painted in happy Caribbean pastels, and by night and day is buzzing with golf-carting visitors from Resorts World and the marinas along the main road of King's Highway. In a prominent location stand the ruins of the Compleat Angler Hotel, Ernest Hemingway's famous haunt, which burned down in 2006. A short walk away on the west coast is Radio Beach (aka Alice Town Beach) and in the center of town is the Bimini Native Straw and Craft Market, the tourist office, the government dock, the marinas, and many restaurants and bars.

In quick succession, Alice Town turns into **Bailey Town**, then **Porgy Bay**—these three towns are separated only by signs heralding the change. Going north you'll see some pretty conch stands, restaurants, and the pink-colored government center and clinic. The beaches up here are less frequented. The north third of the island is the vast Resorts World development with homes, condos, the Hilton hotel, casino, restaurants, and shops and, finally, the amenities-filled, impressive Paradise Beach.

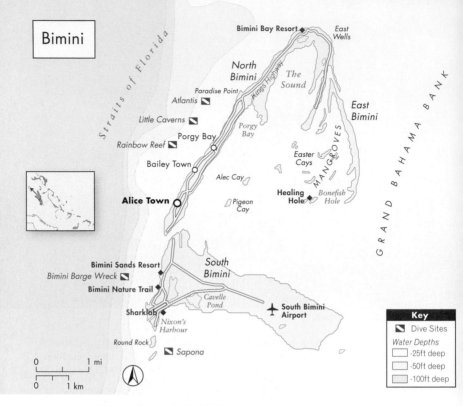

Bimini

GETTING HERE AND AROUND

If arriving by plane, catch a taxi at the South Bimini Airport and a ferry to the new government dock in Alice Town. The entire process costs $5. Once there, walk or take one of the waiting taxis to your accommodations. Ferries cannot take you directly to your hotel or marina because government regulations protect the taxi union.

Most people get around North Bimini on gas-powered golf carts, available for rent from various vendors and resorts from $70 to $100 per day, or $20 for the first hour, and $10 for each additional hour. At smaller rental companies, try bargaining. Note that the speed limit is 25 mph, helmets are required for scooters, and that the roads follow the British system—driving on the left.

Resorts World operates an hourly free tram service from the resort to Alice Town during the day.

Golf Cart Rental Contacts ABC Rentals. ✉ King's Hwy., Alice Town ☎ 242/359–8133 cell ⊕ http://www.biminigolfcarts.com. **Sue & Joys Rentals.** ✉ Alice Town ☎ 242/347–6082. **Uncle Tanny's Golf Cart Rentals.** ✉ Alice Town ☎ 242/347–2480 ⊕ www.uncletannygolfcartrentalsbimini.com.

EXPLORING

Ansil Saunder's Boat Building Shop. In Bailey Town, near the government park, is Ansil Saunder's boatbuilding shop where you can see his beautiful flats fishing boat called the *Bimini Bonefisher*, handcrafted from oak, mahogany, and native horseflesh. Ansil is firstly a bonefisherman of some repute, having scared up a 16-pound, 3-ounce bonefish for Jerry Lavenstein in 1971—the still-standing bonefish world record. Ansil is equally famous for taking Dr. Martin Luther King Jr. on a guided boat tour to the East Bimini wilderness. Dr. King wanted inspiration for an upcoming speech to be given for striking sanitation workers in Memphis. He found it in the mangroves, so rich in life and full of God's Creation, says Ansil, who recited his Creation Psalm to King. Three days after the Memphis speech, Dr. King was killed. To those interested, Ansil proudly shows memorabilia from Dr. King's wife and various VIPs. ⊠ *Bailey Town, on the harbor front* ☎ *242/347–2178 shop* ✉ *Donations accepted.*

Bailey Town. Most of the island's residents live in Bailey Town in small, pastel-color concrete houses, just off King's Highway, north of the Bimini Big Game Club and before Porgy Bay. Bailey Town has two of Bimini's biggest grocery stores where goods and produce come on by mail boat usually on Thursday—so shop Friday! It's also a good place to find a home-cooked meal or conch salad from shacks along the waterfront. Don't miss a bite at Joe's Conch Stand; it's a local institution. ⊠ *North Bimini.*

Bimini Museum. The Bimini Museum, sheltered in the restored (1921) two-story original post office and jail—a two-minute walk from the ferry dock, across from the native straw market—showcases varied artifacts, including Adam Clayton Powell's domino set, Prohibition photos, rum kegs, old cannonballs, Martin Luther King Jr.'s immigration card from 1964, and a fishing log and rare fishing films of Ernest Hemingway. The exhibit includes film shot on the island as early as 1922. The museum is privately managed. ⊠ *King's Hwy., Alice Town* ☎ *242/347–3038, 242/473–1252 cell* ⊕ *www.biminimuseum.com* ✉ *$2 donation requested* ⊙ *Daily 10–7.*

Bimini Roads. Avid divers shouldn't miss a trip to underwater Bimini Roads, aka the Road to Atlantis. This curious rock formation under about 20 feet of water, 500 yards offshore at Bimini Bay, is shaped like a backward letter J, some 600 feet long at the longest end. It's the shorter 300-foot extension that piques the interest of scientists and visitors. The precision patchwork of large, curved-edge stones forms a perfect rectangle measuring about 30 feet across. A few of the stones are 16 feet square. It's purported to be the "lost city" whose discovery was predicted by Edgar Cayce (1877–1945), a psychic with an interest in prehistoric civilizations. Archaeologists estimate the formation to be between 5,000 and 10,000 years old. Carvings in the rock appear to some scientists to resemble a network of highways. ⊠ *North Bimini.*

Dolphin House. Bimini historian and poet laureate Mr. Ashley Saunders has spent decades constructing this eclectic home and guesthouse from materials salvaged from local construction sites and the sea. Mr.

5

You can kayak in North Bimini's mangrove flats.

Saunders offers walking tours of Alice Town which begin with a tour of his structure—named for the 27 mosaic, sculpted, and painted dolphins throughout—then continues through Alice Town to tell the island's history. ⊠ *Alice Town between King's and Queen's Hwys., Alice Town* ☎ *242/347–3201* ✉ *Tours $20 hr* ⊙ *By appointment.*

OFF THE BEATEN PATH

Healing Hole. Hidden in the west coast mangroves of East Bimini is the Healing Hole—a cold spring of freshwater amid the hot sea saltwater with, some say, real, and others, mythical, healing powers. Hard to get to and find, it's best to hire a guide in a shallow boat, or, if you want exercise, in a kayak. You can only get there in mid-to-high tide, and make sure to take insect repellent. You'll see much life above and below water. For eco-lovers and adventure-seekers only.

BEACHES

Alice Town's Radio Beach, Bailey Town's Blister Bay Beach, and Porgy Bay's Spook Hill Beach form an almost continuous stretch of beach for 2 miles, with more sunbathers in the south. In places you can snorkel on shallow reefs offshore. North in Resorts World is the much wider Paradise Beach with rentals, restaurant, and bar. Occasionally giving a refuge of shade, Australian pine trees line the sensational, downy sands—what Hemingway described as "floury white" in *Islands in the Stream.*

Radio Beach/ Blister Bay. Alice Town's Radio Beach and Bailey Town's Blister Bay form a continuous stretch of beach off Queen's Highway, easily accessible in many places. Also called Alice Town Beach, its southern part is often busier and where spring breakers and the young like to party together. CJ's bar and grill, among other stands, is the default

HQ, serving affordable beers, drinks, burgers, and native dinners. Eat inside (away from the flies), on the deck, or on the beach. **Amenities:** food and drink. **Best for:** partiers; swimming. ⊠ *Alice Town.*

Spook Hill Beach. Named for its proximity to the local cemetery and Bimini's memorial park, Spook Hill Beach is quieter than Radio and Blister Bay beaches and caters mostly to families looking for quiet sands and calm waters. Shallow shores are ideal for wading and the crystal clear waters make for great snorkeling. There is a permanent snack bar here and usually a few pop-up beach bars add to the fun. The beach is heavily lined with pine trees and is narrow at high tide. **Amenities:** food and drink. **Best for:** solitude; snorkeling; swimming.

WHERE TO EAT

$$
BAHAMIAN
✕ **Bimini Big Game Bar & Grill.** A favorite place for anglers, this popular restaurant has a large, cool (and insect-free) interior and patio deck with excellent second-story views of the marina, boats passing in the harbor, and the shimmering flats beyond. Enjoy beers, cocktails, and native and American fare at reasonable prices. Open for breakfast, lunch, and dinner, this venerated bar and grill also has TVs for catching up on sports. $ *Average main: 26* ⊠ *Alice Town* ☎ *242/347–3391* ⊕ *biggameclubbimini.com.*

$
BAHAMIAN
✕ **Captain Bob's.** Across from the Sea Crest Marina, centrally located in Alice Town, this casual joint starts serving rib-sticking American and Bahamian breakfasts (try the conch or lobster omelet) at 6:30 am seven days a week. This is an ideal place for anglers to start their day before heading out to the flats or the blue water. Lunches of burgers, conch, soups, salads, and fresh fish are served until 2 pm Monday through Saturday and until 1 pm on Sunday. After a long day on the sea, step in for a hearty dinner (summer only) of stuffed lobster or the popular seafood platter. If you call ahead, fishing lunches to take out on your boat can be prepared. $ *Average main: $15* ⊠ *Queen's Hwy., Alice Town* ☎ *242/347–3260* ▬ *No credit cards* ⊗ *No dinner Fall through Spring.*

$
BAHAMIAN
✕ **Joe's Conch Shack.** Heading from Bailey toward Resorts World, you can't miss this small native-style open-air conch stand between the road and the harbor. Joe personally extracts conch (with his eyes on you) while serving with a big smile. Patrons, both locals and visitors, swear the salad has more conch and is more tender conch here. But there's often a waiting line as it is made fresh by Joe himself. A couple of picnic tables in shade let you munch and sip a beer with harbor views. Joe's is accessible by boat. A truly Bahamian experience that many see as a highlight. $ *Average main: $10* ⊠ *North Bailey Town* ▬ *No credit cards.*

$$$
BAHAMIAN
✕ **Sabor.** This elegant marina-front restaurant at Resorts World is the most formal and stylish place you'll find on Bimini. Dine alfresco or inside and enjoy marina, pool, or display kitchen views while noshing on sophisticated, artistic island and international cuisine. Try the delicious Lobster Bisque or the Trio of Conch for starters, and among the 12 entrées and grilled meats and seafood, try the Porterhouse Steak, the Champagne Lobster Risotto, or the fresh-catch special. The foods' presentation is magnificent and service is willing. Hours vary greatly; call ahead to make sure. $ *Average main: $40* ⊠ *Resorts World Bimini*

5

☎ 242/347–2900, 866/344–8759 🌐 rwbimini.com/dining/on-island-dining ✍ Reservations essential.

WHERE TO STAY

$$ HOTEL 🏨 **Bimini Big Game Club Resort & Marina** (*BBGC*). This king of Alice Town's marina-based resorts has an illustrious fishing history since 1936 and in 2015 enjoyed a $5 million upgrade. **Pros:** major renovation in 2015; excellent marina for fishing boats; great base with good restaurant. **Cons:** only fishing and diving oriented; most rooms ground level; not on the beach. [$] *Rooms from: $211 ✉ King's Hwy., Alice Town ☎ 242/347–3391 resort, 800/867–4764 reservations 🌐 www.biggameclubbimini.com 🛏 35 rooms, 12 cottages, 4 penthouses 🍴 No meals.*

$$ RESORT FAMILY 🏨 **Resorts World Bimini & Marina.** This pastel-splashed luxury resort now boasts a boutique casino and a stunning new Hilton hotel with a rooftop infinity pool, a luxury spa, and a fitness center. **Pros:** top-quality marinas with all services; children's activity center; shuttle service around the property. **Cons:** restaurant opening times irregular; north-end units are long walk from town; beach can get crowded. [$] *Rooms from: $239 ✉ King's Hwy., north of Bailey Town ☎ 888/930–8688 reservations, 242/347–8000 Hilton, 242/347–2900 front desk, 305/374–6664 (ext. 1035) marina 🌐 rwbimini.com 🛏 374 units with 200 rooms and suites at the Hilton 🍴 No meals.*

$ HOTEL 🏨 **Sea Crest Hotel & Marina.** Near Radio Beach, this small marina has two buildings: one with three stories down a little lane leading to the beach and one with two stories on the marina. **Pros:** free Wi-Fi; central location; welcoming service. **Cons:** rooms are motel style; rooms lack decor; no restaurant. [$] *Rooms from: $120 ✉ King's Hwy., Alice Town ☎ 242/347–3071 🌐 www.seacrestbimini.com 🛏 25 rooms, 2 suites.*

NIGHTLIFE

Big John's Bar & Grill. This waterside sports bar and restaurant, patronized by the younger set, is one of the most popular places on-island to party, dance, and grab a cold beer, burger, or native snack. It's open from 11:30 am 'til late. It now sports a snazzy humidor with (apparently) authentic Cuban cigars. Come nightfall Thursday to Saturday, a fabulous local Bimini band plays live music combining pop, Bahamian hits, reggae, and soca. At midnight, a local DJ takes over and spins until 3 am. If you want to book a room in the boutique hotel upstairs be mindful of the loud vibes. There's a $10 cover when live music plays. *✉ King's Hwy., Alice Town ☎ 239/347–3117 🌐 www.biminibigjohns.com.*

End of the World Saloon (*The Sand Bar*). The back door of the small, noisy End of the World Saloon, better known by locals as "Sand Bar," is always open to the harbor. This place—with a sandy floor and visitors' graffiti, business cards, and other surprises on every surface—is a good spot to meet local folks over a beer and a lobster-and-conch pizza, while playing a game of ringtoss. The bar is near the heart of Alice Town, 100 yards from the Compleat Angler ruins, just steps away from Big John's. *✉ King's Hwy., Alice Town.*

OneTwoThreeFloor Sports Bar & Nightclub. Midway on North Bimini, west of the big park in Bailey Town, is the islands' latest addition to the bar-and-nightclub scene. You'll notice a big black wall on King's Highway painted with the club's funny name. Open from noon to 2 am daily, drinks are affordable especially during the Happy Hour, all day until 8 pm. OneTwoThreeFloor serves bar food such as buffalo wings, burgers, and cracked conch snacks, which you can enjoy in cool air-conditioning while watching sports on wide screens from the bar. On weekend nights until 2 am, a DJ plays everything from R&B and hip-hop to pop and golden oldies. The busiest night is Monday when the rest of the island's nightlife is mostly closed. Owner Ambrose Francis is young-spirited, friendly, and pleasing. He also owns the ABC Golf Cart business. ⊠ *King's Hwy., Bailey Town* ✛ *West of big park. Look for building with black wall and mural* ☎ *242/359–8133 cell.*

SHOPPING

Bimini Craft Centre & Straw Market. Near the Government Public Dock in Alice Town, this craft center features the original straw, wood carving, and craft works of myriad islanders. Products are showcased over 17 stalls. A great place for tie-dye resort wear and T-shirts, there's also some amazing food to be had. Make sure to stop at Nathalie's Thompson's Bread stand to try a loaf of decadent Bimini Bread. Think hot challah with sugar glaze. ⊠ *Next to a big pink government building and government dock, Alice Town* ☎ *242/347–3529.*

Trev Inn Marketplace. Trev Inn is probably the largest selection of groceries and produce on North Bimini. It's located four buildings south of the pink-colored Bimini Clinic in Porgy Bay, a short distance from Resorts World. (Also, Brown's in nearby and farther south is Roberts' Grocery Store near the big power station in Bailey Town, and Jontra's near the Bimini Big Game Club.) The mail boat comes in Thursday, so best to shop for fresh produce Thursday pm, Friday, and Saturday. Exploring local grocery stores is quaint and amusing except when you get to the cash register: with costly freight, import duties, and 7.5% VAT tax, expect to pay about double. If you are self-catering, to save money, bring coolers packed with fresh and frozen food. ⊠ *King's Hwy., Porgy Town* ☎ *242/347–2452* ✆ *patricia-roberts@hotmail.com* ✆ *Mon.–Sat. 7 am–10 pm, Sun. 7 am–8 pm.*

SPORTS AND THE OUTDOORS
BOATING AND FISHING

Bimini is not only one of the big game fishing capitals of the world, it also holds six bonefishing world records. Hire one of the island's famous guides—and great characters—to hunt for the spooky "gray ghost." Full-day fishing excursions cost upwards of $600. Reef and deep-sea fishing excursions are also available from $400 for a half day. The best bonefishing guides must be booked well in advance.

Bonefish Ansil. Ansil Saunders holds the world's record for the biggest bonefish ever caught. He's known around town as "Bonefish Ansil" and is one of the most-sought-after bonefishing guides in Bimini. Ansil also has a workshop in Bailey Town where he builds boats. He's most proud to show his memorabilia and autographs when he took Dr. Martin

Luther King Jr. on a nature tour to the mangroves in a boat. ⊠ *Alice Town* ☎ *242/347–2178.*

"Bonefish" Ebbie David. Personality-plus, you'll get more laughs out of Ebbie David than fish—or will you? He's one of Bimini's most famous and highly recommended bonefishing guides. In 2015 he won a coveted Ministry of Tourism Cacique Award for his excellence in the sport and in hospitality. Ebbie now runs his own bonefishing lodge. ⊠ *Alice Town* ☎ *242/347–2053, 242/359–8273 cell.*

"Bonefish" Tommy Sewell. Renowned bonefishing guide Tommy Sewell has over 26 years' experience leading bonefishing expeditions. Although sometimes quiet and thoughtful, Tommy calls himself "the friendly guide" and is, indeed, very obliging and pleasing. Known for delivering excellent customer service, he's proud of the big catches he can hunt down for his guests. ⊠ *Alice Town* ☎ *242/347–3234, 242/473–1089 cell.*

Captain Carson Saunders. For snorkeling and sightseeing tours in relatively calm weather, Captain Carson, based at Bimini Big Game Club, is a great choice for his value. Half days are $400 and full days are $800 in his 25-foot Proline center console. Although it lacks the luxury of bigger cabin cruisers, you'll save time and money. Bring your sunblock. ⊠ *Bimini Bug Game Club Resort & Marina, Alice Town* ☎ *242/464–5810.*

Captain Jerome Stuart. For deep-sea fishing in Bimini, Captain Jerome Stuart is your man. Stuart charges from $1,400 per day, and from $800 per half day for deep-sea fishing, with captain, mate, and gear included. Depending on the season, expect to catch wahoo, yellowfin, marlin, bluefin tuna, and swordfish. ⊠ *Alice Town* ☎ *242/347–2081.*

Fisherman's Village Marina. This 136-slip full-service marina, one of two marinas at Resorts World Resort & Marina, doubles as North Bimini's main shopping village. Adjacent to the reception area , the "village" houses Bimini Undersea dive shop, a liquor and grocery store, an ice-cream shop, a gourmet pizzeria, a café and deli, a clothing boutique, and the surprisingly affordable and good-value Healing Hole Rum Bar & Grill (only open 11 am–4 pm, Monday Wednesday, and Friday). ☎ *242/347–2900* ⊕ *rwbimini.com/dining/on-island-dining.*

Golden Dream Charters. Ex-commercial fisherman and native born Captain Stephen Knowles has a special insight when and where the fish are biting. His Ocean Yachts 46-foot Convertible *Golden Dream* is purpose-made for comfortable, fun fishing. Stephen heads to the Gulf Stream, trolling for big game: blue marlin, sailfish, mahimahi, wahoo, and tuna. Bimini abounds with bottom-fishing spots where he'll set you on groupers, snappers, porgies, and yellowtails. In his 46-foot luxury sportfishing cabin cruiser it's $1,000 for a half day, and $1,800 for a full day. ⊠ *Alice Town* ☎ *242/727–8144 cell, 242/(242) 347–3391 Bimini Big Game Club marina* ✍ *stephenknowles57@hotmail.com.*

SCUBA DIVING AND SNORKELING

The **Bimini Barge Wreck** (a World War II landing craft) rests in 100 feet of water. **Little Caverns** is a medium-depth dive with scattered coral heads, small tunnels, and swim-throughs. **Rainbow Reef** is a shallow dive popular for fish gazing. **Moray Alley** teems with captivating moray eels and

This large bonefish was caught on Bimini's shallow flats.

Bull Run is famous for its profusion of sharks. And, of course, there's **Bimini Road (aka, Road to Atlantis)**, thought to be the famous "lost city." Dive packages are available through most Bimini hotels. You can also check out the best diving options through the **Bahamas Diving Association** (☎ *954/236–9292 or 800/866–DIVE* ⊕ *www.bahamasdiving.com*).

Big Game Dive Shop. The PADI-certified Big Game Dive Shop, located at Bimini Big Game Club Resort & Marina, offers two-tank dives in the morning and one-tank dives in the afternoon. Besides exciting great hammerhead dives (from October to March, and Caribbean Reef and lemon shark dives, Big Game also offers wild–spotted dolphin snorkeling excursions. The operator visits all of Bimini's popular spots: the Sapona Wreck, the Bimini Barge, Atlantis Road, Tuna Alley, Victory Reef, the Nodules, the Strip, Rainbow Reef, and much more. They offer full range of rentals and tank fills, as well as kayaks and paddleboards for exploring the harbor and flats beyond. Novices can safely train in the resort's pool, then grab a quick bite and drink. With everything so convenient, Big Game is an excellent choice for a pure diving vacation. ⊠ *Alice Town* ☎ *242/347–3391 resort, 800/867–4764 toll free in U.S. and Canada.*

Bimini Undersea. Headquartered in Fisherman's Village at Resorts World, Bimini Undersea offers myriad excursions and experiences, including scuba diving, snuba, nature boat tours, fishing, and snorkeling near a delightful pod of Atlantic spotted dolphins. They run Sunset Celebration Cruises and near the marina and on Paradise Beach they offer kayaks and paddleboards. You can also rent or buy snorkel and diving gear. They offer two, two-tank dives a day and introductory scuba lessons.

Dive packages with accommodations at Resorts World are available, and day-trippers are also welcome to join. ✉ *Resorts World Bimini & Marina* ☎ *242/347–2941, 786/462–4641 in U.S. and Canada* ⊕ *www. biminiundersea.net.*

SOUTH BIMINI

Bigger, with nicer beaches and higher elevation than low-lying North Bimini, South Bimini is nonetheless the quieter of the two islands. Home to the island's only airport, it has a smattering of shops near the ferry landing where boats make regular crossings between the two islands, a short five-minute ride. Bimini Sands Resort is the biggest property on the island with its safe-harbor marina, condos, and nature trail. South of the main resort in Port Royal are 80-plus vacation homes, the South Bimini Beach Club and restaurants, and Neal Watson's Bimini Scuba Center. The resort helps preserve the island's eco-focus by staying low-key and keeping much of its land undeveloped. It also helps maintain the little Fountain of Youth Park, the Sharklab, and beautiful beaches.

GETTING AROUND
Visitors do not need a car on Bimini, and there are no car-rental agencies. A taxi from the airport to Bimini Sands Resort is $3. Hitching a ride is common and a kaleidoscopic-colored school bus freely transports guests from the main resort to South Bimini Beach Club and its restaurants on request and at night.

EXPLORING
Bimini Biological Field Station Sharklab. Often featured on the Discovery Channel and other TV shows, the Bimini Biological Field Station Foundation's Sharklab was founded over 25 years ago by Dr. Samuel Gruber, a shark biologist at the University of Miami. Important research on the lemon, hammerhead, nurse, bull, and other shark species has furthered awareness and understanding of the misunderstood creatures. Visitors can tour the lab at low tide. The highlight is wading into the bay where the lab keeps several lemon sharks, rotating them on a regular basis. The tour leader gets in the pen with the sharks, captures one in a net, and speaks about its behaviors and common misconceptions people have of the lemon. Tours are offered daily but visitors must call in advance; the times aim for low tide. ✉ *South Bimini* ✛ *End of long road to south of island, turn left* ☎ *242/347–4538* ⊕ *www.biminisharklab.com* 🎫 *$10 donation desirable* ⊙ *Call ahead for tour time; at low tide only.*

FAMILY **Bimini Nature Trail.** Developed by Bimini Sands Resort on undeveloped property, this mile-loop trail is one of the best of its kind in the Bahamas. Its slight rise in elevation means a lovely shaded walk under hardwood trees such as gumbo-limbos, poisonwood (marked with "Don't Touch" signs), and buttonwood. Check out the ruins of the historic Conch House, a great place for sunset-gazing. There is also a pirate's well exhibit devoted to the island's swashbuckling history. Excellent signage guides you through the island's fauna and flora if you prefer doing a self-guided tour. However, for the best interpretation and learning experience, book a guided tour with Bimini Sand's resident biologists Grant Johnson or Katie Grudecki. Kids always love petting the indigenous Bimini boa on the guided tour. ⊠ *South Bimini* ☎ *242/347–3500 resort* 🖃 *Free. Tours $12 adults, $6 kids* ☉ *Daily sunrise–sunset.*

Fountain of Youth. Famous explorer Juan Ponce de León heard from Indians about a Fountain of Youth possibly located in Bimini, so in 1513, on his way to discovering Florida and the Gulf Stream, he landed on Bimini but never found the fountain. The historical result? Somehow native Biminites adopted a freshwater natural well that was carved out of limestone by groundwater thousands of years ago and used it to commemorate Ponce de León's search. Now there's a plaque to celebrate the myth. So, nonetheless, go there and make a wish (without casting a penny—this is an eco-island). You'll find the Fountain of Youth on the road to the airport.

BEACHES

South Bimini claims Bimini's prettiest beaches, all on its western and southern sides, with some of the best from-shore snorkeling around. In the far south is South Bimini Beach Club with a big area of beach, a pool, tiki hut bar, restaurants, and convenient docks for boats. Neal Watson's Bimini Scuba Center runs dives and dolphin excursions and rents out kayaks and paddleboards. The partiers tend to congregate here leaving the northern beaches relatively secluded.

Bimini Sands Beach. Patrons of Bimini Sands Resort &Marina are not the only ones who love Bimini Sands Beach. In fact, this gorgeous stretch of white-sand beach is so enticing that vacationers on North Bimini and even boating Floridians often take the quick ferry over or cross the Gulf Stream for the day. Beachgoers can set up headquarters at the Bimini Sands Beach Club, where public boat docks (including one with a Customs and Immigration office for Floridian boats), volleyball, tiki umbrellas, restaurants, and bars provide convenience and action. The beach gets particularly busy during spring break. **Amenities:** food and drink; showers; toilets; water sports. **Best for:** partiers; sunrise; swimming; walking. ⊠ *South Bimini.*

Shell Beach. Arguably Bimini's most pristine beach, Shell Beach lies centrally on South Bimini's undeveloped west coast. Head here for seclusion. The beach stretches out, long and natural, and calm waters typically prevail. The snorkeling is also good where reefs are. As the name implies, the beach is strewn with colorful seashells. A small picnic shelter is the only concession to facilities, but head north to Bimini Sands Resort or south to South Bimini Beach Club and you'll find restaurants, bars, pools, and shade. **Amenities:** none. **Best for:** solitude; snorkeling; sunsets; swimming. ⊠ *South Bimini* ☎ *242/347–3500 resort.*

WHERE TO EAT

$$
SEAFOOD
Fodor's Choice
★

✕ **Bimini Twist and Island Sushi.** One of the top dining spots in Bimini, Bimini Twist at the South Bimini Beach Club has an exceptional sushi bar and an elegant dining room. Time your dinner for the dipping sunset show. If you'd rather not do sushi, start with conch, shrimp, lobster, or tomato ceviche. The chef is at the top of his game, and will prepare special requests with panache. Entrées provide good variety from pasta pomodoro and conch linguine to chicken sautéed with mushroom and onions, and sirloin steak. Also next door is Mackey's Sand Bar, the fun place to be on Wednesday nights, with karaoke. The bus from Bimini Sands Resort and the ferry to North Bimini is free. [$] *Average main: $35* ✉ *Bimini Sands Resort* ☎ *242/347–4500* 🌐 *www.thebiminisands.com* 🕒 *No lunch Mon.–Thurs.*

$ BAHAMIAN 🍴 **The Petite Conch.** This second-story cozy, little diner/café overlooks Bimini Sands' Marina and while not serving fancy cuisine, does have some jolly good Bahamian cooks that can satisfy the taste and wholesomeness departments without charging the earth. Very convenient for the resort's and marina's guests, The Petite Conch serves breakfast, lunch, and dinner with American and local favorites. The service is fast and comes with a smile. [$] *Average main: 10* ☎ *242/347–3500* 🌐 *www.thebiminisands.com.*

WHERE TO STAY

$$ RESORT FAMILY Fodor'sChoice ★ 🏨 **Bimini Sands Resort & Marina.** Overlooking the Straits of Florida on a stunning beach, this well-designed property rents one- to three-bedroom condominiums with direct marina access. **Pros:** four good restaurants including a sushi bar; great nature trail on property; good tour operations; full-service marina with customs nearby. **Cons:** limited nightlife on South Bimini (party is daytime here); south beach and near marina has lots of day-trippers; sometimes shortage of lounge chairs. [$] *Rooms from: $250* ✉ *South Bimini* ☎ *242/347–3500 resort, 800/737–1007 in U.S. and Canada* 🌐 *www.biminisands.com* 🛏 *206 condominiums* 🍴 *All meals.*

NIGHTLIFE

Mackey's Sand Bar. With its beachfront location, sand floor, and eight flat-screen TVs, Mackey's Sand Bar is South Bimini's one and only hot spot. Folks often make the water-taxi ride from North Bimini for dinner and cocktailing. Wednesday night is the night to be here. There's decent meals and snacks (pizzas are great), and a supercheap happy hour, karaoke, and live music in spring and summer. Bus transport to the water-ferry dock and to the resort and marina starts at 3 pm and is complimentary. ✉ *South Bimini Beach Club* ☎ *242/347–4500* 🌐 *www.thebiminisands.com.*

SPORTS AND THE OUTDOORS

BOATING AND FISHING

Bimini Sands Marina. This marina on South Bimini is a top-notch 60-slip marina with a fuel dock, and small ship's store, capable of accommodating vessels up to 100 feet. Customs and Immigration clearance is at the airport, a short, 2-mile, $3 taxi ride away. Many local bone- or bottom- or deep-sea-fishing guides and charter operators can be arranged at the front desk. It's easy for charter boats to come from North Bimini only a couple of miles away. ✉ *Bimini Sands Resort & Marina* ☎ *242/347–3500* 🌐 *www.thebiminisands.com.*

SCUBA DIVING AND SNORKELING

Bimini has excellent diving opportunities, particularly for watching marine life. Off the shore of South Bimini the concrete wreck of the SS *Sapona* attracts snorkelers as well as partiers.

Fodor'sChoice ★ **Bimini Sands Resort & Marina.** For guests of the hotel and day-trippers, Bimini Sands Resort & Marina has an excellent range of activities that includes dives and snorkeling on wrecks, reefs, and the Bimini Road to Atlantis. It also offers kayaking trips, boat tours, snorkeling with wild dolphins, shark encounters, and the Bimini Nature Trail. Located here is one of the most reputable names in diving: Neal Watson's Bimini Scuba Center, with its dive shop, equipment rentals, and tank filling all located at the South

PLAN AHEAD

Even though you're going to the laid-back islands, you need to reserve your guides, boats, cars, and golf carts in advance. And if you ask, these friendly islanders might include an airport greeting and transfer to your hotel.

Bimini Beach Club. There, you can also rent kayaks and paddleboards. ✉ *South Bimini* ☎ *242/347-3500* ⊕ *www.thebiminisands.com.*

THE BERRY ISLANDS

5

Discovered by a lucky few and pristine in beauty, the Berry Islands consist of more than two-dozen small islands and almost a hundred tiny cays stretching in a thin crescent to the north of Andros and Nassau. Most of the Berries have breathtakingly beautiful beaches. Although a few of the islands are privately owned, most of them are uninhabited—except by rare birds who use the territory as their nesting grounds, or by visiting yachters dropping anchor in secluded havens. The Berry Islands start in the north at **Great Stirrup Cay** and **Coco Cay** where thousands of cruise passengers enjoy Bahama-island experiences and the Stingray City Bahamas attraction on neighboring Goat Cay. The Berries end in the south at **Chub Cay**, only 35 miles north of Nassau.

Most of the islands' 700 residents live on **Great Harbour Cay**, which is 10 miles long and 1 mile wide. Great Harbour Cay, the largest of the Berry Islands, is tranquil, self-contained, and oriented toward yachting, family, beach, and water-sports vacationing. Its main settlement, **Bullock's Harbour**, aka "the Village," has a couple of good restaurants, two grocery and liquor stores, and small shops. A mile west, the Great Harbour Cay's beach area, partly owned by the company that owns the marina, was developed in the early 1970s. More homes, condos, and villas have been built since then, and many of the older beach villas and cottages have been remodeled. The 65-slip protected marina has also been renovated and is once again popular with yachties. There are no big resorts on Great Harbour; instead, there's a delightful, world-class boutique hotel, a motel, and homes and villas for rent on the marina and beaches. The GHC Property Owners Association is active and provides many fun activities and events, including the partial upkeep of 9 holes of the original golf course. Many private pilots have homes and fly in here. The Berries are reputed to have one of the world's highest concentrations of millionaires per square mile, but, surprisingly, there are no banks or ATMs. So, make sure you bring some cash.

Although the area has long been geared toward deep-sea fishing, in recent years, family, wedding, honeymoon, and beach-seeking vacations and bonefishing have become more popular. In the south, Chub Cay is close to a deep-sea pocket where the Tongue of the Ocean meets the

North West Providence Channel—a junction that traps big game fish. Remote flats south of Great Harbour, from Anderson Cay to Money Cay, are excellent bonefish habitats, as are the flats around Chub Cay. Deeper-water flats hold permit and tarpon.

Chub Cay, a popular halfway point for boaters crossing to and from Florida, is also experiencing a comeback with millions having been recently invested in the Chub Cay Resort & Marina. It's a project in progress. For deep-sea fishing and bonefishing fans, Chub Cay's extensive flats and deep ocean canyons are pure heaven. It's a bit quiet for families where kids have to be kept occupied—unless they are fishermen, divers, and beach fans, too. On Chub, you'll certainly connect with your friends and young ones but make sure you have a boat to get off land and give you freedom to explore, dive, and fish—and unless you want to dine at one place the whole time, bring lots of home-bought supplies: food, drink, etc. in a couple of coolers. Most rentals come with kitchens. Blessed with serenity, sea life, and beaches, the Berries are a tucked-away secret that vacationers wish they could find.

AIR TRAVEL   In the Berry Islands, Great Harbour Cay (GHC) airport receives regular flights from Fort Lauderdale Hollywood International airport (FLL) through Tropic Ocean Airways on Friday and Sunday. From Nassau, two flights a day come in from Le Air. A thrilling way to go is to hire a seaplane. Safari Seaplanes flies from Odyssey Aviation at Nassau Airport, and from Miami's seaplane base on Key Biscayne you can hire Miami Seaplanes to take you. Even more thrilling is a helicopter: ⊕ *Miamiheli.com* flies from South Florida, and Dave Harmon's Ocean Helicopters, based in West Palm Beach, can take three passengers from Executive Flight Support at Nassau Airport. From Fort Lauderdale, Miami, and Nassau, many private charter companies fly into Great Harbour and Chub Cay's (CCZ) private airport.

Chub Cay is served from Nassau (NAS) every Friday and Sunday by Captain Bill Munroe's Bill Air who can vary the aircraft's size according to passenger numbers. It's $75 one way.

On Great Harbour Cay, one of the few taxis will take you to your resort or villa. After that, renting an SUV, golf cart, or at least a bike is sensible, although walking around the Bullock's Harbour village itself is comfortable. On 6-mile-long Chub Cay, it's only a mile from the marina resort to the airport.

BOAT TRAVEL   Great Harbour Cay and Chub Cay are popular yachting destinations and stop-offs for boats going farther afield. Both are ports of entry with friendly service by Customs and Immigration for entry clearance and gaining the mandatory cruising permits. Both have excellent marinas with fuel and full services. From Nassau, the mail boat M/V *Capt. Gurth Dean* sets sail twice or three time a month from Potter's Cay Dock on Wednesday nights, arriving Thursday morning to supply the GHC with groceries, supplies, and general cargo. Some weeks, although not all, the mail boat *Sherice M* leaves Nassau on Wednesday afternoon to arrive in Chub Cay the next morning. For $40 each way you can secure passage—an authentic native adventure if somewhat bare-boned.

Fuel for boaters is also available at Alder Cay and Little Whale Cay, halfway down the chain.

When coming to the Berries think "do-it-by-boat." It's the best way to explore the islands' vast magnificence. Rent a boat or hire a guide to take you snorkeling, beaching, and even dining at the famous outpost Flo's Conch Bar on Little Harbour Cay, 16 miles southeast of Great Harbour. Visit the Stingray City Bahamas tour to snorkel with stingrays off Goat Cay, north of Great Harbour Cay, by catching the company's boat.

Contacts Chub Cay Resort & Marina. ☎ *242/325–1490 marina, 800/662–8555 in U.S. and Canada* ⊕ *www.chubcay.com.* **Great Harbour Cay Marina.** ☎ *242/367–8005 marina, 561/704–4444 in U.S. and Canada* ⊕ *www.great harbourcay.com.*

ISLAND TRANSPORTATION On Great Harbour Cay, you can get most places on foot, but you can also rent a bike, car, or golf cart. Golf-cart rentals start at $60 a day, rattle-trap SUVs from $40, and better cars from $75 up to $90. On Chub Cay you can rent golf carts at the marina and elsewhere. On both islands, transport maybe included in your villa rental. Hopefully, you'll get on to the water and sightsee some Berry magic by renting a small boat or doing some fishing. Make sure you have a good VHF radio and plot your course on a good chart that you can buy at the marinas: these islands have many hazardous reefs and sandbars. Gas is around $5 a gallon.

Contacts Happy People Rentals. ✉ *Great Harbour Cay Marina* ☎ *242/367–8117 shop, 242/359–9052 cell.* **Krum's Rentals.** ☎ *242/367–8370, 242/451–0579 cell.*

BEACHES

Off these always secluded, immaculate beaches, the clarity of Bahamian waters is especially evident when you reach the Berry Islands. Starfish abound, and you can often catch a glimpse of a gliding stingray or eagle ray. You'll find ocean beaches with gentle surf, sultry beaches with sandbar flats where you can walk half a mile, and private coves enclosed by cliffs for ultra-private experiences.

Chub Cay Beach. As well as the 400-yard beach right at the marina, Chub Cay has a splendid 1¼-mile strand with great swimming and nearby snorkeling. The Club House with its pool is a mere 400 yards away for refreshments. **Amenities:** None. **Best for:** swimming; snorkeling. ✉ *Chub Cay's southern coast* ☎ *242/325–1490 Club House and marina office.*

Great Harbour Cay Beach. Two crescents scoop Great Harbour Cay's east coast with 5 miles of almost unbroken powder. Travel north to discover Sugar Beach with its bluff-surrounding private coves. Going south is the thinner Lover's Beach and the very wide Hotel Point Beach. Next is the long, stunning, wide Great Harbour Beach, and finally, Shelling Beach with its shallow, simmering sandbars that invite you to patter yards out from shore. Great Harbour Beach has The Beach Club, a popular daytime bar and grill with a cute arts, crafts, and gift shop. Here, the residents schedule beach volleyball, activities, and

5

games, as well as yoga and exercise classes—and everyone's welcome. **Amenities:** food and drink. **Best for:** sunset; swimming; walking. ✣ *Very near the airport.*

> **EARLY-BIRD DINNERS**
>
> Dinner is commonly served in most restaurants starting at 6 pm and can be over by 8:30. It is always best to call ahead for reservations, and to let the restaurant know you are coming for sure, as hours can be irregular, or restaurants can just decide to close if they think they aren't going to be busy. Some like to have your order ahead of time.

Haines Cay Beach. At low tide, walk across from Shelling Beach estuary, round the point, and walk south a half mile and you'll discover one of the Bahamas' most unspoiled, beautiful beaches. It's 2 miles long with excellent snorkeling on its north end and swimming all along. Wear some sturdy footwear for the land walk. It's also reachable by kayak. There are no trees for shade, so an umbrella, lots of fluids, and sunscreen are advisable. **Amenities:** none. **Best for:** swimming; walking; snorkeling; solitude. ✣ *½ mile west of Shelling Beach.*

Sugar Beach. The northernmost of the island's beaches, rock bluffs divide the gorgeous, fine white sand into "private" beaches of various lengths. Exploring the Sugar Beach caves is an added attraction. Calm waters along these coved beaches make them great for snorkeling. **Amenities:** none. **Best for:** solitude; snorkeling; sunrise; swimming; walking.

WHERE TO EAT

$
BAHAMIAN

🍴 **The Beach Club.** This is the island's cool locale for breakfast and lunch, across the road from the airport, overlooking the beach and turquoise water. At breakfast, go for the eggs and ham with home grits. At lunch, have a grilled cheeseburger or whatever fresh fish is on the menu for the day. Takeout is available, including fishing lunches. Dinner is available on request, but if you eat at the open-air tables, be sure to have insect repellent, especially if the wind is down or at sunset. The club and the island's residents put on fun activities including volleyball, yoga, and exercise classes. Visitors are invited. Also, check out the beautiful tiny shop with arts, crafts, souvenirs, and gifts. [$] *Average main: $16* ✉ *On Great Harbour Cay Beach, near airport* ☎ *242/367–8108* 💳 *No credit cards* 🕒 *No dinner unless requested by group.*

$$
BAHAMIAN
Fodor's Choice ★

🍴 **Carriearl Restaurant.** Guests who discover Carriearl Restaurant are pleasantly stunned that a restaurant of such charm and caliber just happens to be on their tiny island. The warm and capable couple from Manchester, restaurateur Martin "Dronzi" Dronsfield and former British Airways flight attendant Angie Jackson, have managed to fashion one of the Bahamas' most illustrious beachside mansions into a gem of culinary and visual delight. Around the bar, conviviality abounds. Succulent fresh seafood is served with aplomb, yet it's the variety and quality of the international cuisines that many guests applaud. Carriearl's pizzas are the talk of the town. On her years flying around the world, Angie collected a treasure of fascinating exotic art, wall coverings, and sculptures. With them, she's created an eclectic ambience that spreads from the hotel's living area across pretty tables, into the cozy bar, spilling out onto the poolside terraces. Service is eagle-eyed, responsive, and amiable. Marty's bar is clearly the best-stocked on the island, tempting you to challenge the man's mixology skills. You'll be spreading the word about Carriearl's for days, or more likely, years. $ *Average main: $28* ✉ *Great Harbour Cay Beach* ☏ *242/367–8785, 242/451–8785 cell* ⊕ *www.carriearl.com* ⚓ *Reservations essential* ☞ *Breakfast, lunch, and dinner daily for hotel guests. For others: lunch Thurs.–Sat.; Sun. brunch 10 am–2 pm; dinner Wed.–Sat. 6–9:30.*

$$　✕ **Coolie Mae's Sunset Restaurant.** In the native food category, expats,
BAHAMIAN　locals, and visitors rate Mae's food as true-true excellent. Her bright sign makes the casual 60-seat restaurant, on Bullock's Harbour's central seafront, easy to find. A couple of outside tables give heightened views of a sleepy anchorage, the ocean, and gorgeous sunsets. Midday, try the conch salad, panfried grouper, or a tasty burger. Broiled lobster, steaks, pork chops, and fried conch along with peas 'n' rice and macaroni and cheese are dinner specialties. The menu changes daily, but the world-famous guava duff is always available for dessert. Place your order in advance or call a day ahead for a reservation. $ *Average main: $22* ✉ *In the middle of Bullock's Harbour's west peninsula* ☏ *242/367–8730* ▭ *No credit cards* ⊘ *Closed Sun.*

$$　✕ **Rocky Hill Pool Bar & Grill.** Located at the marina, yet not belonging to
BAHAMIAN　it, is "the Pool Bar," a convenient spot for mariners, with a refreshing pool to dip and sip. Under the shady open-air clubhouse or the sunny, bougainvillea-strewn terrace, enjoy tasty American and Bahamian fare and drinks as you mingle with yachties and friendly locals who can advise you on practically anything to see or do. The prices seem rather high for such a casual joint—owners Paul and Janet Rich insist on fine imported ingredients and local fresh seafood. Every Wednesday evening yachties and residents gather in the street to play bocce ball. After a few plonks and free rum punches, you'll discover how friendly the Berry Islands are. $ *Average main: $25* ✉ *At the marina* ☏ *242/367–8051.*

$$　✕ **Tamboo Club.** A tradition at the Great Harbour Marina, this grand
BAHAMIAN　supper club—once a private club for the likes of Cary Grant, Brigitte Bardot, and Walter Cronkite—now holds fun dinner events every two weeks, such as Dining Under the Stars and A Night in Havana. The lively crowd enjoys local and fancier international fare such as grilled seafood, pig roast, rack of lamb, beef tenderloin, pork loin, baked duck, Cornish hen, and Bahamian specialties like smothered chicken with macaroni and cheese. The events, which for this tiny island are always special, gleefully end in dancing. Call ahead to confirm dates. It's as much (perhaps more) a nightspot as a place to eat. $ *Average main: $25* ✉ *Great Harbour Marina* ☏ *242/367–8203* ▭ *No credit cards* ⚓ *Reservations essential.*

WHERE TO STAY

$$　⌂ **Carriearl Boutique Hotel.** Guests staying at this charming boutique hotel
B&B/INN　talk in superlatives. **Pros:** right on 7 miles of silky sand beach; superb
Fodor's Choice　restaurant and bar; excellent, attentive, and friendly service. **Cons:** only
★　four rooms; rooms only for 18 years or older. $ *Rooms from: $255*

Kayaks line the beach at Little Stirrup Cay in the Berry Islands.

☎ *242/367–8785 hotel, 242/451–8785 cell* 🌐 *www.carriearl.com* 🛏 *4 rooms.*

$ HOTEL 🏨 **Chub Cay Resort & Marina.** Chub Cay Resort & Marina is now open again after a rich Texas investor restarted its engines in 2014. **Pros:** the full-service marina is one of the best hurricane holes in the Bahamas; excellent location for flats and offshore fishing; decent on-site restaurant and bar serves three meals. **Cons:** can be noisy and congested with construction; not much to do other than beach, snorkel and fish. [$] *Rooms from: $155* ✉ *Chub Cay* ☎ *242/325–1490, 954/634–7496 in U.S. and Canada* 🌐 *www.chubcay.com* 🛏 *15 rooms, 3 villas (one 2-bed, two 3-bed)* 🍴 *All meals.*

$ RENTAL 🏨 **Great Harbour Cay Rentals.** Two options offer great boat access and docks near Great Harbour Cay Marina on a private peninsula: downstairs is Anglers Roost apartment villa ($150/day), newly remodeled to sleep three, with free dockage, and up above is the Seaside Cottage ($500/day), a lovely four-bedroom house with huge decks, a freshwater pool, an outside bar, and a dock that can take up to two boats under 34 feet and one up to 55 feet in 20-foot depths. **Pros:** off-the-beaten-path; easy boat access to beaches and bonefish flats; private and economical. **Cons:** you need a golf cart to get around and gather supplies. [$] *Rooms from: $125* ✉ *Seaside Cottage is on a private peninsula opposite Great Harbour Marina about 5 mins by boat, 10 mins by golf cart* ☎ *561/313–4760 in U.S. and Canada, 242/367–8155* 🛏 *2 villas, 1 house* 🍴 *No meals.*

$ B&B/INN 🏨 **Great Harbour Inn.** Perched above the marina in Great Harbour Cay, this inn is basic but conveniently located to the marina, about 3/4 mile from the beach. **Pros:** a basic, no-frills economical getaway; near marina. **Cons:** no TV or Internet service; can be hot and buggy when the wind is down. [$] *Rooms from: $130* ✉ *Above Great Harbour Cay marina* ☎ *242/367–8370, 242/451–0579 cell* ▭ *No credit cards* 🛏 *5 suites.*

$ RENTAL Fodor's Choice ★ 🏠 **The Little House On The Berry.** This beautifully designed two-bed, two-bath villa sits on rocky bluff overlooking gorgeous Lover's Beach. **Pros:** beautifully designed and well-equipped kitchen; surprisingly affordable; on the beach. **Cons:** no pets allowed; a mile to nearest grocery store. [$] *Rooms from: $199* ✉ *Lovers Beach, east side of Great Harbour Cay* ☎ *242/451–0936 cell* 🌐 *www.homeaway.com/vacation-rental/p249342#summary* 🛏 *2 rooms* ▭ *No credit cards.*

SPORTS AND THE OUTDOORS

BOATING

The water's depth is seldom more than 20 feet here. Grass patches and an occasional coral head or flat coral patch dot the light-sand bottom. You might spot the odd turtle, and if you care to jump over the boat's side with a mask, you might also pick up a conch or two in the grass. Especially good snorkeling and bonefishing, and peaceful anchorages, can be found on the lee shores of the Hoffmans and Little Harbour cays. When it's open, **Flo's Conch Bar,** at the southern end of Little Harbour Cay, serves fresh conch prepared every way you can imagine.

Great Harbour Cay Marina. In the upper Berry Islands, the full-service Great Harbour Cay Marina has 65 slips for yachts up to 150 feet. Thanks to a new manager and friendly staff, it has been upgraded and has lost the downcast look of former years. Accessed through an 80-foot-wide channel from the west, the marina is loved by yachties because it has almost zero motion even in rough weather: it's a top hurricane hole. They all love the sleepy, Out Island feel and the safe, crime-free island with its gorgeous 6-mile beach. Nevertheless, there's lots to do here: the Property Owners Association organizes petanque in the street with free rum punch on Wednesday evenings; jewelry-craft lessons, cards, and backgammon at Rocky Hill Bar & Grill (where there's a pool); and yoga, exercise classes, and beach volleyball at The Beach Club. You can even play nine holes of golf on the rather weedy course. Fuel is at a separate dock west of the marina. ☎ *242/367–8005 dock, 242/451–0936 cell* 🌐 *www.greatharbourcay.com/WebPages/marina.asp.*

Happy People. At Great Harbour Cay Marina, Elon Rolle, located in a small convenience store on the dock, hires for the day, half day, or hour, an unsinkable 20-foot Boston Outrage with 200HP for $200 a day plus gas (using about $150 for 30 gallons for a day). Snorkeling, spear, and fishing gear are extra, so bring your own. It also comes with VHF radio. If you don't know these waters, it's wise to study a map ($27 from Happy People's shop). If you're a boater, this will be a super vacation highlight, but come prepared with food, water, ice, sunscreen, shade, and gear. ✉ *Great Harbour Cay Marina* ☎ *242/367–8117, 242/367–8761 cell.*

FISHING

Percy Darville's Five Hearts Charters. Percy Darville and crew know the flats of the Berries better than anyone, and his brothers Joe and Jimmy and cousin Clive also guide. The fleet comprises four skiffs in good shape. They also travel the 1½ hours to Chub Cay (due to clients' requests), or anywhere in the Berries. Worldly fishermen who have fished around the Bahamas say the Berries have a higher percentage of larger fish. It's $400 for a half day or $600 for a full day, plus gas. Call the crew as far in advance as possible, as they are in hot demand. ⊠ *Great Harbour Cay* ☎ *242/464–4149 cell, 242/367–8119 home, 242/225–9104 toll free within the Bahamas.*

SNORKELING

FAMILY **Stingray City.** A snorkel trip here by boat to this spot on Goat Island is a favorite experience of both cruise passengers and anyone staying in Great Harbour Cay. Visitors interact in the pristine, sparkling, and shallow water with southern rays. It's by far the most popular attraction in the region. ☎ *242/364–1032 Nassau office, 242/477–0261 excursion manager; call at night* ✉ *Info@StingrayCityBahamas.com* ⊕ *stingray citybahamas.com.*

ELEUTHERA AND HARBOUR ISLAND

WELCOME TO ELEUTHERA AND HARBOUR ISLAND

TOP REASONS TO GO

★ **Play in pink sand:** Glorious, soft pink sand, the ethereal shade of the first blush of dawn, draws beach connoisseurs to Harbour Island. Plenty of pretty pink beaches also dot Eleuthera's east and north coasts.

★ **Ogle island architecture:** Historic homes with storybook gables and gingerbread verandas are the norm on Harbour Island and Spanish Wells. Picturesque Victorian houses overlook Governor's Harbour in Eleuthera.

★ **Savor soulful sounds:** Nights here rock with the Bahamian group Afro Band, the hip-hop of TaDa, the traditional sound of Jaynell Ingraham, and the calypso of Dr. Sea Breeze.

★ **Indulge in alfresco dining:** Harbour Island's intimate restaurants have reinvented regional cuisine. On Eleuthera, Governor's Harbour has a number of laid-back spots with memorable menus and magnificent views.

1 Gregory Town and North Eleuthera. Eleuthera's undeveloped, serene north holds some of the island's most iconic natural wonders: the Glass Window Bridge, a heart-racing span between 80-foot cliffs often buffeted by a raging Atlantic; the 17th-century Preacher's Cave; and the thrilling waves of Surfer's Beach.

2 Hatchet Bay. "The Country's Safest Harbour" is Hatchet Bay's claim to fame. The naturally protected harbor is a popular place to anchor sailboats and fishing vessels.

3 Governor's Harbour. The pretty Victorian town, with a lively harbor that's a frequent stop for mail boats, ferries, and yachts, offers upscale restaurants and down-home conch cafés, boutique inns, and inexpensive apartments.

4 Rock Sound and South Eleuthera. Rock Sound, the original capital of Eleuthera, is a quaint seaside settlement with 19th-century homes. Thirty miles away, yachties stop at Cape Eleuthera peninsula for a few nights of luxury in elegant town houses. Environmentalists also come here from around the world to learn about the self-sustaining Island School.

5 Harbour Island. Dunmore Town, the first capital of the Bahamas, may be the country's loveliest place, with its historic Loyalists' houses. White picket fences, some with cutouts of pineapples and boats, are festooned with red bougainvillea and tumbling purple morning glories. Luxurious inns, renowned restaurants, and the magnificent pink beach attract a parade of celebrities.

6 Spanish Wells. A quaint town of tidy clapboard white houses is on windswept St. George's Cay, a destination for those who don't want to bump elbows with other tourists. Idyllic white- and pink-sand beaches are the main attractions.

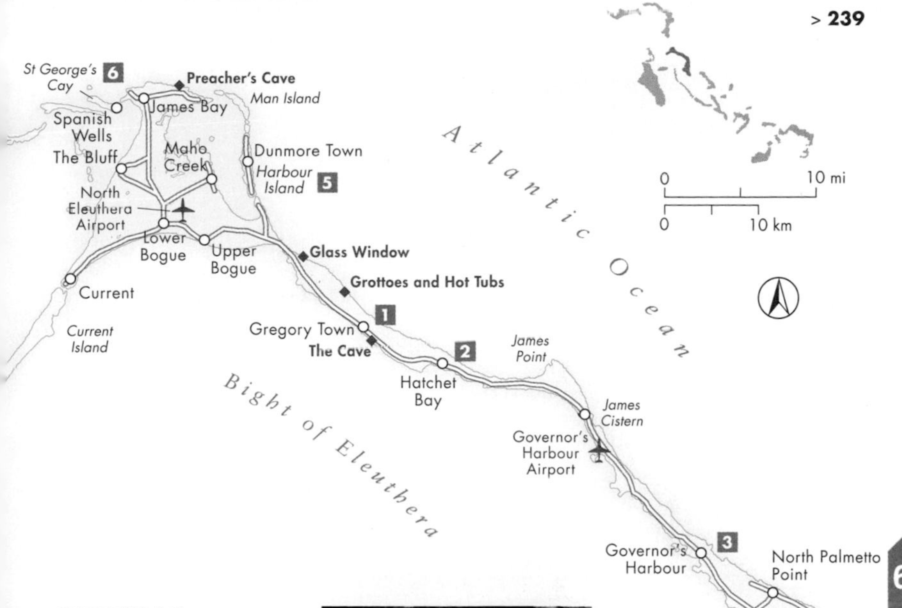

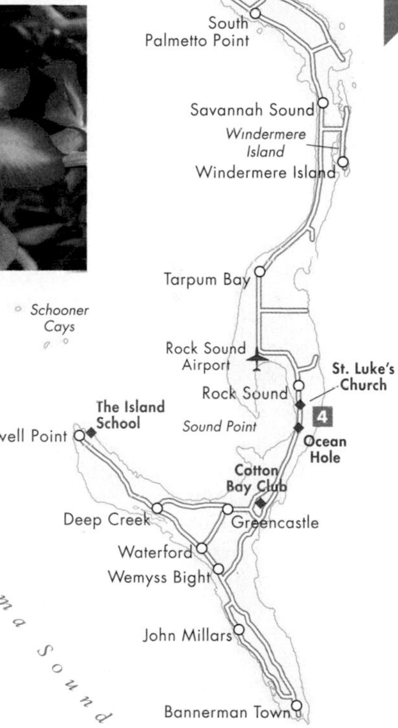

St George's **6**
Cay
Spanish   **Preacher's Cave**
Wells   James Bay   Man Island
The Bluff   Maho
                Creek   Dunmore Town
North   Harbour
Eleuthera   Island **5**
Airport
    Lower   Upper   **Glass Window**
    Bogue   Bogue
Current   **Grottoes and Hot Tubs**
Current   Gregory Town   **1**
Island   The Cave   **2**   James
            Hatchet   Point
            Bay
                James
        Governor's   Cistern
        Harbour
        Airport
                Governor's **3**
                Harbour   North Palmetto
                        Point   **6**
                    South
                Palmetto Point

GETTING ORIENTED

Eleuthera, at the center of the Bahamas chain, is a narrow, 110-mile long iguana-shaped island. The fierce, deep-blue Atlantic is to the east, and the usually placid azure and teal shallows of the Bight of Eleuthera and Great Bahama Bank are to the west. Eleuthera's mainland holds the majority of the island's residents, about 8,000. The rest of the 3,000 residents are split between 3-mile Harbour Island, 1 mile off Eleuthera's northeast coast, and 2-mile Spanish Wells, 1 mile off Eleuthera's northern coast. The island is 200 miles east of Florida and 50 miles east of Nassau.

Savannah Sound
Windermere Island
Tarpum Bay
Schooner Cays
Rock Sound Airport   St. Luke's Church
The Island School   Rock Sound **4**
Powell Point   Sound Point   Ocean Hole
        Cotton Bay Club
Deep Creek   Greencastle
Waterford
Wemyss Bight
John Millars
Bannerman Town

Atlantic Ocean

Bight of Eleuthera

Exuma Sound

0   10 mi
0   10 km

Updated by
Julianne Hoell

You haven't experienced a real escape until you've vacationed in Eleuthera. Simple luxury resorts are the norm, deserted expanses of white- or pink-sand beaches are your playground, and islanders are genuinely friendly. Although the low-key, relax-and-relax-some-more island vacation isn't for everyone, Eleuthera is the place to go when you need to recharge your batteries. Seclusion, sun, and starry skies—just what the doctor ordered.

Eleuthera was founded in 1648 by a British group fleeing religious persecution; the name is taken from the Greek word for freedom. These settlers, who called themselves the Eleutheran Adventurers, gave the Bahamas its first written constitution. "Adventurers" has taken on new meaning as a clarion call to sailors, tourists, and, more recently, retirees looking for adventures of their own.

Largely undeveloped rolling green hills and untrammeled sandy coves, along with sleepy 19th-century towns, offer an authentic Bahamas experience that is quickly disappearing. Try not to notice the ubiquitous HG Christie and Sotheby's "For Sale" signs unless, of course, you're so smitten you want to stay. Rent a car—or even better, an SUV—for washboard back roads, and explore the island's secluded beaches and sandy coves fringing turquoise and aqua water that rivals anything in the Caribbean. The island is among the prettiest in the Bahamas, with gentle hills, unspoiled "bush" (backwoods), and gardens of tumbling purple lantana and sky-blue plumbago. Hotels and inns are painted in the shades of Bahamian bays and sunset, which is best watched from the comfort of inviting verandas and seaside decks.

If you're looking for all of this and a bit more action, ferry over to Harbour Island, Eleuthera's chic neighbor. With its uninterrupted 3-mile pink-sand beach, top-notch dining, and sumptuous inns, the island has long been a favorite hideaway for jet-setters and celebrities. For splendid beaches with few, if any, tourists, head to Spanish Wells, a quiet, secluded island.

Eleuthera and Harbour Island beaches are some of the best in the world, thanks to their pristine beauty and dazzling variety. Deep-blue ocean fading to aqua shallows makes gorgeous backdrops for gourmet restaurants and the wooden decks of fishing shacks. The sand is for bonfires, celebrity-watching, Friday-night fish fries, dancing, and music, as much as it is for afternoon naps and stargazing.

Tranquil coves' sparkling white sand are as calm as a pool on the west side of Eleuthera, while the Atlantic's winter waves challenge skilled surfers on the east side, which has long stretches of pink sand. On Harbour Island, pink sand is on the ocean side and the white-sand coves face the calm channel. Home to shells that tumble in with every wave and starfish resting just offshore, the island's occasional glitz can't compete with the beaches' natural beauty.

PLANNING

WHEN TO GO

High season in Eleuthera runs December through April, when residents of cold-weather climates head to the Bahamas to defrost and soak up some rays. Low temperatures might dip into the 60s, and the water can be chilly. Bring a sweater and a jacket, especially if you are boating. Expect to pay higher rates for rooms, boat rentals, and airfare during this time. For the cheapest hotel rates and some of the best deals on water-sports packages, visit in summer or fall, when the ocean is generally calm and warm. But beware, hurricane season runs June through November, with most risk of storms from August to October. During this time weather can be steamy and rainy.

For those who want to catch some action, the liveliest times to visit Eleuthera are Christmas during the annual Junkanoo celebration, the Pineapple Festival and Conch Fest in June, and the North Eleuthera Sailing Regatta in October. Reserve hotel rooms early.

TOP FESTIVALS

WINTER **Junkanoo** is celebrated in in Rock Sound and Harbour Island on December 26. Celebrations start around 7 pm.

SUMMER **The Eleuthera Pineapple Festival** draws a crowd from all over The Bahamas and internationally. If you like a little competition on your vacation, time your trip to include the Pineappleman Sprint Triathalon.

Conch Fest. Deep Creek's annual Conch Fest in June has lots of conch, Rake 'n' Scrape, and arts and crafts. ⊠ *Rock Sound.*

Eleuthera Pineapple Festival. In June, Gregory Town hosts the four-day Eleuthera Pineapple Festival, with a Junkanoo parade, crafts displays, tours of pineapple farms, the annual 40-mile Cycling Race—as well as an opportunity to sample what Eleuthera natives proclaim to be the sweetest pineapple in the world. ⊠ *Gregory Town.*

FALL **Softball Playoff Games.** Softball is the top sport in Eleuthera, and you can't beat Softball Playoff Games in September for excitement and camaraderie with locals. The winner competes in the national tournament.

6

Games are held in Palmetto Point, Rock Sound, Governor's Harbour, and James Cistern.

North Eleuthera/Harbour Island Sailing Regatta. The North Eleuthera/Harbour Island Sailing Regatta in October provides five days of exciting competition of Bahamian Class A, B, and C boats. Onshore activities based on Harbour Island include live bands, Bahamian music, cultural shows, food, and drink.

GETTING HERE AND AROUND

AIR TRAVEL

Eleuthera has three airports: **North Eleuthera (ELH)**, midisland **Governor's Harbour (GHB)**, and **Rock Sound (RSD)** in the south. Taxis usually wait for scheduled flights at the airports. Taxi service for two people from North Eleuthera Airport to the Cove is $20 ($60 from Governor's Harbour Airport); from Governor's Harbour to Pineapple Fields, $35; from Rock Sound airport to Cape Eleuthera, $70. Visitors going to Harbour Island and Spanish Wells should fly into North Eleuthera Airport.

Contacts North Eleuthera Airport. ✛ *North Eleuthera* ☎ *242/335–1242.* **Governor's Harbour Airport.** ✉ *Governor's Harbour* ☎ *242/332–2321.* **Rock Sound Airport.** ✉ *Rock Sound* ☎ *242/334–2177.*

BOAT AND FERRY TRAVEL

Mail boats leave from Nassau's Potter's Cay for the five-hour trip to Eleuthera. One-way tickets cost $35. M/V *Current Pride* sails to Current Island, Hatchet Bay, the Bluff, and James Cistern on Thursday, returning Tuesday to Nassau. M/V *Bahamas Daybreak III* leaves Nassau on Monday and Wednesday for Harbour Island, Rock Sound, and Davis Harbour, returning to Nassau Tuesday and Friday. The *Eleuthera Express* sails for Governor's Harbour, Rock Sound, Spanish Wells, and Harbour Island on Monday and Thursday, returning to Nassau on Tuesday and Sunday. Contact the **Dockmaster's Office. Bahamas Ferries**, high-speed catamarans, connect Nassau to Harbour Island, Governor's Harbour, and Spanish Wells. The trip takes three hours and costs $155 round-trip.

Contacts Dockmaster's Office. ☎ *242/393–1064.*

CAR TRAVEL

Rent a car if you plan to travel around Eleuthera. North to south is about a three-hour drive. Daily rentals run about $70. Request a four-wheel drive if you plan to visit Preacher's Cave or Surfer's Beach.

Contacts Big Daddy's Rental Cars. ✉ *Governor's Harbour* ☎ *242/332–1592* ⊕ *www.wcbigdaddyrentalcars.com.* **Dingle Motor Service.** ✉ *Rock Sound* ☎ *242/334–2031.* **Gardiner's Automobile Rentals.** ✉ *Governor's Harbour* ☎ *242/332–2665.* **Stanton Cooper.** ✉ *Governor's Harbour* ☎ *242/359–7007.*

GOLF CART TRAVEL

You'll want a golf cart if you spend more than a couple of days on Harbour Island or Spanish Wells. Four-seater carts start at about $50 a day. Carts can be rented at most hotels and at the docks.

Contacts Abner's Rentals. ✉ *Spanish Wells* ☎ *242/333-4090.* **Dunmore Rentals.** ☎ *242/333-2372.* **Johnson's Rentals.** ☎ *242/333-2376.* **Kam Kourts.** ☎ *242/333-2248.*

TAXI TRAVEL

Taxis are almost always waiting at airports and at the North Eleuthera and Harbour Island water taxi docks. Your hotel can call a taxi for you; let them know a half hour before you need it.

Contacts Amos at Your Service. ✉ *Gregory Town* ☎ *242/422-9130.* **Stanton Cooper.** ☎ *242/359-7007.*

HOTELS

Harbour Island, more than any other Out Island, is where the cognoscenti come to bask in ultraluxurious inns and atmospheric small resorts. Follow the celebrities to $600-a-night cottages with views of the pink-sand beach or ultraelegant rooms in Dunmore Town. Eleuthera offers elegant intimate resorts next to pink- and white-sand beaches happily empty of crowds. Those on tight budgets have a range of friendly, tidy, and affordable inns, a few on the beach, for around $100 a night. For urbanites who want all-out American luxury, there are modern town houses with stainless-steel appliances and granite in the kitchens, and bedrooms for the entire family. Whether you spend a lot or a little, the staff on this friendly island will know your name after a day. Many hotels are closed in September and October.

RESTAURANTS

Don't let the outdoor dining on rustic wood tables fool you—Harbour Island and Eleuthera offer sophisticated cuisine that rivals that of any restaurants in Nassau. Although the place is usually casual and you never have to wear a tie, food is taken seriously. Of course, island specialties such as cracked conch, barbecued pork or chicken, and the succulent Bahamian lobster most locals call crawfish still abound, but you'll also find cappuccinos, steak, and lobster ravioli. Stop by Harbour Island's conch shacks on Bay Street north of Government Dock, where you can eat fresh conch salad on decks next to the water.

Most eateries are closed Sunday. Many restaurants have entertainment on regular nights so plan your dining schedule accordingly.

HOTEL AND RESTAURANT PRICES

Restaurant prices are based on the median main course price at dinner, excluding gratuity, typically 15%, which is often automatically added to the bill. Hotel prices are for two people in a standard double room in high season, excluding service and 6%–12% tax.

WHAT IT COSTS IN DOLLARS			
$	$$	$$$	$$$$
Restaurants	under $20	$20–$30	$31–$40	over $40
Hotels	under $200	$200–$300	$301–$400	over $400

GREAT ITINERARIES

IF YOU HAVE 3 DAYS

Fly into North Eleuthera and take the ferry to **Harbour Island**. Base yourself at a hotel near the famous 3-mile pink-sand beach or in historic Dunmore Town. Relax on the beach and have lunch at an ocean-side restaurant. Stroll through **Dunmore Town** in the afternoon, stopping at crafts stands and fashionable shops, admiring colonial houses along Bay Street, and visiting historic churches. At night, dine at one of the island's fine restaurants, such as The Landing, Rock House, Pink Sands, or Acquapazza. On Day 2, go scuba diving or snorkeling, or hire a guide and try to snag a canny bonefish. Visit the conch shacks on Bay Street for a low-key beachside dinner. On Day 3 get some last-minute color on the beach or some in-room spa pampering; stop by Vic-Hum Club or Gusty's for late-night music.

IF YOU HAVE 5 DAYS

Head back to **Eleuthera** for the next two days. Rent a car at the North Eleuthera Airport (reserve in advance) and drive south past the **Glass Window Bridge**, where you can stand in one spot and see the brilliant-blue and often-fierce Atlantic Ocean to the east and the placid Bight of Eleuthera to the west. Continue to **Governor's Harbour**, the island's largest town, and grab lunch at Tippy's or the Beach House, upscale, laid-back beach bistros overlooking the Atlantic Ocean. Stay at one of the beach resorts and enjoy the incredible water views. Head into town if you're looking for some nightlife or dining options.

IF YOU HAVE 7 DAYS

On your last two days, drive back to **North Eleuthera**, base yourself at the Cove, and relax on the resort's two beaches. On your final day take the ferry to **Spanish Wells**, where you can rent a golf cart and spend a half day exploring the tiny town and relaxing on a white-sand beach with no tourists. Or stay put and explore Surfer's Beach.

VISITOR INFORMATION

Contacts Eleuthera Tourist Office. ⊠ *Governor's Harbour* ☎ *242/332–2142* ⊕ *www.bahamas.com.* **Harbour Island Tourist Office.** ⊠ *Dunmore St.* ☎ *242/333–2621.* **Out Islands Promotion Board.** ⊕ *www.myoutislands.com.*

GREGORY TOWN AND NORTH ELEUTHERA

Gregory Town is a sleepy community, except on Friday nights when people are looking for music, whether that is speakers blasting reggae or a local musician playing Rake 'n' Scrape at a roadside barbecue. There's action, too, at Surfer's Beach, where winter waves bring surfers from around the world. They hang their surfboards from the ceiling at Elvina's Bar for free summer storage. The famous Glass Window Bridge is north of town, and Preacher's Cave, landing of the earliest settlers, is on the northern tip of the island. Gregory Town is home to a little more than 400 people, residing in small houses on a hillside that slides down to the sea. The town's annual Pineapple Festival begins on the Thursday

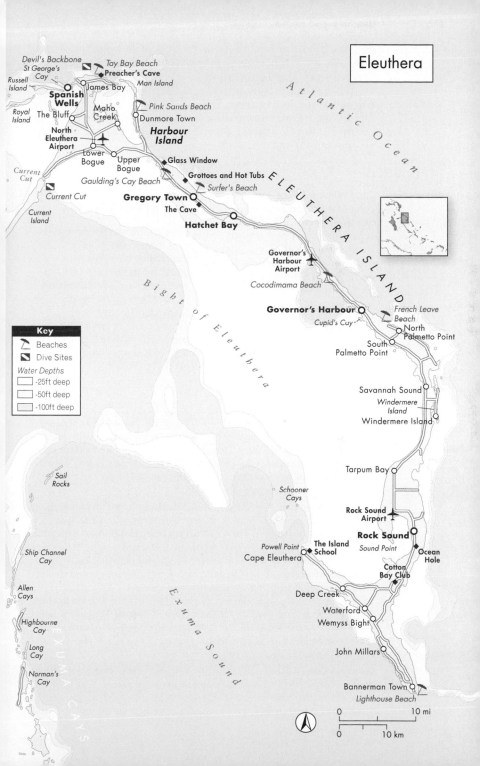

Eleuthera

Atlantic Ocean

Devil's Backbone
St George's Cay
Russell Island
Tay Bay Beach
Preacher's Cave
Man Island
James Bay
Spanish Wells
Royal Island
The Bluff
Maho Creek
Pink Sands Beach
Dunmore Town
Harbour Island
North Eleuthera Airport
Lower Bogue
Upper Bogue
◆ **Glass Window**
Current Cut
Current Island
Gaulding's Cay Beach
Grottoes and Hot Tubs
◆ Surfer's Beach
Gregory Town
The Cave
Hatchet Bay

Bight of Eleuthera

ELEUTHERA ISLAND

Governor's Harbour Airport
Cocodimama Beach
Governor's Harbour
Cupid's Cay
French Leave Beach
North Palmetto Point
South Palmetto Point

Savannah Sound
Windermere Island
Windermere Island

Tarpum Bay

Sail Rocks

Schooner Cays

Rock Sound Airport
Rock Sound
◆ Ocean Hole
Sound Point

Ship Channel Cay

Allen Cays

Powell Point
The Island School
Cape Eleuthera
Cotton Bay Club

Deep Creek
Waterford
Wemyss Bight

Highbourne Cay

Long Cay

John Millars

Exuma Sound

Norman's Cay

EXUMA CAYS

Bannerman Town
Lighthouse Beach

Key
▶ Beaches
◣ Dive Sites
Water Depths
- -25ft deep
- -50ft deep
- -100ft deep

0   10 mi
0   10 km

evening of the Bahamian Labor Day weekend, at the beginning of June, with live music continuing into the wee hours.

GETTING HERE AND AROUND

The North Eleuthera Airport is closer to Gregory Town hotels than the airport in Governor's Harbour. The taxi fare from the North Eleuthera Airport to the Cove Eleuthera, the area's most upscale inn, is $35 for two people. Rent a car at the airport unless you plan to stay at a resort for most of your visit.

EXPLORING

Fodor'sChoice
★

Glass Window Bridge. At a narrow point of the island a few miles north of Gregory Town, a slender concrete bridge links two sea-battered bluffs that separate the island's Central and North districts. Sailors going south in the waters between New Providence and Eleuthera supposedly named this area the Glass Window because they could see through the natural limestone arch to the Atlantic on the other side. Stop to watch the northeasterly deep-azure Atlantic swirl together under the bridge with the southwesterly turquoise Bight of Eleuthera, producing a brilliant aquamarine froth. Artist Winslow Homer found the site stunning, and painted *Glass Window* in 1885. The original stone arch, created by Mother Nature, was destroyed by a combination of storms in the 1940s. Subsequent concrete bridges were destroyed by hurricanes in 1992 and 1999. Drive carefully, because there is frequent maintenance work going on. ⊠ *Queen's Hwy., north of Gregory Town, Gregory Town.*

> **PINEAPPLE EXPRESS**
>
> Pineapples remain Eleuthera's most famous product, even though the industry has been greatly reduced since the late 1800s, when the island dominated the world's pineapple market. These intensely sweet fruits are still grown on family farms, primarily in northern Eleuthera. Don't miss Gregory Town's Pineapple Festival in June.

Grottoes and Hot Tubs. If you're too lulled by the ebb and flow of lapping waves and prefer your shores crashing with dramatic white sprays, a visit here will revive you. The sun warms these tidal pools—which the locals call "moon pools"—making them a markedly more temperate soak than the sometimes chilly ocean. Be careful, and ask locals about high seas before you enjoy. On most days refreshing sprays and rivulets tumble into the tubs, but on some days it can turn dangerous; if the waves are crashing over the top of the cove's centerpiece mesa, pick another day to stop here. ⊠ *Queen's Hwy., Gregory Town ✣ 5 miles north of Gregory Town on the right (Atlantic) side of Queen's Hwy. A Bahamian Heritage sign marks the turn. If you reach the one-lane Glass Window Bridge, you've gone too far.*

Fodor'sChoice
★

Preacher's Cave. At the island's northern tip, this cave is where the Eleutheran Adventurers (the island's founders) took refuge and held services when their ship wrecked in 1648. Note the original stone altar inside the cave. Across from the cave is a long succession of deserted pink-sand beaches. ⊠ *North Eleuthera ✧ Follow the Queen's Hwy. to the T-intersection at the north end of the island. Turn right and follow signs to the cave.*

BEACHES

Gaulding's Cay Beach. Snorkelers and divers will want to spend time at this beach, 3 miles north of Gregory Town. You'll most likely have the long stretch of white sand and shallow aqua water all to yourself, and it's great for shelling. At low tide, you can walk or swim to Gaulding's Cay, a tiny rock island with a few casuarina trees. There's great snorkeling around the island; you'll see a concentration of sea anemones so spectacular it dazzled even Jacques Cousteau's biologists. **Amenities:** none. **Best for:** snorkeling; sunset. ⊠ *Queen's Hwy., across from Daddy Joe's restaurant, Gregory Town.*

> **GREGORY TOWN SOUND**
>
> Grammy Award–winning musician Lenny Kravitz built a multimillion-dollar recording studio called Gregory Town Sound, and he and his band often slip into Elvina's Bar down the road for inspiration. Kravitz, who lives in Gregory Town part-time, has said, "This is the place I love being the most. Some of the nicest people I've ever met in my life are here."

Surfer's Beach. This is Gregory Town's claim to fame and one of the few beaches in the Bahamas known for surfing. Serious surfers have gathered here since the 1960s for decent waves from December to April. If you don't have a jeep, you can walk the ¾ mile to this Atlantic-side beach—take a right onto the paved road past the Hatchet Bay silos, just south of Gregory Town. Look for a young crowd sitting around bonfires at night. **Amenities:** none. **Best for:** surfing; walking. ⊠ *Queen's Hwy., Gregory Town.*

Tay Bay Beach. Steps from historical Preacher's Cave, this beach offers a long expanse of pink powdery sand. The area is remote, so you're likely to have the beach to yourself. There are plenty of palmetto trees to relax underneath for a quiet afternoon. Just offshore is Devil's Backbone, where the Eleutheran Adventurers shipwrecked and sought shelter in the cave. **Amenities:** parking. **Best for:** solitude; walking. ⊠ *North Eleuthera ✧ Follow the Queen's Hwy. to the T-intersection at the north end of the island. Turn right and follow signs to Preacher's Cave.*

WHERE TO EAT

$$$
EUROPEAN
Fodor's Choice
★

✕ **The Cove Eleuthera Restaurant.** The spacious, window-lined dining room serves three meals a day, blending classic Continental with fresh Bahamian fare. An extensive cocktail list from the Freedom Bar includes the Glass Window Bridge—the exquisite landmark of the same name is just a short drive away. It's one of the nicest restaurants on the island. Be sure to order from the sushi bar—you won't be disappointed. $ *Average main: $33* ⊠ *Queen's Hwy., Gregory Town* ☎ *242/335–5142, 888/776–3901* ⊕ *www.thecoveeleuthera.com* ⚓ *Reservations essential.*

6

$$ BAHAMIAN 🍴 **Daddy Joe's.** Located just south of the Glass Window Bridge, this restaurant hosts live bands every Sunday. Order conch bites as a starter to complement the long list of tropical concoctions, including the aptly named "Da Glass Window." In addition to wings and wraps, Daddy Joe's also offers grilled options like fresh seafood and chicken. Call ahead to confirm live music. [$] *Average main: $21* ✉ *Queen's Hwy., Gregory Town* ☎ *242/335–5688* 💳 *No credit cards* ⏲ *Closed Wed.*

$ CAFÉ 🍴 **The Laughing Lizard Café.** This eco-minded café is perched high atop a hill just off the Queen's Highway, north of Gregory Town. The colorful restaurant uses local produce to create island-inspired wraps, panini, and salads. They also have a full bar where you can order tropical smoothies, Bahamian beer, or fresh herbal iced tea. Jamaican owner Petagay Hollinsed-Hartman is committed to a green philosophy—all to-go utensils and plates are biodegradable, and aluminum cans are crushed and sent to Nassau to support the Cans for Kids program. [$] *Average main: $10* ✉ *Queen's Hwy., Gregory Town* ☎ *242/470–6992* 💳 *No credit cards* ⏲ *Closed Sun. and Mon.*

WHERE TO STAY

$$$ RESORT Fodor's Choice ★ 🏨 **The Cove Eleuthera.** Forty secluded acres studded with scenic beach cottages set the tone for this relaxing island escape, which underwent a sweeping renovation in 2013. **Pros:** sandy beaches; top-rated amenities; one of the most luxurious places to stay on the island. **Cons:** need a car if you want to do anything outside the property; resort is quiet and secluded; some lower-budget rooms lack the privacy of the bungalows and villas. [$] *Rooms from: $395* ✉ *Queen's Hwy., Gregory Town* ✥ *1½ miles north of Gregory Town* ☎ *242/335–5142, 888/776–3901* 🌐 *www.thecoveeleuthera.com* 🛏 *57 rooms* 🍽 *No meals.*

NIGHTLIFE

Elvina's Bar and Restaurant. A one-room bar with a small stage and dance floor, Elvina's has been a musical and social institution for 30 years. A live band plays every Saturday, and you can't miss open-mike nights, where you never know who will walk in the door and sing—Kid Rock, Mariah Carey, the Black Crows, or Lenny Kravitz, who lives nearby. The place doesn't really get hopping until after 9 pm. ✉ *Queens Hwy., Gregory Town* ☎ *242/699–5595* ⏲ *Closed Mon. and Wed.*

SHOPPING

Fodor's Choice ★ **Island Made Shop.** This shop, run by Pam and Greg Thompson, is a good place to shop for Bahamian arts and crafts, including Androsia batik (made on Andros Island), driftwood paintings, Abaco ceramics, and prints. Look for the old foam buoys which have been carved and painted into fun faces. ✉ *Queen's Hwy., Gregory Town* ☎ *242/335–5369* ⏲ *Closed on Sun.*

SPORTS AND THE OUTDOORS

ADVENTURE TOURS

Bahamas Out-Island Adventures. This tour operator offers day, half-day, and overnight kayaking, snorkeling, and surfing trips, and offers accommodations at its headquarters at Surfer's Beach. ⊠ *Gregory Town* ☎ *242/335–0349* ⊕ *www.bahamasadventures.com.*

ISLAND TOURS

Arthur Nixon Tours. The caretaker and keeper of the North Palmetto Sound Lighthouse offers tours of the lighthouse and the island. ☎ *242/359–7879.*

Pineapple Tours. Pineapple Tours can help you experience the northern end of Eleuthera. Contact them to set up an individualized tour of the area. ☎ *242/470–7876.*

SCUBA DIVING AND SNORKELING

The **Current Cut**, a narrow passage between North Eleuthera and Current Island, is loaded with marine life and provides a roller-coaster ride on the currents. You'll want a boat and, most important, a guide, as the current is very fast and can be dangerous if you don't know what you're doing. In North Eleuthera, **Devil's Backbone** offers a tricky reef area with a nearly infinite number of dive sites and a large number of wrecks. Contact a local dive shop to schedule a trip.

SURFING

Rebecca's Beach Shop. In Gregory Town, stop by Rebecca's Beach Shop, a general store, crafts shop, and, most important, a surf shop, where local surf guru "Ponytail Pete" rents surfboards, snorkel gear, and more. A chalkboard lists surf conditions and tidal reports. He also gives surf lessons. ⊠ *Queen's Hwy., Gregory Town* ☎ *242/335–5436.*

HATCHET BAY

Hatchet Bay, which has one of mid-Eleuthera's few marinas, is a good place to find a fishing guide and friendly locals. Take note of the town's side roads, which have such colorful names as Lazy Road, Happy Hill Road, and Smile Lane. Just south of town, the Rainbow Inn and restaurant is the hub of activity for this stretch of the island.

"The Country's Safest Harbour" is Hatchet Bay's claim to fame. The naturally protected harbor is a popular place to anchor sailboats and fishing vessels when storms are coming. One of the most memorable days for the harbor, however, wasn't a storm but the day years ago when Jackie Kennedy Onassis came in on a friend's yacht.

The pastoral scenery outside of Hatchet Bay is some of the island's most memorable—towering, long-empty grain silos, windswept green hillsides, and wild cotton, remnants of the old cotton plantations. Don't miss James Cistern, a seaside settlement to the south.

GETTING HERE AND AROUND

Hatchet Bay is equidistant between the Governor's Harbour and North Eleuthera airports. The taxi fare from either airport is about $50 for two people. Rent a car at the airport unless you plan to stay at a resort for most of your visit.

EXPLORING

The Cave. North of Hatchet Bay lies a subterranean, bat-populated tunnel complete with stalagmites and stalactites. Pirates supposedly once used it to hide their loot. An underground path leads for more than a mile to the sea, ending in a lofty, cathedral-like cavern. Within its depths, fish swim in total darkness. The adventurous may wish to explore this area with a flashlight (follow the length of guide string along the cavern's floor), but it's best to inquire first at one of the local stores or the Rainbow Inn for a guide. ☒ *Queen's Hwy.* ✛ *2 miles north of Hatchet Bay, turn left at sign for "Hatchet Bay Caves".*

WHERE TO EAT

$$
ECLECTIC

✕ **The Front Porch.** This little roadside restaurant features a beautiful view of the bay, particularly at sunset when the orange horizon is freckled with the silhouettes of moored sailboats. The menu is island-inspired European cuisine and always includes fresh seafood. In addition to serving lunch and dinner, The Front Porch can also arrange captains and tour guides. Ⓢ *Average main: $24* ☒ *Queen's Hwy.* ☎ *242/335–0727.*

$$$
EUROPEAN

✕ **The Rainbow Inn Steakhouse.** With a classy but no-fuss aura and exhibition windows that face gorgeous sunsets, this restaurant is well known for its steaks, which are flown in daily. Grouper, conch, mahimahi, and cobia are also fresh, caught daily. Guests have 180-degree views of the ocean from the screened patio or dining room. The restaurant has live music on Monday, Wednesday, and Saturday nights (in high season). They are open for breakfast. Ⓢ *Average main: $35* ☒ *Queen's Hwy.* ✛ *2½ miles south of Hatchet Bay* ☎ *242/335–0294* ☯ *Closed Tues. and end of Aug.–Oct.*

$$
BAHAMIAN

✕ **Twin Brothers.** This brightly painted restaurant is famous for its frozen daiquiris. Icy mixes of strawberry and piña colada are swirled into a striking (and delicious) dessert cocktail. Bahamian fare is available at lunch and dinner in the casual outdoor dining area. There's no harbor view, but the alfresco atmosphere is pleasant nonetheless. Ⓢ *Average main: $25* ☒ *West off Queen's Hwy.* ☎ *242/335–0730* ▭ *No credit cards* ☯ *Closed Mon. and Tues.*

WHERE TO STAY

$
RENTAL
Fodor's Choice
★

▥ **Rainbow Inn.** Immaculate, generously sized cottages, some octagonal— all with large private porches—have sweeping views of the ocean. **Pros:** superspacious cottages at reasonable prices; great water views; friendly service. **Cons:** not on the beach; not close to a town or shops; rustic accomodations. Ⓢ *Rooms from: $155* ☒ *Queen's Hwy.* ✛ *2½* *miles south of Hatchet Bay* ☎ *242/335–0294* ⊕ *www.rainbowinn.com* ⊘ *Closed end of Aug.–Oct.* ⇨ *4 cottages, 2 villas* ❍|*Some meals.*

NIGHTLIFE

Dr. Sea Breeze. The debonair Cedric Bethel, better known as Dr. Sea Breeze, strums his acoustic guitar while singing island songs at the Rainbow Inn in Hatchet Bay and Sky Beach Club in Governor's Harbour. To be sure you don't miss him, call beforehand to confirm his schedule.

GOVERNOR'S HARBOUR

Governor's Harbour, the capital of Eleuthera and home to government offices, is the largest town on the island and one of the prettiest. Victorian-era houses were built on Buccaneer Hill, which overlooks the harbor, bordered on the south by a narrow peninsula and Cupid's Cay at the tip. To fully understand its appeal, you have to settle in for a few days and explore on foot—if you don't mind the steep climb up the narrow lanes. The town is a step into a gentler, more genteel time. Everyone says hello, and entertainment means wading into the harbor to cast a line, or taking a painting class taught by Martha's Vineyard artist Donna Allen at the 19th-century pink library on Monday mornings. You can see a current movie at the balconied Globe Princess, the only theater on the island, which also serves the best hamburgers in town. Or swim at the gorgeous beaches on either side of town, which stretch from the pink sands of the ocean to the white sands of the Bight of Eleuthera. There are three banks, a few grocery stores, and some of the island's wealthiest residents, who prefer the quiet of Eleuthera to the fashionable party scene of Harbour Island.

GETTING HERE AND AROUND

Fly into Governor's Harbour Airport north of town, or arrive by mail boat from Nassau. You will want to rent a car at the airport, even if you plan to stay in Governor's Harbour, to best explore the beaches and restaurants. If you stay at Duck Inn or Laughing Bird Apartments, you'll be able to walk to nearby restaurants.

EXPLORING

Haynes Library. The heart of the community, this 19th-century building offers art classes and Tuesday-morning coffee hours for visitors and residents. The library has a wide selection of books and Internet terminals, with gorgeous views of the harbor. ⊠ *Cupid's Cay Rd.* ☎ *242/332–2877* ⊕ *hayneslibrary.blogspot.com* ⊘ *Mon.–Thurs. 9–6, Fri. 9–5, Sat. 10–4* ⊘ *Closed Sun.*

Leon Levy Native Plant Preserve. Walk miles of scenic trails in this 25-acre nature preserve located on Banks Road. Funded by the Leon Levy Foundation and operated by the Bahamas National Trust, the preserve serves as an environmental education center with a focus on traditional bush medicine. Follow the boardwalk over a small waterfall and take the path to the Observation Tower to see hundreds of indigenous trees,

A Governor's Harbour home

plants, and wildlife such as mangroves, five-finger plants, and bull-finches. Group tours are available, or if you'd prefer to tour the preserve on your own, the welcome center will provide you with a map and a plant identification guide. ⌧ *Banks Rd.* ☎ *242/332–3831* ⊕ *www. levypreserve.org* ⌑ *$5* ⊘ *Daily 9–5.*

Windermere Island. About halfway between Governor's Harbour and Rock Sound, distinguished Windermere Island, 5 miles long with a lovely pink-sand beach, is the site of vacation homes of the rich and famous, including Mariah Carey and members of the British royal family. Don't plan on any drive-by ogling of these million-dollar homes, though; the security gate prevents sightseers from passing. ⌧ *Queen's Hwy., Windermere.*

BEACHES

FAMILY **Cocodimama Beach.** Many necklaces and shell decorations come from Cocodimama, which, along with Ten Bay Beach at South Palmetto Point, is well known for perfect small shells. The water at this secluded beach, 6 miles north of Governor's Harbour, has the aqua and sky-blue shades you see on Bahamas posters, and is shallow and calm, perfect for children and sand castles. **Amenities:** parking. **Best for:** sunset. ⌧ *Queen's Hwy.* ⚓ *Look for Cocodimama Charming Resort.*

French Leave Beach. This stretch of pink sand was Club Med's famed beach before the resort was destroyed by a hurricane in 1999, and is now home to the new French Leave Marina Village. The gorgeous Atlantic-side beach is anchored by fantastic bistros like the Beach

House and Tippy's. The wide expanse, ringed by casuarina trees, is often deserted and makes a great outpost for romantics. **Amenities:** food and drink. **Best for:** solitude; swimming; walking. ⌧ *Banks Rd.*

WHERE TO EAT

$ DELI **✕ Banks Road Deli.** For the perfect beach picnic, stop by Banks Road Deli to pick up freshly made sandwiches, chips, and homemade cookies. Located in the same building as Pineapple Field's Gift Store, the deli also serves pastries and coffee in the morning, which you can enjoy in their quiet outdoor seating area. The small gourmet grocery section is great for stocking up on wine and chocolate. $ *Average main: $9* ⌧ *Banks Rd.* ☏ *242/332–2221* ⊕ *www.pineapplefields.com/index.php/dining/banks-road-deli.html* ⊗ *Closed Sun.*

PINK-SAND BEACHES

Contrary to popular opinion, pink sand comes primarily from the crushed pink and red shells of microscopic insects called foraminifera, not coral. Foraminifer live on the underside of reefs and the sea floor. After the insects die, the waves smash the shells, which wash ashore along with sand and bits of pink coral. The intensity of the rosy hues depends on the slant of the sun.

6

$$ EUROPEAN **Fodor's** Choice ★ **✕ The Beach House Tapas Restaurant.** On a gorgeous pink-sand beach, this outdoor restaurant offers stunning views and exquisite Spanish appetizers and entrées such as shrimp with goat cheese and prosciutto, and jumbo crab–and–lobster ravioli. There is live music on Monday and Thursday nights, so be sure to arrive early to secure a table, or sit at the bar for the best view of the band. $ *Average main: $25* ⌧ *Banks Rd.* ☏ *242/332–3387* ⊗ *Closed Sept. No dinner Tues., Wed., and Fri.–Sun.*

$$ BAHAMIAN **✕ Buccaneer Club.** On the top of Buccaneer Hill overlooking the town and harbor, this mid-19th century farmhouse is now a restaurant serving three meals a day, with an outdoor dining area surrounded by a garden of bougainvillea, hibiscus, and coconut palms. The beach is a leisurely five-minute stroll away, and the harbor, where you can also swim, is within shouting distance. Sample such native specialties as grouper, conch, and crawfish. $ *Average main: $21* ⌧ *Haynes Ave.* ☏ *242/332–2000* ⊗ *No dinner Sun. and Wed.*

$ CAFÉ **✕ Da Perk Café.** This tidy restaurant offers free Wi-Fi and is an excellent place to catch up on emails over a homemade quiche and Lavazza coffee. The café is located in the middle of town, making it a convenient spot for a quick bite at breakfast or lunch. With menu items like tuna salad and deli sandwiches, and myriad bottled drink options, Da Perk Café is also a great place to pack your cooler for a fishing excursion. $ *Average main: $8* ⌧ *Queen's Hwy.* ☏ *242/332–2620* ▬ *No credit cards* ⊗ *Closed Sun. No dinner.*

$ BAKERY **✕ Governor's Harbour Bakery.** A Governor's Harbour staple since 1989, this bakery serves up delicious pastries and breads, baked fresh daily. Stop in to pick up come of the popular Danish coffee cake, or sample johnnycakes and hot patties—Bahamian favorites. The bakery also makes fresh doughnuts, éclairs, and other homemade treats. Be

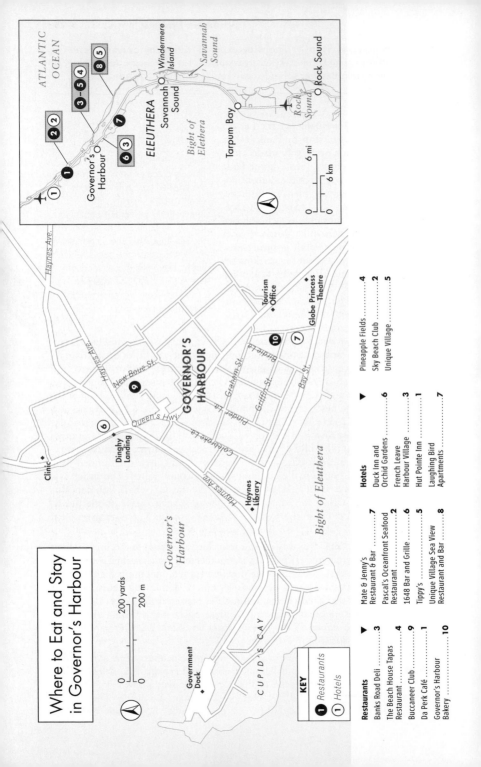

Where to Eat and Stay in Governor's Harbour

KEY

▶ Restaurants

① Hotels

Restaurants ▶

Banks Road Deli **3**
The Beach House Tapas
Restaurant **4**
Buccaneer Club **9**
Da Perk Café **1**
Governor's Harbour
Bakery **10**

Mate & Jenny's
Restaurant & Bar **7**
Pascal's Oceanfront Seafood
Restaurant **2**
1648 Bar and Grille **6**
Tippy's **5**
Unique Village Sea View
Restaurant and Bar **8**

Hotels ▶

Duck Inn and
Orchid Gardens **6**
French Leave
Harbour Village **3**
Hut Pointe Inn **1**
Laughing Bird
Apartments **7**

Pineapple Fields **4**
Sky Beach Club **2**
Unique Village **5**

ATLANTIC OCEAN

ELEUTHERA

Governor's Harbour

Savannah Sound

Windermere Island

Savannah Sound

Bight of Eleuthera

Tarpum Bay

Rock Sound

Rock Sound

6 mi

6 km

Haynes Ave.

Haynes Ave.

New Boue St.

Queen's Hwy.

Colebroke La.

Pinder La.

Graham St.

Griffin St.

Birdie La.

Bay St.

Clinic

Dinghy Landing

Haynes Ave.

Haynes Library

GOVERNOR'S HARBOUR

Governor's Harbour

Bight of Eleuthera

CUPID'S CAY

Government Dock

Government Dock

Tourism Office

Globe Princess Theatre

0   200 yards

0   200 m

sure to buy extra: once you get them home, these pastries tend to disappear quickly. The bakery opens at 7 am and closes at 5 Monday through Friday, at 2:30 on Saturday. [$] *Average main: $4* ✉ *Gibson La.* ☎ *242/332–2071* 💳 *No credit cards* 🕒 *Closed Sun.*

$ PIZZA 🍴 **Mate & Jenny's Restaurant & Bar.** A few miles south of Governor's Harbour, this casual neighborhood restaurant specializes in pizza; try one topped with conch. Sandwiches and Bahamian specialties are also served. The walls are painted with tropical sunset scenes and decorated with photos and random memorabilia, and the ongoing dart games add to the joint's local color. Pizza prices range from $10 to $25, depending on the toppings. [$] *Average main: $14* ✉ *S. Palmetto Point* ☎ *242/332–1504* 💳 *No credit cards* 🕒 *Closed Tues.*

$$ ECLECTIC 🍴 **Pascal's Oceanfront Seafood Restaurant.** In addition to ocean-view seating in its outdoor dining room, Pascal's also features a swim-up bar, perfect for a leisurely lunch. Relax in the infinity-edge pool while you savor a mango daiquiri and cheeseburger, and take in the magnificent view of the Atlantic. Dinner is decidedly more sophisticated, with French-Caribbean options inspired by fresh, locally caught seafood. Pascal's is located on the Sky Beach Club property, and while you are invited to enjoy the pool and beach without being a hotel guest, an afternoon at Pascal's may have you booking your next stay there. [$] *Average main: $23* ✉ *Sky Beach Club, Queen's Hwy.* ☎ *242/332–3422* 🌐 *www.pascalsoceanfront.com.*

6

$$ ECLECTIC 🍴 **1648 Bar and Grille.** Take in the sunset view as you enjoy a glass of wine and an island-inspired pizza at the brand-new 1648 Bar and Grille. Located at French Leave Harbour Village, the restaurant boasts a sweeping view of the Bight of Eleuthera and its stunning turquoise water. The chic atmosphere is just as stunning at night, when the pool becomes a deep, vivid blue as part of the resort's "Dark Sky Paradise" which aims to reduce light pollution, increasing star visibility. [$] *Average main: $28* ✉ *French Leave Harbour Village, Queen's Hwy.* ☎ *242/332–3777* 🌐 *www.frenchleaveeleuthera.com.*

$$ ECLECTIC Fodor's Choice ★ 🍴 **Tippy's.** Despite its barefoot-casual environment (old window shutters used as tabletops, sand in the floor's crevices), the menu at this open-air beach bistro is a sophisticated mix of Bahamian and European cuisine, with items that change daily based on the availability of fresh local products. Expect things like lobster salad, specialty pizzas, and fresh fish prepared with some sort of delectable twist. This place may look like a beach shack, but everything has been well planned—the owners even imported a French chef to satisfy discriminating palates. Try to grab a table on the outdoor deck, which has a fantastic view of the beach. Locals and visitors keep this place hopping year-round, and there's live music on Saturday nights. [$] *Average main: $25* ✉ *Banks Rd.* ☎ *242/332–3331* 🌐 *www.pineapplefields.com/index.php/dining/tippys.html* 🕒 *Closed Mon. and Sept. and Oct.* ✍ *Reservations essential.*

$$ BAHAMIAN 🍴 **Unique Village Sea View Restaurant and Bar.** Bahamas home cooking is the reason to come to this octagonal restaurant, with its pagoda-style natural-wood ceiling, wraparound covered deck, and panoramic view of the beach. The restaurant–bar is a popular spot for locals and visitors, especially for the live music on Tuesday. Specialties include cracked

conch, the chef's snapper special with peas 'n' rice, homemade bread, and coconut tarts for dessert. $ *Average main: $27* ✉ *North Palmetto Point, Banks Rd.* ☎ *242/332–1830* 🌐 *www.uniquevillage.com.*

WHERE TO STAY

$ B&B/INN 🏨 **Duck Inn and Orchid Gardens.** Facing west into the sunset, overlooking beautiful Governor's Harbour, two colonial cottages and a two-story home built in the 1850s are surrounded by a tropical garden with a superb orchid collection. **Pros:** historic buildings; harbor views; lush orchid gardens. **Cons:** not on the beach; only a few restaurants and shops within walking distance. $ *Rooms from: $175* ✉ *Corner of Pine and Queen's Hwy.* ☎ *242/332–2608* 🌐 *www.theduckinn.com* 🛏 *2 cottages* 🍴 *No meals.*

$$$$ RESORT Fodor's Choice ★ 🏨 **French Leave Harbour Village.** This Governor's Harbour resort, which welcomed its first guests in August 2013, offers gorgeous waterfront bungalows, a harbor-view bar and grill, a freshwater pool, and dozens of other luxurious amenities. **Pros:** relatively new resort; beautiful harbor views; luxurious amenities. **Cons:** you'll need a car if you want to explore the island; construction is ongoing; all accommodations are presently harbor-facing, not on the beach. $ *Rooms from: $450* ✉ *Queen's Hwy.* ☎ *814/278–7263* 🌐 *www.frenchleaveeleuthera.com* 🛏 *4 villas* 🍴 *No meals.*

$$ B&B/INN 🏨 **Hut Pointe Inn.** Those looking for history and luxury will find much to like about this historic building constructed in 1944 by the first premier of the Bahamas, Sir Roland Symonette. **Pros:** historic building; wonderfully landscaped grounds; upscale amenities. **Cons:** within a few feet of the Queen's Highway; not on beach; 10 minutes from town. $ *Rooms from: $245* ✉ *Queen's Hwy.* ☎ *760/908–6700, 242/332–3530* 🌐 *www.hutpointe.com* ⏲ *Closed Sept. and Oct.* 🛏 *7 suites* 🍴 *No meals.*

$ B&B/INN 🏨 **Laughing Bird Apartments.** Jean Davies and her son Pierre own these four tidy apartments on an acre of land across the street from Laughing Bird Beach. **Pros:** nice view of harbor through garden foliage; roomy guest rooms with full kitchens; kind and helpful staff. **Cons:** needs refurbishing and redecorating; limited amenities; does not have pool; beach is small and across the street. $ *Rooms from: $120* ✉ *Gibson La.* ☎ *242/332–2012* 🛏 *4 apartments* 🍴 *No meals.*

$$ RENTAL FAMILY Fodor's Choice ★ 🏨 **Pineapple Fields.** Across the street from a pink-sand Atlantic beach and Tippy's oceanfront bistro, Pineapple Fields is the perfect base for a disappearing act. **Pros:** modern facilities and amenities; large units; secluded beach and Tippy's across the street. **Cons:** sterile American-style condo; will need to drive to town; not oceanfront. $ *Rooms from: $220* ✉ *Banks Rd.* ☎ *242/332–2221, 877/677–9539* 🌐 *www.pineapplefields.com* ⏲ *Closed mid-Oct.–mid-Sept.* 🛏 *32 condo units* 🍴 *No meals.*

$$$ RESORT 🏨 **Sky Beach Club.** Perched on 22 acres of oceanfront property, this modern resort rents poolside bungalows and large four-bedroom houses. **Pros:** secluded pink-sand beach; restaurant on-property; close to airport. **Cons:** need a car to get to town; landscaping is not well maintained; faces the less tranquil Atlantic. $ *Rooms from: $395* ✉ *Queen's*

Dr. Sea Breeze performs at the Rainbow Inn.

Hwy. ☎ *242/332–3422* 🌐 *www.skybeachclub.com* 🛏 *3 bungalows, 4 houses.*

$ HOTEL 🏨 **Unique Village.** Just south of Governor's Harbour near North Palmetto Point on marvelous pink Poponi Beach, this resort has large, refurbished rooms with French doors opening to private balconies. **Pros:** on a gorgeous pink beach; steps to large pool and restaurant. **Cons:** must go down many wood stairs to access beach; a 10-minute drive to Governor's Harbour. [$] *Rooms from: $130* ✉ *North Palmetto Point, Banks Rd.* ☎ *242/332–1830* 🌐 *www.uniquevillage.com* 🛏 *10 rooms, 4 villas* 🍴 *No meals.*

NIGHTLIFE

Dr. Sea Breeze. Dr. Sea Breeze plays calypso at Sky Beach Club in Governor's Harbour and at Rainbow Inn, south of Hatchet Bay. Be sure to call ahead to make sure he's scheduled.

Globe Princess. The Globe Princess shows current movies, one show each night at 8:15 pm. Movies change weekly. The concession serves the best hamburgers in town. ✉ *Queen's Hwy.* ☎ 🎟 *$5.50* 🕘 *Closed Thurs.*

Ronnie's Hi-D-Way. With a pool table, outdoor basketball court, and large dance floor, Ronnie's is the most popular local hangout in Governor's Harbour. The scene really takes off on Friday and Saturday nights, when the bar hosts a DJ. If you drop in for a drink on the weekend, expect to stay a while for dancing to popular reggae and hip-hop tunes. ✉ *Cupid's Cay* ☎ *242/332–2307.*

SHOPPING

The Gift Shop at Pineapple Fields. You'll find Bahamian handcrafted art, locally made jewelry, and elegant beachwear in this gift shop, located in the same building as Pineapple Fields' office and Banks Road Deli. ⊠ *Bay St.* ☎ *242/332–2221* ⊕ *www.pineapplefields.com* ☉ *Closed Sun. and Oct.*

SPORTS AND THE OUTDOORS

FISHING

Paul Petty. Paul is one of the best in the business for guiding anglers through the flats in Governor's Harbour. With his help, you're sure to hook a bonefish. He is also a knowledgeable reef-fishing and deep-sea-fishing guide. ⊠ *Governor's Harbour* ☎ *242/332–2963.*

HORSEBACK RIDING

Oceanview Farm. The island's only horseback riding facility offers two trail rides daily, at 9:30 am and 11 am, through mangroves and wild orchids, around a lake, and onto a pink-sand beach. The fee is $100 per person, with group rates available. Prior experience is not necessary, but riders must be 12 years of age or older. Pony rides are available for children ages 5–11. ⊠ *Banks Rd.* ☎ *242/332–3671* ⊕ *www.oceanview242.com* ☉ *Mon.–Sat. 9–4. Closed Sun.*

> **LEARNING IN PARADISE**
>
> The Island School is a pioneering 14-week program for high-school students that's a model of sustainability—students and teachers work together to run a campus where rainwater is captured for use, solar and wind energy are harnessed, food comes from its own small farm, wastewater is filtered and reused to irrigate landscaping, and biofuel is made from cruise ships' restaurant grease to power vehicles and generators. This "mind, body, and spirit experience" aims to inspire students to be responsible, caring global citizens. Call the school and see if someone's available to give a tour. ☎ *242/334-8551.*

ROCK SOUND AND SOUTH ELEUTHERA

One of Eleuthera's largest settlements, the village of **Rock Sound** has a small airport serving the island's southern part. Front Street, the main thoroughfare, runs along the seashore, where fishing boats are tied up. If you walk down the street, you'll eventually come to the pretty, whitewashed St. Luke's Anglican Church, a contrast to the deep-blue and green houses nearby, with their colorful gardens full of poinsettia, hibiscus, and marigolds. If you pass the church on a Sunday, you'll surely hear fervent hymn singing through the open windows. Rock Sound has the island's largest supermarket shopping center, where locals stock up on groceries and supplies.

The tiny settlement of **Bannerman Town** (population 40) is 25 miles from Rock Sound at the island's southern tip, which is punctuated by an old cliff-top lighthouse. Rent an SUV if you plan to drive out to it;

the rutted sand road is often barely passable. The pink-sand beach here is gorgeous, and on a clear day you can see the Bahamas' highest point, Mt. Alvernia (elevation 206 feet), on distant Cat Island. The town lies about 30 miles from the residential Cotton Bay Club, past the quiet little fishing villages of Wemyss Bight (named after Lord Gordon Wemyss, a 17th-century Scottish slave owner) and John Millars (population 15), barely touched over the years.

GETTING HERE AND AROUND

Fly into Rock Sound Airport and rent a car. The airport is just north of town, and The Island School is a 22-mile drive south. If you fly into Governor's Harbour, plan to rent a car at the airport—Rock Sound is about 34 miles south. Taxis are available at both airports, but can be expensive.

A SWINGING TIME

In Eleuthera the game that brings the crowds is fast-pitch softball. The Eleuthera Twin City Destroyers were the men's champions of the 2006 Bahamas Softball Federation tournament. On most any weekend afternoon from March to November you can find the team playing at Rock Sound or Palmetto baseball parks on the island, known as the Softball Capital of the Bahamas. Eleuthera pitchers and brothers Edney and Edmond Bethel are both players for the Bahamas National Team, which has been consistently in the top 10 in the world.

6

EXPLORING

The Mission House. A superb example of an historic Bahamian Colonial building, the Mission House sits on the Rock Sound waterfront and is open to visitors during regular business hours. Originally built in the 1850s, the reconstruction to a Methodist Manse was overseen by volunteer Patricia Rose Maclean, a British designer highly experienced in period restoration. An Internet café, a retail shop for visitors, a museum, and a genealogical facility are planned. ⊠ *Rock Sound* ☉ *Weekdays 9–5.*

Ocean Hole. A small inland saltwater lake a mile southeast of Rock Sound is connected by tunnels to the sea. Steps have been cut into the coral on the shore so visitors can climb down to the lake's edge. Bring a piece of bread or some fries and watch the fish emerge for their hors d'oeuvres, swimming their way in from the sea. A local diver estimates the hole is about 75 feet deep. He reports that there are a couple of cars at the bottom, too. Local children learn to swim here. ⊠ *Queen's Hwy., Rock Sound* ✢ *A Bahamas Heritage sign, across the street from a church, marks the path to the Ocean Hole.*

St. Luke's Anglican Church. This idyllic seaside church on Front Street, which runs along the shore, has a pretty belfry and a garden of poinsettia, hibiscus, and marigolds. ⊠ *Queen's Hwy., Rock Sound.*

BEACHES

Lighthouse Beach. You'll need an SUV to cross the rocky terrain to get to this beach, but the drive is well worth the breathtaking views. Lighthouse beach has it all: dramatic cliffs, a pink sand beach, plenty of shade beneath the trees—and you'll likely have it entirely to yourself. Reefs just off the beach make it a great place to spend the day snorkeling. Be aware that there can be a strong current. **Amenities:** none. **Best for:** solitude; snorkeling; walking. ⊠ *Southern tip of Eleuthera, Bannerman Town.*

WHERE TO EAT

$

BAHAMIAN

FAMILY

✗ **Northside Restaurant & Bar.** If you want an authentic Bahamian meal, look no further than Northside Restaurant & Bar, a Rock Sound establishment famous for its sweeping Atlantic views. Northside's menu varies based on available fresh seafood, but you can always find Bahamian specialities such as baked macaroni and cheese, plantains, and peas and rice. If you're staying on-property, you can let the kitchen know ahead of time what you'd like to eat—they can make almost anything. $ *Average main: $15* ⊠ *Northside Cottages, Rock Sound* ☎ *242/334–2573* ⊕ *www.northsideinneleuthera.com* ⚖ *Reservations essential.*

$$

CARIBBEAN

✗ **Pascal's at Cape Eleuthera.** Located at Cape Eleuthera Resort with a breathtaking sunset view, Pascal's serves both traditional Bahamian fare and French-Caribbean fusion cuisine. The conch fritters are some of the best in the area, and the quesadillas are popular for lunch. Dinner options vary, but often include island-inspired pizzas, fresh fish, and seafood curry. Be sure to try the signature Parrot Punch cocktail. $ *Average main: $25* ⊠ *Cape Eleuthera Resort and Marina, Rock Sound* ☎ *242/334–8500* ⊕ *www.capeeleuthera.com.*

$

BAHAMIAN

✗ **Sammy's Place.** This spotless stop is owned by Sammy Culmer and managed by his friendly daughter Margarita. It serves conch fritters, fried chicken, lobster and fish, and peas 'n' rice. When it's available in season, don't miss the guava duff dessert, sweet bread with swirls of creamy guava. It's open for breakfast, too. $ *Average main: $19* ⊠ *Albury La., Rock Sound* ☎ *242/334–2121* ▭ *No credit cards.*

$

BAHAMIAN

✗ **Ship to Shore.** Menu options change daily, but you'll often find conch burgers, grouper fingers, and chicken wings at this local restaurant. The two flat-screen TVs at the bar make it a popular spot to catch a ball game. If you're in the mood for something sweet, the homemade rum punch recipe is fantastic. $ *Average main: $12* ⊠ *Wemyss Bight* ✛ *3 miles south of Cotton Bay. Drive south on Queen's Hwy. Turn left at old Cotton Bay Club entrance. Continue about 3 miles, restaurant will be on right* ☎ *242/334–0111* ▭ *No credit cards* ☉ *Closed Sun.*

WHERE TO STAY

$$$$

RESORT

FAMILY

▦ **Cape Eleuthera Resort and Marina.** Nestled between the aquamarine and emerald waters of Rock and Exuma sounds, gigantic town homes have two bright bedrooms, each with a full bath, and a stainless-steel kitchen. **Pros:** handsome resort right on the water; professional and friendly staff; gear rental on-site for water and land excursions (some with fee). **Cons:** isolated from rest of island; need a car to leave resort; on-property restaurant is the only dining option nearby. $ *Rooms from: $499* ⊠ *Cape Eleuthera, Rock Sound* ☎ *242/334–8500* ⊕ *www. capeeleuthera.com* ⤙ *14 villas* ⦵ *No meals.*

$ **⊞ Northside Cottages.** These quaint cottages are nestled into a hillside
RENTAL with an extraordinary view of the Atlantic. **Pros:** beachfront; restaurant on-property; friendly staff. **Cons:** steep walk down to the beach; the area is remote; only three cottages on the property. $ *Rooms from: $120* ⊠ *Northshore Dr., Rock Sound* ✦ *Turn off of Queen's Hwy. in Rock Sound onto Fish St. Turn left at T-intersection onto Northshore Dr., then right at the end of the pavement.* ☎ *242/334–2573* ⊕ *www. northsideinneleuthera.com* ⤙ *3 cottages* ⦵ *No meals.*

HARBOUR ISLAND

Harbour Island has often been called the Nantucket of the Caribbean and the prettiest of the Out Islands because of its powdery pink-sand beaches (3 miles' worth!) and its pastel-color clapboard houses with dormer windows, set among white picket fences, narrow lanes, cute shops, and tropical flowers.

The frequent parade of the fashionable and famous, and the chic small inns that accommodate them, have earned the island another name: the St. Bart's of the Bahamas. But residents have long called it Briland, their faster way of pronouncing "Harbour Island." These inhabitants include families who go back generations to the island's early settlement, as well as a growing number of celebrities, supermodels, and tycoons who feel that Briland is the perfect haven to bask in small-town charm against a stunning oceanscape. Some of the Bahamas' most handsome small hotels, each strikingly distinct, are tucked within the island's 2 square miles. At several, perched on a bluff above the shore, you can fall asleep with the windows open and listen to the waves lapping the beach. Take a walking tour of the narrow streets of **Dunmore Town,** named after the 18th-century royal governor of the Bahamas, Lord Dunmore, who built a summer home here and laid out the town, which served as the first capital of the Bahamas. It's the only town on Harbour Island, and you can take in all its attractions during a 20-minute stroll.

GETTING HERE AND AROUND
Access Harbour Island via a 10-minute ferry ride from the North Eleuthera dock. Fares are $5 per person in a boat of two or more, plus an extra dollar to be dropped off at the private Romora Bay Club docks and for nighttime rides.

The best way to get around the island is to rent a golf cart or bike, or hire a taxi, since climbing the island's hills can be strenuous in the midday heat. If you plan to stay in Dunmore Town, you'll be able to walk everywhere.

A stroll through Dunmore Town on Harbour Island is a must for any visitor.

EXPLORING

Lone Tree. If you stroll to the end of Bay Street and follow the curve to the western edge of the island, you'll find the Lone Tree, one of the most photographed icons of Harbour Island. This enormous piece of driftwood is said to have washed up on shore after a bad storm and anchored itself on the shallow sandbar in a picturesque upright position, providing the perfect photo op for countless tourists. ⊠ *Bay St.*

Loyalist Cottage. The most photographed house on the island is the pretty turquoise-and-white Loyalist Cottage, one of the original settlers' homes (circa 1797) on Bay Street. You can't go inside; it's privately owned. Many other old houses are in the area, with gingerbread trim and picket fences. Amusing names include Beside the Point, Up Yonder, and The Royal Termite. ⊠ *Bay St.*

St. John's Anglican Church. The first church built by the Eleutheran Adventurers and the Bahamas' oldest Anglican church was constructed in 1768. It still welcomes churchgoers after almost 250 years. Services are Sunday at 8 am and 7 pm. ⊠ *Dunmore St.*

Straw Crafts. A row of straw-work stands are on Bay Street next to the water, including Pat's, Dorothy's, and Sarah's, where you'll find straw bags, hats, and T-shirts. Food stands sell conch salad, Kalik beer, coconut water, and fruit juices. ⊠ *Bay St.*

BEACHES

Pink Sands Beach. This is the fairest pink beach of them all: 3 miles of pale pink sand behind some of the most expensive and posh inns in the Bahamas. Its sand is of such a fine consistency that it's almost as soft as talcum powder, and the gentle slope of the shore makes small waves break hundreds of yards offshore; you have to walk out quite a distance to get past your waist. This is the place to see the rich and famous in designer resort wear or ride a horse bareback across the sand and into the sea. **Amenities:** food and drink; toilets. **Best for:** partiers; sunrise; swimming; walking.

HEAVENLY MUSIC

The best live music on Harbour Island is at the Lighthouse Church of God on Chapel Street in Dunmore Town on Sunday mornings. Mick Jagger and Lenny Kravitz have dropped by to hear Pastor Samuel Higgs, drummer and bass player, and guitarist Rocky Sanders, both of whom played Europe's clubs for years before settling down on the island.

WHERE TO EAT

Many Harbour Island hotels and restaurants are closed from September through mid- to late October.

$$$ ITALIAN 🍴 **Acquapazza.** Briland's only Italian restaurant offers a change of pace from the island's standard fare, and a change of scenery, too. It's located on the island's south end at the Harbour Island Marina, with a dockside terrace where you can take in the sunset while sipping one of its exclusively imported Italian wines. Chef and owner Manfredi Mancini's hearty portions of fried calamari and pasta *e fagioli* (with beans) don't disappoint, and the seafood entrées are always a good choice. [$] *Average main: $30* ✉ *Harbour Island Marina, south end of island off Queens Hwy., Dunmore Town* ☎ *242/333–3240* 🌐 *www.acquapazzabahamas.com* ✍ *Reservations essential.*

$ CAFÉ 🍴 **Arthur's Bakery and Cafe.** Bread and pastries are baked every morning by *White Shadow* screenwriter and local real-estate agent to the stars Robert Arthur and his Trinidadian wife Anna. The friendly café has a quiet garden nook where you can savor your morning brew with an apple turnover, banana pancakes, or any of the daily breakfast offerings. The most popular item to take back is the jalapeño-and-cheese bread. Internet access is available for customers. [$] *Average main: $14* ✉ *Crown St. and Dunmore St., Dunmore Town* ☎ *242/333–2285* 💳 *No credit cards* 🕒 *Closed Sun.*

$$ DELI 🍴 **Bahamas Coffee Roasters.** This charming café in the middle of Dunmore Town imports coffee beans from around the world and roasts them on-island to produce a number of special blends available to enjoy every morning. The vibe is decidedly surfer-chic, with modern artwork on the walls and picinic bench seating. Join them at brunch for a breakfast burrito with your fresh coffee; or during lunch for a sandwich, all made from local produce and organic meats. [$] *Average main: $20* ✉ *Dunmore St., Dunmore Town* ☎ *242/470–8015* 💳 *No credit cards.*

Where to Eat and Stay on Harbour Island

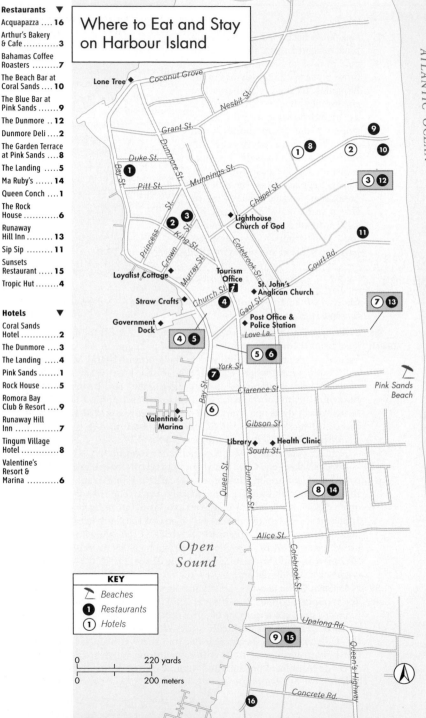

Restaurants ▼

Acquapazza 16
Arthur's Bakery & Cafe 3
Bahamas Coffee Roasters 7
The Beach Bar at Coral Sands 10
The Blue Bar at Pink Sands 9
The Dunmore .. 12
Dunmore Deli 2
The Garden Terrace at Pink Sands 8
The Landing 5
Ma Ruby's 14
Queen Conch 1
The Rock House 6
Runaway Hill Inn 13
Sip Sip 11
Sunsets Restaurant 15
Tropic Hut 4

Hotels ▼

Coral Sands Hotel 2
The Dunmore 3
The Landing 4
Pink Sands 1
Rock House 5
Romora Bay Club & Resort 9
Runaway Hill Inn 7
Tingum Village Hotel 8
Valentine's Resort & Marina 6

$$ ECLECTIC Fodor's Choice ★ 🍴 **The Beach Bar at Coral Sands.** For lunch with a view, try Coral Sands' oceanfront bar and restaurant, just steps from the pink-sand beach. Executive Chef Ken Gomes creates delicious lunch options that go perfectly with a tropical cocktail or a glass of white wine. In addition to seafood options like conch fritters, lobster rolls, and grouper sandwiches, the restaurant also serves fresh salads and gourmet pizzas. [$] *Average main: $20* ✉ *Chapel St., Dunmore Town* ☎ *242/333–2350* 🌐 *www.coralsands.com* 🕒 *Closed Sept. No dinner.*

$$ ECLECTIC 🍴 **The Blue Bar at Pink Sands.** Head to the beach for lunch outside at this lively oceanfront restaurant. Situated just above the pink-sand beach, you'll have an unbeatable view for sipping one of the signature cocktails and enjoying fish tacos, a grouper ciabatta, or any of the other island-inspired menu options. If you're in the mood for a cheeseburger, try the Blue Water Burger on a brioche roll. During the summer, the Blue Bar is also open for dinner. [$] *Average main: $20* ✉ *Pink Sands Resort, Chapel St., Dunmore Town* ☎ *242/333–2030* 🌐 *www.pinksandsresort.com* 🕒 *No dinner except in summer.*

$$$ CARIBBEAN 🍴 **The Dunmore.** Start with a signature cocktail at the handsome mahogany bar before enjoying dinner under the stars on the ocean-view porch at this recently renovated restaurant at The Dunmore. Chef Cindy Hutson creates island-inspired dishes that change seasonally. If it's too chilly for dinner by the beach, you can also choose to sit in the restaurant's charming indoor dining room. [$] *Average main: $36* ✉ *The Dunmore, Gaol La., Dunmore Town* ☎ *242/333–2200* 🌐 *www.dunmorebeach.com* 🕒 *Closed mid-Aug–mid-Nov.* ✍ *Reservations essential.*

6

$ DELI 🍴 **Dunmore Deli.** Patrick Tully's exceptional deli satisfies the epicurean demands of Briland's more finicky residents and visitors, while its shaded wooden porch, filled with hanging plants and bougainvillea, makes this the perfect spot for a lazy breakfast or lunch. Treat yourself to the Briland Bread Toast, the amazingly fluffy take on French toast, or pick up one of the inventive deli sandwiches for a picnic on the beach. While here, you can also stock up on a variety of international coffees, imported cheeses, produce, and other gourmet items you won't find anywhere else on the island. [$] *Average main: $12* ✉ *King St., Dunmore Town* ☎ *242/333–2644* 🕒 *Closed Sun.*

$$$$ CARIBBEAN Fodor's Choice ★ 🍴 **The Garden Terrace at Pink Sands.** Enjoy an elegant candlelit dinner in Pink Sands' exquisitely decorated indoor dining room, or alfresco in their lush garden. Executive Chef Pushkar Marathe emphasizes fresh seafood with his Caribbean bistro cuisine. The menu changes based on the availability of fresh ingredients, but often features fresh ceviche or chilled avocado soup to start, followed by ginger tamarind black grouper or a roasted beef tenderloin. [$] *Average main: $40* ✉ *Pink Sands Resort, Chapel St., Dunmore Town* ☎ *242/333–2030* 🌐 *www.pinksandsresort.com* 🕒 *No lunch* ✍ *Reservations essential.*

$$$$ ECLECTIC Fodor's Choice ★ 🍴 **The Landing.** You never know which actor or rock star you'll rub elbows with—Richard Gere and Dave Matthews like to dine here—at the Hemingway-esque bar, but none of it matters once you've moved on to the dining room and are under the spell of Swedish chef Vincent Vitlock, whose dishes soar with a Southeast Asian flair. Standouts include the goat-cheese ravioli with shrimp, walnut-crusted fresh

Harbour Island is a tranquil place to spend some time.

fish, and banana upside-down cake. One of the Caribbean's top dining destinations, The Landing also offers an impressive wine selection. If the weather is nice, request a romantic table on the porch. [$] *Average main: $45* ✉ *The Landing, Bay St., Dunmore Town* ☎ *242/333–2707* 🌐 *www.harbourislandlanding.com* 🕒 *Closed Wed. No lunch* ✍ *Reservations essential.*

$ BAHAMIAN 🍴 **Ma Ruby's.** Although you can sample local Bahamian fare at this famous eatery, the star of the menu is the cheeseburger, purportedly the inspiration for Jimmy Buffett's "Cheeseburger in Paradise" song. Maybe it's the rustic charm of the breezy patio, or the secret seasonings on the melt-in-your-mouth patty, but this burger served between thick slices of homemade Bahamian bread is definitely otherworldly. Dinner specialties include cracked conch and fish stew. Be sure to save room for Ma's coconut tart or key lime pie. [$] *Average main: $10* ✉ *Tingum Village Hotel, Colebrooke St., Dunmore Town* ☎ *242/333–2161.*

$ BAHAMIAN 🍴 **Queen Conch.** Four blocks from the ferry dock on Bay Street, with a deck overlooking the water, this colorful snack stand—presided over by Lavaughn Percentie—is renowned for its freshly caught conch salad ($10), which is diced in front of you, mixed with fresh vegetables, and ready to eat right at the counter. On weekends, get there early to put in your order, as visitors from the world over place large orders to go. [$] *Average main: $10* ✉ *Bay St., Dunmore Town* ☎ *242/333–3811* 💳 *No credit cards* 🕒 *Closed Sun.*

$$$$
MODERN
AMERICAN
Fodor's Choice
★

✕ **The Rock House.** Splendid harbor views and a transporting Mediterranean-loggia vibe create the perfect backdrop for Chef Jennifer Learmonth's California Continental menu, infused with tropical accents. Imaginative dishes include curried Colorado lamb chops and Thai-style stone crab and lobster spring rolls. The Rock House also takes its drinks seriously, with an extensive list showcasing California boutique wines. Dining here is refined and serene, thanks to the flawless service, so linger over coffee and one of the decadent desserts, like red velvet cake or homemade "hokey pokey" turtle ice cream. Try the restaurant at lunchtime for a peaceful meal with a spectacular view. $ *Average main: $40* ⊠ *The Rock House Hotel, Bay St., Dunmore Town* ☎ *242/333–2053* ⊕ *www.rockhousebahamas.com* ☉ *Closed Aug.–mid-Nov.* ⟍ *Reservations essential.*

$$$$
CARIBBEAN

✕ **Runaway Hill Inn.** Enjoy a moonlit dinner on Runaway Hill's beachfront veranda. The atmosphere feels like a private club with a handsome 1920s interior. Chef Krishna Higgs specializes in Bahamian cuisine, combining local ingredients with global flavors. The menu always features a fresh catch of the day, and often includes Bahamian lobster and stone crabs. $ *Average main: $40* ⊠ *Colebrooke St., Dunmore Town* ☎ *242/333–2150* ⊕ *www.runawayhill.com* ☉ *Closed Mon.* ⟍ *Reservations essential.*

$$
BAHAMIAN
Fodor's Choice
★

✕ **Sip Sip.** Locals and travelers alike seek out this popular snow-cone-green house overlooking the beach for a little "sip sip" (Bahamian for gossip) and delicious inspired food. Chef and owner Julie Lightbourn uses whatever is fresh, local, and in season to create "Bahamian with a twist" dishes, so check what daily specials are on the blackboard. Conch chili is one of her signatures; consider yourself lucky if the lobster quesadillas are available, and don't miss the decadent carrot cake with gingercaramel. Sip Sip is open for lunch only, from 11:30 to 4, and it usually closes on Wednesdays in the summer (call to confirm hours). $ *Average main: $25* ⊠ *Court Rd., Dunmore Town* ☎ *242/333–3316* ☉ *Closed Tues. and mid-Aug.–Nov. No dinner* ⟍ *Reservations not accepted.*

$$
BAHAMIAN
FAMILY

✕ **Sunsets Restaurant.** This waterfront pavilion at the Romora Bay Club perfectly frames sunsets over Harbour Island, so be sure to get here in time to snag a good seat for the show. Popular with locals, the restaurant serves mid-priced Bahamian specialties such as conch fritters for a casual lunch or dinner. The bartender is always happy to create drinks just to suit your vibe. $ *Average main: $20* ⊠ *Romora Bay Club, Dunmore St., Dunmore Town* ☎ *242/333–2325* ⊕ *www.romorabay.com* ☉ *Closed Sept.*

$
PIZZA

✕ **Tropic Hut.** If you're in the mood to dine at home, this centrally located restaurant is the perfect place for pizza take-out. In addition to a multitude of toppings, the menu also includes wings, wraps, burgers, and subs. It may lack the elegant ambience of most Harbour Island restaurants, but for a relatively inexpensive meal, this pizza joint is a great option. $ *Average main: $10* ⊠ *Dunmore St., Dunmore Town* ☎ *242/333–3700* ☉ *Closed Sun.*

6

WHERE TO STAY

$$$ RESORT FAMILY **Coral Sands Hotel.** An elegant yet energetic flair accents this 8-acre oceanfront resort, right on the pink-sand beach. **Pros:** direct ocean access; trendy beach resort vibe; billiard room. **Cons:** rooms vary in quality and style; some rooms can be loud; complimentary breakfast menu has limited options. [$] *Rooms from: $335* ✉ *Chapel St.* ☎ *242/333–2350, 800/468–2799* 🌐 *www.coralsands.com* ⏲ *Closed Sept.* 🛏 *40 rooms* 🍴 *Breakfast.*

$$$$ RESORT **The Dunmore.** This recently renovated hotel with private cottages evokes a 1940s club in the tropics—with its mahogany bar, casual yet elegant dining room, and faded paperbacks in the clubhouse library, it's a favorite with the New England yachting set. **Pros:** on the beach with ocean-side bar service; spacious bathrooms; private terraces and lawn chairs for every cottage. **Cons:** cottages too close for real privacy; small clubhouse; not all cottages have a view of the ocean. [$] *Rooms from: $450* ✉ *Gaol La., Dunmore Town* ☎ *242/333–2200, 877/891–3100* 🌐 *www.dunmorebeach.com* ⏲ *Closed mid-Aug.–mid-Nov.* 🛏 *14 cottages* 🍴 *No meals.*

$$ B&B/INN **The Landing.** Spare white walls and crisp white linens evoke a timeless, understated chic at The Landing, which is acclaimed as much for its singular style as for its superb cuisine. **Pros:** chic and comfortable rooms; glorious outdoor shower; acclaimed dining. **Cons:** 10 am checkout time; limited hotel services; not on the beach. [$] *Rooms from: $225* ✉ *Bay St., Dunmore Town* ☎ *242/333–2707* 🌐 *www.harbourislandlanding.com* ⏲ *Closed mid-Aug.–Oct.* 🛏 *13 rooms* 🍴 *No meals.*

$$$$ RESORT Fodor's Choice ★ **Pink Sands.** Harbour Island's famed beachfront resort has long been praised by celebrities—Martha Stewart, Nicole Kidman, and Brooke Shields—and honeymooners alike for its 25 secluded acres of beautiful rambling gardens and private cottages. **Pros:** truly private cottages; state-of-the-art media room; discreet and well-trained staff. **Cons:** some cottages quite a walk from the main house and beach; need a golf cart to explore Dunmore Town; pool is small and needs updating. [$] *Rooms from: $600* ✉ *Chapel St., Dunmore Town* ☎ *242/333–2030* 🌐 *www.pinksandsresort.com* ⏲ *Closed Sept.* 🛏 *25 cottages* 🍴 *Breakfast.*

$$$ HOTEL Fodor's Choice ★ **Rock House.** With a drawing room straight out of a villa on the Amalfi Coast, the Rock House is Harbour Island's most luxurious boutique hotel. **Pros:** heavenly beds; stellar service; best gym on the island. **Cons:** not on the beach; lack of views from some rooms; not ideal for families with young children. [$] *Rooms from: $300* ✉ *Bay St., Dunmore Town* ☎ *242/333–2053* 🌐 *www.rockhousebahamas.com* ⏲ *Closed Aug.–mid-Nov.* 🛏 *7 rooms, 4 suites* 🍴 *Breakfast.*

$$$$ RESORT FAMILY **Romora Bay Club & Resort.** Three pink Adirondack chairs on the dock welcome you to this colorful and casual resort situated on the bay side of the island. **Pros:** friendly staff; water views from every room; private bay-side beach. **Cons:** sloping steps from dock to cottages are a hassle for luggage; main house has been converted into a resort showroom. [$] *Rooms from: $500* ✉ *South end of Dunmore St., Dunmore Town* ☎ *242/333–2325* 🌐 *www.romorabay.com* ⏲ *Closed Sept.* 🛏 *18 rooms* 🍴 *No meals.*

$$$
B&B/INN

🛏 **Runaway Hill Inn.** This quiet seaside inn on gorgeous, rolling grounds feels far removed from the rest of the island, which is precisely the point. **Pros:** oceanfront location with direct beach access; well-stocked library; intimate character. **Cons:** limited service; not as chic a vibe as nearby resorts. $ *Rooms from: $375* ✉ *Colebrooke St., Dunmore Town* ☎ *242/333–2150, 843/278–1724* ⊕ *www.runawayhill.com* ✪ *Closed mid-Aug.–mid-Nov.* ✈ *10 rooms, 1 cottage, 1 house* ❘○❘ *No meals.*

$
B&B/INN

🛏 **Sugar Apple Bed and Breakfast.** Located in the middle of the island, Sugar Apple has roomy suites, all with modern full kitchens, hand-crafted four-poster beds, and sitting areas. **Pros:** tranquil area; spotless and affordable rooms. **Cons:** a fairly long walk to beach and town; need to rent a golf cart; no ocean views. $ *Rooms from: $149* ✉ *Colebrooke St., Dunmore Town* ☎ *242/333–2750* ✈ *7 suites* ❘○❘ *Breakfast.*

$
B&B/INN
FAMILY

🛏 **Tingum Village Hotel.** Each of the rustic cottages on this property, owned by the Percentie family, is named after a different island of the Bahamas. **Pros:** family-friendly; local flavor; Ma Ruby's restaurant. **Cons:** no-frills interior and furnishings; not on beach or harbor; rustic grounds. $ *Rooms from: $140* ✉ *Colebrooke St., Dunmore Town* ☎ *242/333–2161* ✈ *8 rooms, 6 suites, 2 cottages* ❘○❘ *Breakfast.*

$$
RESORT
FAMILY

🛏 **Valentine's Resort and Marina.** With the largest marina on Harbour Island, equipped with 50 slips capable of accommodating yachts up to 160 feet, this resort is ideal if you are a self-sufficient traveler or family that doesn't require many amenities but enjoys spacious condo-style rooms and water-focused activities. **Pros:** modern rooms; state-of-the-art marina; large swimming pool. **Cons:** not oceanfront; impersonal condo-style quality; lack of hotel service. $ *Rooms from: $295* ✉ *Bay St., Dunmore Town* ☎ *242/333–2142* ⊕ *www.valentinesresort.com* ✈ *41 rooms* ❘○❘ *No meals.*

6

NIGHTLIFE

Beyond the Reef. The party starts at this waterfront bar at sunset and extends well into the evening. Drink specials are available all day and you can find great Bahamian food at any one of its neighboring vendors. ✉ *Bay St., Dunmore Town* ☎ *242/333–3478.*

Daddy D's. This is the place to be on the weekends and holidays in Harbour Island. The dance floor takes off around midnight and is a popular spot for young locals and tourists alike. DJ and owner Devon "Daddy D" Sawyer spins pop music, hip-hop, and reggae tunes late into the night. ✉ *Dunmore St., Dunmore Town* ☎ *242/333–3700.*

Gusty's. Enjoy a brew on the wraparound patio of Gusty's, on Harbour Island's northern point. This lively hot spot has sand floors, a few tables, and patrons shooting pool. On weekends, holidays, and in high season, it's an extremely crowded and happening dance spot, especially after 10 pm. ✉ *Coconut Grove Ave., Dunmore Town* ☎ *242/333–2165.*

Vic-Hum Club. Vic-Hum Club, owned by "Ma" Ruby Percentie's son Humphrey, occasionally hosts live Bahamian bands in a room decorated with classic record-album covers; otherwise, you'll find locals playing Ping-Pong and listening and dancing to loud recorded music, from calypso to American pop and R & B. Mick Jagger and other rock stars have dropped by. Look for the largest coconut ever grown in the Bahamas—33 inches in diameter—on the bar's top shelf. ✉ *Barrack St., Dunmore Town* ☎ *242/333–2161.*

SHOPPING AND SPAS

Most small businesses on Harbour Island close for a lunch break between 1 and 3.

SHOPPING

ART GALLERIES

Princess Street Gallery. Princess Street Gallery displays original art by local and internationally renowned artists, as well as a diverse selection of illustrated books, home accessories, and locally made crafts. ✉ *Princess St., Dunmore Town* ☎ *242/333–2788* ⊙ *Closed Sun.*

CLOTHING

Blue Rooster. This is the place to go for festive party dresses, sexy swimwear, fun accessories, and exotic gifts. ✉ *King St., Dunmore Town* ☎ *242/333–2240* ⊙ *Closed Sun.*

Briland's Androsia. This shop has a unique selection of clothing, beachwear, bags, and home items handmade from the colorful batik fabric created on the island of Andros. ✉ *Coconut Grove Ave., Dunmore Town* ☎ *242/333–2342* ⊙ *Closed weekends.*

Miss Mae's. Miss Mae's sells an exquisite and discerningly curated collection of fashion-forward clothing, accessories, and gifts from international designers and artisans. ✉ *Dunmore St., Dunmore Town* ☎ *242/333–2002.*

The Sand Dollar. This boutique specializes in resort wear made from Trinidadian cloth. You'll also find jewelry, handbags, shoes, and other accessories. ✉ *King St., Dunmore Town* ☎ *242/333–3576* ⊙ *Closed Sun.*

Sugar Mill. Here you can find a glamorous selection of resort wear, accessories, and gifts from designers around the world. ✉ *Bay St., Dunmore Town* ☎ *242/333–3558* ⊙ *Closed Sun.*

FOOD

Patricia's Fruits and Vegetables. This is where locals go for homemade candies, jams, and other Bahamian condiments. Her famous hot sauce and native thyme (sold in recycled Bacardi bottles) make memorable gifts. ✉ *Duke St., Dunmore Town* ☎ *242/333–2289.*

GIFTS AND SOUVENIRS

Bahamian Shells and Tings. This shop sells island wear, souvenirs, and crafts, many handmade on Harbour Island. ✉ *Coconut Grove Ave., Dunmore Town* ☎ *242/333–2839* ⊙ *Closed Sun.*

Dilly Dally. Here you can find Bahamian-made jewelry, maps, T-shirts, CDs, decorations, and other fun island souvenirs. ✉ *Dunmore St., Dunmore Town* ☎ *242/333–3109* ⊙ *Closed Sun.*

Pink Sands Gift Shop. This shop offers a trendy selection of swimwear, accessories, casual clothing, and trinkets. ✉ *Pink Sands Resort, Chapel St., Dunmore Town* ☎ *242/333–2030.*

The Plait Lady. You'll find novelty gifts, locally crafted baskets, and other straw goods at this Bay Street store. ⊠ *Bay St., Dunmore Town* ☎ *242/333–3799* ☉ *Closed Sun.*

The Shop at Sip Sip. The Shop at Sip Sip sells its own line of T-shirts and a small but stylish selection of handmade jewelry, custom-designed totes, Bahamian straw work, and gifts found by owner Julie Lightbourn on her far-flung travels. ⊠ *Court Rd., Dunmore Town* ☎ *242/333–3316* ☉ *Closed Tues. and mid-Aug.–Nov.*

SPAS AND SPA SERVICES

The Island Spa. For romantic couples massages in the privacy of your own room, book Karen at The Island Spa. She makes in-room visits and offers evening beach massages, body scrubs, and aromatherapy. In addition to massages, The Island Spa can also do bridal hair and makeup, manicures, and pedicures—ideal for a destination wedding. ☎ *242/333–3326* ⊕ *www.theharbourislandspa.com* ⌧ *Services: aromatherapy, massage, nail treatment, scrubs, wedding hair and makeup.*

SPORTS AND THE OUTDOORS

BIKING

Michael's Cycles. Bicycles are a popular way to explore Harbour Island; rent one—or golf carts, motorboats, Jet Skis, and kayaks—at Michael's Cycles. ⊠ *Colebrooke St., Dunmore Town* ☎ *242/333–2384.*

BOATING AND FISHING

There's great bonefishing right off Dunmore Town at **Girl's Bank.** Charters cost about $350 for a half day. The Harbour Island Tourist Office can help organize bone- and bottom-fishing excursions, as can all of the major hotels.

Stuart Cleare. Bonefish Stuart is one of Harbour Island's best bonefishing guides. You'll want to call well in advance to arrange a trip with him. ☎ *242/333–2072, 242/464–0148.*

SCUBA DIVING AND SNORKELING

Ocean Fox Diving and Deep-sea Fishing Center. Ocean Fox Diving and Deep-sea Fishing Center provides diving excursions as well as fishing trips with an experienced captain and crew. ⊠ *Harbour Island Club and Marina, Dunmore Town* ☎ *242/333–2323* ⊕ *www.oceanfoxfishing bahamas.com.*

Valentine's Dive Center. This dive center rents and sells equipment and provides all levels of instruction, certification, and dive trips. ⊠ *Valentine's Resort and Marina, Bay St., Dunmore Town* ☎ *242/333–2080* ⊕ *www.valentinesdive.com.*

SPANISH WELLS

Off Eleuthera's northern tip lies St. George's Cay, the site of **Spanish Wells.** The Spaniards used this as a safe harbor during the 17th century while they transferred their riches from the New World to the Old. Residents—the few surnames go back generations—live on the island's eastern end in clapboard houses that look as if they've been transported

from a New England fishing village. Descendants of the Eleutheran Adventurers continue to sail these waters and bring back to shore fish and lobster (most of the Bahamas' langoustes are caught here), which are prepared and boxed for export in a factory at the dock. So lucrative is the trade in crawfish, the local term for Bahamian lobsters, that the 1,500 inhabitants may be the most prosperous Out Islanders.

GETTING HERE AND AROUND

You can reach Spanish Wells by taking a five-minute ferry ride ($7) from the Gene's Bay dock in North Eleuthera. You can easily explore the area on foot, or rent a golf cart.

WHERE TO EAT

$$ BAHAMIAN 🍴 **The Generation Gap.** This casual diner is a hub of activity during lunch hours. In addition to American soda shop favorites like cheeseburgers, subs, and hot dogs, the menu also includes Bahamian fare such as fried grouper sandwiches and conch dishes. The Gap, as it's known locally, serves a great milk shake, and their crushed ice makes it the best spot to stop for a cold drink on the island. [$] *Average main: $24* ✉ *13th and Samuel Guy Sts.* ☎ *242/333–4230* 💳 *No credit cards* 🕒 *Closed Sun.*

$ BAKERY 🍴 **Kathy's Bakery.** Located on the corner of Samuel Guy Street and 17th Street, Kathy's Bakery makes breads, pies, and cakes. You can custom order ahead of time, or choose from the daily selection. The bakery is also home to the island's best johnnycakes, a Bahamian specialty. [$] *Average main: $5* ✉ *17th and Samuel Guy Sts.* ☎ *242/333–4405* 💳 *No credit cards* 🕒 *Closed Sun.*

WHERE TO STAY

$ RENTAL FAMILY 🏨 **Abner's Rentals.** These two-bedroom ocean-side rentals include the discounted use of a golf cart so you can explore the island and pick up groceries at one of the local shops. **Pros:** all four houses have washers and dryers. **Cons:** Spanish Wells is very quiet and remote; limited dining options in the area. [$] *Rooms from: $170* ✉ *Between 12th and 13th Sts.* ☎ *242/333–4890, 954/237–6266* 🌐 *www.abnersvacationrentals.com* 💳 *No credit cards* 🛏 *4 houses* 🍽 *No meals.*

THE EXUMAS

WELCOME TO THE EXUMAS

TOP REASONS TO GO

★ **Party like a local:** Hot spots include the Fish Fry on weekends for conch salad and fresh fish and Chat 'N' Chill on Stocking Island for Sunday pig roasts.

★ **Island-hop:** You'll want to spend a couple of days boating through the 365 cays (one for every day of the year, as the locals say), most uninhabited, some owned by celebrities. Get ready for iguanas, swimming pigs, and giant starfish.

★ **Enjoy empty beaches:** Beautiful stretches of bleach-white sand are yours to explore, and more often than not you'll be the only person on them, even at noon on a Saturday.

★ **Explore the Land and Sea Park:** Underwater attractions in the 176-square-mile Exuma Cays Land and Sea Park, one of the best snorkeling sights in the Bahamas, include queen conchs, starfish, and thriving coral reefs. Keep a lookout for the endangered hawksbill and threatened green and loggerhead turtles.

1 **Great Exuma.** Capital George Town sees most of the action on this mainland, including the 12-day George Town Cruising Regatta and the Bahamian Music and Heritage Festival. But dazzling white beaches and fish fries offering cold Kaliks and conch salad crop up along the coasts of the entire island. Visitors come to fish—especially to stalk the clever bonefish—dive, and snorkel, and stay in atmospheric inns and luxurious resorts, where you can find complete solitude or hopping beach parties.

2 **Little Exuma.** The Tropic of Cancer runs through the chain's second-largest island, which is duly noted on the steps leading to Tropic of Cancer Beach, one of the most spectacular on the island.

3 **The Exuma Cays.** If you're looking for a true escape—a vacation where you're more likely to see

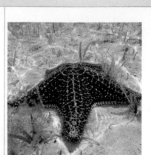

giant starfish, wild iguanas, swimming pigs, dolphins, and sharks than other people—boat over to the cays. This is also where celebrities come to buy their own spectacular islands—Johnny Depp, Faith Hill and Tim McGraw, David Copperfield, and Nicholas Cage all have 'em. The renowned Exuma Cays Land and Sea Park, toward the chain's north end, has some of the most gorgeous crystal clear water and white sand on Earth.

GETTING ORIENTED

Thirty-five miles southeast of Nassau, Allan's Cay sits at the top of the Exumas chain of 365 islands (most uninhabited) that skip like stones for 120 miles south across the Tropic of Cancer. Flanked by the Great Bahama Bank and Exuma Sound, the islands are at the center of the Bahamas. George Town, the Exumas' capital and hub of activity, so to speak, is on Great Exuma, the mainland and largest island, near the bottom of the Exumas' chain. Little Exuma is to the south and connected to the mainland by a bridge. Together, these two islands span 50 miles.

7

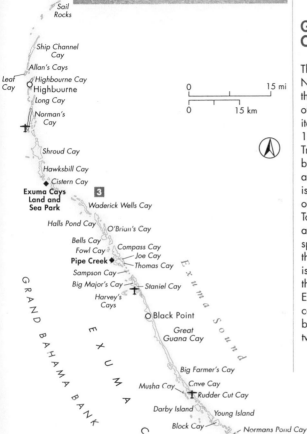

Sail Rocks

Ship Channel Cay

Allan's Cays

Leaf Cay

Highbourne Cay
Highbourne

Long Cay

Norman's Cay

0   15 mi
0   15 km

Shroud Cay

Hawksbill Cay

Cistern Cay

Exuma Cays Land and Sea Park   **3**

Waderick Wells Cay

Halls Pond Cay   O'Brian's Cay

Bells Cay

Fowl Cay   Compass Cay

Pipe Creek   Joe Cay

Thomas Cay

Sampson Cay

Big Major's Cay   Staniel Cay

Harvey's Cays

O Black Point

Great Guana Cay

GRAND BAHAMA BANK

EXUMA CAYS

Exuma Sound

Big Farmer's Cay

Musha Cay   Cave Cay

Rudder Cut Cay

Darby Island

Block Cay

Young Island

Normans Pond Cay

Lee Stocking Island

Brigantine Cays

Barraterre

Starfish Reserve

O Rolleville

Steventon
Queen's Hwy.

Great Exuma Island   **1**

O Mt. Thompson

Exuma Int'l Airport

Moss Town

Fish Fry O

George Town

Channel Cays

Rolle Town O

St. Christopher's

Elizabeth Harbour

Stocking Island

Rolle Town Tombs

Forbes Hill

The Hermitage   **2**

Little Exuma Island

Williams Town

EXUMA CAYS LAND AND SEA PARK

Created by the Bahamas National Trust in 1958, the 176-square-mile Exuma Cays Land and Sea Park was the first of its kind in the world—an enormous open aquarium with pristine reefs, an abundance of marine life, and sandy cays.

The park appeals to divers, who appreciate the vast underworld of limestone, reefs, drop-offs, blue holes, caves, and a multitude of exotic marine life including one of the Bahamas' most impressive stands of rare pillar coral. Since the park's waters have essentially never been fished, you can see what the ocean looked like before humanity. For landlubbers there are hiking trails and birding sites; stop in the main office for maps. More than 200 bird species have been spotted here. At Shroud Cay, jump into the strong current that creates a natural whirlpool whipping you around a rocky outcropping to a powdery beach. On top of the hill overlooking the beach is Camp Driftwood, made famous by a hermit who dug steps to the top leaving behind pieces of driftwood.⊠ *Between Conch Cut and Wax Cay Cut* ☎ *242/225–1791, VHF Channel 9 or 16* ⊕ *www.exumapark.info.*

BEST TIME TO GO
In summer the water is as warm as bathwater and usually just as calm. The park has vastly fewer boats than in the busy winter season, when the channel becomes a blue highway for a parade of sailing and motor vessels. Bring insect repellent in summer and fall.

BEST WAYS TO EXPLORE
By Boat. Boaters can explore the sandy cays and many islets that are little more than sandbars. The water is so clear

it's hard to determine depths without a depth finder, so go slow and use your charts. Some routes are only passable at high tide. Get detailed directions before you go into the park, and be sure to stop by the park headquarters on Warderick Wells Cay for more information. Make sure you have a VHF marine radio on the boat or carry a handheld VHF radio so you can call for help or directions.

On Foot. The park headquarters has a map of hiking trails—most are on Warderick Wells Cay—that range from 2-mile walks to two-hour treks. Wear sturdy shoes, because trails are rocky. You'll see red, black, and white mangroves; limestone cliffs; and lots of birds—white-tail tropic birds, green herons, blue herons, black-bellied plovers, royal terns, and ospreys. Take sunscreen and water, and be aware that there's very little shade.

By Kayak. Visitors do sometimes take kayak trips from neighboring cays into the park and camp on the beach. The park has two kayaks that can be used free of charge by boaters moored in the park. As you paddle, look for sea turtles, which might pop up beside you.

Underwater. You have to go underwater to see the best part of the park—spiny lobsters walking on stilt legs on the sandy floor, sea grass waving in the currents, curious hawksbill turtles (critically endangered), solemn-faced groupers, and the coral reefs that support an

astonishing range of sea life. Bring your own equipment.

FUN FACT

The park has one native land mammal—the hutia, a critically endangered nocturnal rodent that looks similar to a gray squirrel.

MAKING A DIFFERENCE

How successful has the Exuma Cays Land and Sea Park been? About 74% of the grouper in the northern Exumas' cays come from the park. Crawfish tagged in the park have been found repopulating areas around Cat Island 70 miles away. The concentration of conch inside the park is 31 times higher than the concentration outside. This conservatively provides several million conchs outside the park for fishermen to harvest each year.

(above) Boats anchored in the bay at Warderick Wells Cay, the park's headquarters.

Updated by
Julianne Hoell

The Exumas are known for their gorgeous 365 cays—most uninhabited, some owned by celebrities. Get the wind and sea salt in your hair as you cruise through the pristine 120-mile chain. The water here is some of the prettiest in the world, and comes in every shade of blue and green (you'll grow tired trying to name the exact color); beaches are dazzling white. Combine that with fresh seafood and friendly locals, and you have yourself one of the best vacation destinations in the Bahamas.

Yes, the Exumas are Out Islands in the fullest sense of the word; there isn't a casino or cruise ship in sight. Those who love the remote beauty of the windswept cays keep coming back, people like Jimmy Buffett, who once docked his seaplane behind the historic Club Peace and Plenty and amused islanders by fishing from the cockpit. A vacation here revolves around uncrowded beaches, snorkeling, fishing, and enjoying a freshly caught dinner at an outdoor restaurant by the beach.

In 1783 Englishman Denys Rolle sent 150 slaves to Great Exuma to build a cotton plantation. His son Lord John Rolle later gave all of his 5,000 acres to his freed slaves, and they took the Rolle name. On Great Exuma and Little Exuma you'll still find wild cotton, testaments from plantations first established by Loyalists after the Revolutionary War. But today the Exumas are known as the Bahamas' onion capital, although many of the 7,000 residents earn a living by fishing and farming, and, more recently, tourism.

The Exumas attract outdoorsmen and adventurers, particularly fishermen after bonefish, the feisty breed that prefers the shallow sandy flats that surround these islands. And the healthiest coral reefs and fish populations in the country make for excellent diving and snorkeling. But for those simply seeking secluded beaches, starry skies, and a couple of new friends, the Exumas won't disappoint.

You can't go wrong with any of the beaches in the Exumas. They're some of the prettiest in the Bahamas—powdery bleach-white sand sharply contrasts the glittery emerald and sapphire waves. You can even stake your umbrella directly on the Tropic of Cancer. And the best part of all? You'll probably be the only one there.

The Exumas are made up of 365 cays, each and every one with pristine white beaches. Some cays are no bigger than a footprintless sandbar. But you won't stay on the sand long; Perrier-clear waters beckon, and each gentle wave brings new treasures—shells, bits of blue-and-green sea glass, and starfish. Beaches won't be hard to find on the tiny cays; on Great Exuma, look for "Beach Access" signs on the Queen's Highway.

PLANNING

WHEN TO GO

High season is December through April, when weather is in the 70s (although lows can dip into the 60s). Be warned that hotels will sell out for events such as the George Town Cruising Regatta and the Bahamian Music and Heritage Festival in March, and the National Family Islands Regatta in April.

Summer room rates are cheaper than the winter high season, but fall (late August through November) offers the best deals. That's because it's hurricane season (June–November), with the most chance of a storm from August to November. Weather during this time can be rainy and hot. Some inns close for September and October.

TOP FESTIVALS

WINTER **Junkanoo.** The Exumas' Junkanoo Parade on Boxing Day (December 26) starts around 3 pm in George Town, ending at Regatta Park. Dancing, barbecues, and music happen before and after the parade. ⊠ *George Town.*

Annual New Year's Day Cruising Regatta. The Annual New Year's Day Cruising Regatta at the Staniel Cay Yacht Club marks the finale of a two-day celebration.

George Town Cruising Regatta. The George Town Cruising Regatta in March is 12 days of festivities including sailing, a conch-blowing contest, dance, food and entertainment, and sports competitions. ⊠ *George Town.*

Bahamian Music and Heritage Festival. March's Bahamian Music and Heritage Festival brings local and nationally known musicians to George Town, along with arts and crafts, Bahamas sloop exhibitions, storytelling, singing, poetry reading, and gospel music. ⊠ *George Town.*

SPRING **National Family Islands Regatta.** In April the National Family Islands Regatta is the Bahamas' most important yachting event. Starting the race in Elizabeth Harbour in George Town, island-made wooden sloops compete for trophies. Onshore, the town is a weeklong riot of Junkanoo parades, Goombay music, and arts-and-crafts fairs. ⊠ *George Town.*

SUMMER **Junkanoo Summer Festival.** The Junkanoo Summer Festival in June and July is held beachside at the Fish Fry in George Town, and features local and visiting bands, kids' sunfish sailing, arts and crafts, and boatbuilding displays. It takes place Saturdays at noon. ⊠ *George Town.*

FALL **Bahamas Sunfish Festival.** The annual Bahamas Sunfish Festival in October at Little Farmer's Cay features exciting races to prepare young sailors for international competition.

GETTING HERE AND AROUND
AIR TRAVEL
The airport is 10 miles north of George Town. Taxis wait at the airport for incoming flights; a trip to George Town costs $30 for two people; to Williams Town, $80; to February Point, $30; to Emerald Bay, $20; to Barraterre, $50. Each additional person is $3. Staniel Cay Airport accepts charter flights and private planes.

Contacts Exuma International Airport (GGT). ☎ 242/345–0002.

BOAT AND FERRY TRAVEL
The Bahamas Ferries vessels *Seawind* and *Sealink* travel from Nassau to George Town on Monday and Wednesday, arriving in Exuma the next day (on Tuesday and Thursday). The trip takes 10 hours and costs $71 one-way, $130 round-trip.

The mailboat M/V *Grand Master* travels from Nassau to George Town on Tuesday and returns to Nassau on Thursday. The trip takes 14 hours and costs $45 each way. M/V *Captain "C"* leaves Nassau on Tuesday for Staniel Cay, Big Farmer's Cay, and Ragged Island, returning to Nassau on Friday. The trip is 14 hours and costs $45. Contact the Dockmaster's Office for more information.

Elvis Ferguson operates a boat taxi from Government Dock to Chat 'N' Chill on the hour throughout the day. If you plan on leaving the island after 6 pm, tell the captain in advance.

Contacts Dockmaster's Office. ☎ 242/393–1064. **Elvis Ferguson.** ⊠ *Government Dock, George Town* ☎ 242/464–1558.

CAR TRAVEL
If you want to explore Great Exuma and Little Exuma, you'll need to rent a car. Most hotels can arrange car rentals.

Contacts Exuma Car Rentals. ⊠ *George Town Airport, George Town* ☎ 242/345–0090. **Thompson's Rentals.** ⊠ *George Town* ☎ 242/336–2442.

TAXI TRAVEL
Taxis are plentiful on Great Exuma, and most offer island tours. A half-day tour of George Town and Little Exuma is about $150 for two people.

Contacts Exuma Travel and Transportation Limited. ⊠ *George Town* ☎ 242/345–0232. **Kendal "Dr. K" Nixon.** ⊠ *George Town* ☎ 242/422–7399. **Luther Rolle Taxi Service.** ☎ 242/357–0662.

HOTELS
Accommodations in the Exumas are more wide-ranging than on most Bahamian Out Islands. You can stay in simple stilt cottages, fabulous rooms with butler service, atmospheric old inns, modern condo rentals, all-inclusives, eco-lodges, or bed-and-breakfasts—temporary

homes-away-from-home for every taste and price point. Most places have lots of personality and are distinctive in some marvelous way—a great hangout for fishermen, a peaceful place of tranquillity with no distractions, or action-packed resorts with head-spinning activity choices. Meal plans are available at some hotels.

The mainland of Great Exuma has had an energetic growth spurt that includes some of the country's most luxurious hotels, including Sandals Emerald Bay, Grand Isle Resort and Spa; and February Point Resort Estates.

RESTAURANTS
Exuma restaurants are known for terrific Bahamian home cooking—cracked conch, pan-seared snapper caught that morning, coconut fried shrimp, fried chicken served with peas 'n' rice, or macaroni baked with egg and loads of cheese. Try conch salad at the cluster of wooden shacks called the Fish Fry, just north of George Town. Pea soup and dumplings (made with pigeon peas) is a specialty here, and many local restaurants serve it as a weekly lunch special, usually on Wednesday.

Restaurants at larger resorts have upscale dining, including Continental twists on local cuisine—fresh snapper with mango salsa—as well as imported steaks, rack of lamb, and gourmet pizzas.

HOTEL AND RESTAURANT PRICES
Restaurant prices are based on the median main course price at dinner, excluding gratuity, typically 15%, which is often automatically added to the bill. Hotel prices are for two people in a standard double room in high season, excluding service and 6%–12% tax.

WHAT IT COSTS IN DOLLARS			
$	$$	$$$	$$$$
Restaurants	under $20	$20–$30	$31–$40	over $40
Hotels	under $200	$200–$300	$301–$400	over $400

VISITOR INFORMATION
Contacts Exuma Tourist Office. ✉ Queen's Hwy., George Town ☎ 242/336–2430 ⊕ www.exuma.bahamas.com. **Out Islands Promotion Board.** ⊕ www.myoutisland.com.

GREAT EXUMA

George Town is the capital and largest town on the mainland, a lovely seaside community with darling pink government buildings overlooking Elizabeth Harbour. The white-pillared, colonial-style Government Administration Building was modeled on Nassau's Government House and houses the commissioner's office, police headquarters, courts, and a jail. Atop a hill across from it is the whitewashed St. Andrew's Anglican Church, originally built around 1802. Behind the church is the small, saltwater Lake Victoria. It was once used for soaking sisal used for making baskets and ropes. The straw market, a half-dozen outdoor shops

GREAT ITINERARIES

IF YOU HAVE 3 DAYS

Fly into **George Town**, relax on the beach or at the pool, and if it's a Friday night drive to the Fish Fry, a collection of outdoor fish shacks and bars just north of George Town; eat your dinner on a picnic table next to the beach. Finish the night at Club Peace and Plenty, the heart of George Town for more than 50 years. On Day 2, pick an activity: golfing at Sandals Emerald Bay; diving, snorkeling, or kayaking (make arrangements the night before at your resort); bonefishing; or driving to a beautiful secluded beach. Get gussied up (sundresses and linen shirts) for a nice dinner in town. On Day 3, head out to **Stocking Island** for some beach volleyball and that it's-five-o'clock-somewhere cocktail. Stay for dinner and sunset. If it's Sunday, a pig roast at noon brings all the islanders over.

IF YOU HAVE 5 DAYS

On Day 4, head to the **Exuma Cays** for some island-hopping: snorkel in Thunderball Grotto, feed swimming pigs and the rare Bahamian iguanas, or find your own secluded sandbar. Spend the night at Staniel Cay Yacht Club, and enjoy a festive dinner at the bar. On Day 5, head to the Exuma Cays Land and Sea Park, and spend the day snorkeling, hiking, and beach snoozing.

IF YOU HAVE 7 DAYS

For the last two days, on your way back from the cays, relocate to Grand Isle or Sandals Emerald Bay for a luxurious end to your vacation. Relax on the beach, go to the spa, and enjoy that gorgeous blue water one last time. Eat at some of the finer restaurants on the island, or at beach shacks off the resort property.

shaded by a huge African fig tree, is a short walk from town. You can bargain with fishermen for some of the day's catch at the Government Dock, where the mail boat comes in.

Small settlements make up the rest of the island. **Rolle Town,** a typical Exuma village devoid of tourist trappings, sits atop a hill overlooking the ocean 5 miles south of George Town. Some of the buildings are 100 years old. **Rolleville** overlooks a harbor 20 miles north of George Town. Its old slave quarters have been transformed into livable cottages. The Hilltop Tavern, a seafood restaurant and bar, is guarded by an ancient cannon.

GETTING AROUND

If you are going to sightsee on your own and plan to eat at restaurants and visit beaches outside your resort, you should rent a car, since taxis can get expensive. If you plan to stay at your resort most of your vacation, you can use taxis.

EXPLORING

Fish Fry. Fish Fry is the name given to a jumble of one-room beachside structures, such as Charlie's and Honeydew, about 2 miles north of George Town. They're favored by locals for made-to-order fish and barbecue. Some shacks are open weekends only, but most are open

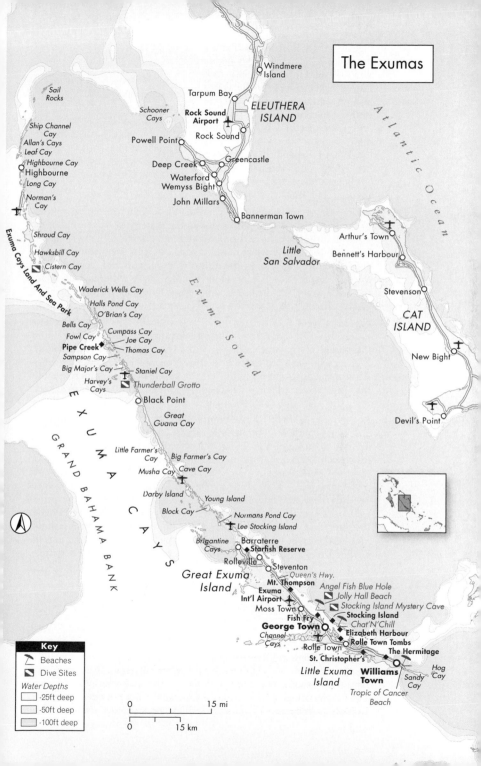

The Exumas

Sail Rocks

Ship Channel Cay
Allan's Cays
Leaf Cay
Highbourne Cay
Highbourne
Long Cay

Norman's Cay

Exuma Cays Land And Sea Park

Shroud Cay

Hawksbill Cay

Cistern Cay

Waderick Wells Cay

Halls Pond Cay
O'Brian's Cay

Bells Cay
Fowl Cay   Compass Cay
Pipe Creek   Joe Cay
Thomas Cay
Sampson Cay
Big Major's Cay   Staniel Cay
Harvey's Cays   Thunderball Grotto

Black Point

Great Guana Cay

Little Farmer's Cay   Big Farmer's Cay
Musha Cay   Cave Cay

Darby Island
Block Cay   Young Island
Normans Pond Cay
Lee Stocking Island

Brigantine Cays   Barraterre
Starfish Reserve
Rolleville
Steventon
Great Exuma Island   Queen's Hwy.
Mt. Thompson
Exuma   Angel Fish Blue Hole
Int'l Airport   Jolly Hall Beach
Moss Town   Stocking Island Mystery Cave
Fish Fry   Stocking Island
George Town   Chat'N'Chill
Channel   Elizabeth Harbour
Cays   Rolle Town Tombs
Rolle Town   The Hermitage
St. Christopher's
Little Exuma   Williams   Hog Cay
Island   Town   Sandy Cay
Tropic of Cancer Beach

EXUMA CAYS

GRAND BAHAMA BANK

Exuma Sound

Windmere Island
Tarpum Bay
Rock Sound Airport   ELEUTHERA ISLAND
Rock Sound
Powell Point
Deep Creek   Greencastle
Waterford
Wemyss Bight
John Millars
Bannerman Town

Little San Salvador

Arthur's Town
Bennett's Harbour

Stevenson

CAT ISLAND

New Bight

Devil's Point

Atlantic Ocean

Key

- Beaches
- Dive Sites

Water Depths
- -25ft deep
- -50ft deep
- -100ft deep

0   15 mi
0   15 km

nightly until at least 11 pm. There's live Rake 'n' Scrape Monday nights and DJs on Friday and Saturday. Eat at picnic tables by the water and watch the fishing boats come into the harbor. This is a popular after-work meeting place on Friday nights, and a sports bar attracts locals and expats for American basketball and football games. ⊠ *Queen's Hwy., George Town.*

Mt. Thompson. From the top of Mt. Thompson, rising from the Three Sisters Beach, there is a pleasing view of the **Three Sisters Rocks** jutting above the water just offshore. Legend has it that the rocks were formed when three sisters, all unwittingly in love with the same English sailor, waded out into deep water upon his departure, drowned, and turned into stone. If you look carefully next to each "sister," you'll see smaller boulders—the children with which the fickle sailor left them. Mt. Thompson is about 12 miles north of George Town, past Moss Town. ⊠ *Queen's Hwy., Mount Thompson.*

Rolle Town Tombs. Seek out the three Rolle Town Tombs, which date back to Loyalists. The largest tomb bears this poignant inscription: "Within this tomb interred the body of Ann McKay, the wife of Alexander McKay who departed this life the 8th November 1792. Aged twenty-six years and their infant child." The tombs are off the main road; look for a sign. The settlement has brightly painted buildings, several more than 100 years old. ⊠ *Rolle Town.*

Fodor's Choice ★ **Stocking Island.** Slightly more than a mile off George Town's shore lies Stocking Island. The 4-mile-long island has only 10 inhabitants, the upscale Hotel Higgins Landing, lots of walking trails, a gorgeous white beach rich in seashells and popular with surfers on the ocean side, and plenty of good snorkeling sites. Jacques Cousteau's team is said to have traveled some 1,700 feet into Mystery Cave, a blue-hole grotto 70 feet beneath the island. Don't miss Chat 'N' Chill, a lively open-air restaurant and bar right on the point. Volleyball games, board games under the trees, and the Conch Bar make for fun in the sun. The restaurant picks up guests at Government Dock on the hour. Stocking Island is the headquarters for the wildly popular George Town Cruising Regatta.

BEACHES

Fodor's Choice ★ **Chat 'N' Chill.** The restaurant and 9-acre playground—an amazing white-sand beach—is the Exumas' party central, particularly for the famous all-day Sunday pig roasts. Play volleyball in the powdery sand, order what's cooking on the outdoor grill—fresh fish, ribs—or chat and chill. There are dances on the beach from January to the end of April when 200-plus sailboats populate the harbor. The new Conch Bar on the beach serves conch fritters, conch salad, and lobster fritters. The beach is quieter on weekdays, and usually not crowded in summer and fall. **Amenities:** food and drink; toilets. **Best for:** partiers. ⊠ *Stocking*

Island ☎ *242/357–0926* 🌐 *www.chatnchill.com.*

Jolly Hall Beach. A curve of sparkling white sand shaded by casuarina trees, this long beach is located just north of Palm Bay Beach Club. It's quiet and the shallow azure water makes it a great spot for families or romantics. When it's time for lunch, walk over to Palm Bay, Exuma Beach Resort, or Augusta Bay, three small nearby inns. Watch your bags when high tide comes in; much of the beach is swallowed by the sea. That's the signal for a cold Kalik and grouper sandwich. **Amenities:** none. **Best for:** solitude; sunrise; swimming; snorkeling. ✉ *Queen's Hwy., George Town.*

PEACOCKS

During your walks, you might glimpse peacocks on Great Exuma. Originally, a peacock and a peahen were brought to the island as pets by a man named Shorty Johnson, but when he left to work in Nassau he abandoned the birds, which gradually proliferated into a colony. The birds used to roam the streets, but development has forced them into the bush, so they are rarer sights these days.

WHERE TO EAT

$ BAHAMIAN Fodor's Choice ★ 🍴 **Big D's Conch Shack.** For the freshest—and according to locals, best—conch salad and the coldest beer, look for the splatter-painted seaside shack a stone's throw from Grand Isle Resort. You can't get a better water view, and the beach is great; bring a swimsuit. [$] *Average main: $10* ✉ *Queen's Hwy., Emerald Bay* ☎ *242/358–0059* 🕑 *Closed Mon.*

$ ECLECTIC 🍴 **Blu Bistro.** With a stunning view of the Three Sisters Rocks, this charming beachfront restaurant offers dinner à la carte every night and themed dinners three times a week: Mexican Wednesdays with margaritas, Indian Fridays, and Bahamian Sundays with barbecue. Blu Bistro also serves lunch on the beachfront terrace every day, but you'll need to call ahead. Menu options include burgers, sandwiches, and chicken tenders. [$] *Average main: $16* ✉ *Exuma Palms Hotel, Queen's Hwy., Mount Thompson* ☎ *242/358–4040* 🌐 *www.exumapalms.com* ✍ *Reservations essential.*

$$ ECLECTIC 🍴 **Catch a Fire Bar and Grill.** Sip a tropical cocktail and enjoy the sunset at this waterfront bar and grill. Tastefully decorated with teak benches, a handsome bar, and infinity pool, Catch a Fire is a fun place to go for dinner and for dancing on Wednesday and Saturday nights when the restaurant has live entertainment. It can be busy, so call ahead for reservations. [$] *Average main: $30* ✉ *George Town* ☎ *242/357–0777* 💳 *No credit cards* 🕑 *Closed Sun.*

$ BAHAMIAN Fodor's Choice ★ 🍴 **Chat 'N' Chill.** Yacht folks, locals, and visitors alike rub shoulders at Kenneth Bowe's funky open-air beach bar on the point at Stocking Island. All of the food is grilled over an open fire; awesome conch burgers with secret spices and grilled fish with onions and potatoes attract diners from all over Great Exuma. Dances and bonfires on the beach during the winter season are famous island-wide. Sunday pig roasts, which start around noon, are legendary, but call first to make sure it's scheduled. Most guests arrive by sailboat but you can get here by water taxi (*242/464–1558; or call Capt. Elvis Ferguson on VHF radio channel 16*) from the Government Dock, which leaves on the hour during the day. [$] *Average main: $14* ✉ *1 Stocking Island* ☎ *242/357–0926* 🌐 *www.chatnchill.com* 💳 *No credit cards.*

THE GOLDEN TICKET

Sandals restaurants aren't open to nonguests—unless you buy a $150 pass that includes all you can eat and drink from 6 pm to 2 am, a $180 pass for 10 am to 6 pm, or an all-day pass for $310.

$ BAHAMIAN 🍴 **Cheater's Restaurant and Bar.** Disregard the lack of ambience; this popular restaurant serves some of the best food on the island. Fresh fish and fried chicken dinners are the house specialties. Free transportation is available to those staying at hotels within 4 miles of the restaurant. [$] *Average main: $15* ✉ *George Town* ✥ *1½ miles south of Queen's Hwy.* ☎ *242/336–2535* 💳 *No credit cards* 🕒 *Closed Sun. and Mon.*

$$ EUROPEAN 🍴 **Club Peace and Plenty.** The legendary hotel's restaurant has a fabulous view of the pool and harbor, along with traditional Bahamian specialties including conch fritters and grilled fish, and a 12-ounce New York strip steak. This is one of the nicer places to dine on the island, perfect for a romantic dinner or family celebration. For breakfast start your day with boiled snapper and johnnycakes or an omelet. [$] *Average main: $29* ✉ *Club Peace and Plenty, Queen's Hwy., George Town* ☎ *242/336–2551* 🌐 *www.peaceandplenty.com.*

$ DELI 🍴 **Driftwood Café.** Located in central George Town just across from the Club Peace and Plenty, this café is a pleasant spot for a cup of coffee and hot breakfast sandwich in the morning. Driftwood Café also offers lunch, with specialties such as quiche, subs, and salads served with fresh lemonade or iced tea. Choose between air-conditioned seating inside, or tables outside on the private terrace. [$] *Average main: $10* ✉ *Queen's Hwy., George Town* ☎ *242/336–3800* 💳 *No credit cards* 🕒 *Closed Sun.*

$ BAHAMIAN 🍴 **Eddie's Edgewater.** Fried chicken, lobster, T-bone steak, and cracked conch are the delicious reasons people eat at this modest lakeside establishment. Stop by on Monday nights for some authentic Bahamian Rake 'n' Scrape music. [$] *Average main: $15* ✉ *Charlotte St., George Town* ☎ *242/336–2050* 🕒 *Closed Sun. No dinner Tues. or Wed.*

$$ BAHAMIAN Fodor's Choice ★ 🍴 **Exuma Yacht Club.** Located in the hustle and bustle of central George Town, the Exuma Yacht Club has a magnificent view of the harbor. Enjoy the ocean breeze from the bar on the balcony, or dine in the chic indoor seating area. The menu includes burgers, salads, and a fresh catch of the day. [$] *Average main: $29* ✉ *Queen's Hwy., George Town* ☎ *242/336–2579* 🌐 *www.theexumayachtclub.com* 🕒 *Closed Sun.*

$$$ CARIBBEAN 🍴 **Latitudes.** Enjoy the ocean view at Exuma Beach Resort for lunch, dinner, or over one of their famous cocktails. Highlights of the lunch menu are the ½-pound gourmet Angus beef burger, sushi-grade ahi tuna wrap, and flatbread pizzas. Dinner options include the popular mango-chutney shrimp curry and grilled Bahamian lobster. Latitudes has live entertainment on Sunday, Tuesday, and Friday nights, and Happy Hour on Sunday. Be sure to try one of their signature cocktails: the 22.5 degrees North is named for the latitude of the Tropic of Cancer, which runs

7

through Exuma, and the Chocolatini is the best dessert in the house. [$] *Average main: $36* ✉ *Queens Hwy., George Town* ☎ *242/336–3100.*

$$$ EUROPEAN Fodor's Choice ★ 🍴 **Palappa Pool Bar and Grill at Grand Isle Resort.** This poolside restaurant serves three meals a day and offers a stunning view of the ocean. The extensive menu equally features American classics and Bahamian specialties. Dinner highlights include ahi tuna steak, shrimp pasta, prime rib eye, and baby back ribs. A fun drink list including many frozen concoctions complements the food. [$] *Average main: $37* ✉ *Grand Isle Resort, Queen's Hwy., Emerald Bay* ☎ *242/358–5000* 🌐 *www.grandisleresort.com* ✍ *Reservations essential.*

$ DELI 🍴 **Prime Island Meats and Deli.** Stop by this deli to stock up on gourmet meats, cheeses, and wine for your stay. Owners Ron and Susan Kemp also sell delicious chicken salad, crab salad, potato salad, and more. All are homemade and perfect for a beach picnic. The rotisserie chicken is extremely popular, as is the quality beef. [$] *Average main: $8* ✉ *Queen's Hwy., George Town* ☎ *242/336–3627* 🌐 *www.primeislandmeats.com* ⏲ *Closed Sun.*

$ BAHAMIAN 🍴 **Splash Bar & Grill.** Restaurant highlights for lunch are fish burgers, conch burgers, and regular burgers. Dinner specialties include grilled grouper, cracked conch, and pizza. The restaurant circles a lively bar, a popular hangout for locals as well as guests who enjoy the view of the harbor and Stocking Island. [$] *Average main: $13* ✉ *Queen's Hwy., George Town* ☎ *242/336–3587* 🌐 *www.hideawayspalmbay.com.*

$ BAHAMIAN 🍴 **Towne Café.** This George Town restaurant serves breakfast (especially popular on Saturday)—consider trying the stew' fish or chicken souse—and lunches of grilled fish or seafood sandwiches with three sides. It's open until 3 pm. Don't miss the baked goods, especially the giant cinnamon rolls. [$] *Average main: $14* ✉ *Marshall Complex, Queen's Hwy., George Town* ☎ *242/336–2194* 💳 *No credit cards* ⏲ *Closed Sun.*

WHERE TO STAY

$$ RESORT Fodor's Choice ★ 🏨 **Augusta Bay Bahamas.** The perfect balance of luxury and casual chic, without the megaresort feel, this 16-room resort on 300 feet of narrow beach is a mile north of George Town. **Pros:** luxurious rooms; great water views; friendly service. **Cons:** beach almost disappears at high tide; need a car to drive to town and shops. [$] *Rooms from: $277* ✉ *Queen's Hwy., George Town* ☎ *242/336–2250* 🌐 *www.augustabaybahamas.com* 🛏 *16 rooms* 🍽 *Breakfast.*

$ HOTEL 🏨 **Club Peace and Plenty.** The first Exumas hotel and granddaddy of the island's omnipresent Peace and Plenty empire, this pink, two-story lodge is in the heart of the action in George Town. **Pros:** guests are in middle of the George Town action; friendly staff; ocean-view balconies in some rooms. **Cons:** no beach; have to take a water taxi to Stocking Island. [$] *Rooms from: $180* ✉ *Queen's Hwy., George Town* ☎ *242/336–2551, 800/525–2210* 🌐 *www.peaceandplenty.com* 🛏 *32 rooms* 🍽 *No meals.*

$ B&B/INN 🏨 **Coral Gardens Bed and Breakfast.** Extremely popular with Brits and Europeans, the sprawling two-story B&B, owned and run by British expats Betty and Peter Oxley, is on a hilltop with an inviting veranda. **Pros:** superb hilltop view of water in the distance; friendly hosts; free

Sandals Emerald Bay on Great Exuma has one of the island's best beaches.

Wi-Fi. **Cons:** not on the beach; need a car to go to George Town and the beach. [$] *Rooms from: $99* ⊠ *12 Garden Rd., off Queen's Hwy., George Town* ✛ *3 miles north of George Town* ☎ *242/336–2880,* ⊕ *www.coralgardensbahamas.com* ⊘ *Closed Sept.–mid-Oct.* ⤴ *3 rooms, 2 apartments* ⍟ *Breakfast.*

$ **Exuma Beach Resort.** This newly renovated beachfront resort just
RESORT outside of George Town boasts eight guest rooms and one exceptional suite. **Pros:** modern accommodations; centrally located. **Cons:** backs into main road; resort can feel cramped. [$] *Rooms from: $175* ⊠ *Queen's Hwy., George Town* ☎ *242/336–3100* ⤴ *7 rooms, 2 suites* ⍟ *Breakfast.*

$$$$ **February Point Resort Estates.** This gated residential community and
RESORT resort is made up of 40 villas and privately owned homes—27 of the
FAMILY villas are available as guest accommodations. **Pros:** elegant accommodations that feel like an ultraluxurious home away from home; waterfront restaurant on-property. **Cons:** more like a gated community than a resort; ongoing construction can be noisy. [$] *Rooms from: $650* ⊠ *Queen's Hwy., George Town* ☎ *242/336–2695* ⊕ *www.februarypoint.com* ⤴ *27 villas.*

$$$ **Grand Isle Resort and Spa.** This luxurious 78-villa complex boasts
RESORT one of the island's few spas, an infinity pool overlooking the ocean,
FAMILY and a poolside patio restaurant. **Pros:** the ultimate in luxury accom-
Fodor'sChoice modations; friendly staff; on-site spa and restaurant. **Cons:** 20-minute
★ drive from George Town and not much to do near the resort; lacks local flavor. [$] *Rooms from: $300* ⊠ *Off Queens Hwy., Emerald Bay* ☎ *242/358–5000* ⊕ *www.grandisleresort.com* ⤴ *78 villas* ⍟ *No meals.*

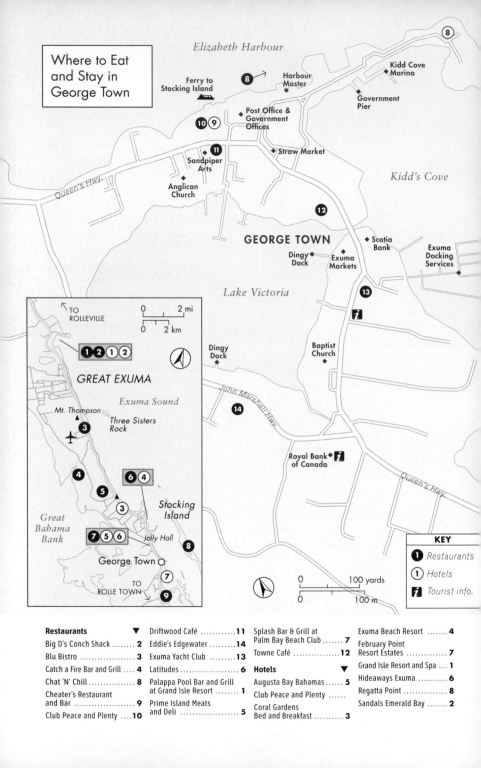

Where to Eat and Stay in George Town

Elizabeth Harbour

Ferry to Stocking Island

8

Harbour Master

Kidd Cove Marina

Government Pier

10 **9**

Post Office & Government Offices

11

Sandpiper Arts

Straw Market

Kidd's Cove

Anglican Church

Queen's Hwy.

12

GEORGE TOWN

Dingy Dock

Exuma Markets

Scotia Bank

Exuma Docking Services

Lake Victoria

13

🛈

Dingy Dock

Baptist Church

John Marshall Hwy.

14

Royal Bank of Canada 🛈

Queen's Hwy.

Inset Map

↖ TO ROLLEVILLE

0   2 mi
0   2 km

1 2 1 2

GREAT EXUMA

Exuma Sound

Mt. Thompson ▲

Three Sisters Rock

3

4

5

3

6 4

Stocking Island

Great Bahama Bank

7 5 6

Jolly Hall

8

George Town ○

TO ROLLE TOWN

7

9

0   100 yards
0   100 m

KEY

1 *Restaurants*
① *Hotels*
🛈 *Tourist info.*

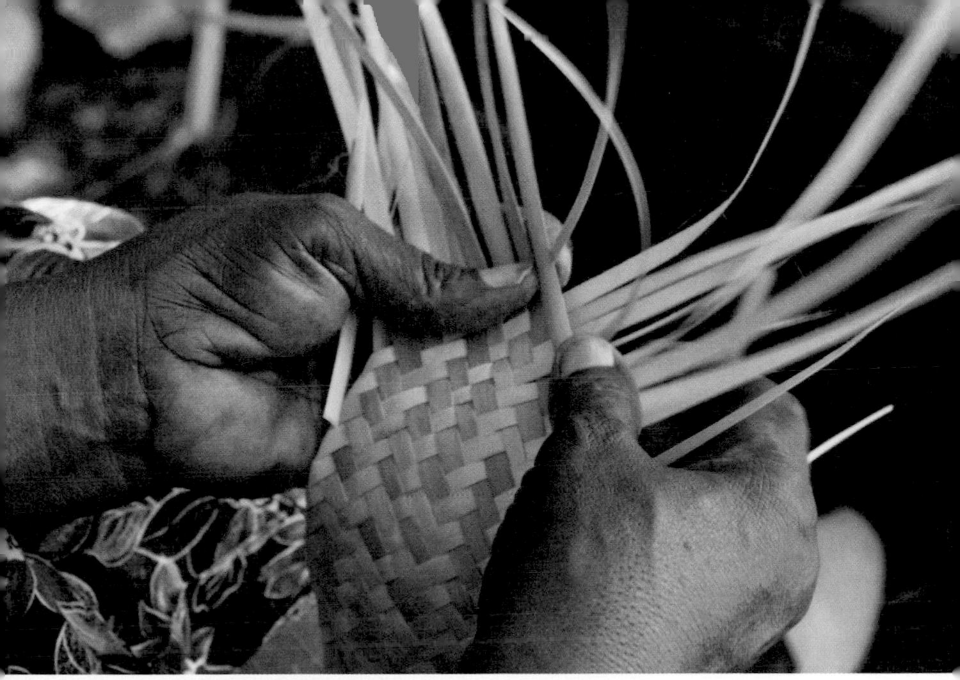

The Straw Market in George Town features handmade crafts.

$$ RESORT FAMILY **Hideaways Exuma.** Formerly called Palm Bay, one of George Town's most modern accommodations, is all about light and color. **Pros:** roomy accommodations; friendly young staff. **Cons:** beach all but disappears at high tide; accommodations are close together. [$] *Rooms from: $250* ✉ *Queen's Hwy.* ↕ *1 mile from George Town* ☎ *888/396–0606, 242/336–2787* 🌐 *www.hideawayspalmbay.com* 🛏 *43 rooms* 🍴 *No meals.*

$ HOTEL **Regatta Point.** Soft pink with hunter-green shutters, this handsome two-story guesthouse overlooks Kidd Cove from its own petite island. **Pros:** in George Town but has the feel of a private island; has beach and fantastic harbor views. **Cons:** water at the beach doesn't look clean; no restaurant; cash only. [$] *Rooms from: $184* ✉ *Kidd Cove, George Town* ☎ *242/336–2206, 800/561–7954* 🌐 *www.regattapointbahamas.com* 💳 *No credit cards* 🛏 *6 suites* 🍴 *No meals.*

$$$$ RESORT **Sandals Emerald Bay.** The former luxurious Four Seasons is now the even more luxurious Sandals Emerald Bay, an all-inclusive resort of pink and aqua buildings facing a 1-mile-long stretch of powdery white sand. **Pros:** spa and golf on-property; magnificent beach and swimming pools; great water sports. **Cons:** the resort is isolated; lacks Bahamian flavor. [$] *Rooms from: $750* ✉ *Queen's Hwy., Emerald Bay* ☎ *242/336–6800, 800/726–3157* 🌐 *www.sandals.com* 🛏 *245 suites* 🍴 *All-inclusive.*

NIGHTLIFE

Club Peace and Plenty. In season, the Thursday-night poolside bashes at Club Peace and Plenty, fueled by live bands, keep Bahamians and vacationers on the dance floor. ⊠ *Queen's Hwy., George Town* ☎ *242/336–2551.*

Eddie's Edgewater. On Monday, head to Eddie's Edgewater for rousing Rake 'n' Scrape music. The front porch is a popular spot, where locals hang out all week long. ⊠ *Charlotte St., George Town* ☎ *242/336–2050.*

Fish Fry. There's always something going on at the Fish Fry, a cluster of shacks 2 miles north of George Town. A DJ is usually there on Friday and Sunday. ⊠ *Queen's Hwy., George Town.*

> ### TAKING PICS OF THE WATER
>
> "My pictures will never show the incredible shades of blue in this water." You're likely to hear this on your vacation, maybe straight from your own mouth. Here are a few tips: shoot early—before 9—on a sunny day, or late in the afternoon. Make sure the sun is behind you. Use a tripod, or hold the camera still. Find a contrasting color—a bright red umbrella or a yellow fishing boat.

SHOPPING AND SPAS

SHOPS

Exuma Markets. At this grocery store located in the center of George Town, yachties tie up at the skiff docks in the rear, on Lake Victoria. Emergency email and faxes for visitors are also accepted here. ⊠ *Across from Scotia Bank, Queen's Hwy., George Town* ☎ *242/336–2033.*

Sandpiper Arts & Crafts. Here you can find upscale souvenirs, from high-quality cards and books to batik clothing and art. ⊠ *Queen's Hwy., George Town* ☎ *242/336–2084* ⊘ *Closed Sun.*

Straw Market. The Straw Market offers a wide range of Bahamian straw bags, hats, and beachwear at a half-dozen open-air shops under a huge African fig tree. Prices are negotiable. ⊠ *Queen's Hwy., George Town* ⊘ *Closed Sun.*

SPAS

Red Lane Spa. Located on the Sandals Emerald Bay property, this elegant spa has 16 treatment rooms, a steam room, and a fitness center. Couples massages and "sun lover" relief are among the treatments offered. The spa is also open to nonguests, but you'll need to call ahead to make your appointment. ⊠ *Sandals Emerald Bay, Queen's Hwy., Emerald Bay* ☎ *242/336–6800* ⊕ *www.sandals.com* ⚲ *Steam room. Gym with: cardiovascular machines, free weights, weight-training equipment. Services: body wraps, facials, massage, scrubs, nail treatment. Classes and programs: Pilates, yoga.*

SeaStar Spa. Seawater therapy, or the art of marine healing, is the philosophy at SeaStar Spa, located at Grand Isle Resort. Relax in one of three treatment rooms, including one designed especially for couples. The spa is open every day and offers a number of massages, scrubs, and wraps utilizing natural ingredients such as ginger, lime, coconut, and island spices. SeaStar also has a special "children's spa" menu which includes shorter massages and pedicures as well as hair braiding. ⌂ *Grand Isle Resort, Emerald Bay* ☎ *242/358–5000* ⊕ *www.grandisleresort.com* ⌘ *Services: aromatherapy, massage, nail treatment, scrubs.*

SPORTS AND THE OUTDOORS

ADVENTURE TOURS

Island Boy Adventures. Floating down the lazy river at Moriah Harbor Park, taking a boat trip through the Exuma Cays to swim with the pigs, and going diving for lobster are just a few of the activities offered by experienced Captains Evvie and Tonio. If you're not sure what to choose, let Island Boy Adventures help you plan your day—they won't disappoint. ⌂ *George Town* ☎ *242/357–0459* ⊕ *www.islandboy adventures.com.*

BOATING

Because of its wealth of safe harbors and regatta events, the Exumas are a favorite spot for yachtsmen. Renting a boat allows you to explore the cays near George Town and beyond, and a number of area hotels allow guests to tie up rental boats at their docks. For those who want to take a water jaunt through Stocking Island's hurricane holes, sailboats are ideal.

FISHING

In the shallow flats off Exuma's windward coast the elusive bonefish, the "ghosts of the sea," roam. Patient fishermen put featherweight, thumbnail-size flies on the lines, calculate the tides and currents, and cast out about 50 feet in hope of catching one. For sure success, avid fishermen pay guides about $300 a day to help them outsmart the skinny gray fish that streak through crystal water. Most hotels can arrange for expert locals guides, and a list is also available from the Exuma Tourist Office. The season is year-round and highly prized among fly-fishermen.

Exuma Bonefish Guides Association. These guides are all highly qualified to help you hook a bonefish. A full day on the flats costs $380. ⊕ *www. exumabonefish.com.*

Fish Rowe Charters. This charter company has a 40-foot Hatteras that holds up to four fishermen. Deepwater charters run $800 for a half day, $1,200 for ¾ day, and $1,600 for a full day. ☎ *242/357–0870* ⊕ *www. fishrowecharters.com.*

Steve Ferguson. Stevie is an experienced guide who will help you hook feisty bonefish. ☎ *242/422–7033* ⊕ *www.bonefishstevie.com.*

GOLF

Sandals Emerald Reef Golf Club. Golf legend Greg Norman designed the 18-hole, par-72 championship course, featuring six ocean-side holes, at Sandals Emerald Bay, the island's only golf course. There are preferred tee times for hotel guests. ⌂ *Sandals, Queen's Hwy., Emerald Bay* ☎ *242/336–6800* ⊕ *www.sandals.com* ⌘ *$175 for guests; $185 for nonguests. Admission includes golf cart* ⛳ *18 holes, 7000 yards, par 72.*

7

You'll swim among multicolored tropical fish at Staniel Cay.

KAYAKING

Gully's Sea Kayaking. Gully rents kayaks for $60/day for a single and $80/day for a double. Discounts are available for longer rentals. ☎ *242/524–4213*.

SCUBA DIVING

The popular **Angel Fish Blue Hole**, just minutes from George Town, is filled with angelfish, spotted rays, snapper, and the occasional reef shark. However, while it is full of mesmerizing schools of colorful fish, it is for experienced divers only.

Dive Exuma. This outfitter provides dive instruction, certification courses, and scuba trips. Two-tank dives are $135; blue-hole one-tank dives are $85. ☎ *242/357–0313, 242/336–2893* ⊕ *www.dive-exuma.com*.

SNORKELING

Minn's Water Sports. Minn's rents snorkeling gear for $10/day. ✉ *Queen's Hwy., George Town* ☎ *242/336–2604* ⊕ *www.mwsboats.com*.

TENNIS

February Point. Nonguests can use the two Laykold cushion–surfaced courts and adjacent fitness center at February Point for $16 a day. ✉ *February Point Resort, Queen's Hwy., George Town* ☎ *242/336–2661* ⊕ *www.februarypoint.com*.

LITTLE EXUMA

Scenes from two *Pirates of the Caribbean* movies were filmed on the southern end of Little Exuma—only 12 square miles—and on one of the little cays just offshore. The movies' stars, Johnny Depp and Orlando Bloom, often roamed around the island and ate at Santana's open-air beach shack, the island's best-known restaurant. But that's just one of the reasons people are drawn to this lovely island connected to Great Exuma to the north by a narrow bridge. Rolling green hills, purple morning glories spilling over fences, small settlements with only a dozen houses, and glistening white beaches make a romantic afternoon escape. Near **Williams Town** is an eerie salt lake, still and ghostly, where salt was once scooped up and shipped away. You can hike old footpaths and look for ruins of old plantation buildings built in the 1700s near the Hermitage, but you'll have to look beneath the bushes and vines to find them. Little Exuma's best beach is Tropic of Cancer Beach (also known as Pelican's Bay Beach); it is a thrill to stand on the line that marks the spot. You're officially in the tropics now.

GETTING HERE AND AROUND

You need a car or a scooter to explore Little Exuma. It's possible to walk or ride a bike around the island, but it's hot and there's very little shade.

VISITOR INFORMATION

People-to-People Program. To get to know Exuma islanders better, hook up with the People-to-People Program. The group hosts a tea where visitors can learn about bush medicine and other aspects of local life. ☎ *242/356–0435, 242/336–2430* ⊕ *www.bahamas.com/ people-to-people.*

EXPLORING

Hermitage. The Hermitage estate ruins are testaments to the cotton plantation days. The small settlement was built by the Ferguson family from the Carolinas who settled here after the American Revolutionary War. Visitors can see the foundations of the main house and tombs that date back to the 1700s. The tombs hold George Butler (1759–1822), Henderson Ferguson (1772–1825), and Constance McDonald (1755–1759). A grave is believed to be that of an unnamed slave. ⊠ *Williams Town.*

St. Christopher's Anglican. This is the island's smallest church, built in 1939 when the parish priest, Father Marshall, heard that a schooner loaded with timber from the Abacos had wrecked off Long Island. He visited the local Fitz-Gerald family and suggested they use the timber to build a church, which they did. Visitors can see the church and pews, all built of salvaged wood. ⊠ *Queen's Hwy., Ferry.*

BEACHES

Fodor's Choice ★ **Tropic of Cancer Beach** (*Pelican's Bay Beach*). This is the beach most visitors come to the Exumas for, although don't be surprised if you're the only one on it at noon on a Saturday. It's right on the Tropic of Cancer; a helpful line marking the spot on the steps leading down to the sand makes a great photo op. The beach is a white-sand crescent in a protected cove, where the water is usually as calm as a pond. A shady wooden cabana makes a comfortable place to admire the beach and water. *Pirates of the Caribbean* 2 and 3 were filmed on nearby Sandy Cay. Have lunch at the cast's favorite place, the open-air Santana's in Williams Town, a 10-minute drive from the beach. **Amenities:** none. **Best for:** solitude; snorkeling; swimming; walking. ✉ *Williams Town.*

WHERE TO EAT

$ BAHAMIAN Fodor's Choice ★ 🍴 **Santana's Grill Pit.** This seaside open-air restaurant—you can't miss the orange-and-yellow building—is the hot spot in Little Exuma, and the closest restaurant to the Tropic of Cancer Beach. Dinner highlights include cracked lobster, cracked conch, shrimp, and grilled grouper, all served with peas 'n' rice or baked macaroni and cheese. Ask to see the photo book of celebrities who have eaten here; it was popular with the *Pirates of the Caribbean* cast and crew. [$] *Average main: $16* ✉ *Queen's Hwy., Williams Town* ☎ *242/345–4102* 💳 *No credit cards* 🕒 *Closed Sun.*

WHERE TO STAY

$$$ HOTEL 🏨 **Turquoise Cay.** In the place of the old Peace and Plenty Bonefish Lodge, the island's first luxury boutique hotel opened in summer 2013. **Pros:** the resort has docks if you choose to rent a boat; peaceful; great sunset views. **Cons:** secluded; need a car to leave the property. [$] *Rooms from: $400* ✉ *Queen's Hwy., Ferry* ☎ *242/345–5010* 🌐 *www.turquoisecay.com* 🛏 *8 rooms* 🍽 *No meals.*

THE EXUMA CAYS

A band of cays—with names like **Rudder Cut**, **Big Farmer's**, **Great Guana**, and **Leaf**—stretches northwest from Great Exuma. It will take you a full day to boat through all 365 cays, most uninhabited, some owned by celebrities (Faith Hill and Tim McGraw on Goat Cay, Johnny Depp on Halls Pond Cay, and David Copperfield on Musha Cay). Along the way you'll find giant starfish, wild iguanas, swimming pigs, dolphins, sharks, and picture-perfect footprintless sandbars. The Land and Sea Park, toward the northern end of the chain, is world-renowned.

GETTING HERE AND AROUND

Most people visit the cays with their own boats; you'll need one to island-hop, although you can fly into Staniel Cay. The channels are confusing for inexperienced boaters, especially at low tide, and high tide can hide reefs and sandbars just underneath the surface. If this sounds nerve-racking, look into booking a boat tour. Once on a cay, most are small enough to walk. Golf carts are popular on Staniel Cay.

Island of the Stars

The Bahamas have served as a source of inspiration for countless artists, writers, and directors. The country's movie legacy dates back to the era of silent films, including the now-legendary original black-and-white version of **Jules Verne**'s *20,000 Leagues Under the Sea,* which was filmed here in 1907. Since the birth of color film, the draw has only increased—directors are lured by the possibility of using the islands' characteristic white sands and luminous turquoise waters as a backdrop. Among the more famous movies shot in the Bahamas are *Jaws: The Revenge,* the cult favorite whose killer shark has terrified viewers for more than four decades; *Flipper,* the family classic about a boy and a porpoise; *Splash,* whose main character is a mermaid who becomes human; and *Cocoon,* about a group of elderly friends who discover an extraterrestrial secret to immortality. Most recently, parts of the two sequels to *Pirates of the Caribbean, Dead Man's Chest* and *At World's End,* were shot on location in the Exumas. *Thunderball* and *Never Say Never Again* were both shot on location in Staniel Cay, one of the northernmost islands of the Exumas chain.

Ernest Hemingway wrote about the Bahamas as well. He visited Bimini regularly in the 1930s, dubbing it the "Sportsfishing Capital of the World." His hangout was the Compleat Angler,

a bar that housed a small Hemingway museum until it burned down in January 2006. Among the items the museum displayed were Hemingway's drawings for *The Old Man and the Sea*—rumor has it that the protagonist looks suspiciously like one of the Angler's former bartenders.

The Bahamas not only seem to spark the imaginations of artists, but have also become a playground for the rich and famous. **Lenny Kravitz** and **Patti LaBelle** own homes in Eleuthera, while the stars of *Cocoon,* the late **Hume Cronyn** and **Jessica Tandy,** were regular visitors to Goat Cay, a private island just offshore from George Town, Exuma. **Johnny Depp** purchased a cay in the Exumas after filming on location for *Pirates of the Caribbean,* and **Nicolas Cage** and **Faith Hill** and **Tim McGraw** own private islands in the area as well. Many world-famous celebrities and athletes hide out at **Musha Cay,** an exclusive retreat in the northern part of the Exumas, where a week's stay sets you back $24,750 for the entire island. **David Copperfield** bought Musha and its five houses in 2006 for $50 million, renaming it Copperfield Cay. Although the cay won't name its guests, the all-knowing taxi drivers at the George Town airport mention **Oprah Winfrey** and **Michael Jordan** as a couple of the esteemed visitors.

7

EXPLORING

Allan's Cay. Allan's Cay is at the Exumas' northernmost tip and home to the rare Bahamian iguana. Bring along some grapes and a stick to put them on, and these little guys will quickly become your new best friends. ⊠ *Allan's Cay.*

FAMILY **Big Major's Cay.** Just north of Staniel Cay, Big Major's Cay is home to the famous swimming pigs. These guys aren't shy; as you pull up to

The famous swimming pigs of Big Major's Cay will be happy to meet you at your boat.

the island they'll dive in and swim out to greet you. Don't forget to bring some scraps; Staniel Cay restaurant gives guests bags before they depart. ⊠ *Big Major's Cay.*

Compass Cay. Explore the many paths on the island, which is 1½ miles long and 1 mile wide, or sit on the dock and watch the sharks swim below—don't worry, they're harmless nurse sharks. There are four houses for rent on the island, all come with a 13-foot Boston Whaler. There's also a small convenience store stocked with snacks and beverages. ⊠ *Compass Cay.*

Exuma Cays Land and Sea Park. Created by the Bahamas National Trust in 1958, the 176-square-mile Exuma Cays Land and Sea Park was the first of its kind in the world—an enormous open aquarium with pristine reefs, an abundance of marine life, and sandy cays.

The park appeals to divers, who appreciate the vast underworld of limestone, reefs, drop-offs, blue holes, caves, and a multitude of exotic marine life including one of the Bahamas' most impressive stands of rare pillar coral. Since the park is protected and its waters have essentially never been fished, you can see what the ocean looked like before humanity. For landlubbers there are hiking trails and birding sites; stop in the main office for maps. More than 200 bird species have been spotted here. At Shroud Cay, jump into the strong current that creates a natural whirlpool whipping you around a rocky outcropping to a powdery beach. On top of the hill overlooking the beach is Camp Driftwood, made famous by a hermit who dug steps to the top, leaving behind pieces of driftwood. ⊠ *Park Headquarters, Warderick Wells Cay* ☎ *242/225–1791* ⊕ *www.exumapark.org* ☞ *VHF Channel 9 or 16.*

Little Farmer's Cay. If you're looking for a little civilization, stop off at Little Farmer's Cay, the first inhabited cay in the chain, about 40 minutes (18 miles) from Great Exuma. The island has a restaurant and a small grocery store where locals gather to play dominoes. But don't expect too big of a party; just 70 people live on the island. A walk up the hill will reward you with fantastic island views. ⊠ *Little Farmer's Cay.*

Norman's Cay. North of the Exuma Cays Land and Sea Park is Norman's Cay, an island with 10 miles of rarely trod white beaches, which attracts an occasional yachter. It was once the private domain of Colombian drug smuggler Carlos Lehder. It's now owned by the Bahamian government. Stop by Norman's Cay Beach Club at MacDuff's for lunch or an early dinner and that it's-5-o'clock-somewhere beach cocktail. ⊠ *Norman's Cay.*

Pipe Creek. Boaters will want to explore the waterways known as Pipe Creek, a winding passage through the tiny islands between Staniel and Compass cays. There are great spots for shelling, snorkeling, diving, and bonefishing. Staniel Cay is a good place for lunch or dinner.

Staniel Cay. This is the hub of activity in the cays, and a favorite destination of yachters. That's thanks to the Staniel Cay Yacht Club, the only full-service marina in the cays. Shack up in one of the cotton candy–color cottages, some perched on stilts right in the water. The club's restaurant is the place to be for lunch, dinner, and nightlife. The island has an airstrip, one hotel, and paved roads. Virtually everything is within walking distance. Oddly enough, as you stroll past brightly painted houses and sandy shores, you are as likely to see a satellite dish as a woman pulling a bucket of water from a roadside well. At one of three grocery stores, boat owners can replenish their supplies. The friendly village also has a small red-roof church, a post office, and a Bahamian bread vendor. Staniel Cay is a great home base for visiting the Exuma Cays Land and Sea Park. ⊠ *Staniel Cay.*

Starfish Reserve. Just off the mainland of Great Exuma, locals call the water surrounding the first few cays the Starfish Reserve, where tons of giant starfish dot the shallow ocean floor. Though it's not technically a protected area, starfish here are abundant. As long as you don't keep them out of the water for too long, it's okay to pick them up.

Thunderball Grotto. Just across the water from the Staniel Cay Yacht Club is one of the Bahamas' most unforgettable attractions: Thunderball Grotto, a lovely marine cave that snorkelers (at low tide) and experienced scuba divers can explore. In the central cavern, shimmering shafts of sunlight pour through holes in the soaring ceiling and illuminate the glass-clear water. You'll see right away why this cave was chosen as an exotic setting for such movies as 007's *Thunderball* and *Never Say Never Again*, and the mermaid tale *Splash*. ⊠ *Staniel Cay.*

Warderick Wells Cay. Next to the park headquarters in Exuma Cays Land and Sea Park is a lovely white beach, but you won't be looking at the sand when you first arrive. The beach is dominated by the stunningly huge skeleton of a sperm whale that died in 1995 because it consumed plastic. The skeleton was fortified in its natural form and makes an emotion-packed statue that no artist could duplicate. Equally striking

7

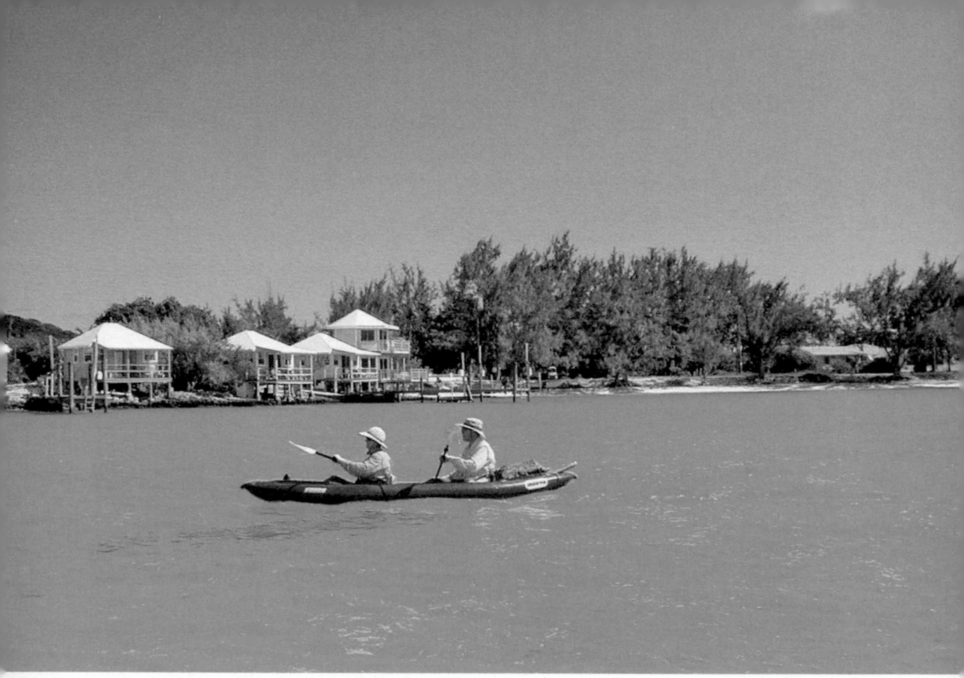

Staniel Cay Yacht Club attracts fishermen and non-fishermen.

is the gorgeous blue shades of water and the glistening white sand. Check out the snorkel trail in the park when you've soaked in enough sun. ✉ *Warderick Wells Cay.*

WHERE TO EAT

$ BAHAMIAN 🍴 **Norman's Cay Beach Club at MacDuff's.** The outdoor patio strung with Christmas lights gives this beach bar a lost-island vibe. Inside the screened patio, at dinner you have a choice of three entrées: grilled chicken, grilled fish, or cracked conch. For lunch there are burgers, grilled fish sandwiches, and salads. Meals are washed down with tasty cocktails from the full bar; enjoy out on the patio with a backdrop of the glorious ocean. If you're coming for dinner, you must call by 3. [$] *Average main: $16* ✉ *Norman's Cay* ☎ *242/357–8846* ⏲ *Closed Tues.* ✍ *Reservations essential.*

$$ BAHAMIAN 🍴 **Staniel Cay Yacht Club.** Hand-painted tablecloths cover the tables in the dining room that serves Bahamian specialties such as cracked conch, fresh grouper, snapper, and grilled lobster with homemade bread. Many of the herbs come fresh from the restaurant's garden. Don't miss the key lime pie for dessert. A dinner bell rings when dinner is ready and diners move from the bar to the dining room. You must place your dinner order by 4 pm. Three meals are served daily. [$] *Average main: $30* ✉ *Staniel Cay* ☎ *242/355–2024* 🌐 *www.stanielcay.com.*

WHERE TO STAY

$$$$
RENTAL

⊞ **Compass Cay.** Four spacious houses on the island, which is 1½ miles long and 1 mile wide, are so far apart and separated by lush palm and hardwood hammocks that you feel you have the island to yourself. **Pros:** remote tranquility; boat included. **Cons:** expensive to get to. $ *Rooms from: $650* ✉ *Compass Cay* ☎ *772/532–4793* ⊕ *www. compasscaymarina.com* ⤴ *4 villas* ⊠ *No meals.*

$$$$
RENTAL

⊞ **Norman's Cay Beach Club at MacDuff's.** There might be some rust on the refrigerator, but these three pastel villas are adorable, and just what you need for a true Out Island vacation. **Pros:** Out Island tranquillity; close to park; good restaurant on-site. **Cons:** expensive to get there; no Wi-Fi available. $ *Rooms from: $750* ✉ *Norman's Cay* ☎ *242/357–8846* ⤴ *3 villas* ⊠ *Breakfast.*

$
RENTAL
Fodor'sChoice
★

⊞ **Staniel Cay Yacht Club.** The club once drew such luminaries as Malcolm Forbes and Robert Mitchum. **Pros:** simple cottages that give an authentic Bahamian experience; great restaurant. **Cons:** expensive to get to if you don't have your own boat or plane. $ *Rooms from: $185* ✉ *Staniel Cay* ☎ *242/355–2024, 954/467–6658* ⊕ *www.stanielcay.com* ⤴ *14 cottages* ⊠ *No meals* ☞ *All-inclusive rate is available.*

NIGHTLIFE

Staniel Cay Yacht Club. Staniel Cay Yacht Club has a relatively busy bar, hopping with yachters from all over the world. ✉ *Staniel Cay* ☎ *242/355–2024.*

SPORTS AND THE OUTDOORS

BICYCLING

Staniel Cay Yacht Club rents beach cruisers if you want to pedal around the island.

BOATING AND FISHING

Staniel Cay Yacht Club. Rent a 13- or 17-foot Whaler and arrange for a fishing guide at Staniel Cay Yacht Club, a prime destination for serious bonefishers. Regular excursions can also be arranged for any resort guest. ✉ *Staniel Cay* ☎ *242/355–2024* ⊕ *www.stanielcay.com.*

GUIDED TOURS

BOAT TOURS

Charter World. This company offers a variety of yacht charters. ☎ *954/603–7830* ⊕ *www.charterworld.com.*

Exuma Cays Adventures. This company offers several tour options, including a trip through the Exuma Cays, a snorkeling excursion to Long Island, and tours of Elizabeth Harbour in a glass-bottom boat. ☎ *242/357–0390* ⊕ *www.exumacaysadventures.com.*

Exuma Water Sports. Come here for guided Jet Ski tours through the Exuma Cays, as well as a scenic boat cruise that includes snorkeling at Thunderball Grotto. ☎ *242/357–0770, 242/357–0100* ⊕ *www.exuma watersports.com.*

7

Four C's Adventures. Various private and group charters are available through Four C's Adventures, including snorkeling, fishing, and sightseeing tours. ☎ *242/464–1720, 242/355–5077* ⊕ *www.exumawater tours.com.*

ISLAND TOURS

Exuma Travel and Transportation Limited. This company provides bus tours of Great Exuma and Little Exuma and can accommodate large parties. ☎ *242/345–0234.*

Kendal "Dr. K" Nixon. Dr. K gives tours of Great Exuma and Little Exuma by car, for up to six passengers. ☎ *242/422–7399.*

Luther Rolle. Luther's four-hour guided tour of the island by car is fully customizable, and can be split between days to best suit your vacation schedule. ☎ *242/357–0662.*

SCUBA DIVING AND SNORKELING

Exuma Cays Land and Sea Park and **Thunderball Grotto** are excellent snorkeling and dive sites.

THE SOUTHERN
OUT ISLANDS

WELCOME TO THE SOUTHERN OUT ISLANDS

TOP REASONS TO GO

★ **Stage a disappearing act:** Discover your inner castaway on islands way off the trampled tourist track. Pink or white sand, calm azure coves, or rolling ocean waves—you'll have your pick.

★ **Tell your own tall fishing tale:** Whether deep-sea fishing past the Wall off southern Inagua or bonefishing in the crystal clear shallows on Cat Island's east coast, your fish-capades will be ones to remember.

★ **Explore historic lighthouses:** Surrounded by treacherous shoals and reefs, the southern Out Islands have the country's most famous 19th-century lighthouses, most of which you can climb for stunning views.

★ **Feast on the reefs and walls:** Spectacular diving and snorkeling, and even specialty shark dives, are on the menu for nature lovers when visiting these secluded southern isles with their calmer, clearer waters undisturbed by cold fronts.

1 Cat Island. Stunning pink and white beaches, the highest hilltop in the country (the 206-foot Mt. Alvernia), 200-year-old deserted stone cottages, and superb diving and fishing attract loyal visitors. More than a half-dozen small resorts offer low-key luxury for those who want an Out Island experience with creature comforts.

2 San Salvador. Located on one of the largest reefs in the world, the tiny island's crystal clear waters are a scuba diver's dream. The beach at Club Med is gorgeous, with soft white sand and dazzling turquoise water.

3 Long Island. Ringed with stunning beaches that reach to the west out into the Bahamas Banks and string along the easterly reef-strewn Atlantic deep blue coast, this island is off the beaten path, yet offers resorts and inns that provide ample comfort, myriad activities, dining, and full service. It boasts a rich history, the world's deepest blue hole, and is populated by friendly, accommodating people.

4 Crooked and Acklins islands. These islands make great outposts for the self-sufficient adventurer and escape artists. Fishing and

Arthur's Town
Cat Island 1
New Bight
Mt. Alvernia
Port Howe
Exuma Sound
Conception Cay
Stella Maris
Great Exuma Island
Deadman's Cay
Ragged Island Range

more fishing are the reasons to come here, except when you take the day off to dive and snorkel. The Wall, a famed dive site about 50 yards off Crooked Island's coast, drops from 45 feet to thousands.

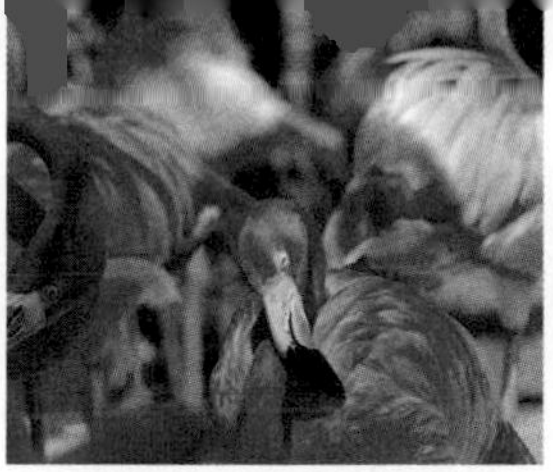

GETTING ORIENTED

The southernmost Bahamas islands are remote, exposed to the open Atlantic, and ruggedly dramatic. One hundred thirty miles southeast of Nassau, Cat Island lies to the west of diminutive San Salvador, about the size of Manhattan. Long Island, which is indeed long, stretches 80 miles across the Tropic of Cancer, due south of Cat Island. Windswept Crooked and Acklins islands, each with about 400 residents, are southeast of Long Island. And way down at the southernmost point of the country is Inagua, only 55 miles northeast of Cuba and 60 miles north of Haiti.

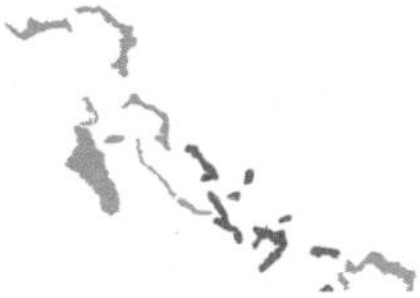

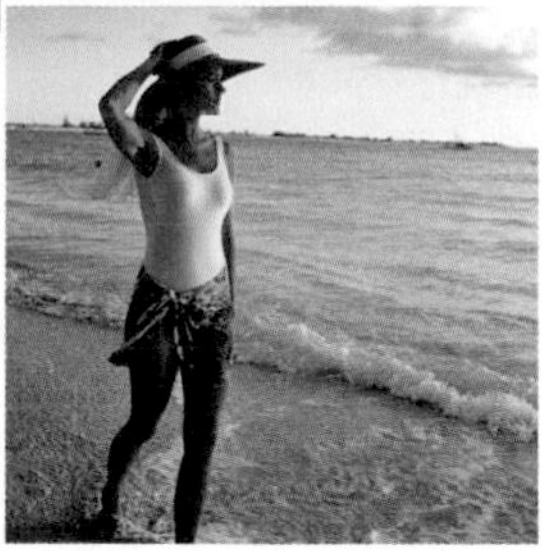

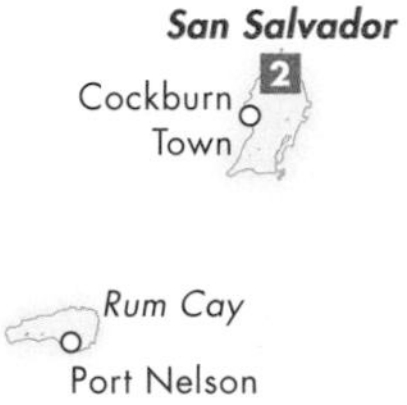

San Salvador
2
Cockburn Town
Rum Cay
Port Nelson

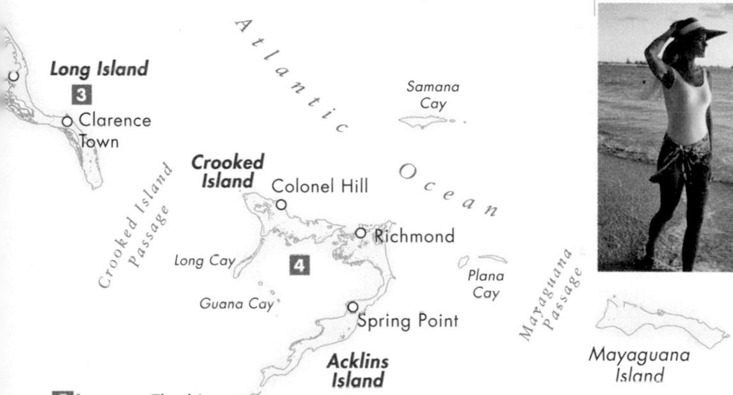

Atlantic Ocean
Long Island
3
Clarence Town
Samana Cay
Crooked Island
Colonel Hill
Richmond
Crooked Island Passage
Long Cay
4
Guana Cay
Spring Point
Plana Cay
Mayaguana Passage
Mayaguana Island
Acklins Island

[5] Inagua. The biggest attraction here is undoubtedly the island's 80,000 pink flamingos. The first sighting is a thrilling shock to the senses; some birds stand as tall as 5 feet. Flocks, ranging in size from a half dozen to hundreds, live all over the island, but the highest concentration are at the salt ponds and in the park. Anglers come to fish with famed fishing guide Ezzard Cartwright, and to dive in search of the Spanish galleons that sank off the coast.

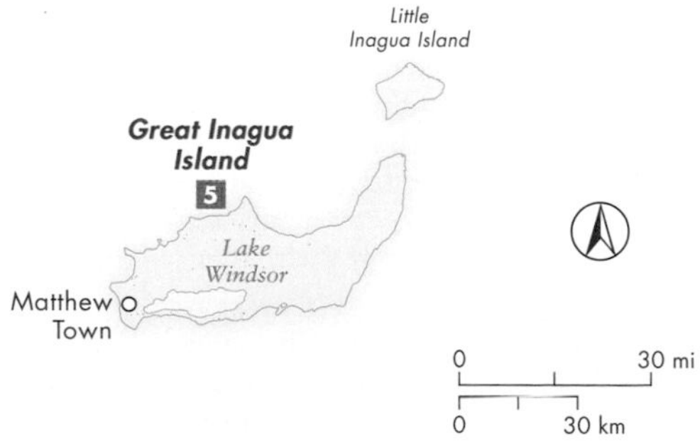

Little Inagua Island
Great Inagua Island
5
Lake Windsor
Matthew Town
0
30 mi
0
30 km

INAGUA NATIONAL PARK

Nothing quite prepares you for your first glimpse of the West Indian flamingos that nest in Inagua National Park: brilliant crimson-pink, up to 5 feet tall, with black-tipped wings. A dozen flamingos suddenly fly across a pond, intermixed with fantastic pink roseate spoonbills.

It's a moving experience, and yet because of the island's remote location, as few as 50 people witness it every year. By 1952, Inagua's flamingos had dwindled to about 5,000. The gorgeous birds were hunted for their meat, especially the tongue, and for their feathers. The government established the 287-square-mile park in 1963, and today 80,000 flamingos nest on the island, the world's largest breeding colony of West Indian flamingos. The birds like the many salt ponds on Inagua that supply their favorite meal—brine shrimp.

You must contact the **Bahamas National Trust**'s office (☎ *242/393–1317* ⊕ *www.bnt.bs*) or **Warden Henry Nixon** (☎ *242/225–0977*) to make reservations for your visit. All visits to the park are by special arrangement. *10 miles west of Matthew Town.*

BEST TIME TO GO
Flamingos are on the island year-round, but for the greatest concentration, visit during nesting season, from the end of February through June. Early morning and late afternoon are the best times to come. If you visit right after their hatching, the flocks of fuzzy, gray baby flamingos—they can't fly until they're older—are entertaining.

BEST WAYS TO EXPLORE

With a guide. Park warden Henry Nixon or Deputy Randolph Burrows lead all tours into the park and to Union Creek Reserve. They'll drive you by small flocks of flamingos in the salt ponds and answer questions. Nixon is difficult to reach by phone, but your best chance is in the early evening.

By kayak. You can't kayak in the park's salt ponds because they're too shallow, but you can in Lake Windsor, also called Lake Rosa, a huge inland lake. Its eastern half is in the park. Because of badly washed-out dirt roads, a truck is necessary to reach the lake.

On foot. The best way to see flamingos up close is by parking the car and walking, or sitting quietly for a while in a thicket of mangroves. Flamingos are skittish and easily spooked. Although the ponds and mangroves look a lot like the Florida Everglades, there are no alligators or poisonous snakes here. Make sure you have insect repellent on before you take off; the mosquitoes are brutal.

FLAMINGO FACTS

Flamingos are the country's national bird, and they're protected from hunters by law.

Female flamingos lay one egg a year, and both parents take turns sitting on it for 28 days. Both parents also produce milk in the crop at the base of the neck for the chick, for three months. The parents'

feathers turn white while they feed the chick because they lose carotene.

Flamingos are monogamous and usually mate for life, but are extremely social birds that like to live in groups.

Their "knees," which seem to bend backward, are actually ankles (the knees are tucked under their feathers). What looks like the leg is actually the foot extending from the ankle.

Standing on one leg is the most comfortable position for a flamingo.

Brine shrimp, the flamingo's main source of food, is what gives the mature bird its brilliant deep pink.

8

RAKE 'N' SCRAPE

There's something about Rake 'n' Scrape music that makes you want to dance. The contagious, unique cadence accompanied by the "chink-chink," "kalik-kalik," "scratch-scratch" sound created by the unique instruments, made mostly from recycled objects, brings on a particularly strong urge to get up and shake it.

Most closely linked in sound, rhythm, and composition to zydeco music out of New Orleans, Rake 'n' Scrape is folk music at its best. It's unclear just where Rake 'n' Scrape originated, but most believe it has roots in Africa, made the voyage to the Bahamas with slaves, and was adapted over the years. Today's Rake 'n' Scrape was cultivated on remote Cat Island. Lacking money for and access to modern things, the resourceful locals made use of whatever supplies were available. Years later, many of these musicians could have their pick of shiny, finely tuned instruments, but they stick with what they know makes beautiful music.

HAVE A LISTEN

International recording artist and Cat Island native **Tony McKay**, who went by the stage name Exuma, incorporated Rake 'n' Scrape into his music. He paid homage to the style with the song "Goin' to Cat Island."

George Symonette's "Don't Touch Me Tomato" gained infamy in a recent television commercial for Cable Bahamas. Symonette is associated with Goombay, a music style popular in Nassau in the 1950s. Goombay soon died out, giving way to closely related Rake 'n' Scrape.

Comprised of six Harbour Island natives, **the Brilanders** have toured with

Jimmy Buffet. Their hit song "Backyard Party" is a sound-track standard at just about any Bahamian party.

INSTRUMENTS

An authentic Rake 'n' Scrape band uses recycled objects to make music. An ordinary saw held in a musician's lap, then bent and scraped, becomes an instrument. A piece of wood, some fishing line, and a tin washtub is a good stand-in for the brass section. Plastic juice bottles are filled with pigeon peas, painted in bright colors, and turned into maracas. Add a goatskin drum, and you have all you need for a Rake 'n' Scrape ensemble, although many bands now add a concertina, guitar, or saxophone.

MAJOR PLAYERS

Authentic Rake 'n' Scrape is a dying art. The handful of groups scattered throughout the Bahamas are comprised of older men, as younger Bahamians prefer more modern sounds. Today **Ophie and the Websites**, **The Brilanders**, **Thomas Cartwright**, and **Bo Hogg** are among the few groups still performing old-style Rake 'n' Scrape. Other modern Bahamian musicians, such as **K.B.**, **Phil Stubbs**, and **Ronnie Butler**, work the sound and rhythm into their own signature styles.

The popular four-day **Rake 'n' Scrape Festival** each June on Cat Island hosts dozens of bands from all over the Bahamas and the Caribbean.

On Harbour Island, **Gusty's** and **Vic-Hum Club** usually work at least one night of Rake 'n' Scrape into the weekly live music schedule. **The Brilanders** often play at **Seagrapes**.

DANCE LIKE A LOCAL

The Rake 'n' Scrape rhythm is so captivating that even the most rhythmically challenged will be hard-pressed to stand still. As the first beats are played, look around and see what the old folk do. It's not unusual to see a man stick his leg out (whether he's sitting or standing), lift his pants leg a bit, and let his footwork get fancy.

At festivals, schoolchildren usually dance the quadrille or heel-toe polka. If you ask a Bahamian to show you how to "mash de roach" or dance "the conch style," they may jump up and put on a show.

8

Updated by
Bob Bower

Wild and windswept, the southern Bahamian islands are idyllic Edens for those adventurers who want to battle a tarpon, dive a "wall" that drops thousands of feet, photograph the world's largest group of West Indian flamingos, or just sprawl on a sun-splashed beach with no sign of life—except maybe for a Bahama parrot pelting seeds from a guinep tree.

The quiet, simpler way of life on the southern Out Islands is startlingly different from Nassau's fast-paced glitz and glamour, and even more secluded than the northern Out Islands. You won't find huge resorts, casinos, or fast-food restaurants here, not to mention stoplights. Instead, you'll be rewarded with a serene vacation that will make your blood pressure drop faster than a fisherman's hook and sinker.

Sportsmen are drawn to the southern islands to outsmart the swift bonefish, and fish for marlin, black and bluefin tuna, wahoo, and swordfish. Yachties roam these islands on their way to the Caribbean, and vacationers rent Hobie Cats and kayaks. On all these islands, divers and snorkelers come to see healthy reefs and abundant underwater wildlife and even sharks. Romantics and honeymooners head south for the glorious sunsets viewed from the verandas of beachside cottages, and for the lovely pink beaches. Bird-watchers arrive with binoculars in hand to see the green and red Bahama parrots, Bahama pintails, tricolored and crested night herons, and, of course, flamingos. They can also try to spot the Bahama woodstar hummingbird, which is very similar to one of the world's newest discovered species, the Inaguan lyretail hummingbird.

The friendliness of residents is well known, but visitors are often taken aback by their instant inclusion in the community. You can't walk 100 feet without someone offering a welcome ride on a hot day. Ask an islander where a certain restaurant is and they will walk with you until you see it. On Inagua, express any disappointment such as not seeing a flamingo up close, and the person standing behind you at the store will get on their cell phone. (There's a big flock now at the Town Pond!) The scenery is gorgeous, but this genuine rapport is what brings regulars back time and again to these tiny communities.

PLANNING

WHEN TO GO

Few visitors make it to these southern islands, but those who do come at different times. Europeans tend to arrive in summer and stay for a month or longer. Sailors come through on their way to the Caribbean in fall and return to the Bahamas in summer on trips back to the United States. Fishermen arrive all year and divers like the calm seas in summer. Those looking for a winter warm-up visit from December to April, when temperatures are in the 70s. These months have the lowest rainfall of the year, but the ocean is chilly and rough for divers and boaters. Christmas, New Year's, and Easter are usually booked, so reserve rooms months in advance.

Many inns and resorts are closed in September and October for hurricane season, which technically runs from June through November. Mosquito repellent is usually needed year-round, but is imperative in summer and fall, especially after a period of rain when both mosquitoes and no-see-ums come out in full force. Note that they remain in the sand on your feet and towels even after you leave the beach, so make sure to rinse or leave your towel outside your room.

The southern islands are generally warmer than Nassau, but you may need a windbreaker in winter, particularly on a boat. If possible, time your visit for Junkanoo on New Year's morning, sailing regattas in June and July, and special events such as the Cat Island's Rake 'n' Scrape Festival in early June.

TOP FESTIVALS

WINTER **Junkanoo.** Inagua puts on a spirited Junkanoo parade on Boxing Day, December 26, and New Year's Day. Parades start at 4:30 am; you have to make the decision to stay up all night or get up early. There's food at the Fish Fry at Kiwanis Park in the center of town, where the parades end. ⊠ *Matthew Town.*

SUMMER **Long Island Sailing Regatta.** The annual Long Island Sailing Regatta, featuring Bahamian-made boats, is a three-day event the first weekend of June. Held in Salt Pond, the regatta is the island's biggest event and the Bahamas' second-largest regatta, attracting contestants from all over the islands. Booths featuring handmade crafts and Bahamian food and drink dot the site and local bands provide lively entertainment beginning at sundown. Salt Pond is 10 miles south of Simms. ⊠ *Salt Pond* ⊕ *www.thelongislandrunnernews.com.*

Cat Island Rake 'n' Scrape Festival. The Cat Island Rake 'n' Scrape Festival in early June is one of the country's top festivals and celebrates the Bahamas' indigenous Rake 'n' Scrape music. Leading Bahamian musicians, The Spank Band, accompany the country's most popular performers such as K.B., Geno D, D Mack, Ancient Man, the Lassie Doe Boys, and many more. Choirs and dance troupes such as the Folkloric Dancers add variety. Enjoy food, drinks, crafts, and after-parties in nearby restaurants. Between 1,000 and 3,000 people attend, so accommodations are hard to find if you book late. Two mail boats, Bahamasair,

Hurricane Joaquin

Hurricane Joaquin proved to be a particularly destructive storm in the southern Bahamas in October 2015. As the tropical storm escalated rapidly to become a Category 4 hurricane, it also moved through the region very slowly, causing widespread damage both from its high winds and its strong tidal surge. Islands that took direct hits included Crooked and Acklins Islands, southern Long Island, Rum Cay, Samana Cay, and San Salvador. Many of the hotels, fishing lodges, and restaurants on those islands suffered serious damage and will require significant repairs. At this writing travel and tourism to the region was expected to be affected through at least February 2016, but for those establishments that suffered more catastrophic damage, recovery could take much longer. Be sure to verify any reservations and accommodations.

SkyBahamas, and private charters serve the festival. ⊠ *Arthur's Town Airport Park, North Cat Island* 🖭 *$15.*

GETTING HERE AND AROUND

AIR TRAVEL

All of the southern Out Islands have at least one airport, and several have multiple airports, so be careful to fly into the airport closest to your resort or you may pay for a long taxi ride. Flights are primarily from the Nassau hub using local airlines and charter companies. San Salvador has scheduled flights from Montreal in Canada, Fort Lauderdale in Florida, and from Paris in France. ⇨ *See individual island sections for more details.*

BOAT AND FERRY TRAVEL

Mailboats link all of these islands to Nassau, and, only for a popular festival, Bahamas Ferries may add a special service to supply the extra demand. ⇨ *See individual island sections for more details.* If you plan to use the mailboat for transportation, you can and should also check schedules by calling the Dockmaster's Office in Nassau. They do change frequently.

CAR AND TAXI TRAVEL

You can rent a car on all the islands. Taxi service is also available. Regardless, transportation tends to be expensive because of the isolation and cost of fuel.

HOTELS

The inns in the southern Out Islands are small and intimate, and usually cater to a specific crowd such as anglers, divers, or those who just want a quiet beach experience. Club Med–Columbus Isle, an upscale resort on San Salvador, is the exception, with 236 rooms (with more being built) and a wide range of activities.

Most inns are on the beach, and many have one- and two-bedroom cottages with private verandas. Most inns offer three meals a day for their guests, kayaks, and bikes, and will pick you up at the airport, arrange car rentals, fishing guides, and dive trips. Off-season rates usually begin in May, with some of the best deals available in October, November, and early December. Club Med–Columbus Isle offers early-bird booking bonuses and runs pricing promotions year-round.

RESTAURANTS

Out Island restaurants are often family-run and focus on home-style dishes. You'll probably eat most of your meals at your hotel, since there aren't many other places. If you want to dine at a restaurant or another inn, it's crucial to call ahead. Dinner choices largely depend on what the fishermen and mail boats bring in; be prepared for few choices. If you are renting, make sure to bring lots of food and snacks. Here, they are double or triple the costs from home and the variety is limited. Use dry ice and coolers.

Although served at a couple of places, don't expect fine dining or gourmet food but instead anticipate tasty Bahamian fresh fish, lobster, conch, fresh-baked bread, and coconut tarts—along with a smattering of American and international dishes. Fish, lobster, and conch—which is served stewed, as a salad, or cracked (battered and deep fried)—is served at almost every restaurant for lunch and dinner. Chicken served many ways is a Bahamian staple and the skills of Bahamian cooks to prepare tasty chicken are legendary. These islands have breezy roadside conch stands—typically near a settlement or a beach or with sea views—that deserve a special trip from your hotel. On Friday and Saturday nights many restaurants and bars crank up the music and visitors and locals will drink and dance 'til late.

HOTEL AND RESTAURANT PRICES

Restaurant prices are based on the median main course price at dinner, excluding gratuity, typically 15%, which is often automatically added to the bill as well as the new 7.5% VAT tax. Hotel prices are for two people in a standard double room in high season, excluding service and the 7.5% VAT tax. Some resorts can charge a 6% resort levy that goes to the Bahama Out Island Promotion Board. These BOIPB hotels typically offer a high standard of service.

8

WHAT IT COSTS IN DOLLARS			
$	$$	$$$	$$$$
Restaurants	under $20	$20–$30	$31–$40	over $40
Hotels	under $200	$200–$300	$301–$400	over $400

VISITOR INFORMATION

Contacts The Bahamas Ministry of Tourism. ☎ *242/302–2000 in Nassau* ⊕ *www.bahamas.com.*

CAT ISLAND

You'll be purring on Cat Island's exquisite pink-sand beaches and sparkling white-sand-ringed coves, as calm and clear as a spa pool. Largely undeveloped, Cat Island has the tallest hill in the Bahamas, a dizzying 206 feet high, with a historic tiny stone abbey on top, a lovely spot for reflection or a picnic. The two-lane Queen's Highway runs the 48-mile length of the island from north to south, mostly along the western gorgeous sandy coastline, through quaint seaside settlements and past hundreds of abandoned stone cottages. Some are 200-year-old slave houses, crumbling testaments to cotton and sisal plantation days, while others were just too old to have modern utilities so were abandoned. Trees and vines twist through spaces that used to be windows and roofs and the deep-blue ocean can be seen through missing walls. In 1938 the island had 5,000 residents and today only about 1,500. Many of the inhabitants left the cottages long ago out of necessity, to find work in Nassau and Florida, but the houses remain because they still mark family land.

Cat Island was named after a frequent visitor, the notorious pirate Arthur Catt, a contemporary of Edward "Blackbeard" Teach. Another famous islander is Sir Sidney Poitier, who grew up here before leaving to become a groundbreaking Academy Award–winning movie actor and director.

GETTING HERE AND AROUND

AIR TRAVEL Cat Island has two airports: Arthur's Town (ATC) in the north and the New Bight (TBI) midisland. Two airlines fly in from Nassau to both airports: Southern Air four days a week, and SkyBahamas daily. (SkyBahamas has a connecting flight from Fort Lauderdale to Nassau in the early morning four days a week, providing convenient connections from Florida). To reach these southern islands from Nassau, Stella Maris Air Service has a great reputation and, from Fort Lauderdale or Miami, you can arrange a charter through Eastern Air Express, Monarch Air Group, or Triton Airways to fly you direct, avoiding Nassau. For the best price, call around for a plane with the right number of seats. If you are going to Fernandez Bay Village or Hawk's Nest Resort, fly into the Bight. If you are going to Pigeon Cay, Orange Creek Inn, Shanna's Cove, or Tailwinds, fly to Arthur's Town. ⇨ *For contact information of individual airlines, see also Air Travel in Travel Smart.*

Airport Contacts Arthur's Town Airport. ⊠ *Arthur's Town* ☎ *242/354–2236.* **New Bight Airport.** ⊠ *New Bight* ☎ *242/342–2016.*

BOAT TRAVEL Mail boats that bring supplies to the island each week make an adventurous mode of transportation. You'll ride with groceries, large and small appliances, automobiles, and sometimes even livestock. All boats depart from Potter's Cay in Nassau. Schedules change frequently. The *Lady Emerald* sails to Arthur's Town on Thursdays, and the *New G* sails on Wednesday evening to Smith's Bay, near New Bight in the south. Both take around 10 hours and are $60 one-way).

CAR TRAVEL The New Bight Service Station and Gilbert's New Bight Market rent cars on the southern end of Cat Island and will pick you up from the New Bight Airport. Robon Enterprises rents cars for the north (for those flying into Arthur's Town). It's important to rent a car from an agency that services the end of the island where you are staying because companies will not deliver cars to renters at the opposite end of the island. However, all inns and resorts can arrange rental cars for you upon arrival, and many people arrange their cars through their lodging.

Rates depend on the number of days you're renting but are expensive, averaging $85 per day plus gas (which is also very expensive).

The best way to enjoy the overall Cat Island experience is to rent a car, at least for one day, and do some exploring on your own. You'll need one if you want to check out various settlements, as they're not within walking distance. The two-lane, potholed Queen's Highway runs the 48-mile length of the island from north to south. You can also tour the island with a guide from Cat Island Experience.

Car Rental Contacts Gilbert's Car Rentals and Market. ⊠ *Across from Gilbert's Inn, New Bight* ☎ *242/342–3011.* **New Bight Car Rentals.** ⊠ *New Bight* ☎ *242/342–3014.* **Robon Enterprises Car Rental.** ⊠ *In Bennett's Harbour, near Arthur's Town Airport, Arthur's Town* ☎ *242/354–6120, 242/359–9725.*

TAXI TRAVEL Taxis wait for incoming flights at the New Bight and Arthur's Town airports, but be warned that fares can be expensive, starting at about $20 for the 10-minute trip from the New Bight Airport to the community of New Bight. Most inns and resorts will make arrangements for airport transfers, often complimentary.

ARTHUR'S TOWN AND BENNETT'S HARBOUR

Arthur's Town's claim to fame is that it was the boyhood home of actor Sidney Poitier, who wrote about growing up here in his autobiography. His parents and relatives were farmers. The village has a BTC Bahamas telephone station, a few stores, and Pat Rolle's **Cookie House Bakery** (☎ *242/354–2027*)—an island institution that serves lunch and dinner by the order, so call ahead. Or just stop by to say hello, as Pat is a wealth of island knowledge and more than happy to bend your ear.

When you drive south from Arthur's Town, which is nearly at the island's northernmost tip, you'll wind along a road that passes through small villages and past bays where fishing boats are tied up. Fifteen miles south of Arthur's Town is Bennett's Harbour, one of the island's oldest settlements. Fresh-baked breads and fruit are sometimes sold at makeshift stands at the government dock, and there is good bonefishing in the creek.

WHERE TO EAT

$ ✕ **Da Smoke Pot.** Cold beer, Bahama Mama rum drinks, conch anyway
BAHAMIAN   you want it, and the local Tough Skins live Rake 'n' Scrape music—Da Smoke Pot is an authentic Bahamian experience, named for the old local tradition of lighting green brush in the evening to keep the bugs at bay. Julian and the band will even let you take a turn playing on the saw with a screwdriver, while they sing and play along with you. You can't help but leave with a smile on your face. It's located near Arthur's Town's only beach, serving lunch and dinner except on Monday. $ *Average main: $15* ⊠ *Arthur's Town* ☎ *242/354–2094* ▬ *No credit cards* ⊗ *Closed Mon.* ⚸ *Reservations essential.*

$$ ✕ **Sammy T's Restaurant and Bar.** Before sitting down to dinner on the
BAHAMIAN   wooden deck outside, grab a drink and take a stroll down the boardwalk bridge to the beach—a great place to see the sunset. The outside deck

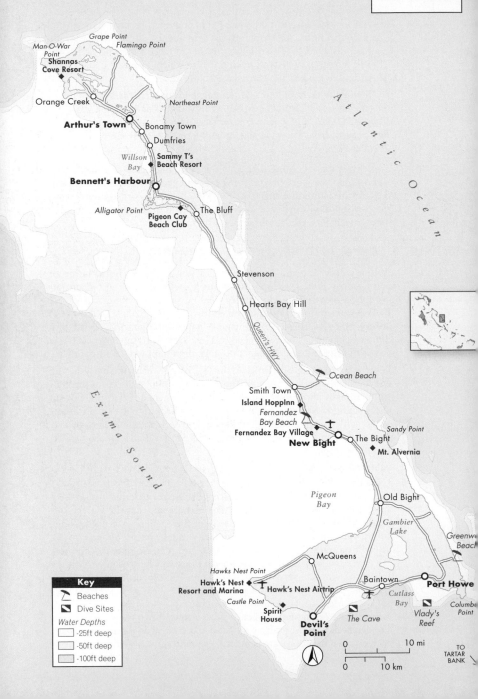

The Hermitage on Mt. Alvernia in Cat Island's most iconic sight.

also has a pool table and darts for added entertainment. The setting far outweighs the food, but each meal is served with a warm and friendly smile. Breakfast includes omelets and fresh fruits. For lunch the salads are fresh and served with Sammy T's secret dressing, and the burgers are big and tasty. The evening menu includes fish, shrimp, lobster, or conch prepared any way you want it, with traditional Bahamian sides like peas 'n' rice, fried plantains, and coleslaw. Call ahead because the restaurant closes if business is slow. The bar stays open after dinner with demand. [$] *Average main: $25* ✉ *Bennet's Harbour, north Cat Island, Bennett's Harbour* ☎ *242/354–6009* 🌐 *www.catislandbeachresort.com* 🕒 *Closed Sept.* ✍ *Reservations essential.*

$$$ EUROPEAN Fodor's Choice ★ 🍴 **Shanna's Cove Restaurant.** This resort restaurant boasts a beautiful towering view above the sea and the north point of the island and offers three meals a day on the breezy veranda or in the cool interior. Owners Frank and Gabi, and chef Simon, take their European cuisine seriously and they please and surprise hotel guests and those from other resorts who drive far to dine here. Replete with homemade breads, cheeses, viands, and fruits (or eggs cooked-to-order) breakfast is a delight while the lunch menu features large fresh salads and homemade 12-inch pizzas. Dinner's three-course menu varies nightly and might include rack of lamb, pork tenderloin, steaks, lobster, or grilled fish. Call well in advance (or you may feel unwelcome). If you don't like what's being served just ask Frank or Gabi to cook you something else. The cocktails and coffee at the cute bar are also good. [$] *Average main: $40* ✉ *Shanna's Cove, north of Orange Creek, Arthur's Town* ☎ *242/354–4250* 🌐 *www.shannas-cove.com* 💳 *No credit cards* 🕒 *Closed Sept.*

$ ✕ **Yardie's Restaurant, Bar & Conch Stand.** Yardie's owners, Odette & Der-
JAMAICAN rick Rolle, serve up large-sized genuine Jamaican and Bahamian dishes such as jerk chicken, steamed pork chops, curried mutton, barbecue ribs, and their famous, fresh conch salad. If you really want an island meal, try the breakfast grits with tuna or corned beef. A fun fact for the kids is that Yardie's is the only stop on the island for ice cream. This place is no frills, but a great shady spot to stop for lunch, a snack, or just a cold drink and a game of dominoes. $ *Average main: $14* ✉ *North Cat Island* ☎ *242/354–6076* ⊟ *No credit cards.*

WHERE TO STAY

$ ⛫ **Pigeon Cay Beach Club.** In a wide bay a half mile off the main road
RESORT just south of Alligator Point, this family-owned-and-operated resort has seven deluxe cottages and a "big house" with several rooms that are colorfully decorated and perched steps away from a secluded 3-mile stretch of pristine sugary white beach. **Pros:** fully equipped kitchens in rooms; Wi-Fi; bicycles, kayaks, and snorkel gear available; cars available for a small fee. **Cons:** no TV; surcharge for airport transfers; meals are served only a few times a week, so plan to cook for yourself; don't forget your insect repellent. $ *Rooms from: $160* ✉ *Rokers ✛ 3 miles south of Bennetts Harbour* ☎ *242/354–5084* ⊕ *www.pigeoncaybahamas.com* ⇗ *11 rooms, some in big house or cottages* ⏐⊙⏐ *No meals.*

$ ⛫ **Sammy T's Beach Resort.** Tucked away in a small cove on a dream
RESORT beach, this tranquil, friendly resort has seven one- and two-bedroom villas. **Pros:** private beach is great for sunsets; staff will arrange daily fishing/snorkeling excursions and rental cars. **Cons:** villas are not on the beach; facilities and villas are worn; pool has been filled in with a rock garden. $ *Rooms from: $160* ✉ *Bennett's Harbour* ☎ *242/354–6009* ⊕ *www.catislandbeachresort.com* ☾ *Closed Sept.* ⇗ *7 villas* ⏐⊙⏐ *No meals.*

$$ ⛫ **Shanna's Cove Resort.** This quiet and secluded owner-run beach resort,
RESORT built in 2009, is perched high on the hill on the northern tip of Cat Island, granting sweeping views of the beautiful beach at Shanna's Cove and the north of the island. **Pros:** stunning, private beach; excellent on-site restaurant; nicely designed, roomy cottages with air-conditioning; a real Out Island experience. **Cons:** no TVs; isolated from the rest of the island; rooms just steps away from the beach; no children under 18. $ *Rooms from: $215* ✉ *North of Orange Creek, Arthur's Town* ☎ *242/354–4249* ⊕ *www.shannas-cove.com* ☾ *Closed Sept.* ⇗ *5 villas* ⏐⊙⏐ *No meals.*

NIGHTLIFE

Da Hot Spot Restaurant & Karaoke Bar. Owners Ted and Melony, also a fabulous cook, entertain locals and visitors with great native food and karaoke. Noted for the Bahamian touches, like coconutty skyjuice, the 46-ounce Como Hill cocktail, and other drinks served in pea cans. Some claim Melony's food, served on palms and sea grape leaves, is the best they had. This place—spurred on by tuneful locals and visitors pumping out a great selection of music—can rock until 3 am. If the music's too loud, you can dine and drink on the deck. This is the north's best nightlife spot, but it's a decent place to eat if you want to kill two birds with one stone. ✉ *North Cat Island, Arthur's Town* ☎ *242/354–2076* 💲 *Free.*

SPORTS AND THE OUTDOORS
SCUBA DIVING

Coral Reefs teeming with fish and mysterious shipwrecks, make great diving off the north end of the island, where visibility ranges from 165 to 200 feet thanks to a natural filtering system of limestone and rich fauna.

Diving with Shanna's Cove Resort. This is not a certified dive shop, but Frank, one of the owners of Shanna's Cove, is a master diver and takes only up to four divers at a time—making it very safe for beginners and pros alike. Shanna's offers north Cat Island's amazing range of dives: from wrecks to walls, and reefs with amazing visibility, all from the 22-foot catamaran. Diving spots can be reached within 5 to 30 minutes. Well-maintained equipment is available for rent. ✉ *Shanna's Cove Resort, North of Orange Creek, Arthur's Town* ☎ *242/354–4249, 242/359–9668 cell* ⊕ *www.shannas-cove.com* ◷ *Closed Sept.*

NEW BIGHT

Yachts large and small anchor off the coast of Regatta Beach, and boaters dingy in to the Custom House, located in a small collection of government buildings, in this pretty little community, the largest town on the island. Houses face the Queen's Highway, which twists through green hills. Yachties and visitors stock up at the small grocery store and a bakery. The island's most iconic sight is **Mt. Alvernia**, which is crowned with a historic little abbey. There's also a colorful **Fish Fry**, a collection of fish shacks on Regatta Beach that's a lively hangout at nights and on weekends, lovely old churches, and eerie abandoned stone cottages, many of which are plantation ruins. The town sits along a thin, Australian pine–lined white beach on the west coast and has peaceful saltwater estuaries, nesting areas for great blue herons, egrets, and pelicans.

EXPLORING

Fodor's Choice ★ **The Hermitage.** At the top of 206-foot Mt. Alvernia, the highest point in the Bahamas, the Hermitage is the final resting place of Father Jerome who lived quite an astonishing life. Born John Hawes, he was an architect who traveled the world and eventually settled in the Bahamas. An Anglican who converted to Roman Catholicism, he built many structures including in the Bahamas a hermitage on Mt. Alvernia; two churches, St. Paul's and St. Peter's, in Clarence Town, Long Island; as well as the St. Augustine Monastery in Nassau. He retired to Cat Island to live out his last dozen years as a hermit, and his final, supreme act of religious dedication was to carve the steps up to the top of Mt. Alvernia. Along the way, he also carved the Stations of the Cross. At the summit, he built an abbey with a small chapel, a conical bell tower, and living quarters comprising three closet-size rooms. He died in 1956 at the age of 80 and was supposedly buried with his arms outstretched, in a pose resembling that of the crucified Christ.

8

The pilgrimage to the Hermitage begins next to the commissioner's office at New Bight, at a dirt path that leads to the foot of Mt. Alvernia. Don't miss the slightly laborious climb to the top. The Hermitage provides a perfect place to pause for quiet contemplation. It also has glorious views of the ocean on both sides of the island. A caretaker clears the weeds around the tomb—which islanders regard as a shrine—and lights a candle in Father Jerome's memory. ⊠ *New Bight.*

BEACHES

Fernandez Bay Beach. Imagine the perfect calm cove in the tropics—a 1-mile stretch of glistening, pristine white sand, inviting shade under coconut palms and sea grape trees, quaint resort cottages and verandas facing the spectacular sand, and calm azure water. Two resorts (Fernandez Bay Village and Island HoppInn) have restaurants and bars built on decks overlooking the water and they each rent kayaks and paddleboards to guests. The beach is often deserted, so dinner for two might really mean just that. **Amenities:** food and drink; water sports. **Best for:** solitude; snorkeling; sunset; swimming; walking. ⊠ *Just north of New Bight Airport* ☎ *242/342–3043.*

Ocean Beach. On the eastern Atlantic side, four miles from Queen's Highway at Smith's Bay is Ocean Beach, 1.8 miles of wide powdery white sand with a frequent breeze. There's no shade here and you should bring whatever water-sports toys you can. When conditions are right it's good for surfing and, when calm, paddleboarding or kayaking and snorkeling on the nearby reefs. High on the dune crest is Ocean Dream Beach Resort, a quaint four-cottage inn, with a restaurant and bar serving Greek and Bahamian food. Bring water and snacks. Only reasonably accessed by car or bike. **Amenities:** food and drink. **Best for:** snorkeling ⊠ *4 miles east of Smith's Bay, Smith Bay* ☎ *242/342–2052 Hotel.*

WHERE TO EAT

$$$$
INTERNATIONAL
FAMILY

✗ **Fernandez Bay Village Restaurant.** Fernandez Bay Village's Clubhouse serves delicious breakfasts buffet-style with seating on the beachfront terrace or inside—everywhere with splendid views of the beautiful bay. The breakfast buffet is loaded: pile on pastries, home-baked breads, croissants, bacon, sausage, grits, pancakes, cereals, yogurt, and fruit. And staying guests can enjoy healthy snacks, fresh fruit, coffee, and punch all day. For lunch, order from a menu that includes salads, burgers, and sandwiches. In fact, the cooks will cook up almost anything you desire. FBV's sumptuous dinner buffets can include lobster in white sauce, grouper almandine, pork loin, filet mignon, and a grilled catch of the day along with scalloped potatoes, salads, and fresh-baked breads.

At the tiki hut with its honor bar, enjoy pre- and after-dinner drinks and a clever assembly of bar games. Make friends with guests or gather close to a bonfire on the beach. FBV is a popular spot for private pilots who fly in for the day or longer. It also has a kids' menu. As always in the Out Islands, book in advance. $ *Average main: $48* ✉ *Fernandez Bay Village* ✈ *1 mile northwest of New Bight Airport* ☎ *242/342–3043 resort, 954/474–4821 Fort Lauderdale, 800/940–1905 toll free in U.S. and Canada* ⊕ *www.fernandezbayvillage.com* ☾ *Closed mid-Aug.–Oct.* ⚴ *Reservations essential.*

$$

BAHAMIAN

FAMILY

✕ **Island HoppInn Tiki Bar and Restaurant.** Island HoppInn's open-air restaurant and bar is right on the beach, just steps away from the tranquil lapping waters of Fernandez Bay. The 24-seat patio has a barbecue grill for cooking up fresh fish of the day, shrimp, lobster, steaks, and ribs. Owner-chef Cathy Perdok is renowned for her conch chowder, fish and vegetable stews, fresh-baked breads, and killer desserts. She will also cater to food allergies and vegetarian and vegan diets. Guests staying at the inn, which has a bed-and-breakfast casualness, mix in by cooking their own dinners at times. The service is good and very personal, the crowd (when there is one) a lot of fun, and the tropical rum drinks are a mellowing delight. $ *Average main: $30* ✉ *Island HoppInn, Fernandez Bay Village* ☎ *234/542-4657, 216/337–8800, 740/777–4477* ⊕ *www.islandhoppinn.com* ▭ *No credit cards* ⚴ *Reservations essential.*

$$

GREEK

✕ **Mermaid's Restaurant at Ocean Dream Resort.** A pleasant surprise for a remote Out Island, this spacious, clean restaurant with a stunning location above Ocean Beach serves Greek (and Bahamian) food. Tables in the cool inside and on the breezy outside patio seat 20 guests each, and Mermaid's also has a nice bar with imported Mythos beer. Popular Greek and Bahamian dishes are served, often mixing fresh Bahamian produce with imported Greek specialties. Try Greek salad, tzatziki, or calamari for appetizers and a gyro or chicken, pork or shrimp souvlaki with Greek fries for a main course. The Bahamian curried lobster and the honey- and walnut-infused baklava are to die for. Locals rate it highly and visitors come in tow. $ *Average main: $30* ✉ *1½ miles east of Smith's Bay, along rugged white road, Smith Bay* ☎ *242/342–2052* ⊕ *www.oceandreambeachresort.com* ⚴ *Reservations essential* ▭ *No credit cards.*

WHERE TO STAY

$$

RESORT

Fodor's Choice

★

🏨 **Fernandez Bay Village.** This owner-run resort is one of the Bahamas' most famous and successful resorts and one of the best kick-back retreats anywhere. **Pros:** a "wow" beachfront location; private spacious accommodations; friendly accommodating staff; lots of water sports there and activities off-site. **Cons:** no TV; Wi-Fi in the main clubhouse only; insect repellent needed outside in the evening. $ *Rooms from: $283* ✉ *1 mile north of New Bight Airport* ☎ *242/342–3043, 800/940–1905 toll free* ⊕ *www.fernandezbayvillage.com* ⇶ *2 villas, 5 houses, 7 cottages, 2 suites* ☞ *Meal plan can be included.*

8

Tiki Bar is the place to hang out at Fernandez Bay Village resort.

NIGHTLIFE
Regatta Beach Fish Fry. For an authentic Bahamian experience, don't miss the Regatta Beach Fish Fry on Regatta Beach, just south of the government buildings in the town center. On weekends, at least two fish shacks open late in the afternoon and stay lively on into the night. Duke's Deck offers excellent conch salad and you can watch him make it from start to finish, including cracking the conch from the shell. Cedell's Sunshine Take Away gathers a regular crowd for her food (great fritters!). On weekends, Hidden Treasures offers Rake 'n' Scrape music performed by famed Bo Hog and the Rooters from around 8 pm. It's a great place for sunset watching and mingling with locals. ⊠ *Regatta Beach*.

SHOPPING
Pam's Boutique. This little shop at Fernandez Bay Village has reasonably priced resort wear including sarongs, Haviana flip-flops, logo hats, and T-shirts. They also sell jewelry, bags, coffee cups, postcards, local art, and books. This is one of your few chances to get a Cat Island T-shirt. ⊠ *Fernandez Bay Village* ☎ *242/342–3043, 800/940–1905, 954/474–4821.*

SPORTS AND THE OUTDOORS
FISHING
Cat Island Fishing. On Cat Island you have myriad ways to fish: deep-sea, bone-, fly-, and bottom-fishing. Several expert guides can do all but each has his own specialty. Mark Keasler is great for bonefishing, Nathaniel Top Cat is great for deep-sea trolling, and Carl Pinder is great for reef fishing. Call Fernandez Bay to let them find out who is available for which type of fishing. They also do snorkeling tours and beach picnics.

✉ *Fernandez Bay Village* ☎ *242/342–3043, 800/940–1905, 954/474–4821* ⊕ *www.fernandezbayvillage.com/fishing.html.*

TOURS

The Cat Island Experience. C&O Tours, comprising Pastor Chris, son Danny, and wife Olive King, have eight-seater air-conditioned vans for guided tours of Cat Island. They have a tour for the north and one for the south and both include much of the same thing. They'll customize your tour. The tour in the south includes beaches, Mt. Alvernia, the mini-monastary on the Bahamas' highest point at 206 feet, a step-down well, bat caves, cotton plantations and ruins, the old cotton railroad, an old lighthouse, churches, and also the modern structures and utilities. Chris and family can answer your many questions and give good, historical background. It's one of the most rewarding activities, giving you a lasting connection to the island. ✉ *New Bight* ☎ *242/464–6181 Chris* ✉ *$175 for half day, $350 for full day.*

PORT HOWE

At the conch shell–lined traffic roundabout at the southernmost end of the Queen's Highway, you must turn either east or west; head east out toward Port Howe, believed by many to be Cat Island's oldest settlement. Nearby lie the ruins of the **Deveaux Mansion**, a stark two-story, whitewashed building overrun with vegetation and pretty much unexploreable. Once it was a grand house on a cotton plantation, owned by Captain Andrew Deveaux of the British Navy, who was given thousands of acres of Cat Island property as a reward for his daring raid that recaptured Nassau from the Spaniards in 1783. Just beyond the mansion ruin is the entrance road to the Greenwood Beach Resort, which sits on an 8-mile stretch of unblemished, velvet pink-sand beach, but its fate as an operational hotel was up in the air at this writing.

BEACHES

Greenwood Beach. An 8-mile stretch of pink sand on the Atlantic Ocean makes this one of the most spectacular beaches on Cat Island. Hypnotized by the beauty, most visitors walk the entire beach, some even farther to an adjoining sandy cove accessible only by foot. After such a long walk, a dip in the shallows of the turquoise ocean is pure bliss. The beach is on the remote southeastern end of the island and is home to just one hotel, Greenwood Beach Resort, which, if open, is a good place for a munch and a drink. Along with its dive center, Greenwood has sporadically been closed, especially in summer. **Amenities:** none. **Best for:** solitude; snorkeling; swimming; walking. ✉ *Greenwood Beach Resort, 3 miles northeast of Port Howe along a bumpy road* ⊕ *www.greenwoodbeachresort.com.*

DEVIL'S POINT

The small village of Devil's Point, with its bright-walled, thatch-roof houses, lies at the southern tip of the Queen's Highway 9 miles southwest of Old Bight. Beachcombers will find great shelling on the pristine beach; keep an eye out for dolphins, which are common in these waters.

Fernandez Bay Beach is a perfect, calm cove for swimming.

From Devil's Point, drive north through the arid southwest corner of the island to **McQueens**, then west to the area's biggest resort, Hawk's Nest Resort, which has an airstrip, marina, restaurant, and bar. This resort is well known to serious anglers and divers, who often fly in to the resort's private airstrip and stay a week doing little else but fish or dive. The southwest end of the island teems with great diving walls, reefs, and wrecks with an abundance of marine life and coral heads.

WHERE TO EAT

$$ ✕**Hawk's Nest Resort Restaurant and Bar.** High-beamed ceilings, tiled
BAHAMIAN floors, blue-and-lime-green walls, and blue ceramic-topped tables create a cheerful vibe to go with the Bahamian comfort-food menu. Start your day with fresh juices and a full breakfast. For lunch and dinner, there are burgers and Bahamian specialties such as cracked conch, lobster and fish, or the touted conch tacos. You can eat on the terrace by the pool or inside with ocean views. The bar runs on the honor system and the 60-inch TV can catch you up on news, sports, and everything else you're happy to miss while lounging in paradise. $ *Average main: $30* ✉ *Hawk's Nest Resort* ✛ *7½ miles by road northwest of Devil's Point* ☎ *242/342–7050, 954/376–3865* ⊕ *www.hawks-nest.com* ⊗ *Closed mid-Sept.–Oct.* ⌕ *Reservations essential.*

WHERE TO STAY

$ ⊡**Hawk's Nest Resort and Marina.** Catering to private pilots, yachters, and
RESORT serious fishermen, this small laid-back resort at Cat Island's southwestern tip has its own 3,100-foot runway and a 28-slip full-service marina with a dive shop for guests. **Pros:** good native and international food; three meals a day; fully stocked honor bar; PADI certified and great

dive spots and shallow walls. **Cons:** if you want to explore the rest of Cat Island, it's a long drive; good swimming beach a few yards from main clubhouse. [$] *Rooms from: $165* ✉ *Devil's Point* ✥ *From Devil's Point village, go 4 miles north and 3½ miles west along a white road* ☎ *242/342–7050 resort, 954/376–3865 in U.S. and Canada* 🌐 *www.hawks-nest.com* 🕓 *Clubhouse and hotel closed Sept. and Oct.* 🛏 *10 rooms* 🍴 *Breakfast.*

$ RENTAL 🏠 **Spirit House.** Three miles west of Devils Point, sitting on a 70-foot height and next to a stunning beach cove, Spirit House is an exotic and idyllic private house for rent for 8 or 10 people at $5,000/week. **Pros:** private escape with your own beach; superbly equipped inside and out; 20-foot Mako speedboat for fishing and snorkeling; TV/DVD and lots of games for fun. **Cons:** off the grid, powered by solar, wind, and generator; miles to airport and bigger village; remote: you'll be self-entertaining. [$] *Rooms from: $179* ✉ *Devil's Point* ✥ *A mile down rough road, northwest of Devil's Point settlement* ☎ *242/424–6542* 🌐 *www.spirithousebahamas.com* 🛏 *5 bedrooms* 🍴 *No meals.*

SPORTS AND THE OUTDOORS

FISHING

Hawk's Nest Marina. Blue-water angling boat owners make a point of using Hawk's Nest Marina to access the dynamite offshore fishing. Look for wahoo, yellowfin tuna, dolphin, and white and blue marlin along the Exuma Sound drop-offs, Devil's Point, Tartar Bank, and Columbus Point. March through July is prime time with multiple annual fishing tournaments on the books. Winter fishing, December through February, is also good for wahoo. You can arrange bonefishing through the marina with a top guide. ✉ *Hawks Nest Resort and Marina* ☎ *242/342–7050, 954/376–3865* 🌐 *www.hawks-nest.com.*

8

SCUBA DIVING

Cat Island's south coast offers some of the country's best diving. The walls start from very shallow depths, allowing long dive times and great photography. Some of the area's best dive sites, which are most easily reached from Hawk's Nest Marina, are: **Hole in The Wall:** (12 miles, 50–100 feet) Spectacular break in the wall and entrance to a small channel with lobster or spotted drums. Impressive archway, black coral, stingray, sharks, dog snapper, barracudas, and groupers; all kinds of soft and hard coral. **The Oz:** (7 miles, 55–100 feet) Tunnels and canyons overgrown with soft corals, turtles, reef sharks, reef fish of any color, hogfish, Nassau and other grouper, and oceanic triggerfish. Spectacular when leading to the wall. **Tartar Bank:** (6 miles, 40–60 feet) Has strong currents, for pro divers only. Offshore pinnacle, reef sharks, white-tip sharks, big turtles, and more. **Fish Bowls:** (20–30 feet) From micro to macro, a photographer's paradise includes schools of goat fish, Atlantic spadefish, yellowtail, and mutton snapper. White spotted eels are numerous, along with nurse sharks and lobster. See a spider crab refuge and cleaning station as you follow the reef's ledge. Dives at Hawk's Nest must be booked a month in advance.

Hawk's Nest Marina Dive Shop. Hawk's Nest at one time was the only PADI-certified dive operation on Cat Island. Nowadays, certified diver

Randy Holder conducts guided diving adventures (albeit for guests only), rents diving and snorkeling gear, and has equipment and sundries for sale. The running time to dive sites off the southern tip of the island is 15 to 30 minutes in the shop's 43-foot custom dive boat, outfitted with VHF and GPS. Call ahead for bookings. Dives must be booked one month in advance. $250 minimum to take the dive boat out. Ask for package rates. ✉ *Devil's Point* ✚ *From Devil's Point, go 4 miles north and 3½ miles along white road* ☎ *242/342–7050, 954/376–3865* ⊕ *www.hawks-nest.com.*

SAN SALVADOR

On October 12, 1492, Christopher Columbus disrupted the lives of the peaceful Lucayan Indians when he landed on the island of Guanahani, which he renamed San Salvador. Apparently he knelt on the beach and claimed the land for Spain. (Skeptics of this story point to a study published in a 1986 *National Geographic* article in which Samana Cay, 60 miles southeast, is identified as the exact point of the weary explorer's landing.) Three monuments on the island commemorate Columbus's arrival, and the 500th anniversary of the event was officially celebrated here.

The island is 14 miles long—a little longer than Manhattan Island—and about 6 miles wide, with a lake-filled interior. Some of the most dazzling deserted beaches in the country are here, and most visitors come for Club Med's unique blend of fun and activities; others, for the peaceful isolation and the diving. There are more than 50 dive sites and world-renowned offshore fishing and good bonefishing. The friendly locals have a lot to be proud of for their special island and their warmth shows it.

GETTING HERE AND AROUND

AIR TRAVEL The island has one airport, in Cockburn Town (ZSA) which is modern, comfortable, and has a long runway. A new fuel depot and FBO by Odyssey Aviation means even more long-haul flights will commence and private aircraft can easily refuel here. XL, the French charter vacation company, flies from Paris on Wednesday, Air Canada from Montreal on Tuesday, and at least one carrier such as Spirit Airlines or American Eagle once a week from Fort Lauderdale or Miami. From Nassau, Southern Air has 13 flights each week in and out of San Sal, and Bahamasair has daily flights. A host of charter companies fly in from Florida and Nassau. If you have a group of six or more, a direct flight from Florida can be worthwhile, for convenience if not for saving dollars. Club Med's website has packages that include air charters, and Riding Rock Resort and Marina can arrange them as well.

Contacts San Salvador Cockburn Town Airport. ☎ *242/331–2131.*

BOAT TRAVEL Mail boats that bring supplies to the island each week make an adventurous mode of transportation. M/V *Lady Emerald* sails from Nassau three times a month (also going to Cat Island), and M/V *Lady Francis* does the same (also going to Rum Cay). Both leave Nassau on Thursday at teatime and arrive the next morning. You'll ride with groceries, large and small appliances, automobiles, and sometimes even livestock. All boats depart from Potter's Cay in Nassau. Schedules change frequently so best to call the Dockmaster's Office in Nassau to get the latest information.

BIKE TRAVEL For a short visit to Columbus Cross or the lighthouse, a bike is a sufficient mode of transportation. Bike rentals are available at Club Med and Riding Rock Resort.

CAR TRAVEL If you want to see the entire island, rent a car. Queen's Highway forms an oval that skirts the island's coastline, and road conditions are excellent. Car rentals are about $85 a day.

Contacts D&W Car Rental. ☎ *242/331–2484, 242/331–2488, 242/331–2184.* **Riding Rock Resort and Marina.** ☎ *800/272–1492, 242/331–2631.*

SCOOTER TRAVEL Scooters are a fun, breezy, and convenient way to get around the entire island.

Contacts K's Scooter Rentals. ✉ *Cockburn Town Airport* ☎ *242/331–2125, 242/331–2651, 242/225–7392.*

TAXI TRAVEL Club Med meets all guests at the airport. Riding Rock, five minutes away, provides complimentary transportation for guests. If you want to take your own taxi, it's approximately $10 to either resort.

Contacts Clifford "Snake Eyes" Fernander. ☎ *242/331–2676, 242/427–8198 cell.* **Nat Walker.** ☎ *242/331–2111.*

FERNANDEZ BAY TO RIDING ROCK POINT

In 1492 the inspiring sight that greeted Christopher Columbus by moonlight at 2 am was a terrain of gleaming beaches and far-reaching forest. The peripatetic traveler and his crews—"men from Heaven," the locals called them—steered the *Niña, Pinta,* and *Santa María* warily among the coral reefs and anchored, so it's recorded, in **Fernandez Bay.** A cross erected in 1956 by Columbus scholar Ruth C. Durlacher Wolper Malvin stands at his approximate landing spot. An underwater monument marks the place where the *Santa María* anchored. Nearby, another monument commemorates the Olympic flame's passage on its journey from Greece to Mexico City in 1968.

Fernandez Bay is just south of what is now the main community of **Cockburn Town,** midisland on the western shore. This is where the airport is, and where the weekly mail boat docks. This small village's narrow streets contain two churches, a commissioner's office, a police station, a courthouse, a library, a clinic, a drugstore, and a telephone station.

From Cockburn Town to Club Med, you'll pass **Riding Rock Point.** All fish excursions leave from the marina. Riding Rock Resort makes a good spot to stop for a drink, meet locals and divers, and buy a local T-shirt.

BEACHES

Fodor's Choice ★ **Bonefish Bay.** The 3-mile beach in front of Club Med has bright white sand as fine as talcum powder, and water that is such a bright neon shade of turquoise it seems to glow. It might possibly be the most gorgeous water you ever lay eyes on. There are activities, such as waterskiing,

8

snorkeling, sailing, kayaking, and paddleboarding in front of Club Med, but the beach is long enough that you'll be able to find an isolated spot. To join in all the fun activities and partying, buy a day pass at the front desk. **Amenities:** food and drink; showers; toilets; water sports. **Best for:** partiers; snorkeling; swimming; windsurfing. ✉ *Club Med—Columbus Isle, Cockburn Town.*

WHERE TO EAT

$$$$ ECLECTIC

🍴 **Christopher's at Club Med.** Christopher's is the huge open-air and air-conditioned buffet restaurant, and although breakfast and lunch are similar each day, the dinner buffet changes themes nightly. So even after a week it doesn't get boring and the team dress up displays and food islands beautifully. Caribbean Night has local fare, such as conch and fresh fish, and other themes include French, Mexican, and Mediterranean. Carving stations and European pastries and breads are impossible to skip, and simple pastas and pizzas are mainstays for the finicky eater. Don't forget the chocolate-chip bread—so good you'll order some loaves to bring back with you. If you're not staying at Club Med, a dinner pass will cost you $64 and is good from 7:30 pm to 1 am, including an open bar and the night's scheduled entertainment. All-you-can-eat breakfast passes are $20 and good from 8 to 10 am; lunch passes are $35, 12:30 to 2:15 pm. The staff, both local and imported, are super-friendly and if you're lucky, will sit with you explaining all the resort and island have to offer. [$] *Average main: $60* ✉ *Club Med—Columbus Isle, Cockburn Town* ✥ *3 miles north of Riding Rock Point* ☎ *242/331–2000* 🌐 *www.clubmed.com* ✍ *Reservations essential.*

$$ ITALIAN Fodor's Choice ★

🍴 **Guanahani Beach Club Restaurant.** At this resort restaurant, fresh fruit smoothies, panini on crusty French bread, fresh salads, and various authentic four-course Italian dinners, are all made to order by owner-chef Elena Sparta. As examples, you could enjoy: mille-feuille of smoked salmon and tomatoes; fettuccine with crab; shrimp with lime, basil, and herbs; lemon and rosemary risotto; or duck breast in Cointreau and orange sauce. The outside patio is beautiful and overlooks stunning Snow Bay; inside, you'll find an all-white contemporary dining room and bar complete with couches and coffee tables for lounging. It's a superb, romantic addition to dining in the Out Islands. [$] *Average main: $30* ✉ *Snow Bay, Sunrise Rd., Cockburn Town* ☎ *242/452–0438* 🌐 *www.guanahanibeachclub.com* ▭ *No credit cards* ⏲ *Often closed June–Oct.* ✍ *Reservations essential.*

$ BAHAMIAN

🍴 **The New Columbus Tavern.** Enthusiastically recommended by locals (ask anyone at the airport), the New Columbus Tavern in Victoria Hill, between Club Med and the airport, serves devilishly good lobster, conch, and fresh seafood treats at an affordable price. The menu is also diverse with burgers, pizza, pastas, and salads. [$] *Average main: $13* ✉ *Victoria Hill* ☎ *242/331–2788* ▭ *No credit cards.*

$ BAHAMIAN

🍴 **Paradis Restaurant and Bar.** A typical Bahamian enclosed restaurant with a small trail to the gorgeous beach, Paradis has a daily changing menu written on a chalkboard. Home-cooked Bahamian and American food such as burgers, conch, ribs, and the fresh catch of the day are tastily prepared. The restaurant is popular with both locals and visitors and

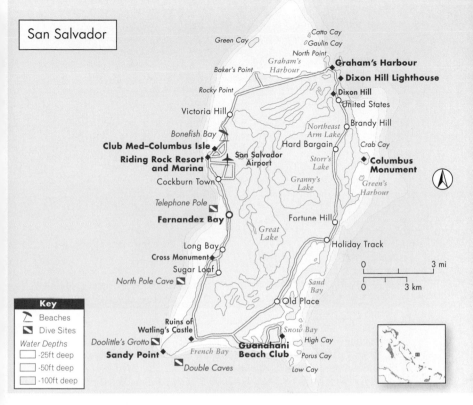

San Salvador

Key
- 🏖 Beaches
- 🔲 Dive Sites

Water Depths
- ☐ -25ft deep
- ☐ -50ft deep
- ☐ -100ft deep

offers complimentary Wi-Fi. [$] *Average main: $16* ✉ *Cockburn Town* ✛ *Just north of the airport near Club Med* ☎ *242/331–2400.*

$$

CARIBBEAN

✕ **Riding Rock Seafront Restaurant.** Eat inside this 60-seat restaurant, take a table on the patio by the pool, or sit on the back patio overlooking the ocean. Androsia-print tablecloths add a colorful tropical flair. Fruit, fresh-baked breads, pancakes, and eggs any style with bacon and grits are a good way to start the day. Burgers, sandwiches, conch chowder, and cracked conch are lunch favorites. The just-off-the-boat catch of the day—wahoo, mahimahi, tuna, grouper, snapper—grilled with lemon and butter, or baked with tomatoes and spices, is the dinner specialty. Broiled or stuffed lobster (in season), barbecue shrimp, steaks, and chicken round out the choices, though all are not available each evening as the menu changes based on availability. During slower seasons or depending on resort guests, the restaurant is not always open, and each meal is set between certain hours—make sure to call ahead. [$] *Average main: $25* ✉ *Riding Rock Resort and Marina, Cockburn Town* ☎ *242/331–2631, 954/453–5031* ⊕ *www.ridingrock.com* ☉ *Sometimes closed during slow season* ⌀ *Reservations essential.*

$$$$

SEAFOOD

✕ **Watling's at Club Med.** Watling's, the specialty seafood restaurant at Club Med, offers table service and is open for late lunches and dinner on certain days each week; reservations must be made a day ahead and it's worth the charge if you're a guest of the resort. If you're not

San Salvador has several popular diving sites.

staying at Club Med, a dinner pass will cost you $60-plus and is good from 7:30 pm to 1 am, including an open bar and the night's scheduled entertainment. [$] *Average main: $60* ✉ *Club Med–Columbus Isle, Cockburn Town* ☎ *242/331–2000* 🌐 *www.clubmed.com* 💳 *No credit cards* ✍ *Reservations essential.*

WHERE TO STAY

$$$$ RESORT FAMILY 🏨 **Club Med–Columbus Isle.** This 89-acre oceanfront village is one of Club Med's most luxurious resorts, with state-of-the-art dive facilities and every water sport and activity imaginable. **Pros:** gorgeous beachfront location; revolving dinner themes; full-service dive shop. **Cons:** no children under two; long walk to outlying rooms; fee for in-room Wi-Fi. [$] *Rooms from: $500* ✉ *Cockburn Town* ✣ *½ mile by road from the airport terminal* ☎ *888/932–2582, 242/331–2000* 🌐 *www.clubmed.com* 🛏 *216 rooms in two-story bungalows* 🍴 *All-inclusive.*

$$$ RESORT Fodor's Choice ★ 🏨 **Guanahani Beach Club.** This cozy, small, owner-operated resort is elegant and sophisticated, offering both quiet solitude on a stunning private beach and serious adventure for sports enthusiasts. **Pros:** excellent on-site restaurant; simple and chic villas; private beach adorned with loungers and hammocks. **Cons:** no children under 16; credit cards not accepted; far from other island amenities so you will probably want a rental car. [$] *Rooms from: $325* ✉ *Snow Bay, Sunrise Rd., Cockburn Town* ☎ *242/452–0438* 🌐 *www.guanahanibeachclub.com* 🕓 *Closed late Aug.–mid-Oct.* 🛏 *3 villas* 🍴 *Some meals.*

$ B&B/INN 🏨 **Riding Rock Resort and Marina.** Good for serious divers, this modest motel-style resort is a long-standing property on San Salvador and has a restaurant on-site serving breakfast, lunch, and dinner when enough guests warrant. **Pros:** budget-friendly alternative to other resorts; friendly, accommodating staff; rooms are standard but clean. **Cons:** boats are not always available during slow season; diving is not daily and dependant on resort guests; small, rocky beachfront. [$] *Rooms from: $162* ✉ *Cockburn Town* ✥ *½ mile southwest of airport terminal* ☎ *800/272–1492, 242/331–2631* 🌐 *www.ridingrock.com* 🛏 *30 rooms* 🍴 *All meals.*

NIGHTLIFE

Club Med–Columbus Isle. Evening passes to Club Med cost $64 and include themed dinners, nightly entertainment, and all you can drink from 7:30 pm to 1am. The predinner cocktail parties and beachside tiki hut parties are lively affairs with skilled DJs and rapid-fire, charming bartenders. This place is big enough to slink away to a romantic spot on your own. Entertainment gets going after dinner with staff shows in the big-stage, open-air theater. ✉ *Club Med, Cockburn Town* ☎ *888/932–2582, 242/331–2000.*

The Driftwood Bar at Riding Rock Resort. Driftwood decorated with messages, stickers, and accolades from regular visitors covers the walls and hangs from the ceilings of this little bar, giving it real character. Fishermen and scuba divers from all over the world gather frequently to tell tall tales, making it a favorite evening hangout. Try your luck at the ringtoss game, catch up on sports from home on the big-screen TV, or grab a cold Kalik or frozen piña colada (touted as the best on the island) and enjoy the sunset on the open-air back patio overlooking the sea. ✉ *Riding Rock Resort, Cockburn Town* ☎ *242/331–2631, 800/272–1492, 954/453–5031* 🌐 *www.ridingrock.com* 🕒 *Daily 4 pm–11 pm.*

8

SHOPPING

Club Med – Columbus Isle. Club Med has a boutique that's clearly the best souvenir, swimsuit, resort-wear shop on the island. It's an independent French franchise chain that has excellent shopping. Browse 45 Club (Club Med's logo brand), Hip Way, Fila, Carrera, Le Mar, gorgeous Colombian swimwear, Havaiana flip-flops, sunglasses, hats, and souvenirs. Great gifts to return home with are the Bahamian-made John Waltlings Fine Rums and Red Turtle Vodka. ✉ *Club Med, Cockburn Town* ☎ *242/331–2000* 🕒 *Daily 9 am–8 pm.*

Simply Bahamian. A small local crafts and liquor store across the street from the airport sells locally made purses and sarongs featuring Andros batik. ✉ *Cockburn Town.*

SPORTS AND THE OUTDOORS

SCUBA DIVING

San Salvador is famous for its vibrant wall dives and abundant marine life, including hammerhead sharks, sea turtles, Eagle rays, and more. The **Telephone Pole** is a stimulating wall dive where you can watch stingrays, grouper, snapper, and turtles in action.

Riding Rock Resort & Marina. The dive operation here (both SSI and PADI recognized) uses mostly buoyed sites to avoid damaging the marine environment by dropping anchor. The 42- and 46-foot dive boats are spacious and comfortable. Resort and certification courses are offered, and all new computerized dive gear and camera gear are available for rent. There's also a modern underwater photographic facility. Complete dive packages, including meals and accommodations, are available through Riding Rock Resort and Marina. However, dive trips are not offered daily so book well in advance. Riding Rock also rents bicycles and golf carts and can arrange half-day and full-day reef, inshore, and offshore fishing trips. The offshore waters hold tuna, blue marlin, dorado, and, in winter, wahoo. ⊠ *Riding Rock Resort and Marina, Cockburn Town* ☎ *800/272–1492, 242/331–2631, 954/453–5031* ⊕ *www.ridingrock.com.*

Fodor's Choice ★ **Seafari Dive Center at Club Med Columbus Isle.** The diving operation at Club Med is now run separately by Seafari International, and all dive trips and certifications (PADI and CMAS) are exclusive to Club Med guests only. If you are not staying at Club Med, you must buy a Day Pass ($64), which is all-inclusive of meals and other resort activities, in addition to paying for any dives. This professional dive center consistently offers three dives a day, in addition to a weekly night dive, to over 35 dive sites with permanent moorings. Divers go out on one of two catamarans, 54 and 52 feet. A hyperbaric chamber is on-site, and the staff consists of 10 dive instructors and four dive masters. All necessary equipment is available for rent including underwater cameras, dive computers, and Nitrox. ⊠ *Club Med, Cockburn Town* ☎ *242/331–2000, 242/331–2195* ⊕ *www.clubmed.us.*

TOURS

Fernander Tours. In addition to being a taxi driver and island tour guide extraordinaire, Mr. Clifford Fernander is friendly and full of information for the inquisitive tourist. He and Bruno Fernander offer tours for Club Med guests. Afterward, you'll feel San Salvador is like a second home. ⊠ *Cockburn Town* ☎ *242/331–2676, 242/427–8198.*

FAMILY **Lagoon Tours.** Cruise through secluded Pigeon Creek, on the island's beautiful southeast corner, in a flat-bottom boat that maxes at five people to view baby sharks, sea turtles, and starfish, and top off the trip shell hunting on High Cay. Lagoon Tours caters to all interests from nature walks and historical tours to bird-watching and excursions through the quiet waters of the lagoons. This family-run company is very proud of San Salvador Island and they are happy to show you their favorite off-the-beaten-path spots, with a smile and a cooler full of refreshments. They also conduct kayaking, nature, and bird-watching tours. ⊠ *Cockburn Town* ☎ *242/452–0102 cell, 242/331–2459* ⊕ *www. lagoon-tours-bahamas.com.*

Nat Walker's Island Adventures. As the island's Warden for the Bahamas National Trust, Nat Walker has a unique understanding of the island's nature and history, and he will customize island tours to include visits to monuments, private beach picnics, native restaurants, shopping, and the like. You can choose to see the archaeological site where its earliest inhabitants, the Lucayan Indians, lived; five monuments at Landfall Park commemorating Columbus's arrival in the Americas; a hand-operated Dixon Hill Lighthouse (one of three in the Bahamas); Watling's Estate 18th-century plantation ruins; the New World Museum; and the

Gerace Research Centre. Nathaniel also has 25-seat buses and rental cars and he arranges private beach picnics and snorkeling and reef tours. ✉ *Sugar Loaf* ☎ *242/331–2111, 242/464–9038.*

WATER SPORTS

Club Med – Columbus Isle. If you are not a guest at Club Med, you can buy a day pass for $64 which gives you access to water sports (including daily guided snorkeling trips, Hobie Cat sailing, paddleboards, kayaks, and windsurfing) and regular sports activities (including group power walks and jogging, beach volleyball, tennis, various aerobics classes, yoga, and tai chi). The day pass includes lunch and all you can drink and is good from 10:30 am to 6:30 pm. ✉ *Club Med, Cockburn Town* ☎ *242/331–2000* ⊕ *www.clubmed.us.*

Guanahani Surf & Sail Center. San Salvador is one of the last "uncrowded kitesurfing paradises," with ideal wind conditions and year-round warm waters. Licensed by IKO (International Kiteboarding Organization), the Guanahani Surf & Sail Center offers in-depth kiteboarding instruction for every level. Led by qualified trainers with Cabrinha kites and boards, courses last anywhere from 3 to 10 hours, and are best done over the course of a few days. The flat, calm, shallow waters in Snow Bay offer the perfect practice and play area. ✉ *Snow Bay, Sunrise Rd., Cockburn Town* ☎ *242/452–0438* ⊕ *www.guanahanibeachclub.com.*

ELSEWHERE ON SAN SALVADOR

Sometimes you just don't want to stay put at the resort. San Salvador's off-the-beaten-path places require some work, but make interesting sightseeing. The Gerace Research Centre and the lighthouse are not difficult to get to, but the "other" Columbus monument requires a little more work and an adventurous spirit.

EXPLORING

Columbus Monuments. Christopher Columbus has more than one monument on San Salvador Island commemorating his first landfall in the New World on October 12, 1492. The simple white cross erected in 1956 at Landfall Park in Long Bay is the easiest to find, on Queen's Highway just outside Cockburn Town. (Also on the site is the Mexican Monument which housed the Olympic flame in 1968 on its journey from Greece to Mexico City. The flame has never been lit since, but this location is popular for weekend family picnics and local gatherings.) The older and more difficult to find is the Chicago Herald Monument erected in 1891 to celebrate the 400th anniversary of the explorer's landing. No roads lead to this monument—a sphere hewn from native limestone—so you'll have to trek through East Beach on Crab Cay by foot, which is fun for the more adventurous. ✉ *Queen's Hwy., Cockburn Town* ⊕ *www.bahamas.com/islands/san-salvador.*

Dixon Hill Lighthouse. A couple of miles south of Graham's Harbour stands Dixon Hill Lighthouse. Built around 1856, it's the last hand-operated lighthouse in the Bahamas. The lighthouse keeper must wind the apparatus that projects the light, which beams out to sea every 15 seconds to a maximum distance of 19 miles, depending on visibility. A climb to the top of the 160-foot landmark provides a fabulous view of the island, which includes a series of inland lakes. The keeper is present 24 hours a day. Knock on his door and he'll take you up to the top and explain the machinery. Drop $1 in the box when you sign the guest book on the way out. ⊠ *Cockburn Town ⚓ Northeast sector of the island.*

Graham's Harbour and Gerace Research Centre. Columbus describes Graham's Harbour in his diaries as large enough "to hold all the ships of Christendom." A former U.S. Navy base near the harbor houses the Gerace Research Centre, previously known as the Bahamian Field Station. The GRC is a center for academic research in archaeology, biology, geology, and marine sciences, backed by the College of the Bahamas and affiliated with many U.S. universities. It provides accommodations, meals, and air transportation arrangements for students and researchers from all over the world who come to study in this unique environment. ☎ *242/331–2520* ⊕ *www.geraceresearchcentre.com.*

Sandy Point. Sandy Point anchors the island's southwestern end, overlooking French Bay. Here, on a hill, you'll find the ruins of **Watling's Castle,** named after the 17th-century pirate. The ruins are more likely the remains of a Loyalist plantation house than a castle from buccaneering days. A 5- to 10-minute walk from Queen's Highway will take you to see what's left of the ruins, which are now engulfed in vegetation.

SPORTS AND THE OUTDOORS
SCUBA DIVING
For more information about these and other sites and for dive operators on the island, contact the Riding Rock Resort and Marina or Seafari at Club Med.

Doolittle's Grotto is a popular site featuring a sandy slope down to 140 feet. There are lots of tunnels and crevices for exploring, and usually a large school of horse-eye jacks to keep you company. As the name implies, **Double Caves** has two parallel caves leading out to a wall at 115 feet; there's typically quite a lot of fish activity along the top of the wall. **North Pole Cave** has a wall that drops sharply from 40 feet to more than 150 feet; coral growth is extensive, and you might see a hammerhead or two.

LONG ISLAND

Long Island lives up to its name—80 gorgeous miles are available for you to explore. The Queen's Highway traverses its length, through the Tropic of Cancer and many diverse settlements and farming

---

HISTORIC LIGHTHOUSES

Since the 19th century, sailors' lives have depended on the lighthouse beacons that rotate over the southern islands and the treacherous reefs that surround them. But for landlubbers, these lighthouses also offer bird's-eye vantage points. Visit the 115-foot Bird Rock Lighthouse on Crooked Island, the Castle Island Lighthouse on Acklins Island, the Inagua Lighthouse, and San Salvador's Dixon Hill Lighthouse.

communities. The island is 4 miles at its widest, so at hilly vantage points you can view both the white cliffs and the raging Atlantic on the east side, and the gentle surf coming to you like a shy child on the Caribbean side. It is truly spectacular.

Long Island was the third island discovered by Christopher Columbus, and a monument to him stands on the north end. Loyalist families came to the island in support of the Crown, and to this day there are Crown properties all over the island, deeded by the king of England. Fleeing the Revolution, their attempt at re-creating life in America was short-lived. The soil and lack of rainfall did not support their crops, cotton being their mainstay. Today you can see wild cotton growing in patches up and down the island, along with the ruins of the plantations.

Fishing and tourism support the 3,000 residents of Long Island. Farms growing bananas, mangoes, papaya, and limes also dot the landscape. Boatbuilding is a natural art here, and in the south you can always see a boat in progress as you travel the Queen's Highway.

Progress has come to the island slowly. There is now high-speed Internet and cell-phone service, but shops and modern forms of entertainment are still limited. People who come to Long Island don't seem to mind; they're here for the beauty, tranquillity, and the friendly people. Deep-sea fishing and diving are readily available, and bonefishing flats attract sportfishermen from all over the world. The beaches provide breathtaking views, shelling, exploring, and magnificent pieces of sea glass. The laid-back lifestyle is reminiscent of a slower, gentler time.

GETTING HERE AND AROUND

AIR TRAVEL Long Island has two airports: Deadman's Cay (LGI) in the middle south and Stella Maris Airport (SML) in the far north. Bahamasair and Southern Air airlines provide daily service from Nassau to Stella Maris and Deadman's Cay airports. Pineapple Air flies daily from Nassau into Stella Maris and twice a week into Deadman's Cay. Stella Maris Resort has its own excellent air charter service to and from Nassau and between many southern islands including the Exumas. Other charter services are available from Nassau and Fort Lauderdale. Hawkline Aviation is an FBO at Stella Maris, a good fuel stop for private pilots going farther afield.

Guests staying at Cape Santa Maria or Stella Maris Resort should fly into Stella Maris Airport. Chez Pierre Bahamas' guests can fly into either airport, although the Stella Maris Airport is a bit closer. All others should fly into Deadman's Cay Airport midisland. Flying into the wrong airport will cost you not only an hour's drive, but also $100 or more in taxi fares. Listen carefully to the arrival announcement when you approach Long Island; most commercial airlines stop at both airports.

Contacts Deadman's Cay Airport. ⊠ *Deadman's Cay* ☎ *242/337–1777, 242/337–7077.* **Stella Maris Airport.** ⊠ *Stella Maris* ☎ *242/338–2006.*

BOAT TRAVEL Mail boats that bring supplies to the island each week make an adventurous mode of transportation. You'll ride with groceries, large and small appliances, automobiles, and sometimes even livestock. All boats depart from Potter's Cay in Nassau. Schedules change frequently. M/V

8

Isolated French Bay is on the southern end of San Salvador.

Mia Dean or its substitute ship the M/V *Sea Spirit* (that also goes on to Acklins and Crooked Islands) leaves Tuesday for Clarence Town in south Long Island and returns Thursday (18 hours; $60 one-way). The *Island Link*, a faster RORO boat, leaves Tuesday with stops in Salt Pond, Deadman's Cay, and Seymour's, returning Thursday (eight hours; $70 one-way). Bahamas Ferries, also a RORO that takes vehicles, and with its faster, more comfortable passenger lounge, leaves Nassau Monday and gets into Simms, north Long Island, having stopped in George Town, Exumas.

CAR TRAVEL A car is absolutely necessary to explore the island or visit any place outside your resort. The Queen's Highway curls like a ribbon from north to south, ending abruptly at the ocean in the north and at a stop sign in the south. It's narrow, with no marked center line, which makes bikes and scooters dangerous modes of transportation. The highway is easily traversed, but some off-roads require four-wheel drive, such as the road to the Columbus Monument, which is rocky and treacherous. The roads to Adderley's Plantation and Chez Pierre's are rough, but a passable adventure.

Most hotels will arrange car rentals, and can have your car waiting on-site or at the airport. Rentals range from $60 to $85. Some include gas; all have a limited number of vehicles. It's best to go for an a SUV or compact SUV with all-wheel drive if you have a choice.

Keep your gas tank full; although there are service stations along the highway, hours can be irregular and some take only cash. Some gas stations are closed on Sunday, so if that's your departure day, be sure to fill up the night before so the tank will be full when you return the car. Gas is expensive in the Outer Islands.

Contacts Mr. T's Car Rental. ✉ *Mid–Long Island, Deadman's Cay* ☎ *242/337–1054, 242/357–1678.* **Omar's Rental Cars.** ✉ *Cape Santa Maria Resort, Cape Santa Maria* ☎ *800/926–9704, 242/338–5273.* **Seaside Car Rentals.** ✉ *Salt Pond, midisland, Deadman's Cay* ☎ *242/338–0041, 242/338–0140.* **Unique Wheels Rental.** ✉ *Clarence Town, south Long Island* ☎ *242/225–7720, 242/225–8630* ⊕ *www.uniquewheelsrental.net.* **Williams Car Rental.** ✉ *Glintons, just north of Stella Maris* ☎ *242/338–5002.*

TAXI TRAVEL Taxis meet incoming flights at both airports. From the Stella Maris Airport, the fare to Stella Maris Resort is $10 per couple; to Cape Santa Maria, the fare is $30 per couple. Guests staying at Chez Pierre Bahamas pay $40 from the Stella Maris Airport and $60 from Deadman's Cay. Winter Haven provides free transportation from the Deadman's Cay Airport. A full-day tour of the island by taxi would cost about $350, and a half-day tour would be about $120. However, all taxis are privately owned, so rates can be negotiated. It is generally cheaper to rent a car for the duration of your trip than it is to pay taxi fares every time you want to go somewhere.

Contacts Jerry's Taxi Service. ✉ *Alligator Bay, near Simms, north Long island, Stella Maris* ☎ *242/338–8592, 242/472–8065.* **Leonard Darville.** ☎ *242/472–0024.* **Omar Daley.** ✉ *North Long Island, Stella Maris* ☎ *242/357–1043, 242/338–2031.* **Scofield Miller Taxi.** ✉ *Millers, mid-north Long Island* ☎ *242/338–8970.*

TOURS

Bahamas Discovery Quest. Discover the beauty of Long Island in a variety of adventures on land and sea: deep-sea, deep-drop, and reef fishing; snorkeling; sponging; crabbing for land crabs at night; sea life ecotours; hiking; beaching; shelling; and historical tours with Long Island native, Charles Knowles, who will take you off the beaten path to meet farmers and taste native dishes you wouldn't easily find on your own. ✉ *Deadman's Cay* ☎ *242/472–2605, 242/337–6024.*

Omar's Long Island Guided Tours. Now based at Cape Santa Maria Resort in the far north, Omar is more than just a tour guide. Raised on Long Island, he's fun and friendly and full of knowledge about the land and the people, and he will cater tours to your interests—from showing you the best spots to jump into Dean's Blue Hole, to introductions to native straw and seashell artisans. However, that's just the start of his long list of services: He's also a dive master and boat captain who will feed sharks and lead you through wrecks, a taxi driver who can transport you to and from the airport to your hotel, and the owner of Omar's Rental Cars if you want to explore the island on your own. ✉ *Cape Santa Maria Resort, Cape Santa Maria* ☎ *242/338–5273, 242/357–1043 cell, 242/357–1477 cell, 800/926–9704 toll free in U.S. and Canada* ⊕ *www.capesantamaria.com.*

VISITOR INFORMATION

Contacts Long Island Ministry of Tourism. ✉ *Salt Pond, mid–Long Island* ☎ *242/338–8668.*

NORTH LONG ISLAND: CAPE SANTA MARIA TO GRAY'S

In the far north you will find two large resort communities: **Cape Santa Maria** and **Stella Maris**. Scattered between are the small settlements of **Seymour's, Glinton's,** and **Burnt Ground**. Columbus originally named the island's northern tip Cape Santa Maria after the largest of his three ships. The beach here is gorgeous, full of private homes and resort villas, and a restaurant, bar, and gift shop that are open to the public. North of the Cape Santa Maria Resort are the **Columbus Monument**, commemorating Columbus's landing on Long Island, and **Columbus Cove**, where he made landfall. Twelve miles south of the Cape, Stella Maris, which means Star of the Sea, is home to the so-named resort. The Stella Maris Airport sits on the property, along with private homes, restaurants and bars, the magnificent **Love Beaches**, a full-service marina, and a tackle and gift shop—all open to the public. Just north of Stella Maris, off Queen's Highway, are the ruins of the 19th-century **Adderley's Plantation**.

Traveling south about 8 miles, you'll come to **Simms**, one of Long Island's oldest settlements. The Tropic of Cancer cuts through the island close to here, dividing the subtropics from the tropics.

Farther south are the idyllic communities of **Thompson Bay** and **Salt Pond**; both providing safe harbors for those who visit by sailboat. Salt Pond, a hilly bustling settlement so named for its many salt ponds, hosts the annual Long Island Regatta. Continuing south, you will pass the settlements of **the Bight** and **Gray's** before reaching **Deadman's Cay**.

EXPLORING

Adderley's Plantation. Just north of the Stella Maris Airport, west of the main road, are the ruins of 19th-century Adderley's Plantation, a cotton plantation that once occupied all of Stella Maris. Clearly marked, the road is marginally passable by car. It is about a 1-mile drive and then a fairly long walk. The walking path is marked by conch shells, and leads to the cotton plantation ruins. Seven buildings are practically intact up to roof level, but it is overgrown with vegetation. For historians, it is well worth the time. ⊠ *North of Stella Maris Airport, Stella Maris.*

Columbus Monument. Two miles north of Cape Santa Maria is the Columbus Monument, commemorating Columbus's landing on Long Island. The road to the monument is off the Queen's Highway, and while the sign is often not visible, any Long Islander will gladly give you directions. The 3-mile treacherous road is too rough for vehicles without four-wheel drive, and most rental car companies won't let you drive it without an SUV, yet it is an extremely long hike. At the end of the road is a steep hill, called Columbus Point, and a climb to the summit affords a spectacular vista. This is the highest point on Long Island, and the second highest in the Bahamas. Farther north on Queen's Highway is Columbus Harbour, on Newton's Cay. Columbus made landfall in this cove, protected by limestone outcroppings. The more adventurous can follow the beach to the left, where a rough walking path leads to three other coves; each one a delight. Two coves up you will find sea glass scattered on the beach like sparkling jewels, and by climbing through limestone formations, you will discover another cove perfect for snorkeling. ⊠ *North of Cape Santa Maria Resort, Cape Santa Maria.*

BEACHES

Cape Santa Maria Beach. Known as one of the Bahamas' top beaches, and located on the leeward side of the island at Cape Santa Maria Resort, the water colors here range from pale blue to aqua to shades of turquoise. The 4-mile stretch of soft white sand beckons you to stroll, build sand castles, sun worship, or wade into the calm shallow waters. In the early morning, you're likely to see a ray swimming along the shore. The resort has a beachside restaurant and lounge chairs for guests, in addition to kayak and paddleboard rentals, but there's also plenty of sand to find a secluded stretch all your own. **Amenities:** food and drink; water sports. **Best for:** solitude; snorkeling; sunset; swimming; walking. ⊠ *Cape Santa Maria Resort, Cape Santa Maria.*

WHERE TO EAT

After a period of rain, the mosquitoes and no-see-ums come out, so bring mosquito repellant with you when dining outdoors.

$$
SEAFOOD
FAMILY

✕ **Cape Santa Maria Beach House Restaurant and Bar.** Upstairs in the Cape Santa Maria Beach House, guests enjoy sweeping vistas of the turquoise bay during the day, and bobbing boat lights in the evening along with the gentle sounds of the sea. Breakfast can be light with yogurt parfait and a seasonal fruit medley, or a splurge with banana bread French toast topped with caramelized plantains or Bahamian-style eggs Benedict. Sit under a colorful umbrella on the oceanfront deck for lunch with a pizza, wrap, or fancy salad. For dinner, delight in Caribbean coconut shrimp, fresh grouper, or Bahamian lobster tail—just don't miss the chocolate drizzled rum cake! Full bar service is available in the open-air, screened-in oceanfront bar and a lively happy hour takes place every evening from 5 to 7, with complimentary conch fritters. This is one of the best spots on the island to grab a drink and watch the sunset. $ *Average main: $29* ⊠ *Cape Santa Maria Resort, Cape Santa Maria* ☎ *242/338–5273, 800/926–9704* ⊕ *www.capesantamaria.com* ✆ *Closed Sept. and Oct.* ⌂ *Reservations essential* ⌕ *Meal plans and kid's menu available.*

$$
ECLECTIC
Fodor's Choice
★

✕ **Chez Pierre Bahamas.** At this airy oceanfront restaurant a few steps from the beach, Chef Pierre has been serving sumptuous cuisine since 2002. This curmudgeonly chef serves the best food on the island, hands down. Specialties include pasta dishes with shrimp and scallops, fresh fish, and pizzas that are to die for. Bahamian lobster, steaks, and chicken, along with vegetarian dishes, are also available, and the salads (big enough to share) are both fresh and beautiful. A full bar is available on the honor system and you're expected to get your own drinks, since Pierre runs the place almost single-handedly. The surly host greets you himself; make sure you are on time for your reservation or he'll be tempted not to serve you at all! But pay no mind, as the food is well worth it and there is a smile hidden deep beneath his brusque outer shell. To get here, watch for the sign on Queen's Highway between the settlements of Weymss and Miller's. $ *Average main: $27* ⊠ *Miller's Bay* ☎ *242/338–8809, 242/357–1374* ⊕ *www.chezpierrebahamas.com* ⌂ *Reservations essential.*

$
BAHAMIAN
FAMILY

✕ **Moonshine Bar & Grill.** The views surrounding Stella Maris Resort Club's new poolside bar are as beautiful as the frozen fresh-fruit daiquiris they serve. Once a week, the delightful Bodo, legendary local

8

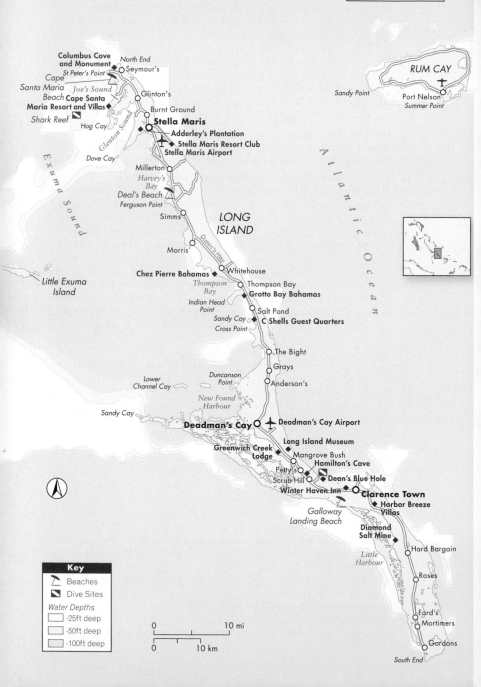

Long Island

Conception
Island

Conception Island
National Park

Wedge Point

RUM CAY

Sandy Point

Port Nelson

Summer Point

**Columbus Cove
and Monument**
St Peter's Point
*Cape
Santa Maria
Beach* **Cape Santa
Maria Resort and Villas**
Shark Reef

North End
Seymour's

Glinton's

Burnt Ground

Stella Maris

Joe's Sound

Hog Cay

Glenton Sound

Dove Cay

Adderley's Plantation
Stella Maris Resort Club
Stella Maris Airport

Millerton

*Harvey's
Bay*

Deal's Beach

Ferguson Point

Simms

**LONG
ISLAND**

Atlantic Ocean

Exuma Sound

Morris'

Queen's Hwy

Chez Pierre Bahamas

Whitehouse

*Thompson
Bay*

Thompson Bay

Grotto Bay Bahamas

*Little Exuma
Island*

*Indian Head
Point*

Salt Pond

C Shells Guest Quarters

Sandy Cay

Cross Point

The Bight

Grays

*Lower
Channel Cay*

*Duncanson
Point*

Anderson's

*New Found
Harbour*

Sandy Cay

Deadman's Cay
Deadman's Cay Airport

Long Island Museum

**Greenwich Creek
Lodge**

Mangrove Bush

Petty's
Hamilton's Cave

Scrub Hill
Dean's Blue Hole

Winter Haven Inn
Clarence Town

*Galloway
Landing Beach*

**Harbor Breeze
Villas**

**Diamond
Salt Mine**

Hard Bargain

*Little
Harbour*

Roses

Ford's

Mortimers

Gordons

South End

Key
Beaches
Dive Sites
Water Depths
-25ft deep
-50ft deep
-100ft deep

0   10 mi

0   10 km

guitarist and Rake 'n' Scrape musician, plucks your heartstrings with Bahamian and calypso songs. On the bar's west side is the sunbaked pool with lounges; to the south, a kids' playground and beachy cove; and to the north, a long boardwalk to a carved-out ocean pool and spectacular views of the coastal bluffs with the waves breaking over the coral reefs. Go for a snorkel when it's calm or enjoy the bar decks when the breeze is up. The menu offers Bahamian and American fare. The panini and bratwurst are favorites. [$] *Average main: $14* ✉ *Stella Maris Resort Club, Stella Maris* ☎ *242/338–2050* 🌐 *www.stellamarisresort.com.*

$$ SEAFOOD 🍴 **Stella Maris Resort Club Restaurant & Bar.** Charming and experienced Chef Bruno and his capable team do a superb job pleasing upmarket American and European palates. For breakfast, browse the buffet or order a full breakfast from the menu. Lunch includes a choice of conch chowder, club sandwiches, burgers, and salads which you can enjoy in the cool inside or on the stone terrace. For dinner, the kitchen prepares the freshest fish in a variety of ways, along with Bahamian lobster tail, a seafood platter, and cracked conch, an island favorite. Steaks, lamb, pork, chicken, hamburgers, pastas, salads, and vegetarian dishes are served. Fresh fruit and ice cream make for a great hot-weather dessert. The liqueur coffees are delicious. You can order from the bar menu until 9 pm or have pizza delivered to your room. [$] *Average main: $26* ✉ *Stella Maris Resort Club, Stella Maris* ☎ *242/338–2050* ⏲ *Closed Sept.* ✍ *Reservations essential.*

WHERE TO STAY

$ B&B/INN FAMILY 🏨 **C Shells Guest Quarters.** These quaint self-catering, full-kitchen suites sit just steps away from a quiet private beach on Salt Pond, with a large grassy garden space—perfect for family picnics, naps in the hammock, and a vacation without the bustle of a busy resort. **Pros:** centrally located on private beach; friendly, accommodating owners; cable TV and Wi-Fi; affordable. **Cons:** no maid service; no on-site restaurant; rental car is essential to explore the island. [$] *Rooms from: $100* ✉ *Salt Pond* ☎ *242/338–0103, 954/889–5075* 🌐 *www.cshellsguestquarters.com* 🛏 *4 suites* 🍽 *No meals.*

8

$$$ RESORT FAMILY Fodor's Choice ★ 🏨 **Cape Santa Maria Beach Resort and Villas.** This stunning resort consists of spacious, new beachfront villas that sleep up to eight and beachfront one-bed and two-bed bungalows that each have a screened-in veranda—all overlooking serene turquoise waters on a gorgeous 4-mile-long white-sand beach. **Pros:** only 15 minutes from Stella Maris Airport; friendly staff arranges excursions; great swimming beach; high-quality accommodations. **Cons:** secluded location means you'll need a rental car to explore. [$] *Rooms from: $325* ✉ *Galliot Cay, off Seymour's, Cape Santa Maria* ☎ *242/338–5273, 800/663-7090 toll free in U.S. and Canada, 250/598-3366 free outside U.S. and Canada* 🌐 *www.capesantamaria.com* ⏲ *Closed Sept. and Oct.* 🛏 *20 bungalows, 18 luxury villas* 🍽 *No meals* ☞ *Kids 12 and under stay free.*

$ RESORT 🏨 **Chez Pierre Bahamas.** Lining lovely Miller's Bay beach, this rustic, remote resort has six simple cabins on stilts right on the beach, making it a real "get-away-from-it-all" place (guests should be self-sufficient and adventurous). **Pros:** breezy porches are screened in: wake up to

Cape Santa Maria Beach Resort is the best on the island.

the sounds of the sea; large private beach; excellent on-site restaurant serves three meals a day. **Cons:** must rent a car to explore the island; no air-conditioning; bathroom water is slightly salty. $ Rooms from: $155 ⊠ Miller's Bay ☎ 242/338–8809, 242/357–1374 cell ⊕ www. chezpierrebahamas.com ⇱ 6 cottages ❍ Some meals.

$
B&B/INN

☷ **Grotto Bay Bahamas.** In the settlement of Salt Pond is this small private hideaway, a labor of love for owners Kris and Jean who offer two lovely guest rooms with sweeping decks facing the ocean on the lower level of their home. **Pros:** centrally located for exploring north and south; personalized service; beautiful lush landscaping. **Cons:** no in-house restaurant, bar, or meals; you need to rent a car to explore the island. $ Rooms from: $120 ⊠ Salt Pond ☎ 242/338–0011 ⊕ www. grottobaybahamas.com ⊟ No credit cards ⇱ 2 rooms ❍ No meals.

$$
RESORT
FAMILY
Fodor'sChoice
★

☷ **Stella Maris Resort Club.** Stella Maris is more than a resort, it is a longstanding family-fun community that sits atop a hilly ridge offering many accommodations choices (including private homes), complemented by multiple pools, breathtaking views of the Atlantic, fun bars and restaurants, and activities for every interest. **Pros:** all accommodations have an ocean view or balcony; great service and organized, headed by several families; super for events or big groups; three high-quality meals a day. **Cons:** long walks between rooms, clubhouse, beach bar; rooms somewhat dated but clean and comfortable; not beachfront but free bus to other beaches. $ Rooms from: $205 ⊠ Stella Maris ☎ 800/426–0466, 242/338–2050 resort ⊕ www.stellamarisresort.com ⇱ 16 rooms, 4 cottages, 6 houses ❍ No meals.

NIGHTLIFE

Stella Maris Resort. This resort often has live music on the weekends, including Rake 'n' Scrape. Every Thursday night is their Rum Punch Party, which includes rum punch, conch fritters, and dinner. Cost is $55 for nonguests. The clubhouse bar, with a pool table and foosball, has a huge rum collection and the restaurant has an excellent selection of wines. Ask about the frequent (in winter) Cave Party where folks gather round and dine on barbecued treats in a cave. Call ahead to make reservations. ✉ *Stella Maris Resort Club, Stella Maris* ☎ *242/338–2050.*

SHOPPING

Bonafide Bonefishing Fly Shop. This fly and tackle shop and souvenir boutique, usually open Monday, Wednesday, and Friday 9 am to 5 pm, is located in Stella Maris on Queens Highway. In addition to fishing gear, they sell cold drinks and snacks, souvenirs, gifts, apparel, and jewelry. James "Docky" Smith is the fishing guru behind Bonafide Bonefishing. A native to Long Island, he is a popular and knowledgeable bonefishing guide who "knows the flats." ✉ *Queens Hwy., Stella Maris* ☎ *242/338–2035, 242/357–1417, 242/338–2025* 🌐 *www.bonafidebonefishing.com.*

Cape Santa Maria Resort. There is a small gift shop in the lobby with clothes, swimsuits, native straw works, island books, souvenirs, cold drinks, and sundries. ✉ *Cape Santa Maria Resort's Beach House lobby, Cape Santa Maria* ☎ *242/338–5273, 800/926–9704* 🌐 *www.capesantamaria.com.*

Hillside Supply & Price Buster. Hillside is probably the largest store on Long Island and the ideal place to stock up if you're self-catering or want snacks in between mealtimes. Here you can find lots of fresh produce and dairy items (that you can't import into the Bahamas), dry foods, toiletries, and supplies. In the back of the store you will find just about anything, from snorkeling gear and ice chests to towels. Hillside can also tell where and how to get fresh lobster, snapper, grouper, and more. There are seafood vendors living nearby. ✉ *Salt Pond, mid–Long Island* ☎ *242/338–0022* ⏲ *Closed Sun.*

Tingum's Boutique. *Tingums* is Bahamian for "I don't know what to call it." This cute gift shop sells clothing, jewelry, gifts, souvenirs, books, and toiletries. ✉ *Stella Maris Resort Club, Stella Maris* ☎ *242/338–2050.*

SPORTS AND THE OUTDOORS

DIVING AND SNORKELING

Conception Island Wall is an excellent wall dive, with hard and soft coral, plus interesting sponge formations. The M/V *Comberbach*, a 103-foot British freighter built in 1948, sank off Cape Santa Maria in 1984, and was scuttled by the Stella Maris Resort in 1986 to create an artificial reef and excellent dive site. Take a guided diving excursion to **Shark's Reef** and watch a scuba master safely feed dozens of sharks.

FAMILY **Cape Santa Maria Resort.** This resort uses expert divers and guides for myriad diving and snorkeling trips to various reefs, walls, and wrecks around Long Island as well as trips to Conception Island; dive and snorkel equipment is available for rent. In addition, visitors can rent stand-up paddleboards and Hobie Cat sailboats to explore the coast of

8

Cape Santa Maria Beach and its surrounding bays. ⊠ *Cape Santa Maria Resort, Cape Santa Maria* ☎ *242/338–5273, 800/926–9704* ⊕ *www.capesantamaria.com.*

Stella Maris Marina & Stella Maris Water Sports. Stella Maris Marina & Stella Maris Water Sports, with three dive boats, are operated by the original owners who, with Joerg Freise, started the Bahamas' first-ever dive operation back in 1963. Today, his son Pascal and Omar Daley, two PADI instructors, run the operation ,which is still famous for shark dives. Most dives are personalized for singles, couples, families, and small groups, and include diving and snorkeling along the calm lee-side as well as reefs and walls along the more adventurous Atlantic northeast shore. You can still dive on the world's first developed shark Reef. Other dives include the Comberbach Freighter (100 feet); Dean's Blue Hole, the deepest known blue hole in the world; and Conception Island Wall (45 feet to bottomless) with huge beautiful interconnecting coral heads, turtles, rays, sharks, and the occasional big game fish. The company also offers Dive and Stay packages, Overnight Dive Cruises for groups, and snorkeling and fishing trips. The marina, with its haul-out rails taking boats up to 100 feet and its machine shop, is the Bahamas' most southerly full-service marina. ⊠ *Queen's Hwy., Stella Maris* ✛ *1 mile south of airport and Stella Maris Resort Club* ☎ *242/338–2055, 242/357–1130, 242/338–2033* ⊕ *www.stellamarisresort.com/scuba-diving/.*

FISHING

Bonafide Bonefishing. James "Docky" Smith is highly regarded as one of the best bonefishing guides in the Bahamas. He does full- and half-day bonefishing excursions, as well as reef-fishing trips. He is also an expert fly-casting instructor. Book well in advance. His operation is based out of the Bonafide tackle shop in Stella Maris, open three days a week, which rents conventional and fly-fishing gear, prepares snacks and box lunches, and sells a range of tackle, clothing, and flies. Full days of bonefishing are $500 (maximum two anglers); reef, bottom, or deep-sea fishing are $1,200 (maximum six anglers). Call ahead. ⊠ *Near Stella Maris Resort, Queen's Hwy., Stella Maris* ☎ *242/338–2025, 242/357–1417* ⊕ *www.bonafidebonefishing.com.*

SOUTH LONG ISLAND: DEADMAN'S CAY TO GORDON'S

The most populated area on the island is **Deadman's Cay**. This umbrella central settlement covers all the communities stretching from **Gray's** to the north to **Scrub Hill**, and is the social, economic, and educational center of the island. The Deadman's Cay Airport is in Lower Deadman's Cay and the infamous Max's Conch Bar is only a short distance to the south. Shops, restaurants, and bars dot this area, along with amazing views of the Bahamas Banks.

Past Scrub Hill is **Dean's Blue Hole**, the deepest blue hole in the world. Free-diving contests, without use of any breathing apparatus, are held here each year, and divers come from all over the world to challenge the record. Fantastic snorkeling can be had around the blue hole's edges.

Clarence Town is the capital of Long Island and home to the Flying Fish Marina in one of the prettiest and safest harbors in the Out Islands.

Situated at the top of the highest hills in town are the twin-towered Moorish style churches of **St. Paul's** and **St. Peter's**, designed by Father Jerome. Clarence Town is the last large settlement on the south end of the island.

South of Clarence Town you will find **Galloway Landing**, a long stretch of amazing beaches and saltwater canals dug into the limestone hills by the now defunct Diamond Salt Mine. From here to **Gordon's** is the most undeveloped stretch of the island. Plantation ruins are at **Dunmone's**, secluded beaches at **Ford's**, and the incredible pink flamingos at Gordon's along with the biggest assortment of sea glass.

EXPLORING

Some of the biggest changes on Long Island have taken place at **Flying Fish Marina** (⊕ *www.flyingfishmarina.com*) in Clarence Town. The full-service, 20-slip marina offers fuel, a new store, and a new, upscale restaurant.

Fodor's Choice ★ **Dean's Blue Hole.** Known as the deepest blue hole in the world with a depth of 663 feet, Dean's Blue Hole is the most amazing sight on the island and one of the most popular photo sites in the land. A blue hole is a term for a water-filled sinkhole with an entrance below the water level. Free divers from around the world gather here annually to take the plunge. In 2010 William Trubridge broke the world record free-diving to 302 feet without fins. Dean's Blue Hole is surrounded by a pretty cliff and a superb beach. The shallows at the edge of the hole are perfect for snorkeling and swimming, and the more adventurous visitors can jump into the water from the cliffs above. To find the blue hole, watch for the well-marked sign on your left (going east on Queen's Highway) after passing through Scrub Hill. ⊠ *Just south of Scrub Hill on east coast, north of Clarence Town, Clarence Town.*

Hamilton's Cave. The largest cave system in the Bahamas, Hamilton's Cave features stalactites and stalagmites, and passages over 45 feet wide and 9 feet high. The Lucayan Indians were thought to have lived here about AD 500 and many Lucayan artifacts were discovered in 1936. Leonard Cartwright will take you on a guided tour, complete with flashlights, as you explore inside the dark depths of his childhood playground. For added excitement, plan to go closer to dusk when the resident bats are most active! ⊠ *Queen's Hwy., Deadman's Cay* ☎ *242/337–0235, 242/472–1796* ⊠ *$10 Adults, $5 Children.*

The Long Island Museum and Library. The Long Island Museum and Library is housed in a beautiful little pink cottage with native trees in front. Patty will share the history of Long Island and show you artifacts collected by local Long Islanders in hopes of preserving their cultural heritage. It's a fascinating collection and exhibit, professionally designed by the Bahamas, Antiquities, Monuments and Museum Corporation. Native wares, homemade jellies, and other island goods are for sale, in addition to books on Long Island and a popular Bahamian calendar painted in watercolors by local artist Nick Maillis. ⊠ *Buckley's, near Scotia Bank, Queen's Hwy.* ☎ *242/337–0500* ⊕ *www.ammcbahamas. com/Runtime/LongIslandMuseum.aspx* ⊠ *Adults: $3, kids 6–12 yrs: 50 cents; kids under 6: free* ⊙ *Weekdays 8–4, Sat. 9–1* ⊙ *Closed Sun.*

8

A gray shark circles a boat off Long Island.

St. Paul's & St. Peter's Churches. The twin, towered Moorish churches of St. Paul's (Anglican) and St. Peter's (Catholic) are two of the island's most celebrated landmarks. Father Jerome, often referred to as the hermit of Cat Island, built St. Paul's when he was Anglican; later, after converting to Catholicism, he built St. Peter's. The architecture of the two churches is similar to the Spanish missions in California. The churches are open sporadically, but tours are available through the Ministry of Tourism. ⊠ *Atop of Clarence Town Hill, Clarence Town.*

BEACHES

Galloway Landing Beach. This remarkable beach on the southeast coast of the island, south of Clarence Town, is relatively unknown and visited mostly by the locals. Swim and sun at the first beach, or walk a short distance south to an even more wonderful and secluded stretch of sand. Here, canals carved into the limestone hills by the now defunct Diamond Salt Mine are filled with the palest blue ocean water and are home to small marine life. It's a wonderful area to kayak, snorkel and swim, and collect sea glass. A bit farther south, a narrow bridge leads to beyond-stunning lagoons and ocean flats. **Amenities:** none. **Best for:** solitude; snorkeling; swimming; walking. ⊠ *Clarence Town ✛ 2.4 miles southwest of Clarence Town.*

WHERE TO EAT

$ ✕**Forest 2 Take-Away.** This family-owned and -operated takeout res-
BAHAMIAN taurant is a favorite with the locals for tasty, native food and value. It offers barbecued ribs, cracked conch, conch burgers, fish fingers, chicken snacks and dinners, and the ever-popular Forest Burger, a hamburger with boneless ribs and sautéed onions. Call ahead for your order

or sit and wait with a cold beer. There's a shady shack with picnic tables adjoining. [$] *Average main: $12* ✉ *Just off Queen's Hwy., Deadman's Cay* ☎ *242/337–1246, 242/337–1246* 💳 *No credit cards* ⏲ *Closed Sun.*

$ BAHAMIAN 🍴 **Max's Conch Bar and Grill.** This island treasure, possibly the island's most-recommended dining spot, is praised up and down by locals and visitors alike. Quintessentially Bahamian, you can sit all day on a stool at the colorful roadside hexagonal gazebo or at a table in the garden patio amid chickens and a goat, nursing beers and nibbling on excellent conch salad prepared right in front of you. Become a veritable expert on Long Island and its people with gregarious Max and the sweet, chatty Liz. Such is the charm of this laid-back watering hole, visitors come back again and again. Their recipes are old-time Bahamian, hard to find elsewhere. Be sure to try the conch fritters, steamed snapper, and breadfruit chips, or any of the daily specials such as pot roast and crawfish stuffed potatoes. Max also offers complimentary Wi-Fi for those needing to stay connected. [$] *Average main: $15* ✉ *Deadman's Cay* ☎ *242/337–0056* ⏲ *Closed Sun.*

$ BAHAMIAN 🍴 **Outer Edge Grill at Flying Fish Marina.** Reopened with new management, Outer Edge Grill is what local Long Islanders call a "poop deck," meaning a restaurant on the water. Open daily for lunch and dinner, Outer Edge serves up Bahamian favorites like conch fritters and fish fingers, along with sweet-potato french fries, mozzarella sticks, and homemade desserts. This is one of only a few restaurants open on Sunday. [$] *Average main: $12* ✉ *Clarence Town Harbour, Flying Fish Marina, just down from Winter Haven Inn, Clarence Town* ☎ *242/337–3445 restaurant, 954/654–7084 in U.S. and Canada, 242/337–3430 marina resort* 🌐 *www.flyingfishmarina.com* 💳 *No credit cards.*

$$ AMERICAN 🍴 **Rowdy Boys Bar and Grill at Winter Haven Inn.** Don't let the name scare you—it's named after the Knowles family's well-known construction company and the owners' two sons. Breakfast, lunch, and dinner can be served in the cool inside or out, and feature authentic Bahamian and American fare. The restaurant overlooks the roaring Atlantic, with a beach nearby, a big pool, a whirlpool, and a tiki bar on the large outside deck. The chef-owners Chloe (pronounced "Klo") and Bert Knowles serve some of the best food on the island (with Bahamian stewed fish for breakfast)—and the prices are affordable (Delmonico steak for just $32 and lobster for $28). Clean, bright, popular with the locals, and with ocean views, it's a great place to enjoy a drink and hearty meal. If you can catch their Friday Pig Roast, you'll enter succulence heaven. This is one of the few restaurants open on Sunday. [$] *Average main: $24* ✉ *Winter Haven Inn, Clarence Town* ☎ *242/337–3062* 🌐 *www.winterhavenbahamas.com* ✍ *Reservations essential.*

$ BAHAMIAN 🍴 **Seaside Village at Jerry Wells.** Located at the end of Jerry Wells Road, this charming, authentic conch shack stuck out on a dock in the water is truly local, offering friendly service, fun music, and good food. Sling back in the hammock, catch some tunes and breeze as you (if you're lucky) watch the almost-tame osprey, "Iron", snack on fish morsels. House favorites include fresh conch salad (watch Kenny pull the conch straight from the water), grilled lobster, and grouper made any way you want it—all go best with a cold Kalik. Some visitors rate the fresh conch salad as the best, noticing the great care Kenny takes to make it. Seaside Village is open on Sunday. [$] *Average main: $15* ✉ *Jerry Wells Rd., on west coast just south of Deadman's Cay Airport, Deadman's Cay* ☎ *242/337–0119, 242/357–1080 cell* 💳 *No credit cards.*

WHERE TO STAY

$ B&B/INN 🏨 **Greenwich Creek Lodge.** One of Long Island's newest places is the tranquil Greenwich Creek Lodge on the west waters of Cartwright's. **Pros:** on the water with boat access; serves three meals a day and has a bar; free Wi-Fi and TV/DVD available; swimming pool and small gym. **Cons:** beach 2 miles away; no TVs in rooms. [$] *Rooms from: $165* ✉ *Off Queen's Hwy., in Cartwright's, 3 miles south of Deadman's Cay Airport, Deadman's Cay* ☎ *242/337–6278 resort, 242/359–0980 cell* 🌐 *greenwichcreeklodge.com* 🛏 *11 rooms* 🍴 *Some meals.*

$$ RENTAL 🏨 **Harbor Breeze Villas.** Long Island's newest luxury villas are nestled among garden pathways atop a hillside, each with private balconies affording views of Clarence Town Harbour and the Atlantic Ocean. **Pros:** owner rents cars and will stock your villa with groceries ahead of your arrival; complimentary transfers to Arthur's Town Airport; laundry facilities on-site. **Cons:** no on-site restaurant or bar; not on beach; office can be hard to reach by phone. [$] *Rooms from: $200* ✉ *Lochabar, just south of Clarence Town, Clarence Town* ☎ *242/225–3086, 242/225–7720, 242/357–9531 cell* 🌐 *www.harborbreezevillas.com* 🛏 *14 villas* 🍴 *No meals.*

$ HOTEL 🏨 **Winter Haven Inn.** In the heart of Clarence Town, this small, colorful inn has two-story houses with rooms overlooking the indigo waters of the Atlantic. **Pros:** complimentary airport transfers; good on-site restaurant serves three meals a day; complimentary Wi-Fi. **Cons:** no kitchen facilities in-room; you must rent a car for exploring; rough, rocky beach not good for swimming. [$] *Rooms from: $150* ✉ *Clarence Town* ☎ *242/337–3062, 866/348–5935* 🌐 *www.winterhavenbahamas.com* 🛏 *12 rooms* 🍴 *No meals.*

NIGHTLIFE

Lloyd's Sporting Lounge. The long name is Lloyd's Sporting Lounge & Entertainment Center and, for Long Island, it has quite a bit. This new, comfortable, and smartly designed sports bar and lounge has big-screen TVs for sports, and five pool tables. In a separate room they also have a dance/disco to the live tunes of the D Changes Band and DJs every Friday and Saturday night. It's $10 for gents, ladies are free. Lloyd's hosts frequent pool tournaments and people flock to enjoy happy hour from 5 to 7 pm weekdays when beer buckets are four for $12. Other times, beers and rum and Cokes are a reasonable $4.50. Their food is also good and affordable: Long Island mutton, chicken, steaks, seafood, and various fettuccine main courses average $11 for chicken to $32 for T-bone steak. Lloyd's is well thought out and rather luxurious for the Out Islands—very enjoyable especially for big-group entertainment and dining, to catch sports on TV, or to dance to some live music. ✉ *Queen's Hwy., opposite Turtle Cove Rd. that leads to Dean's Blue Hole, Clarence Town* ☎ *242/337–5762.*

SHOPPING

It's All Under the Sun. As the name suggests, this "department store" has everything from a café with used books and Wi-Fi to office supplies, toys, baby stuff, souvenirs, beach bags, hats, and snorkeling and fishing gear. Owner Cathy Darville also sells fruit smoothies, deli sandwiches, and, to bribe the kids while you browse, frosty treats, orange creamsicles, cotton candy, and bubble gum. ✉ *Off Queen's Hwy. in Mangrove Bush, near Cartwirght's settlement* ☎ *242/337–0199* ☽ *Closed Sun.*

Sea Winds Super Mart and Supplies. This is probably the second-largest grocery store on the island and has everything you need for a picnic or to stock your vacation kitchen. Toiletries and other supplies are available. There are several other shops in this "strip mall," including Yukon Jack's Wholesale and Retail Liquor. ✉ *Off Queen's Hwy., in Petty's, Clarence Town* ☎ *242/337–0212.*

SPORTS AND THE OUTDOORS

DIVING AND SNORKELING

Surrounded by a beautiful powder-beach cove, the area surrounding **Dean's Blue Hole** offers a great place for a beach picnic if it's not too windy. Visitors can jump into the blue hole from various locations on the overhanging cliff above, some at 25 feet above the water. Snorkelers will see a variety of tropical fish and marine life, and Stella Maris Water Sports at Stella Maris Marina offers guided dive trips; flashlights included and necessary! While Dean's Blue Hole is safe for swimming, it is recommended that all swimmers be competent or wear life jackets.

FAMILY **Bahamas Discovery Quest.** This company, owned by Charles Knowles whose love for his island is obvious, offers full- and half-day snorkeling trips, along with many other unique island escapades including sponging, crabbing, beaching, and shelling, and different types of fishing. Also, he has two places to stay in Stella Maris and one in Salt Pond. ☎ *242/472–2605, 242/337–6024.*

FISHING

Long Island Bonefish Lodge. This modern lodge offers all-inclusive stay/fish/dine packages for fly-fishermen. Packages include three meals and fishing from 8 am to 4 pm. LIBL specializes in and encourages DIY fishing where, although your guide is present, you're mostly in your own privacy, and he can boat you to other flats to find success. Most of Long Island's vast flats are wadable shallows. The main clubhouse has gorgeous flats views. The two duplexes are modern, comfortable, and neat and sleep a total of eight. ✉ *Deadman's Cay* ☎ *242/472–2609* ⊕ *longislandbonefishinglodge.com/www/* 🖃 *$1,850 per person double occupancy. All-inclusive stay/fish/dine package Oct.–May.*

Samuel Knowles Bonefish Adventures. Since 2002, Samuel Knowles Bonefish Adventures has drawn a loyal following of saltwater anglers from around the globe, earning a reputation as one of the most popular bonefishing programs in the islands. The main attraction is their expert guides, who are Long Island natives, fourth- and fifth-generation bonefishermen, and champions of four of the five Bahamas bonefishing tournaments. Their location at the center of Long Island's pristine shoreline, with unique landlocked flats, creates an unforgettable fishing adventure

8

for all ages and experience levels. They offer stay/fish/dine packages at Smith-Wells Bonefish Lodge: $2,395 for seven nights/six days fishing. ✉ *Deadman's Cay* ☎ *242/337–0246, 242/357–1178* ⊕ *www. deadmansbones.com.*

Winter Haven Inn. Winter Haven Inn organizes fishing and boating adventures through various local guides. ✉ *Clarence Town* ☎ *242/337–3062* ⊕ *www.winterhavenbahamas.com.*

CROOKED AND ACKLINS ISLANDS

Crooked Island is 30 miles long and surrounded by 45 miles of barrier reefs that are ideal for diving and fishing. They slope from 4 feet to 50 feet, then plunge to 3,600 feet in the **Crooked Island Passage,** once one of the most important sea roads for ships following the southerly route from the West Indies to the Old World. If you drive up to **the Cove** settlement, you get an uninterrupted view of the region all the way to the narrow passage at **Lovely Bay** between Crooked Island and Acklins Island. Two lighthouses alert mariners that they are nearing the islands.

The tepid controversy continues today over whether Columbus actually set foot on Crooked Island and its southern neighbor, Acklins Island. What's known for sure is that Columbus sailed close enough to Crooked Island to get a whiff of its native herbs. Soon after, the two islands became known as the "Fragrant Islands." Today Crooked and Acklins islands are known as remote and unspoiled destinations for fishermen, divers, and sailors who value solitude. Here phone service can be intermittent, Internet connections can be hard to find, and some residents depend on generators for electricity. Even credit-card use is a relatively new development. The first known settlers didn't arrive until the late 18th century, when Loyalists brought slaves from the United States to work on cotton plantations. About 400 people, mostly fishermen and farmers, live on each island today. Two plantation-era sites, preserved by the Bahamas National Trust, are on Crooked Island's northern end, which overlooks Crooked Island Passage that separates the cay from Long Island. Spanish guns have been discovered at one ruin, **Marine Farm,** which may have been used as a fortification. An old structure, **Hope Great House,** has orchards and gardens.

AIR TRAVEL Crooked and Acklins have one airport each: Colonel Hill Airport (CRI) on Crooked Island and Spring Point Airport (AXP) on Acklins Island. Neither is open unless there's a flight expected. Bahamasair and Pineapple Air fly from Nassau to Crooked and Acklins islands twice a week. The flights are quite early in the morning, making it hard to fly in from overseas without staying one night in Nassau. Many Crooked Island visitors have found a solution to that: fly in on a private aircraft direct from the United States. The private 3,500-foot airstrip at Crooked Island Lodge is complimentary for hotel guests. Nonguests pay landing and parking fees. This airstrip is most convenient for private and charter flights if you're staying in the area of Pittstown and Landrail Point. Ask your hotel to make arrangements for picking you up at the airport in case there are no taxis.

Hotels will arrange airport transportation. Generally someone from even the smallest hotel will meet you at the airport, despite the fact that taxis are usually waiting on flights.

Contacts Acklins Island Spring Point Airport. ✉ *Midway along Acklins Island* ☎ *242/344–3169* 🌐 *www.bahamasair.com or www.pineappleair.com.* **Crooked Island Colonel Hill Airport.** ✉ *On the northeast side of Crooked Island* ☎ *242/344–2357.*

BOAT TRAVEL Mail boats that bring supplies to the islands each week make an adventurous mode of transportation. You'll ride with groceries, large and small appliances, automobiles, and sometimes even livestock. All boats depart from Potter's Cay in Nassau. Schedules change frequently. M/V *Sea Spirit* sails Tuesday at 3 pm to Acklins Island, Crooked Island, and Long Cay, returning Friday morning (30 hours; $90 one-way).

Ferry service between Cove Landing, Crooked Island, and Lovely Bay, Acklins Island, usually operates twice daily on varying schedules between 9 and 4.

Contacts Ferry Service. ☎ *242/344–2197 ferry, 242/344–2415 Island Administrator's Office.*

CAR TRAVEL There are many car-rental operators but to get a good one, reserve a car through your hotel prior to your arrival, but even with a reservation, be prepared for the possibility of not having one. Gas is also not always available on the island, as it's delivered by mail boats, which are sometimes delayed. Fortunately, it's easy to get a ride to most places with locals. They are very friendly and want to help all the time.

EXPLORING

Bird Rock Lighthouse. The sparkling white Bird Rock Lighthouse (built in 1876) once guarded the Crooked Island Passage. The rotating flash from its 115-foot tower still welcomes pilots and sailors to the Crooked Island Lodge, currently the islands' best lodging facility. This lighthouse is located 1 mile offshore and can only be reached by boat. ✉ *Bird Rock* ✣ *On separate island off northwest point of Crooked Island.*

Castle Island Lighthouse. On a separate island on Acklins' southwest point, and only reachable by boat, is the Castle Island Lighthouse (built in 1867). It formerly served as a beacon for pirates who used to retreat there after attacking ships. ✉ *Castle Island.*

WHERE TO STAY

$ RENTAL 🏨 **Casuarina Pine Villas.** Six modern cottages sit on a ½-mile stretch of white-sand beach between Landrail Point and Pittstown Point Landings. **Pros:** beachfront location; spacious economical accommodations; great place to hang out, fish, and relax. **Cons:** you need to arrange transportation to do anything; take plenty of insect repellent. [$] *Rooms from: $145* ✉ *Landrail Point* ☎ *242/344–2197* 💳 *No credit cards* 🛏 *6 cottages* 🍴 *No meals.*

$$ B&B/INN 🏨 **Crooked Island Lodge.** A true anglers' paradise, this is one of the best fishing destinations in the Bahamas and Caribbean for bone- and

deep-sea fishing. **Pros:** mind-bending ocean and beachfront location; bar and restaurant that serves three meals a day; private airstrip for easy access. **Cons:** take a lot of insect repellent and have it on when you step out of the plane; don't go unless you want remote, private, and nothing to do but fish and relax. $ *Rooms from: $150* ✉ *Pittstown Point Landing* ☎ *242/344–2507, 888/344–2507 toll free in U.S. and Canada* 🌐 *www.crookedislandlodge.com* 🛏 *12 rooms* 🍴 *All meals.*

$ B&B/INN **Tranquility On The Bay.** On beautiful scallop-shaped 3-mile-long Winding Bay, lies Tranquility On The Bay, a recently built lodge with five spacious air-conditioned rooms, and a clubhouse with dining room and bar. **Pros:** beautiful beach with free snorkeling and kayaking; near the airport; newly built with good amenities. **Cons:** transport to boat launch in Turtle Sound is $60; quiet—you'll be self-entertaining. $ *Rooms from: $145* ✉ *Winding Bay, 3 miles west of Colonel Hill Airport* ☎ *242/557–9951* 🌐 *www.tranquillitybayresort.com* 🛏 *5 rooms* 🍴 *No meals.*

SPORTS AND THE OUTDOORS

FISHING

Crooked Island has a number of highly regarded bonefishing guides with quality boats and fly-fishing tackle. Most can be booked through Tranquillity On The Bay or the Crooked Island Lodge, but the guides also take direct bookings. Be aware that telephone service to and from Crooked and Acklins islands is not always operational.

You can stalk the elusive and swift bonefish in the shallows, or go deep-sea fishing for wahoo, sailfish, and amberjack.

Michael Carroll (☎ *242/344–2037*), **Derrick Ingraham** (☎ *242/344–2023*), **Elton "Bonefish Shakey" McKinney** (☎ *242/344–2038*), **Randy McKinney** (☎ *242/344–2326*), **Jeff Moss** (☎ *242/344–2029*), and **Clinton** and **Kenneth "The Earlybird" Scavalla** (☎ *242/344–2011 or 242/422–3596*) are all knowledgeable professional guides. **Captain Robbie Gibson** (☎ *242/344–2007*) has a 30-foot Century boat and is the most experienced reef and offshore fishing captain on Crooked Island, where astounding fishing in virgin waters is the rule. Many wahoo weighing more than 100 pounds are landed each season with his assistance. Robbie's personal-best wahoo is a whopping 180 pounds. He's also a skilled guide for anglers pursuing tuna, marlin, sharks, barracuda, jacks, snapper, and grouper.

SCUBA DIVING

Captain Robbie Gibson. In addition to fishing expeditions, Captain Robbie Gibson offers scuba diving, snorkeling, and day tours. ☎ *242/344–2007, 242/422–4737.*

INAGUA

Inagua does indeed feel like the southernmost island in the Bahamas' 700 mile-long chain. Just 50 miles from Cuba, it's not easy to get to—there are only three flights a week from Nassau, and you must overnight there to catch the 9 am flight. At night the lonely beacon of the **Inagua**

8

Deep-sea fishing in the Southern Out Islands

Lighthouse sweeps the sky over the southern part of the island and the only community, **Matthew Town,** as it has since 1870. The coastline is rocky and rugged, with little coves of golden sand. The terrain is mostly flat and covered with palmetto palms, wind-stunted buttonwoods, and mangroves ringing ponds and a huge inland saltwater lake. Parts of it look very much like the Florida Everglades, only without the alligators and poisonous snakes.

Matthew Town feels like the Wild West, with sun-faded wooden buildings and vintage and modern trucks usually parked in front. It's obviously not a tourist mecca, but it's a shame that more people don't make it here. They are missing one of the great spectacles of the Western Hemisphere: the 70,000-some West Indian pink-scarlet flamingos that nest here alongside rare Bahama parrots and roseate spoonbills. If you're not a bird lover, there's extraordinary diving and fishing off the virgin reefs. Although there are few tourists, this remote island is prosperous. An unusual climate of little rainfall and continual trade winds creates rich salt ponds. The Morton Salt Company harvests a million tons of salt annually at its Matthew Town factory, where most of the 1,000 Inaguans work.

GETTING HERE AND AROUND

AIR TRAVEL Inagua has one airport: Matthew Town Airport (IGA). Bahamasair has flights on Monday, Wednesday, and Friday from Nassau. Hotels will arrange airport transportation. Generally someone from even the smallest hotel will meet you at the airport, but taxis sometimes meet incoming flights.

Contacts Inagua Matthew Town Airport. ✉ *Matthew Town* ☎ *242/339–1680 Only answered Mon., Wed., and Fri. when a flight is expected, 242/339–1415 Airport* ⊕ *www.bahamasair.com.*

BOAT TRAVEL   The M/V *Lady Mathilda* sails once a week or three times a month, first to Abraham's Bay, and then to Matthew Town, Inagua. Not only is the boat characteristically cluttered with all sorts of cargo, the service is sporadic—so, always call the captain on the scheduled sailing day, Thursday, or the Potter's Cay Dockmaster's Office in Nassau to check sailing times. She departs from Potter's Cay in Nassau and the journey in good seas takes 36 hours and is a rather pricey $100 one-way. If bad weather is approaching, she may not even leave harbor, skipping a week and leaving you stranded. The whole process is an authentic Bahamian adventure. Take your camera!

CAR TRAVEL   You can rent a car for about $80 a day, but there are few rental cars on the island, so call in advance. If you are driving outside Matthew Town, you will need an SUV or truck to navigate dirt roads. If you plan to stay in Matthew Town, you can easily walk everywhere.

Contacts Ingraham Rent-A-Car. ☎ *242/339–1677.*

TOURS

Great Inagua Tours. Contact Colin Ingraham, a veteran tour guide, who specializes in birding and island sightseeing. He can also arrange deep-sea fishing and snorkeling on the reefs. ✉ *Burnside St., Matthew Town* ✛ *Southwest Inagua* ☎ *242/453–0429.*

EXPLORING

Erickson Museum and Library. The Erickson Museum and Library is a welcome part of the community, particularly the surprisingly well-stocked, well-equipped library. The Morton Company built the complex in the former home of the Erickson family, who came to Inagua in 1934 to run the salt giant. The museum displays the island's history, to which the company is inextricably tied. The posted hours are not always that regular. The Bahamas National Trust office, and the office of the Inagua National Park, is also here, but hours are unpredictable. ✉ *Gregory St. on the northern edge of town across from the police station, Matthew Town* ☎ *242/339–1863* 🎟 *Free* ☉ *Weekdays 9–5, Sat. 10–1* ☉ *Closed Sun.*

Inagua Lighthouse. From Southwest Point, a mile or so south of Matthew Town, you can see Cuba's coast—slightly more than 50 miles west—on a clear day from atop Inagua Lighthouse, built in 1870 in response to the number of shipwrecks on offshore reefs. It's a grueling climb—the last 10 feet are on a ladder—but the view of the rugged coastline and Matthew Town is worth the effort. Look to the west to see the hazy mountains of Cuba. Be sure to sign the guest book, just inside the door to the lighthouse. ✉ *Gregory St., 1 mile south of Matthew Town.*

Fodor's Choice ★   **Inagua National Park.** Nothing quite prepares you for your first glimpse of the West Indian flamingos that nest in Inagua National Park: brilliant crimson-pink, up to 5 feet tall, with black-tipped wings. A dozen flamingos suddenly fly across a pond, intermixed with fantastic pink roseate spoonbills.

It's a moving experience, and yet because of the island's remote location, only about 50 people witnessed it in 2009. By 1952, Inagua's flamingos had dwindled to about 5,000. The gorgeous birds were hunted for their meat, especially the tongue, and for their feathers. The government established the 183,740-acre wildlife sanctuary and national park in 1963, and today more than 60,000 flamingos nest on the island, the world's largest breeding colony of West Indian flamingos. The birds thrive in the many salt ponds (owned by the Morton Salt Company) that supply their favorite meal—brine shrimp. Bird-watchers also flock here to spy gull-billed terns, egrets, herons, burrowing owls, pintail ducks, sandpipers, snowy plovers—over 130 species in all. The Inaguan lyre-tail is one of the world's most recently announced species. Wild boar and feral donkeys, left here after a brief French occupation in 1749, are harder to see.

To make reservations, you must contact the Bahamas National Trust's office (*242/393–1317 www.bnt.bs*) or Warden Henry Nixon (*242/225–0977*). All visits to the park are by special arrangement. ⊠ *Matthew Town* ✛ *10 miles west of Matthew Town* ⊕ *www.bnt.bs* ▤ *Student group rates: $10 per person; visitors: $25 per person, commercial visitors: $75 per person. Rates include: park user fee and the BNT warden's time. Not included: vehicle rental and fuel and park warden gratuity (optional).*

Morton Salt Company. Marveling at the salt process lures few visitors to Inagua, but the Morton Salt Company is omnipresent on the island: it has more than 47 square miles of crystallizing ponds and reservoirs. More than a million tons of salt are produced every year for such industrial uses as salting icy streets. (More is produced when the northeastern United States has a bad winter.) Even if you decide not to tour the facility, you can see the mountains of salt, locally called the Salt Alps, glistening in the sun from the plane. In an unusual case of industry assisting its environment, the crystallizers provide a feeding ground for the flamingos. As the water evaporates, the concentration of brine shrimp in the ponds increases, and the flamingos feed on these animals. Free tours are available by reservation at the salt plant in Matthew Town. ⊠ *Matthew Town* ☎ *242/339–1300, 242/457–6000* ⊕ *www.mortonsalt.com.*

BEACHES

Farquarson Beach. Ten-and-a-half miles north of Matthew Town is the island's nicest (at least the most accessible) beach where locals come out to chill. There's no shade; instead you'll have to keep cool in the mesmerizing turquoise waters. Bring sunscreen, bug spray, umbrellas or portable shade, lots of fluids in a cooler, and some beach toys and snorkeling gear. **Amenities:** none. **Best for:** solitude; snorkeling. ☎ *242/339–1271 Evamae Palacious, Inagua's tourism representative.*

WHERE TO EAT

$ BAHAMIAN 🍴 **Cozy Corner.** Cheerful and loud, this lunch spot—locals just call it Cozy's—is the best on the island. It has a pool table and a large seating area with a bar. Stop in for a chat with locals over a Kalik and a Bahamian conch burger. Cozy's also serves excellent island-style dinners on request—steamed crawfish, grilled snapper, baked chicken and fries, homemade slaw, macaroni and cheese, and fresh johnnycake. If it's not open when you stop by, you might still be able to get food and a drink if you ask. Best to call ahead. [$] *Average main: $9* ✉ *William and North Sts., Matthew Town* ☎ *242/339–1440* 💳 *No credit cards* 🕒 *Closed Sun.*

$ BAHAMIAN 🍴 **S sin L Restaurant & Bar Lounge.** One of the newer places to dine and even party is at S sin L in Matthew Town, where you can also work off the calories as it becomes, at least on weekends, Inagua's dance hotspot. In a comfortable, smart, air-conditioned dining room, you can enjoy delicious fresh native breakfasts, lunches, and dinners with some American fare as well. The bar gets lively, too, so take a chance to enjoy some Bahama Mamas. When the live calypso and Bahamian Goombay music plays, there are plenty of real Inaguan Bahama Mamas shaking their thing. After drinks and dessert shoot some pool. [$] *Average main: $15* ✉ *East St., Matthew Town* ☎ *242/339–1677* 🌐 *www.facebook.com/SnLBar.*

WHERE TO STAY

$ B&B/INN 🏨 **Enrica's Inn Guest House.** This affordable inn is a block from the sea and consists of three brightly colored, two-story Bahamian-colonial-style cottages with five guest rooms in each. **Pros:** inexpensive and three meals on request; efficient and friendly service; walking distance to town. **Cons:** no pool or beach views. [$] *Rooms from: $85* ✉ *Victoria St., Matthew Town* ☎ *242/339–2127* 🌐 *www.enricasinn.com* 💳 *No credit cards* 🛏 *15 rooms* 🍽 *No meals.*

$$ B&B/INN 🏨 **The Great Inagua Outback Lodge.** The Great Inagua Outback Lodge is the dream of Inaguan Henry Hugh who wanted to relax in his own quiet island paradise. **Pros:** comfortable, new with modern amenities, satellite TV, Wi-Fi, and mobile; right on water and close to beach and flats; full meals in stay/fish/dine packages. **Cons:** long and extremely bumpy road; remote; no pool. [$] *Rooms from: $284* ✉ *Matthew Town* ✣ *15 miles from Matthew Town, along northern road and the beach road* ☎ *716/479–2327 in U.S. and Canada* 🌐 *www.ccoflyfishing.com/greatinagua.html* 🛏 *2 rooms* 🍽 *All meals.*

$ B&B/INN 🏨 **The Main House.** The Morton Salt Company operates this small, affordable guesthouse. **Pros:** very inexpensive; clean; walking distance to a couple of bars and restaurants. **Cons:** no Internet service; power plant can be noisy. [$] *Rooms from: $60* ✉ *Kortwright St., Matthew Town* ☎ *242/339–1267* 🌐 *www.inaguamainhouse.com* 💳 *No credit cards* 🛏 *6 rooms.*

$ RENTAL 🏨 **Sunset Apartments.** This is your only option for a room with a water view, and a great place to watch sunsets. **Pros:** great place for bonefishing; Ezzard is a wonderful host and a top fly-fishing guide. **Cons:** no Internet service; little to do but fish and bird-watch; you need to pay in cash. $ *Rooms from: $150* ⊠ *Matthew Town* ☎ *242/339–1362* ▤ *No credit cards* ⇨ *2 apartments* ❍ *No meals.*

NIGHTLIFE

Da After Work Bar. This local bar on Gregory Street (the main street) next to Kiwanis Park is the most popular hangout in town and a good place to meet the mayor and other town notables. It's also a nice spot for watching games of Whist and Dominoes. Typically they close on Sunday, but if you stop by they will still be happy to sell you a cold drink! ⊠ *Gregory St., Matthew Town* ☎ *242/339–3001* ☽ *Usually closed Sun.*

The Fish Fry. A collection of fish shacks next to the water is open on weekends, with DJs occasionally in the covered pavilion next door. ⊠ *Matthew Town.*

Super D Nightclub. On weekends, this is one place you find some action and dancing. No food is served but drinks run aplenty. ⊠ *Matthew Town.*

SPORTS AND THE OUTDOORS

BIRDWATCHING

Great Inagua Tours. Mr. Colin Ingraham has been a tour guide for over 22 years, and while he specializes in birding and island sightseeing, he can also take you fishing for tuna or wahoo, or snorkeling on the reefs. Apparently, there is no scuba dive operator on the island despite Inagua's magnificent reefs. ⊠ *Matthew Town* ☎ *242/339–1336, 242/453–0429 cell.*

FISHING

Ezzard Cartwright. One of Inagua's leading bonefishing and deep-sea fishing guides, Ezzard Cartwright has been featured in outdoors and fishing magazines and on ESPN Outdoors shows. He is one of few locals with access to Lake Windsor, home to tarpon and snook as well as bonefish that can only be reached by boat. Call him if you're a hard-core fisherman who wants to fish for eight hours a day. He's usually booked from January to June for bonefishing, so reserve early. ⊠ *Matthew Town* ☎ *242/339–1362.*

TRAVEL SMART
BAHAMAS

GETTING HERE AND AROUND

■ AIR TRAVEL

Most international flights to the Bahamas connect through airports in Florida, New York, Charlotte, or Atlanta. The busiest airport in the Bahamas is in Nassau, which has the most connections to the more remote Out Islands. If you're traveling to these more remote islands, you might have to make a connection in both Florida and Nassau—and you still may have to take a ferry or a water taxi to your final destination.

A direct flight from New York City to Nassau takes approximately three hours. The flight from Charlotte to Nassau is two hours, and the flight from Miami to Nassau takes about an hour. Most flights between the islands of the Bahamas take less than an hour. You'll probably spend more time on the ground waiting than in the air.

Airline Security Issues Transportation Security Administration. ⊕ www.tsa.gov.

AIRPORTS

The major gateways to the Bahamas include Lynden Pindling International Airport (NAS) on New Providence Island, and Freeport Grand Bahama International Airport (FPO) on Grand Bahama Island. There are no hotels near either airport. ⇨ *For more airports, see individual chapters.*

Airport Information Grand Bahama International Airport. ☎ 242/352–2205. **Lynden Pindling International Airport.** ☎ 242/702–1010.

FLIGHTS

Air service to the Bahamas varies seasonally, with the biggest choice of flights usually available in the Christmas to Easter window.

Local carriers come and go, especially in the Out Islands, which are served mostly by smaller commuter and charter operations. Schedules change frequently. The smallest cays may have scheduled service only a few days a week. In the Out Islands, ask your hotel for flight recommendations, as they are likely to have the most up-to-date information on carriers and schedules; some can even help you book air travel.

Major Airlines American Airlines. ☎ 800/433–7300. **Delta Airlines.** ☎ 800/221–1212. **JetBlue.** ☎ 800/538–2583. **Southwest.** ☎ 800/435–9792. **United.** ☎ 800/864–8331. **US Airways.** ☎ 800/428–4322.

Smaller Airlines Apollo Jets. ✉ *Fort Lauderdale* ☎ 888/908–5934 ⊕ *www.apollojets.com.* **Bahamasair.** ☎ 242/702–4140, 800/222–4262. **Bahamas Express.** ☎ 754/200–0005 ⊕ *flybahamasexpress.com.* **Bill Air.** ☎ 242/434–0374. **Cherokee Air.** ☎ 242/367–1920 ⊕ *www.cherokeeair.com.* **Dave Harmon's Bahamas Helicopters.** ✉ *North Palm Beach County Airport, 11550 Aviation Rd #1, West Palm Beach* ☎ 561/625–1900 ⊕ *www.oceanhelicopters.com.* **Eastern Air Express.** ☎ 954/772-3363 ⊕ *www.easternairexpress.com.* **Flamingo Air.** ☎ 242/351–4963 ⊕ *www.flamingoairbah.com.* **Glen Air.** ✉ *Andros Town* ☎ 242/471–1860. **Golden Wings Charter.** ☎ 242/377–0039 ⊕ *www.goldenwingscharter.com.* **Island Air.** ☎ 800/444–9904 ⊕ *www.islandaircharters.com.* **LeAir.** ☎ 242/377–2356 ⊕ *www.flyleair.com.* **MiamHeli.com.** ☎ 786/507–5200 ⊕ *www.miamiheli.com.* **Miami Seaplane.** ✉ *3401 Rickenbacker Causeway, Key Biscayne* ☎ 305/361–3909 ⊕ *www.miamiseaplane.com.* **Monarch Air Group.** ☎ 954/359–0059 ⊕ *monarchairgroup.com.* **Performance Air.** ☎ 242/341–3281 ⊕ *www.performance-air.com.* **Pineapple Air.** ☎ 242/328–1329 ⊕ *www.pineappleair.com.* **Safari Seaplanes.** ✉ *Odyssey Aviation, Lynden Pindling International Airport, Nassau* ☎ 242/362–4006. **Silver Airlines.** ☎ 800/229–9990 in U.S. and Canada, 954/935–7587 from Fort Lauderdale, 844/674–5837 toll free from Bahamas ⊕ *www.silverairways.com.* **Sky Bahamas.** ☎ 242/377–8993, 954/357–0696 ⊕ *www.skybahamas.net.* **Southern Air.** ☎ 242/377–2014 ⊕ *www.*

southernaircharter.com. **Stella Maris Air Service.** ✉ *Stella Maris Airport* ☏ *242/338–2050 reservations, 242/357–1182 pilot's cell phone* ⊕ *http://www.stellamarisresort.com/air-service/.* **Trans Island Airways.** ✉ *Odyssey Aviation, Lynden Pindling International Airport, Nassau* ☏ *242/427–8888 in Nassau, 954/727–3377 in Fort Lauderdale* ⊕ *sales@transislandairways.com.* **Triton Airways.** ☏ *954/961–8485* ⊕ *www.tritonairways. com.* **Tropic Ocean Airways.** ✉ *Sheltair Aviation, 1100 Lee Wagener Blvd., Fort Lauderdale* ☏ *954/210–5569, 800/767–0897* ⊕ *flytropic.com.* **Watermakers Air.** ✉ *2331 N.W. 55th Court, Hangar 19, Fort Lauderdale* ☏ *954/771–0330* ⊕ *www.watermakersair. com.* **Western Air.** ☏ *242/329–4000* ⊕ *www. westernairbahamas.com.*

▮ BOAT TRAVEL

BOATS AND FERRIES

If you're adventurous and have time to spare, take a ferry or one of the traditional mail boats that regularly leave Nassau from Potter's Cay, under the Paradise Island Bridge. Although fast, modern, air-conditioned boats now make some of the trips, certain remote destinations are still served by slow, old-fashioned craft. Especially if you choose the mailboat route, you may even find yourself sharing company with goats or chickens, and making your way on deck through piles of lumber and crates of cargo; on these lumbering mail boats, expect to spend 5 to 12 or more hours slowly making your way between island outposts. These boats operate on Bahamian time, which is a casual unpredictable measure, and the schedules can be thrown off by bad weather. Mail boats cannot generally be booked in advance, and services are limited. In Nassau, check details with the dockmaster's office at Potter's Cay. One-way trips can cost from $35 to $100.

Within the Bahamas, Bahamas Ferries has the most (and most comfortable) options for island-hopping, with air-conditioned boats that offer food and beverages served by cabin attendants. Schedules do change rather frequently; if you're planning to ferry back to an island to catch a flight, check and double-check the departure times, and build in extra time in case the weather's bad or the boat inexplicably doesn't make the trip you'd planned on. Ferries serve most of the major tourist destinations from Nassau, including Spanish Wells, Governor's Harbour, Harbour Island, Abaco, Exuma, and Andros. The high-speed ferry that runs between Nassau and Spanish Wells, Governor's Harbour, and Harbour Island costs $81 one-way, and takes about two hours each way.

Local ferries in the Out Islands transport islanders and visitors from the main island to smaller cays. Usually, these ferries make several round-trips daily, and keep a more punctual schedule than the longer-haul ferry.

It's possible to get to Grand Bahama by ferry from Florida. Balearia Bahamas Express sails from Fort Lauderdale's Port Everglades (Terminal 1) and provides fast ferry service, making a day trip possible, while Bahamas Paradise Cruise Line sails from the Port of Palm Beach in Riviera Beach and is more like a small cruise ship, though hotel packages can include transportation to Grand Bahamas.

If you're setting sail yourself, note that cruising boats must clear customs at the nearest port of entry before beginning any diving or fishing. The fee is $150 for boats up to 30 feet and $300 for boats longer than 30 feet, which includes fishing permits and departure tax for up to three people. Each additional person above the age of three will be charged the $25 departure tax. Stays of longer than 12 months must be arranged with Bahamas customs and immigration officials.

Boat and Ferry Contacts Bahamas Ferries.
☏ *242/323–2166* ⊕ *www.bahamasferries. com.* **Bahamas Paradise Cruise Line.** ✉ *1 E. 11th St., Riviera Beach* ☏ *800/995–3201 Reservations, 800/374–4363 Customer Service*

⊕ *www.bahamasparadisecruise.com.* **Balearia Bahamas Express.** ✉ *Port Everglades, Terminal 1* ☎ *866/699–6988* ⊕ *www.ferryexpress. com.* **Potter's Cay Dockmaster.** ☎ *242/393– 1064.* **Resorts World Bimini Superfast Ferry.** ☎ *888/930–8688* ⊕ *rwbimini.com/ plan-your-trip/cruise-itineraries.*

▮ CAR TRAVEL

International rental agencies are generally in Nassau, and you will rent from privately owned companies on the small islands. Be warned that you might have to settle for a rusty heap that doesn't have working seat belts. Check it out thoroughly before you leave. And assume that companies won't have car seats—bring your own.

To rent a car, you must be 21 years of age or older.

It's common to hire a driver with a van, and prices are negotiable. Most drivers charge by the half day or full day, and prices depend on the stops and distance, although half-day tours are generally $50 to $100 for one to four people. Full-day tours are $100 to $200. It's customary to pay for the driver's lunch. All tour guides in the Bahamas are required to take a tourism course, pass a test to be a guide, and are required to get a special license to operate a taxi.

GASOLINE

The cost of fuel in the Bahamas is usually at least twice that in the United States, and be prepared to pay in cash. Stations may be few and far between on the Out Islands. Keep the tank full. You can ask for a handwritten receipt if printed ones are not available. Gas stations may be closed Sunday.

PARKING

There are few parking meters in the Bahamas, none in downtown Nassau. Police are lenient with visitors' rental cars parked illegally and will generally just ask the driver to move it. Parking spaces are hard to find in Nassau, so be prepared to park on a side street and walk. Most hotels offer off-street parking for guests. There are few parking lots not associated with hotels.

ROADSIDE EMERGENCIES

In case of a road emergency, stay in your vehicle with your emergency flashers engaged and wait for help, especially after dark. If someone stops to help, relay information through a small opening in the window. If it's daylight and help does not arrive, walk to the nearest phone and call for help. In the Bahamas, motorists readily stop to help drivers in distress.

Ask for emergency numbers at the rental office when you pick up your car. These numbers vary from island to island. On smaller islands the owner of the company may want you to call him at his home.

RULES OF THE ROAD

Remember, like the British, islanders drive on the left side of the road, which can be confusing because most cars are American with the steering wheel on the left. It is illegal, however, to make a left-hand turn on a red light. Many streets in downtown Nassau are one-way. Roundabouts pose further confusion to Americans. Remember to keep left and yield to oncoming traffic as you enter the roundabout and at "Give Way" signs.

▮ TAXI TRAVEL

There are taxis waiting at every airport and outside all the main hotels and cruise-ship docks. Beware of "hackers"—drivers who don't display their license (and may not have one). Sometimes you can negotiate a fare, but you must do so before you enter the taxi.

You'll find that Bahamian taxi drivers are more talkative than their U.S. counterparts. When you take a taxi to dinner or to town, it's common for the driver to wait and take you back, which doesn't cost more. A 15% tip is suggested.

ESSENTIALS

▮ ACCOMMODATIONS

The lodgings we list are the cream of the crop in each price category. We always list the facilities that are available—but we don't specify whether they cost extra: when pricing accommodations, always ask what's included.

APARTMENT AND HOUSE RENTALS

Contacts Bahamas Home Rentals. ☎ 888/881–2867 ⊕ www.bahamasweb.com. **Bahamas Vacation Homes.** ☎ 242/333–4080 ⊕ www.bahamasvacationhomes.com. **Hope Town Hideaways.** ☎ 242/366–0224 ⊕ www. hopetown.com. **Villas & Apartments Abroad.** ✉ East Village ☎ 212/213–6435 ⊕ www. vaanyc.com. **Villas of Distinction.** ✉ Roslyn ☎ 800/289–0900 ⊕ www.villasofdistinction. com. **Villas International.** ✉ 17 Fox La., San Anselmo ☎ 800/221–2260 ⊕ www. villasintl.com. **Wimco.** ✉ Box 1461, Newport ☎ 800/449–1553 ⊕ www.wimco.com.

▮ COMMUNICATIONS

INTERNET

Wireless Internet service is becoming more available throughout the islands, but there are still pockets where service is impossible or difficult to get, and it's likely to be slower than you may be accustomed to. If Internet is important, ask your hotel representative about service before traveling.

If you're carrying a laptop into the Bahamas, you should fill out a Declaration of Value form upon arrival, noting make, model, and serial number. The Bahamian electrical current is compatible with U.S. computers.

PHONES

Bahamas Telecommunications Company (BTC) is the phone company in the Bahamas. Pay phones are fast becoming a thing of the past, as most visitors use their cell phones and Internet when they need to keep in touch. Your best bet is to purchase a BTC VOIP Talk It Up calling card. You can use these cards to call within the country or to the United States.

Check with your calling-card provider before traveling to see if your card will work in the islands (on the smaller cays it almost certainly won't) and to see about surcharges. Always ask at your hotel desk about what charges will apply when you make card calls from your room as these can be steep. There's usually a charge for making toll-free calls to the United States. To place a call from a public phone using your own calling card, dial 0 for the operator, who will then place the call using your card number.

When you're calling the Bahamas, the country code is 242. You can dial any Bahamas number from the United States as you would make an interstate call.

CALLING WITHIN THE BAHAMAS

Within the Bahamas, to make a local call from your hotel room, dial 9, then the number. Some 800 and 888 numbers—particularly airline and credit card numbers—can be called from the Bahamas. Others can be reached by substituting an 880 prefix and paying for the call. Dial 916 for directory information and 0 for operator assistance.

CALLING OUTSIDE THE BAHAMAS

In big resorts instructions are given by the room phones on how to make international calls and the costs, which differ from resort to resort. In small inns, especially those in the Out Islands, you may not be able to get an AT&T, Sprint, or other operator or international operator, but the hotel front desk can usually do it for you.

The country code is 1 for the United States.

Access Codes AT&T USADirect. ☎ 800/872–2881. **MCI Call USA.** ☎ 800/888–8000. **Sprint.** ☎ 866/313–6672.

Phone Company BTC. ☎ *242/302–7000* ⊕ *www.btcbahamas.com.*

MOBILE PHONES

Some U.S. cell phones work in the Bahamas; check with your provider before your trip. The BTC has roaming agreements with many U.S. companies, including AT&T, T-Mobile, and Sprint. Roaming rates vary depending on the carrier.

In order to bypass hefty roaming fees, purchase a SIM card for about $15 at any BTC location; this will allow you to use your own cell phone while in the Bahamas. (You'll also need a BTC pre-paid minutes card, but these cards can be purchased for as little as $10.) You can rent GMS cellular phones from companies such as Cellular Abroad, which charges $1.14 to $1.32 a minute on calls to the United States plus the rental of the phone, starting at $69 for a week or less. Service is improving but is still spotty, and on the Out Islands, cell phones may not work at all.

▌ CUSTOMS AND DUTIES

Customs allows you to bring in one liter of wine or liquor and one carton of cigarettes in addition to personal effects, purchases up to $100, and all the money you wish.

Certain types of personal belongings may get a raised eyebrow—an extensive collection of DVDs, for instance—if they suspect you may be planning to sell them while in the country. However, real hassles at immigration are rare, since officials realize tourists are the lifeblood of the economy.

You would be well advised to leave pets at home, unless you're considering a prolonged stay in the islands. An import permit is required from the Ministry of Agriculture and Fisheries for all animals brought into the Bahamas. The animal must be more than six months old. You'll also need a veterinary health certificate issued by a licensed vet. The permit is

good for one year from the date of issue, costs $10, and the process must be completed immediately before departure.

U.S. residents who have been out of the country for at least 48 hours may bring home $800 worth of foreign goods duty-free, as long as they have not used the $800 allowance or any part of it in the past 30 days.

Contacts Ministry of Agriculture and Marine Resources. ☎ *242/397–7400.* **U.S. Customs and Border Protection.** ⊕ *www.cbp.gov.* **U.S. Embassy.** ☎ *242/322–1181* ⊕ *www.nassau.usembassy.gov.*

▌ EATING OUT

The restaurants we list are the cream of the crop in each price category. You'll find all types, from cosmopolitan to the most casual restaurants, serving all types of cuisine. Unless otherwise noted, the restaurants ⇨ *listed in this guide* are open daily for lunch and dinner.

For information on food-related health issues, see Health below. For dining price categories, consult the price charts found near the beginning of each chapter. For guidelines on tipping, see Tipping below.

PAYING

The U.S. dollar is on par with the Bahamian dollar and both currencies are accepted in restaurants. Most credit cards are also accepted in most restaurants. Typically, you will have to ask for your check when you are finished.

RESERVATIONS AND DRESS

Reservations are sometimes necessary in Nassau and on the more remote islands, where restaurants may close early if no one shows up or says they're coming. We mention dress only when men are required to wear a jacket or a jacket and tie. Otherwise, you can assume that dining out is a casual affair.

WINES, BEER, AND SPIRITS

Kalik and Sands beers are brewed in the Bahamas and are available at most restaurants for lunch and dinner.

▌ELECTRICITY

Electricity is 120 volts/60 cycles AC, which is compatible with all U.S. appliances.

▌EMERGENCIES

The emergency telephone number in the Bahamas is 919 or 911. Pharmacies usually close at 6 pm although some in New Providence are always open. Emergency medicine after hours is available only at hospitals, or, on remote Out Islands, at clinics.

Emergency Contacts Bahamas Air Sea Rescue Association. ☎ *242/325 8864* ⊕ *www.basra.org.* **United States Embassy.** ☎ *242/322–1181* ⊕ *www.nassau.usembassy. gov.*

▌HEALTH

FOOD AND WATER

The major health risk in the Bahamas is traveler's diarrhea. This is most often caused by ingesting fruits, shellfish, and drinks to which your body is unaccustomed. Go easy at first on new foods such as mangoes, conch, and rum punch. There are rare cases of contaminated fruit, vegetables, or drinking water.

If you're susceptible to digestive problems, avoid ice, uncooked food, and unpasteurized milk and milk products, and stick to bottled water, or water that

has been boiled for several minutes, even when brushing your teeth.

Drink plenty of purified water or tea; chamomile is a good folk remedy. In severe cases, rehydrate yourself with a salt-sugar solution (½ teaspoon salt and 4 tablespoons sugar per quart of water).

DIVING

Do not fly within 24 hours of scuba diving. Always know where your nearest decompression chamber is *before* you embark on a dive expedition, and how you would get there in an emergency. The only chambers in the Bahamas are in Nassau and San Salvador, and emergency cases are often sent to Miami.

Decompression Chamber Bahamas Hyperbaric Centre. ☎ *242/362–5765.* **Bahamas Medical Center.** ⊠ *Gambier* ☎ *242/302–4610* ⊕ *www.bahamasmedicalcenter.com.*

INSECTS

No-see-ums (sand fleas) and mosquitoes can be bothersome. Some travelers have allergies to sand-flea bites, and the itching can be extremely annoying. To prevent the bites, use a recommended bug repellent. To ease the itching, rub alcohol on the bites. Some Out Island hotels provide sprays or repellents but it's a good idea to bring your own.

SUNBURN

Basking in the sun is one of the great pleasures of a Bahamian vacation, but take precautions against sunburn and sunstroke.

On a sunny day, even people who are not normally bothered by strong sun should cover up with a long-sleeve shirt, a hat, and pants or a beach wrap while on a boat or midday at the beach. Carry UVA/UVB sunblock (with an SPF of at least 15) for your face and other sensitive areas. If you're engaging in water sports, be sure the sunscreen is waterproof.

Wear sunglasses, because eyes are particularly vulnerable to direct sun and reflected rays. Drink enough liquids—water or fruit juice preferably—and avoid coffee, tea, and alcohol. Above all, limit your sun time for the first few days until you become accustomed to the rays. Do not be fooled by an overcast day. The safest hours for sunbathing are 4–6 pm, but even then it's wise to limit initial exposure.

MEDICAL INSURANCE AND ASSISTANCE

The most serious accidents and illnesses may require an airlift to the United States—most likely to a hospital in Florida. The costs of a medical evacuation can quickly run into the thousands of dollars, and your personal health insurance may not cover such costs. If you plan to pursue inherently risky activities, such as scuba diving, or if you have an existing medical condition, check your policy to see what's covered.

Consider buying trip insurance with medical-only coverage. Neither Medicare nor some private insurers cover medical expenses anywhere outside the United States. Medical-only policies typically reimburse you for medical care (excluding that related to preexisting conditions) and hospitalization abroad, and provide for evacuation. You still have to pay the bills and await reimbursement from the insurer, though.

Another option is to sign up with a medical-evacuation assistance company. A membership in one of these companies gets you doctor referrals, emergency evacuation or repatriation, 24-hour hotlines for medical consultation, and other assistance. International SOS Assistance Emergency and AirMed International provide evacuation services and medical referrals. MedjetAssist offers medical evacuation.

Medical Assistance Companies AirMed International. ⊕ www.airmed.com. **International SOS Assistance Emergency.** ⊕ www. internationalsos.com. **MedjetAssist.** ⊠ Helena ⊕ www.medjetassist.com.

Medical-Only Insurers International Medical Group. ☎ 800/628–4664 ⊕ www. imglobal.com. **International SOS.** ⊕ www.

internationalsos.com. **Wallach & Company.** ☎ 800/237–6615 ⊕ www.wallach.com.

▌HOLIDAYS

The grandest holiday of all is Junkanoo, a carnival that came from slaves who made elaborate costumes and instruments such as goatskin drums. Junkanoo is celebrated on Boxing Day, the day after Christmas, and New Year's Day (the bands compete in all-night parades that start in the wee hours). Don't expect to conduct any business the day after the festivities.

During other legal holidays, most offices close, and some may extend the holiday by keeping earlier (or no) hours the day before or after.

In the Bahamas official holidays include New Year's Day, Majority Rule Day (Jan. 10), Good Friday, Easter, Easter Monday, Whit Monday (last Mon. in May), Labour Day (1st Mon. in June), Independence Day (July 10), Emancipation Day (1st Mon. in Aug.), National Heroes Day (Oct. 12), Christmas Day, and Boxing Day (Dec. 26).

▌HOURS OF OPERATION

Banks are generally open Monday–Thursday 9 or 9:30 to 3 or 4 and Friday 9 to 5. However, on the Out Islands banks may keep shorter hours—on the smallest cays, they may be open only a day or two each week. Most Bahamian offices observe bank hours.

Hours for attractions vary. Most open between 9 and 10 and close around 5.

Though most drugstores typically abide by normal store hours, some stay open 24 hours.

Most stores, with the exception of straw markets and malls, close on Sunday.

▌MAIL

Regardless of whether the term "snail mail" was coined in the Bahamas, you're likely to arrive home long before your postcards do—it's not unheard of for letters to take two to four weeks to reach their destinations. No postal (zip) codes are used in the Bahamas—all mail is collected from local area post-office boxes.

First-class mail from the Bahamas to the United States is 65¢ per half ounce; you'll pay 50¢ to mail a postcard. Postcard stamps good for foreign destinations are usually sold at shops selling postcards, so you don't have to make a special trip. From the United States a postcard or a letter sent to the Bahamas costs 98¢.

SHIPPING PACKAGES

If you want to ship purchases home, take the same precautions you take in the United States—don't pack valuables or fragile items.

Express Services Copimaxx. ✉ *Nassau* ☎ *242/328–2679.* **FedEx.** ✉ *242/352–3402 Freeport, 242/322–5656 Nassau, 242/367–2817 Abaco, 242/368–2540 Andros, 242/332–2720 Eleuthera, 242/337–6786 Long Island, 649/946–2542 Grand Turk, 649/946–4682 Providenciales, 800/247–4747 U.S. international customer service.* **Mail Boxes Etc.** ✉ *Nassau* ☎ *242/394–1508.*

■ MONEY

Generally, prices in the Bahamas are slightly higher than in the United States. Businesses don't care whether you pay in U.S. dollars or Bahamian dollars, since they're the same value, but don't count on them being able to give you U.S. currency change. In the Out Islands you'll notice that meals and simple goods can be expensive; prices are high due to the remoteness of the islands and the costs of importing.

ATMs are widely available, except on the most remote islands, but often the currency dispensed is Bahamian. If you have any left at the end of your stay, you can exchange it at the airport.

Prices here are given for adults. Substantially reduced fees are almost always available for children, students, and senior citizens.

ATMS AND BANKS

There are ATMs at banks, malls, resorts, and shops throughout the major islands. For excursions to remote locations, bring plenty of cash; there are few or no ATMs on some small cays, and on weekends or holidays, those that exist may run out of cash.

Banks are generally open Monday–Thursday 9 or 9:30 to 3 or 4 and Friday 9 to 5. However, on the Out Islands, banks may keep shorter hours—on the smallest cays, they may be open only a day or two each week.

■ TIP→ PINs with more than four digits are not recognized at ATMs in the Bahamas. If yours has five or more, remember to change it before you leave.

CREDIT CARDS

When you book your hotel accommodations, be sure to ask if credit cards are accepted; some smaller hotels in the islands do not take plastic.

It's a good idea to inform your credit-card company before you travel, especially if you don't travel internationally very often. Otherwise, the credit-card company might put a hold on your card owing to unusual activity—not a good thing halfway through your trip.

Although it's usually cheaper (and safer) to use a credit card abroad for large purchases (so you can cancel payments or be reimbursed if there's a problem), note that some credit-card companies *and* the banks that issue them add substantial percentages to all foreign transactions, whether they're in a foreign currency or not. Check on these fees before leaving home, so there won't be any surprises when you get the bill.

CURRENCY AND EXCHANGE

The U.S. dollar is on par with the Bahamian dollar and is accepted all over the Bahamas. Bahamian money runs in bills of $1, $5, $10, $20, $50, and $100.

Since U.S. currency is accepted everywhere, there really is no need to change to Bahamian. Also, you won't incur any transaction fees for currency exchange, or worry about getting stuck with unspent Bahamian dollars. Carry small bills when bargaining at straw markets.

▮ PACKING

Aside from your bathing suit, which will be your favorite uniform, take lightweight clothing (short-sleeve shirts, T-shirts, cotton slacks, lightweight jackets for evening wear for men; light dresses, shorts, and T-shirts for women). If you're going during high season, between mid-December and April, toss in a sweater for the occasional cool evening. Cover up in public places and downtown shopping expeditions, and save that skimpy bathing suit for the beach at your hotel.

Some of the more sophisticated hotels require jackets for men and dresses for women at dinner. The Bahamas' casinos do not have dress codes.

▮ PASSPORTS AND VISAS

U.S. citizens need a valid passport when entering and returning from the Bahamas, but do not need a visa.

U.S. Passport Information U.S. Department of State. ☏ 877/487–2778 ⊕ travel.state.gov/passport.

▮ SAFETY

There has been a significant spike in violent crime in Nassau, mostly in off-the-beaten-path locations. Exercise caution in these areas: be aware of your wallet or handbag at all times, and keep your jewelry in the hotel safe. Be especially wary in remote areas, always lock your rental vehicle, and don't keep any valuables in the car, even in the locked trunk.

Women traveling alone should not go out walking unescorted at night in Nassau or in remote areas. To avoid unwanted attention, dress conservatively and cover up swimsuits off the beach.

General Information and Warnings U.S. Department of State. ⊕ www.travel.state.gov/travel.

▮ TAXES

There's no sales tax in the Bahamas, but starting January 2015, a 7.5% VAT was added to most goods and services; the $15 departure tax is usually included in the price of commercial airline tickets.

Tax on your hotel room is 6%–12% in addition to VAT, depending on the island visited; at some resorts, a small service charge of up to 5% may be added to cover housekeeping and bellman service.

▮ TIME

The Bahamas lie within the eastern standard time (EST) zone, which means that it's 7 am in the Bahamas (or New York) when it's noon in London and 10 pm in Sydney. In summer the islands switch to eastern daylight time (EDT).

▮ TIPPING

In the Bahamas, service staff and hotel workers expect to be tipped. The usual tip for service from a taxi driver or waiter is 15% and $1–$2 a bag for porters. Most travelers leave $1 to $3 per day for their hotel maid, usually every morning since the maid may have a day off. Many hotels and restaurants automatically add a 15% gratuity to your bill; if not, a 15% to 20% tip at a restaurant is appropriate (more for a high-end establishment). Bartenders generally get $1 to $2 per drink.

▮ TRIP INSURANCE

Comprehensive trip insurance is valuable if you're booking a considerably expensive or complicated trip (particularly to an isolated region) or if you're booking far in advance. Comprehensive policies typically cover trip cancellation and interruption, letting you cancel or cut your trip short because of illness, or, in some cases, acts of terrorism in your destination. Such policies might also cover evacuation and medical care. (For trips abroad you should have at least medical-only coverage. ⇨ *See Medical Insurance and Assistance under Health.*) Some also cover you for trip delays because of bad weather or mechanical problems as well as for lost or delayed luggage.

Another type of coverage to consider is financial default—that is, when your trip is disrupted because a tour operator, airline, or cruise line goes out of business. Generally you must buy this when you book your trip or shortly thereafter, and it's available to you only if your operator isn't on a list of excluded companies.

Always read the fine print of your policy to make sure that you're covered for the risks that most concern you. Compare several policies to be sure you're getting the best price and range of coverage available.

Insurance Comparison Info Insure My Trip. ☎ 800/487-4722 ⊕ www.insuremytrip.com. **Square Mouth.** ☎ 800/240-0369 ⊕ www. squaremouth.com.

Comprehensive Insurers AIG Travel Guard. ☎ 800/826-4919 ⊕ www.travelguard.com. **Allianz Global Assistance.** ☎ 866/884-3556 ⊕ www.allianztravelinsurance.com. **CSA Travel Protection.** ☎ 877/243-4135 ⊕ www. csatravelprotection.com. **HTH Worldwide.** ☎ 888/243-2358 ⊕ www.hthworldwide.com. **Travel Insured International.** ☎ 800/243-3174 ⊕ www.travelinsured.com. **Travelex Insurance.** ☎ 800/228-9792 ⊕ www.travelex-insurance.com.

❚ VISITOR INFORMATION

Contacts Bahamas Ministry of Tourism. ☎ 800/224-2627 ⊕ www.bahamas.com. **Bahama Out Islands Promotion Board.** ☎ 954/475-8315 ⊕ www.myoutislands.com. **Caribbean Tourism Organization.** ⊕ www. onecaribbean.org. **Grand Bahama Island Tourism Board.** ☎ 800/545-1300 ⊕ www. grandbahamavacations.com. **Harbour Island Tourism.** ⊕ www.harbourislandguide.com. **Nassau/Paradise Island Promotion Board.** ⊕ www.nassauparadiseisland.com.

USEFUL WEB SITES

BahamasIslands.com. ⊕ www.the-bahamas-islands.com. **Bahamasnet.com.** ⊕ www. bahamasnet.com. **Bahamas Visitors Guide.** ⊕ www.bahamasvisitorsguide.com. **Nassau Guardian.** ⊕ www.thenassauguardian.com.

INDEX

PHOTO CREDITS

Front cover: Chris Schmid/Aurora Photos/Offset [Description: Paradise Island, Nassau, Bahamas.] 1, The Bahamas Ministry of Tourism. 2, Ray Wadia/The Bahamas Ministry of Tourism. 5. The Bahamas Ministry of Tourism. Chapter 1: Experience the Bahamas: 8-9, Reinhard Dirscherl/age fotostock. 16(left), The Bahamas Ministry of Tourism. 16 (top right), PBorowka/Shutterstock. 16 (bottom right), zxvisual/iStockphoto. 17 (top left), ruben i/Flickr. 17(bottom left), Jeff Greenberg/Alamy. 17 (right), Tish 1/Shutterstock. 19, The Bahamas Ministry of Tourism. 20, New Jersey Birds/Flickr. 21 (left), Cheryl Blackerby. 21 (right), Lars Topelmann/The Bahamas Ministry of Tourism. 22 (left, top right, and bottom right), The Bahamas Ministry of Tourism. 22 (bottom center), Cheryl Blackerby. 24 (left), The Bahamas Ministry of Tourism. 24(right), Mark gerardot/Tiamo. 25 (left), t.blue/Flickr. 25 (top right), Jonathunder/wikipedia.org. 25 (bottom right), Greg Johnston/Cape Santa Maria Beach Resort. 26 (left), Graycliff Hotel. 26 (top right), Steve Snodgrass/Flickr. 26 (bottom right), Henrik Bruun. 27 (left), Craig Dennis. 27 (right), Ramona Settle. 33, Dirscherl Reinhard/age fotostock. 34 and 35 (all), The Bahamas Ministry of Tourism. 36, frantisekhojdysz/Shutterstock. 38, Ray Wadia/The Bahamas Ministry of Tourism. 39 (both), 40, and 41 (top left and bottom left), The Bahamas Ministry of Tourism. 41 (right), Ray Wadia/The Bahamas Ministry of Tourism. 42, The Bahamas Ministry of Tourism. Chapter 2: New Providence and Paradise Islands: 43, Macduff Everton/Atlantis. 44 (top), Roland Rose. 44 (bottom), Lijuan Guo/Shutterstock. 45, Macduff Everton/Atlantis. 46, Daniel Korzeniewski/iStockphoto. 51, The Bahamas Ministry of Tourism. 56, Laurin Johnson/iStockphoto. 61, Ramunas I Dreamstime.com. 74, Graycliff Hotel. 77, Bruce Wolf. 82, Ramona Settle. 85, Walter Bibikow/age fotostock. 86 (left), biskuit/Flickr. 86 (right), Jef Nickerson/Flickr. 87 (top), Bahamas Ministry of Tourism. 87 (bottom), Peter Adams/age fotostock. 88, Shane Pinder/Alamy. 89 (top), JTB Photo/photolibrary.com. 89 (bottom), Shane Pinder/Alamy. 94-95, Remedios Valls Lopez/age fotostock. 96, Lars Topelmann/The Bahamas Ministry of Tourism. Chapter 3: Grand Bahama Island: 101, Denis Jr. Tangney/iStockphoto. 102 (left), Thomas Lorenz/Shutterstock. 102 (right) and 103, The Bahamas Ministry of Tourism. 104, Degas Jean-Pierre / age fotostock. 105 (top), Thomas Lorenz/Shutterstock. 105 (bottom) and 106, The Bahamas Ministry of Tourism. 113, Charles Stirling (Travel) / Alamy. 125, Our Lucaya Beach and Golf Resort. 126, The Bahamas Ministry of Tourism. 131, Davis James/age fotostock. 135, Dirscherl Reinhard/age fotostock. 139, The Bahamas Ministry of Tourism. Chapter 4: The Abacos: 143, SuperStock/age fotostock. 144, Island Effects/iStockphoto. 146, FLPA/age fotostock. 147 (top), flickerized/Flickr. 147 (bottom), Kate Philips/iStockphoto. 148, The Bahamas Ministry of Tourism. 159, Sunpix Marine/Alamy. 162, DEA/A VERGANI/age fotostock. 175, Imagestate/age fotostock. 180, Ramona Settle. Chapter 5: Andros, Bimini, and the Berry Islands: 189, Greg Johnston/age fotostock. 190 (left), The Bahamas Ministry of Tourism. 190 (right), andydidyk/iStockphoto. 191 (top and bottom) and 192, Lars Topelmann/The Bahamas Ministry of Tourism. 199, Juliet Coombe/age fotostock. 205, Greg Johnston/age fotostock. 213, Tiamo Resort. 217, BARBAGALLO Franco / age fotostock. 220, Mark Conlin/Alamy. 225, Larry Larsen / Alamy. 234, Amy Strycula / Alamy. Chapter 6: Eleuthera and Harbour Island: 237, The Bahamas Ministry of Tourism. 238 (center), pics721/Shutterstock. 238 (right), Jon Beard/Shutterstock. 239, Cookie Kincaid. 240, Erikruthoff81 I Dreamstime.com. 252, Greg Johnston/age fotostock. 257, Cheryl Blackerby. 262-63, The Bahamas Ministry of Tourism. 264, Greg Johnston/The Bahamas Tourist Office. 268, Alvaro Leiva/age fotostock. 274-75, Ian Cumming/age fotostock. Chapter 7: The Exumas: 277, ARCO/F Schneider / age fotostock. 278 (all) and 279 (top), Staniel Cay Yacht Club. 279 (bottom), The Bahamas Ministry of Tourism. 280 and 281 (bottom), The Bahamas Ministry of Tourism. 281 (top), Ray Wadia/The Bahamas Ministry of Tourism. 282, The Bahamas Ministry of Tourism. 289, Cheryl Blackerby. 293, Ramona Settle. 295, Cheryl Blackerby. 298, Staniel Cay Yacht Club. 302, Cheryl Blackerby. 304, Staniel Cay Yacht Club. Chapter 8: The Southern Out Islands: 307, Greg Johnston/age fotostock. 308 (top), The Bahamas Ministry of Tourism. 308 (bottom), Ray Wadia/The Bahamas Ministry of Tourism. 309 (left), Nina Herne/iStockphoto. 309 (right), The Bahamas Ministry of Tourism. 310, Cheryl Blackerby. 311 (top), Patrick Swint/Flickr. 311 (bottom), stephan kerkhofs/Shutterstock. 312, Jeff Greenberg / Alamy. 313 (top), Cheryl Blackerby. 313 (bottom), mweichse/Shutterstock. 314, Greg Johnston/Cape Santa Maria Beach Resort. 321, Michael DeFreitas / age fotostock. 326, Ray Wadia/The Bahamas Ministry of Tourism. 328, Greg Johnston/age fotostock. 332, The Bahamas Ministry of Tourism. 340, Greg Johnston/age fotostock. 346, Greg Johnston/Cape Santa Maria Beach Resort. 350 BARBAGALLO Franco / age fotostock. 355, Greg Johnston/age fotostock. 358, Greg Johnston/Cape Santa Maria Beach Resort. Back cover, from left to right: travelpixpro/iStockphoto; frantisekhojdysz/Shutterstock; Island Effects/iStockphoto. Spine: Shutterstock / Kovnir Andrii.

NOTES

NOTES

NOTES

ABOUT OUR WRITERS

For over two decades, **Bob Bower** has worked at his family business, Star Publishers Ltd., in Nassau, where he has written and edited publications such as the *Bahamas Tourist News,* and the promotion boards' newspapers, the *Bahama Out Island Travel Guide* and the *Nassau/Paradise Island Tourist News.* Born in Nassau and schooled in the United Kingdom, Bob lived in Australia for seven years, where he co-partnered Blaze Communications, a successful, rising public relations and advertising firm in Sydney. Bob loves travel, particularly the Bahama Out Islands. His further journeys have taken him to the Caribbean, Spain, Malta, France, Belgium, Ireland, the United Kingdom, the United States, and Canada. Since 1987 Bob has resided in Nassau with his wife and three children and loves his faith, reading, travel, and photography.

 A born-and-bred Tar Heel with roots in North Carolina, **Julianne Hoell** began her love affair with the Bahamas after visiting New Providence in 1994. Following completion of a journalism degree from UNC-Chapel Hill, she moved to Eleuthera and began traveling to neighboring islands in search of the perfect conch salad and sunset view. Her answer is forthcoming as she continues to write about the Caribbean's best restaurants and hotels.

Born in England and raised in the Bahamas, **Jessica Robertson** has traveled the world for work and play but calls Nassau home. She has visited just about all of the populated islands in the Bahamas, as well as some occupied only by hermit crabs and seagulls, and works as the online editor for *The Tribune,* the country's daily newspaper.

 Jamie Werner is a freelance writer and photographer based in St. Lucia. She spent over four years relishing the island life on Grand Bahama, and prior to that she lived throughout the Caribbean with her husband and young children: in Aruba, Trinidad, Barbados, and the Dominican Republic, where she taught writing and high school literature. She studied at Sydney University in Australia and the University of Arizona, earning degrees in journalism and photography. Raised in Wyoming and Colorado, her roots are well planted in the mountain ranges of the western United States, but her heart is happiest on the beach with a book and a paddleboard.